STATI [illegible] JR
POLITICS & INTERNATIONAL RELATIONS

USING

IBM SPSS STATISTICS

STATISTICS FOR POLITICS & INTERNATIONAL RELATIONS USING IBM SPSS STATISTICS

HELEN M. WILLIAMS

Los Angeles | London | New Delhi
Singapore | Washington DC | Melbourne

Los Angeles | London | New Delhi
Singapore | Washington DC | Melbourne

SAGE Publications Ltd
1 Oliver's Yard
55 City Road
London EC1Y 1SP

SAGE Publications Inc.
2455 Teller Road
Thousand Oaks, California 91320

SAGE Publications India Pvt Ltd
B 1/I 1 Mohan Cooperative Industrial Area
Mathura Road
New Delhi 110 044

SAGE Publications Asia-Pacific Pte Ltd
3 Church Street
#10-04 Samsung Hub
Singapore 049483

Editor: John Nightingale
Assistant editor: Eve Williams
Production editor: Victoria Nicholas
Marketing manager: Susheel Gokarakonda
Cover design: Stephanie Guyaz
Typeset by: C&M Digitals (P) Ltd, Chennai, India
Printed in the UK

First published 2020

Library of Congress Control Number: 2019943591

British Library Cataloguing in Publication data

A catalogue record for this book is available from the British Library

ISBN 978-1-4739-0270-1
ISBN 978-1-4739-0271-8 (pbk)

CONTENTS

ONLINE RESOURCES

Statistics for Politics and International Relations Using IBM SPSS Statistics is accompanied by a full companion website, which you can access at:
https://study.sagepub.com/statsforpoliticsandirusingspss

Containing resources for both lecturers and students, the website compliments and builds on the material presented in the book, and includes the following:

FOR INSTRUCTORS AND STUDENTS

Syntax files that students and instructors can run to get the same outputs. Accompanied by annotations, they work as how-to guides for ensuring that you arrive at the same tables, charts and answers that are in the book.

Access to an IR dataset compiled from UN Human Development statistics. The UN Human Development data has been collected annually by the UNDP since 1990. It collects a wide variety of data to measure development and quality of life beyond economic indicators. It combines several variables to create a Human Development Index each year, which ranks how countries are doing overall, including variables like literacy, health, poverty and employment.

FOR INSTRUCTORS

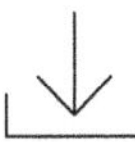

Exhibits of Tables and Figures which includes all the tables and figures found in each chapter. These exhibits have been enlarged and resized so that they can be utilised for teaching purposes in large lecture halls. They can be easily reprinted or imported into revision documents for your learning experience.

FOR STUDENTS

For every chapter you will find the following:

A list of web links. These carefully curated web links – including blogs, datasets and webpages – provide students with the most relevant research material.

Videos from experts on how to tackle certain aspects of SPSS, from entering data and defining variables in SPSS to creating a scatterplot.

Annotated further reading. These books and articles directly compliment the subject matter for every chapter and support further study.

1

INTRODUCTION

Many – probably even most, but I don't have the statistics on this – political science and international relations students do not embark on their degree knowing that they might have to undertake statistical analysis, and even fewer students react to finding this out with excitement. I could probably wallpaper my entire house with student evaluations questioning why this is necessary for their degree and what it has to do with the things they are learning elsewhere, such as political philosophy. This lack of enthusiasm is also frequently reflected in the staff who are teaching statistics, who may be from a different discipline entirely or may have been delegated this teaching task as a form of drawing the short straw in the allocation of teaching. These unenthusiastic teachers may then perpetuate the cycle of unenthusiasm by teaching statistics the way they were taught, which is often a highly mathematical approach that seems far removed from the realities of studying *politics*. Yet statistics can be one of many fascinating ways to learn more about the world we live in, to examine how other people perceive the world, to measure the impact of moments of change on people's worldview.

My introduction to social statistics as a student still sits fresh in my mind. I was taught in precisely the unenthusiastic, mathematical method, which led to little comprehension of what was going on and intense student frustration. One particular moment stands out, when we had listened for 30 minutes in an overheated computer lab to a lecture about chi squared statistics (we get to those in Chapter 6, if you want to skip ahead and find out what this means). One brave student put up their hand and said, 'But I don't understand what chi squared *is*.' Rather than pausing to explain that this is a simple expression of whether we think people's answers to two different questions are actually related to each other, or whether it might just be a fluke, the teacher launched into ten minutes of algebra, showing us the mathematics behind the calculation. No one asked a question again. What the student (and all of us) was wondering was, 'How do I apply this? Why should I use it? How does it help me to understand the world better?' That lesson laid the cornerstone to my approach to teaching statistics: it is important, especially at the introductory level, to focus on *applied* statistics – what the numbers help us to understand, not how to carry out the mathematical calculations by hand.

The second frustration I encountered as a student was that all social science (in this case, psychology, health science, political science, sociology and education) students were taught together, using generic examples. I was already baffled by the language of statistics and a completely new computer program that did not function like other programs; but then I could not recognize any of the examples we looked at in teaching. Why, for example, were we looking at the mode number of cars for female heads of household versus male heads of household? (Which was followed up for at least two weeks, judging by my notes, with further examples about what proportion of households had three or more cars, which ethnic group had the most cars, which class had the most cars, etc.) How was this going to help me understand my substantive field of study better? This forms the other cornerstone of my approach to teaching statistics: embedding in the subject content is key to fostering deeper understanding rather than rote learning based on mimicking what the teacher tells you to do in order to produce a certain table.

This book takes what some might consider to be a heretical approach to learning statistics. There are very few equations in the entire book, and those that appear are calculations that you can perform on the cheapest of non-scientific calculators; and these equations are generally only provided for students who want to take the next step with their results. Rather than inundating you with a completely disorientating environment that contains new software, new mathematics and generic examples that you cannot easily assimilate, this book approaches learning statistics from the perspective of answering questions about the world. Most chapters examine a small range of research questions, formulate hypotheses and test them against data. Many of the end-of-chapter activities are also based on this approach, walking you through the scientific research cycle of research question (RQ), theory, hypotheses and data to answer the question. Throughout, the approach is one focused on understanding what you have produced at a deep enough level that you understand how to transfer these ideas to other examples, contexts and datasets.

WHO THIS BOOK IS FOR

This book is designed for students with no background in statistics, IBM SPSS Statistics ('SPSS') or both. All of the examples are worked through by showing you how to test the data using the statistics software program SPSS, but that does not make it inapplicable to students who are learning how to use other software packages, if you are looking for some additional explanation about what the numbers mean. The questions posed should relate to topics that you would encounter on a political science or international relations degree. The chapters that use the European Social Survey (ESS) are Eurocentric, in some cases very UK-centric, reflecting the context in which I am based. However, the chapters that use the UN dataset engage with a much broader sweep of countries around the world. There are many excellent datasets available publicly, often pre-formatted for use in SPSS, so you should not feel constrained by the datasets or examples used in this book.

This book does not assume any mathematics knowledge beyond the equation of a straight line. Success in applied statistics is not connected to any innate mathematics or statistics ability. It is based on confidence. The best way to build confidence is through practice. This book is the result of ten years of teaching statistics to (often petrified) political science and international relations undergraduates; it has been six years in the writing. The examples flow smoothly (I hope), but behind all of the final materials included in this book are hundreds of examples that I tried out that didn't work. Students learning statistics often think that they have done something wrong when they try combination after combination of variables with no statistically significant findings. What they have actually done is experience the frustration of the research process. Because we often only publish statistically significant results, students do not see the masses of insignificant results we have accumulated in the meantime. So, if your tests don't go smoothly, if things go wrong, if you accidentally ruin your dataset, know that this is a very important part of becoming proficient in applied statistics.

Because this book is aimed at an introductory level, assuming no prior knowledge of statistics, it does not cover more advanced techniques or less common tests. This is not to make a judgement on their utility, but rather to avoid overwhelming you with information and to cover roughly the content you would expect to cover at an introductory level. As such, some of the most well-known techniques *not* covered are: bootstrapping, weighting data, factor analysis, factorial ANOVA, ANCOVA and MANCOVA. This book is also based on secondary data analysis (data that someone else collected), so it does not give extensive detail on how to enter your own data into SPSS.

HOW TO USE THIS BOOK

Each substantive chapter includes a chapter overview, how-to boxes showing you how to produce each test and additional activities to apply your knowledge. Where relevant, there are also indications of further reading to expand your knowledge at a level of depth not covered in this book. This book is laid out in such a way that each chapter follows logically on from the previous one and often speaks to ideas and examples that were raised previously. As such, it is laid out less as a how-to manual that is easy to dip in and out of. That said, each of the statistical techniques taught is identified in a stand-alone box, and the list of boxes after the Table of Contents will help you to locate the test you are looking for.

Chapter 2 provides a general justification for the approach to the social world taken in this book. This is, depending on who you ask, either vitally necessary or utterly unnecessary for embarking on quantitative analysis. When I started writing this book, I was steeped in a department that came down firmly in the camp that questions of ontology, epistemology and methodology should inform every aspect of our lives, and I had wonderful colleagues who have written extensively on these debates. I have since moved to a department where such questions have been relegated to a second-year option, and no one gets into a rousing argument about the epistemological implications of quantitative versus qualitative approaches. Thus, depending on the approach taken at your university, you may find this chapter incredibly helpful in distilling the implications of what can become very abstract, theoretical debates; or you might skip over it completely on the grounds that you are being compelled to learn statistics anyway, so it does not really matter whether you believe in quants or not.

The second half of Chapter 2 provides a much more practical overview of a selection of the many places that you can find quantitative data as well as introducing you to the datasets used in this book. Chapter 3 provides a general orientation to SPSS, helping you to find your way around its various windows and files. The rest of the core chapters are split into three groups: Chapters 4 to 6 show you techniques for working with categorical data; Chapters 7 and 8 show you techniques for working with continuous data; and Chapters 9 and 10 show you techniques that combine categorical and continuous data. The final chapter covers writing about data, distilling information from the previous chapters on how to talk about and present statistical findings.

It is possible that you may get answers that differ from those in this book, even when you have followed the precise example used. This may arise because you are using a more recent version of the public data files (this book is based on ESS round 7, version 3) or because of updates to SPSS (this book was created using IBM SPSS version 24). You can check whether you have used the technique correctly, even if there are minor differences in your output, by comparing your results to the syntax printed in the book, which is also available on the companion website.

FURTHER READING

Field, A. (2017) *Discovering Statistics Using IBM SPSS Statistics*. London: Sage.
For students looking to cover more advanced material. Also available for other software packages.

Pallant, J. (2016) *SPSS Survival Manual*. Maidenhead: McGraw-Hill Education.
Serves as a how-to manual that covers more advanced techniques.

Salkind, N. (2016) *Statistics for People Who (Think They) Hate Statistics*. London: Sage.
Good for explaining the ideas behind statistics. Includes a short SPSS guide.

Urdan, T. (2017) *Statistics in Plain English*. Abingdon: Routledge.
Gives a clear introduction to statistics by hand. Good explanations of some of the tricky concepts of statistics; can be useful as a reference guide when you don't understand some of the concepts.

2

APPROACHES TO THE SOCIAL WORLD

CHAPTER SUMMARY

This chapter addresses the philosophical foundations underpinning research in politics and social science, introducing the core concepts of ontology, epistemology and methodology. It examines some of the assumptions that underlie different approaches to research, looking at choice of methods and inductive versus deductive starting points. The chapter then introduces quantitative data: What is it? Where does it come from? What can we do with it? It discusses the main ways that we can collect and analyse quantitative data. The final part of the chapter provides an overview of common sources of secondary data: that is, data that other people have already collected that is available to you. It finishes with a brief background of the datasets that are used for the examples and exercises in the rest of the book.

OBJECTIVES

In this chapter, you will learn:

- Key differences between inductive and deductive approaches to research
- What ontology is and the main divisions among researchers
- What epistemology is and the main divisions among researchers
- How ontology and epistemology affect a researcher's methodology
- What quantitative data and secondary data are
- How to find the main datasets used in this book.

INTRODUCTION

Many students are required to take an introduction to the philosophy of social research as part of their degree. This is rarely popular and is often taught from an abstract perspective that leaves all but the diehard philosophers emerge frustrated and determined never to think about the ideas again, while their philosophical peers engage eagerly in hours-long debates about the existence of reality. Despite the abstraction with which the ideas of ontology, epistemology and methodology are often introduced, our positions on these debates unconsciously underpin how we see the world, our belief system and how we undertake research. This chapter introduces you to these ideas in what I hope is a gentle manner, emphasizing their real-world application and implications, and how they impact our approach to research. The second half of this chapter introduces some of the many secondary datasets that are available to you, assuming that you emerge from the discussion of ontology and epistemology convinced that quantitative data is a valid way to learn about the social world.

PHILOSOPHICAL FOUNDATIONS

Researchers in the social sciences – which include politics and international relations as well as other subjects like human geography, sociology and economics – often use terms like ontology, epistemology and methodology. These terms all fall under the umbrella of the philosophy of research, and the position that researchers take on each of these affects the kind of research they undertake and how they interpret their results. As Moses and Knutsen (2012: 4) explain, these 'three musketeers of metaphysics' answer fundamental questions about the nature of the world and knowledge:

1. What is the world really made of? (ontology)
2. What is knowledge? (epistemology)
3. How do we know? (methodology)

Training in the philosophy of research – including ontology, epistemology and methodology – forms a core element of social science degrees at most universities. This is because our ontological and epistemological viewpoints on the nature of reality and knowledge inherently affect our methodological decisions, whether we are conscious of it or not. Thus, while it might initially seem irrelevant to talk about the philosophical underpinnings of research in a statistics textbook, it is actually very important for understanding why researchers might eventually choose to use quantitative methods to understand the social world. Understanding the underlying philosophy also helps you to identify the strengths and weaknesses of taking a quantitative approach to research.

In the first half of this chapter, we will walk through what the terms 'ontology', 'epistemology' and 'methodology' mean. In the second half of the chapter, we will look at how these affect the methods a researcher chooses and introduce the research cycle.

Ontology

Ontology translates roughly from ancient Greek as 'the study of being'. Ontology is important for research because different ontological positions entail different approaches to the very existence of facts and truth. Ontological claims are 'claims and assumptions that are made about the nature of social reality, claims about what exists, what it looks like, what units make it up and how these units interact with each other. In short, ontological assumptions are concerned with what we believe constitutes social reality' (Blaikie, 2000: 8). Or, as Furlong and Marsh (2010: 185) explain, 'The main issue is whether there is a "real" world "out there" that is...independent of our knowledge of it.' Competing ontologies disagree about the existence of objective truth and facts.

If this sounds too abstract, think about the rise of the term 'post-truth politics'. Perhaps the most widely quoted recent example of this occurred in January 2017, when newly inaugurated President Trump's senior aide, Kellyanne Conway, waded into a debate instigated by Sean Spicer, the press secretary, who had asserted that the crowd at Trump's inauguration 'was the largest audience to ever witness an inauguration, period, both in person and around the globe' (Hunt, 2017). When reporters confronted Conway with photographs that showed smaller crowds at Trump's inauguration than Obama's four years earlier, Conway retorted, 'You're saying it's a falsehood...Sean Spicer, our press secretary, gave alternative facts to that.' NBC presenter Chuck Todd then countered, 'Look, alternative facts are not facts. They are falsehoods' (NBC, 2017).

What does this have to do with ontology?

Conway and Todd were representing opposing ontological positions. Todd, and most of the US mainstream media, were taking an objectivist (also referred to as foundationalist or realist) approach to the situation. Such an approach assumes that there are objective facts that we can find out through research; if we do our research properly, we should all reach the same conclusion about the 'facts' of the situation. Conway, many members of the Trump administration, and much of the 'alt-right' media represent a constructionist (also referred to as constructivist, anti-foundationalist or relativist) approach. Constructionist approaches mean that 'facts' and 'reality' are social constructs and that there is not a single objective 'truth' about a given situation. This is exemplified in phrases like 'post-truth politics', 'alternative facts' and 'your truth is not my truth'. When opposing ontologies collide, whether in a press room or in social research, the difference is so fundamental that the two sides are irreconcilable. This is why, for example, detailed refutations of Spicer's assertion, using photographs, Metro journeys, crowd estimators and other metrics, failed to shift Conway's position.

Our ontological position matters in social research because it has drastic implications for what research we think can even be undertaken as well as whether we can make any transferrable conclusions from our findings. As Bryman (2008: 19) explains about the constructionist position, 'The term has also come to include the notion that researchers' own accounts of the social world are constructions. In other words, the researcher always presents a specific version of social reality, rather than one that can be regarded as definitive. Knowledge is viewed as indeterminate.' For those who approach research from a constructionist position, 'reality', 'truth' and 'facts' are created by actors. For objectivists, however, 'social phenomena and their meanings have an existence that is independent of social actors' (Bryman, 2008: 19). These are fundamentally different answers to the questions, 'What is there to be known? What is reality?'

Objectivists (or foundationalists) and constructionists (or anti-foundationalists) often express exasperation with each other, with neither recognizing the other's ontological objections to their methods of enquiry into the social world. Some famous objectivists commonly studied in the history of Western political thought include Aristotle, Descartes and Locke. Their theories were based on using deductive reasoning to identify infallible basic knowledge about the world. Famous constructionists include Nietzsche and Foucault, who developed theories based on relativism, emphasizing the conditionality of human practices and questioning the existence of a single, knowable truth.

Epistemology

Epistemology translates roughly from ancient Greek as 'the study of knowledge'. Epistemological positions are important for research because different epistemological positions take different approaches to finding out about the world. Epistemological positions are inherently connected to ontological positions: each epistemological position is only fundamentally compatible with one ontological approach or the other.

There are three main epistemological positions: positivism, realism (including the sub-strand critical realism) and interpretivism (also referred to as relativism). Alternative classification systems use the terminology scientific/positivist and hermeneutic/interpretivist. Did you notice that we have already encountered 'realism' as an ontological position in the previous section as another name for an objectivist ontology? Despite the confusing re-use of terms, it is important to distinguish between a realist (/objectivist/foundationalist) ontology; a realist epistemology; and other uses of realism, such as the core theory of international relations associated with Hans Morgenthau.

In this section, we will work our way through these three epistemological approaches, linking ontology to methodology. Furlong and Marsh (2010: 192) clarify the link between ontology, epistemology and methodology this way: those who take a constructivist approach 'focus on the *meaning* of behaviour. The emphasis is upon *understanding*...Understanding relates to human reasoning and intentions as grounds for social action. In this tradition, it is not possible to establish causal relationships between phenomena that hold across time and space' (emphasis in the original). In other words, interpretivists (who are inherently also constructivists) try to understand behaviour in a single time and place without making claims that this information applies to any other time, place or people. On the other hand, those who take an objectivist approach focus on explanation. In the context of social research, this means identifying causal relationships, and generalizing lessons from one situation to apply to other times, places or people, including making predictions about the future.

Positivism

Positivism has its origins in the empiricist – not to be confused with empirical! – tradition based on Hume's argument that knowledge starts with observation using the senses: 'we should "reject every system...however subtle or ingenious, which is not founded on fact and observation", and accept only argument derived from experience' (Hume, 1975: 1.10/173–4, cited in Morris and Brown, 2014). Firmly based in this tradition, Auguste Comte coined the term 'positivism' to characterize the final stage in the search for truth with two goals: 'to generalize our scientific conceptions, and to systematize the art of social life' (Comte,

1908: 3). He outlined a systematic approach to the study of the social world, naming this 'sociology'. This position developed into epistemological positivism, which contends that:

1. There is an objective reality.
2. We can learn about it by observation through our senses.
3. We can generalize things that we learn from direct experience to make conclusions about the way the world works.
4. We can use the same approaches to the study of the social world as the study of the natural world.

Positivism is based on the scientific method: observation of a phenomenon leads to a hypothesis, which we test empirically, then create a theory based on our results. Positivists contend that the natural and social worlds are fundamentally the same and can be studied using the same techniques. They argue that if we adopt a rigorous, scientific methodology to study human behaviour, we will be able to establish theories of causality similar to laws governing the natural world, such as the theories of gravity and evolution. When social researchers in the 1960s applied the tenets of positivism and empiricism to the scientific study of human behaviour, they became known as behaviouralists.

A pure behaviouralist approach only takes into account observable behaviours. This sets it directly at odds with interpretivism and epistemological realism because it excludes phenomena that cannot be observed directly as well as socially constructed reality. Another critique of positivism is its apparent lack of acknowledgement of the hermeneutics of research: interpretivists criticized positivists for failing to acknowledge the influence of the researcher's bias in the processes of data collection and analysis. Researchers' prior knowledge and experience affect 'both the facts we focus on and how we interpret them' (Furlong and Marsh, 2010: 195), which means that we cannot attain the level of objectivity envisaged by positivism. A final critique of positivism rejects its origins in the natural sciences approach. This critique asserts that there are fundamental differences between the functioning of the natural and social worlds. For example, critics of taking a natural sciences approach to social sciences highlight the inconsistency of human behaviour, which does not seem to obey natural laws with the same consistency as the natural world. The vagaries of human agency and thought mean that, presented with the same situation twice, someone might make a very different choice in each case. We can detect general trends by looking at population level (such as identifying the impact of education on a variety of social values), but there are always exceptions to the explanations, and social sciences have yet to come up with any theories that could be elevated to the status of natural laws.

Interpretivism

Interpretivism starts from a fundamental disagreement with positivist assumptions. Arising during the 'post-behavioural revolution' that brought forward many criticisms of positivism, interpretivism disagrees that the social and natural worlds are fundamentally similar. As a result, the use of a natural sciences approach is not appropriate for the study of the social world. Interpretivist epistemology aligns with constructionist ontology, meaning that reality is socially constructed. If reality is socially constructed and does not exist outside of our experience of it, then we cannot explain or make predictions about the social world; all we can do is understand it.

The difference between explanation and understanding, as used in social research, is not immediately obvious, so we will pause for clarification. Explanation means forming theories about causal relationships that can be used to predict results in other times or contexts. Explanation seeks an answer to the question, 'Why?' Even asking this question implies that we think there is underlying causality. For example, if we ask, 'Why did Trump win the US presidential election in 2016?', we are implying that we think there was a certain set of prior conditions (cause) that resulted in Trump's win (effect). A positivist researcher approaching this question might look at variables like unemployment levels, wage growth and support for the Republican Party to build a model that would predict a Trump win – and would also predict the winner of future elections where the conditions were similar. Researchers seeking explanation are looking for 'facts' and tend to ignore individuals and their values.

Understanding, as used in interpretivism, is based on Max Weber's concept of *Verstehen* – though Weber himself was uninterested in wading into such epistemological debates and even proposed 'explanatory understanding' as an approach to researching the social world. In the context of social research, this means trying to understand the meanings and motivations an individual attributes to their own actions. This includes understanding the actor's feelings, values and personal experience of the social world. As Pope and Mays (1995: 43) maintain, the goal is 'the development of concepts which help us to understand social phenomena in natural (rather than experimental) settings, giving due emphasis to the meanings, experiences, and views of all the participants'. In fact, as you might note from the reference, Pope and Mays are making an argument for bringing interpretivist research methods into natural sciences research – the opposite of the positivist argument advocating the use of natural sciences research methods to study the social world.

The key to the difference between interpretivist 'understanding' and positivist 'explanation' lies in the extrapolations from the knowledge gained. While positivists also seek to understand a given situation, they then use this knowledge to propose laws about human behaviour; interpretivists, on the other hand, do not attempt to form generalizations or make predictions based on the understanding they have gained. Interpretivist understanding also means recognizing not only the subjectivity of the agents but also the researcher's own subjectivity: while positivists attempt to keep both their and their research subjects' values separate from the formulation of laws governing human behaviour, interpretivists recognize that values are inherently intertwined not only with the actors' own understanding of their behaviour but also with the researcher's interpretation of this understanding.

Yet at the extremes of positivism and interpretivism, their approaches in application can look remarkably similar. For example, positivists attempt to take a completely neutral approach to studying the social world, avoiding interpretation guided by their own feelings; interpretivists taking a grounded theory approach also attempt to 'unlearn' their understanding of the social world and to make their minds a blank slate when observing the behaviour of others. The existence of widespread methodological similarities, despite ontological and epistemological differences, has received some attention in recent years (Halperin and Heath, 2017; Hopf, 2007).

Realism

Encompassing subsets including critical realism (Bhaskar, 1978), scientific realism (Halperin and Heath, 2017: 34–41) and metaphysical realism (Khlentzos, 2016); realist epistemology aligns with objectivism in that it is based on the assumption that there is an objective reality and that we can find out about it through research. However, it diverges from positivism in its recognition of 'hidden structures' that cannot be observed directly using the senses. Adherents to realism contend that these unobservable phenomena cause changes to observable phenomena and that failure to take them into account when theorizing, as positivists do, leads to flaws in the resulting explanations. Realists differ from interpretivists in their belief in the existence of an objective reality.

To think about this another way, we can use the structure versus agency debate in the social sciences to illustrate the differences between the epistemological positions. Structures have an existence independent of agents and constrain the choices agents make; this means that structures exist prior to agency. This exemplifies the combination of objective ontology and positivist epistemology. Agency, on the other hand, proposes that the world is socially constructed and that actors create and change the structures that exist. This exemplifies the combination of constructionist ontology and interpretivist epistemology. Realists take a middle ground, theorizing a dynamic relationship between structure and agency. In this case, realists' explanations of social phenomena rely both on constructed reality and the structures that both influence and are influenced by social actors. Because of the fluid middle ground that realists occupy, their position is not always recognized as a third epistemological position (Furlong and Marsh, 2010: 191).

WHAT DOES THIS MEAN IN REAL-WORLD RESEARCH?

Let's think about public opinion polling, specifically with regards to support for political parties. Approaches to and interpretations of polls can help to exemplify the impacts of different epistemologies. Opinion polls have become a staple characteristic of the electoral cycle in countries like the UK and the United States. Yet over the course of a year, they predicted the wrong result in the UK's referendum on European Union (EU) membership (June 2016), the US presidential election (November 2016) and the UK's general election (June 2017). We can interpret the failure of these polls from the three main epistemological standpoints.

We will start with interpretivism. Interpretivism rejects the idea of generalization across time, place and people. In this case, the failure of the polls to predict the correct outcome is wrong because they sought to make a prediction about future behaviour based on the answers people gave to the opinion poll on the day of polling (time) instead of simply using the polls to understand how people were feeling about politics on a given day. The polls violate generalization of place because they make conclusions about what will happen on a national level without taking into context how people behave differently in different regions. Finally, an interpretivist epistemological position is fundamentally incompatible with quantitative approaches to social research. Interpretivists reject the idea of a sample being able to tell us anything about a population as a whole; here, they would say that the opinion poll only tells us about how the people in the sample felt on the day of the poll, not how other people with similar characteristics, or even the same person on a different day, might behave in the future. Instead, an interpretivist researching voter behaviour would be likely to take a qualitative approach that contextualizes the voter's behaviour, especially trying to understand the social meaning of the action.

Positivists and most realists, on the other hand, believe in generalizability of sample data. Because these approaches use validity, reliability and replicability as core requirements of research, their explanations for the failure of the polls revolve around problems with the sample and the questionnaire. These explanations have highlighted, for example, the strong university-educated bias of the samples, leading to an overrepresentation of liberal-leaning views. Defenders of the polls would also note that they did not technically 'get it wrong': the results were within their calculated margin of error, but the media and public interpretation of the numbers usually fail to take this into account. Many of the projections also omitted undecided answers, a common approach in reporting survey data; but the population who made up their mind at the last minute was large enough to change the outcome.

Methodology

If it seems like we are wandering back into abstract territory that has little to do with real-world research – much less with learning how to do applied statistics – then learning about methodology should bring the two together.

At its simplest, a methodology tells researchers what you did, how you did it and why you did it that way. A quick look at the word root again gives us an insight into the meaning. 'Methodology' also has its origins in ancient Greek, translating roughly as 'study of the pursuit of knowledge', with the 'pursuit' implying a logical process. It means explaining how you gathered and analysed your data, identifying the process clearly enough that other researchers could look at the same data using your approach and come to roughly the same conclusions. The approach you take, however, is dependent not only on your research question but also on your underlying ontological and epistemological assumptions. It is important to note that *methodology* and *method* are not synonyms, though they are frequently misused as such. The method is the actual *tool* you use to collect or analyse data (see Table 2.1 for examples). The methodology is the *reason* you chose that method and the *explanation* about how you applied that method. A methodology also includes a discussion of how you broke down abstract concepts to make them measurable (operationalization). It answers the question, 'How do I know it when I see it?' Let's think about this by working through an example.

Table 2.1 Examples of methods of data collection and analysis

	Collection	**Analysis**
Quantitative	Survey	Descriptive statistics
	Experiment	Inferential statistics
	Quantitative observation	Quantitative content analysis
Qualitative	Interview	Discourse analysis
	Focus group	Grounded theory
	Qualitative observation	Narrative analysis
	Document review	Framework analysis

We will start with a research question: 'How has the rate of poverty changed in the UK?' The core concept here is poverty. What does this mean? How do we know it when we see it? How can we measure it? Though this might initially seem straightforward, we shall see why it is anything but. The ontological, epistemological and methodological approach a researcher takes to poverty results in very different conclusions.

Let's start with defining poverty. In 1995, the United Nations defined poverty as:

> [a] condition characterised by severe deprivation of basic human needs, including food, safe drinking water, sanitation facilities, health, shelter, education and information. It depends not only on income but also on access to services. (UN, 1995: 2.19)

This is an absolute definition of poverty and led UN members to agree a series of quantifiable measures for each of these characteristics and set specific targets for these measures as part of the Millennium Development Goals in 2000. Perhaps the most well-known of these targets was to halve the proportion of people across the world living on less than USD 1 a day. Choosing the measure of USD 1 a day implies specific underlying approaches to ontology, epistemology and methodology. First, it assumes that there is an absolute measure for poverty (objectivist ontology). Second, it assumes that poverty is external to the social context (positivist epistemology) and, third, that we can measure poverty using numbers (quantitative methodology).

This approach has come under considerable criticism, including from the UN itself, for being arbitrary and de-contextualized (e.g. Woodward, 2010). For example, it does not take into account the differing costs of living in different cities, regions and countries, which proponents of relative measures of poverty would argue are essential. If we look at various definitions of poverty, we can divide them into three categories: absolute poverty, relative poverty and subjective poverty. Advocates of subjective measures of poverty would argue that one's perceived level of poverty (constructed reality) is more important than one's absolute level of poverty (objective reality), because perceived deprivation has a greater impact on other deprivation indicators – such as unemployment, indebtedness, educational attainment and family breakdown – than absolute measures.

Before researchers have even defined poverty, they run into an ontological debate: is there an objective definition of poverty, or is poverty a social construct? We could align the categories above with ontological approaches, placing absolute and relative poverty in the objectivist camp, and subjective poverty in the constructivist camp. The reason these categories align with opposing ontologies becomes more evident when we look at the different conclusions about the state of poverty to which these different definitions lead. To do this, we will look at a range of poverty measures used in the UK.

The UK government defines absolute poverty as those living in poverty compared to the median household income in a fixed year, adjusted for inflation – a measure that is still more relative than the UN's measure of USD 1 a day. According to the UK definition, absolute poverty dropped from 40 per cent of households in 1995–6 to roughly 20 per cent in 2015–16, using the post-housing costs measure. The UK government defines relative poverty as having a household income after taxes, benefits and housing costs that is less than 60 per cent of national median household income. According to this measure, the percentage of households living in relative poverty has stayed almost flat over time, with roughly one-quarter of UK households living in relative poverty. However, because this is a relative measure, the proportion of households living in relative poverty actually decreased following the 2008 recession because the median income nationally decreased.

The UK government includes a measure of subjective poverty when it includes being unable to afford an annual holiday, a car, a telephone or mobile phone, or a washing machine as 'essential items' in its material deprivation measure on the grounds that not having these items puts a household 'at risk of social exclusion' (ONS, 2017). Proponents of absolute poverty measures reject many of these as being unnecessary luxuries, with annual holidays drawing particular ire (Fogg and Wallace, 2014). Those who reject these measures generally adhere to an absolute definition of poverty as being unable to afford items that are essential to human survival, such as food, clean water and shelter. The Poverty and Social Exclusion Survey uses the public perception of the minimum income necessary to maintain a 'decent' standard of living (subjective poverty). According to this measure, the proportion of people in poverty doubled between 1983 and 2012 (PSE, 2013).

As we can see from just these three approaches, poverty is variously decreasing, staying the same, or increasing. Which indicator we think best encapsulates 'reality' depends very much on our ontological, epistemological and methodological standpoint. This is a book about analysing statistics, which means it is necessarily based on an objectivist ontological position: there would be no point in analysing survey data if we took an extreme constructionist position, arguing that samples cannot tell us anything about populations and that there is no objective truth to be found. In terms of the epistemology, this book does *not* take an interpretivist approach; the study of social statistics naturally places this book into either a positivist or realist epistemological approach. We do not take a position here on the behaviouralist debate; rather, we are equipping you with the tools to analyse quantitative data and to formulate a reasoned critique of the methodology, data and method.

Research cycle

The final element of this discussion of the philosophical foundations of research looks at different starting points in the process of research, which are often referred to as inductive and deductive approaches to research. Although many students have been taught that inductive and deductive approaches align with a specific set of ontological and epistemological assumptions, this does not hold up if we examine induction and deduction in greater detail. As Colin Hay (2002: 30) notes, '*Inductive* approaches to political analysis take as their starting point the (supposedly) neutral and dispassionate assessment of empirical evidence' (emphasis in the original). Thus far, we could be talking about behaviouralists or grounded theorists: both take as their starting point the observation of the social world. In both cases, theory emerges out of observation. Deductive approaches, on the other hand, start with propositions or hypotheses drawn from previous research, which are then subjected to testing. Deductive logic is inherent in carrying out a literature review or writing an essay: you review what others have written before, subject it to testing and propose a new understanding or confirm someone else's explanation.

While many students have been taught that inductive approaches align with positivism and empiricism, such pigeon-holing seems to be a fundamental misunderstanding of induction, deduction and methodology. For example, both Hume's and Comte's positivist approaches specify observation of the world as the starting point of research; the observation of recurrent patterns should then lead to the formulation of a theory, which should be tested and refined. On the other hand, grounded theorists take as their starting point the collection of qualitative data, guided at most by a research topic or question; they then see what theories emerge from the data. It is difficult to label this as anything other than an inductive starting point or to discern great differences between this approach and the approach taken by positivists.

It is more helpful to think of inductive and deductive approaches to research as part of a research cycle rather than a linear process; a researcher joins the cycle at the point that is most logical for the research they are carrying out. For example, a researcher might join the research cycle at the inductive entry point if they are looking at an area where there is little prior research; there are therefore no previously extant theories for them to test, making a deductive starting point illogical. Instead, they start with observation, which leads to a preliminary account of what is happening. What they do at this point will depend upon whether they are seeking understanding or explanation; either way, they have reached the deductive stage of the research cycle. If they are looking for understanding, they would then need to approach the people involved in their research to see whether what they understand of the phenomena aligns with their interpretation of it. If they are looking for explanation, they would then need to apply the logic of their explanation of the phenomenon to a different time, place or group of people to test whether the explanation still holds up.

On the other hand, a researcher might start their research project at the deductive entry point. This is especially common for early-career researchers, such as undergraduate students, who are taking a theory-testing approach. When beginning on the deductive side of the cycle, the researcher starts with a pre-existing theory or explanation. From this, they formulate a framework of what they are looking for and apply this to a phenomenon. During the analysis of their data – whether qualitative or quantitative – they run across some unexpected findings. Here they enter the inductive phase, asking themselves how they can understand/ explain these findings and generating some possible reasons that will then need to be verified.

Most researchers will not complete the whole research cycle in a single research project. Instead, they may highlight 'avenues for further research', identifying a research agenda to explore the phenomenon further, whether at a micro (e.g. individual) or a macro (e.g. societal) level. In fact, when there is a large accumulation of research where other researchers have not followed up on previous research, one approach is to undertake a literature review, which is essentially researching the findings of other researchers. This is an important stocktaking exercise within social sciences to identify gaps in previous research.

QUANTITATIVE DATA

The rest of this book introduces you to techniques for analysing quantitative data. Before moving into the practical how-to, however, we need to define what we mean by quantitative data. 'Data' is just a simple term to refer to a collection of information about the world. Despite how the word is often used, data can be both qualitative (like archived documents, speeches, videos, interview transcripts and photographs) and quantitative (like government statistics, results of closed survey questions and counts of word usage). Data that social researchers use is usually classified as qualitative or quantitative. At its most basic, data that is described using numbers is called quantitative, while data that is described using words is qualitative. Quantitative data comes from counting, at its most basic answering the question, 'How many?' You might count the number of people belonging to each ethnic group in a country; or how many people know how to read; or the number of times countries have gone to war with each other.

Many researchers specialize in either quantitative or qualitative approaches, both because of their own ontological and epistemological beliefs, and because of the amount of training required to become an expert in applying research methods. There is, however, also a strong argument to be made for combining different methods (also called methodological triangulation) – or at the very least choosing the most appropriate method to answer your research question, rather than choosing your research question according to what you can research using your preferred method.

The difference between quantitative and qualitative approaches is rarely as clear-cut as many researchers make it seem, however. To a certain extent, it comes down to a question of scale: when dealing with large amounts of information, whether it started out as words or numbers, we will usually end up using numbers to describe it. It is simply easier for us to make sense of a large volume of data by quantifying it. On the other hand, we will frequently end up focusing on descriptions when working with small quantities. It is therefore perhaps more helpful to frame things in terms of small-*N* (few cases) and large-*N* (many cases). Small-*N* research will usually focus on going into great depth about a few cases, maybe even a single case, trying to provide thick description. Large-*N* research will usually try to detect patterns that can only be seen when looking at large numbers of cases. Even large-*N* research starts out with formulating words to ask questions and select answer choices; and small-*N* research over time can lead to the accumulation of so much data that researchers begin to talk about it using numbers.

The most common way to collect quantitative data for political researchers is through closed questionnaires, but data can also be collected through observation and amassing documents. Using observation, for example, a researcher could record the number of people who entered a particular polling place on an election day, possibly also recording visible characteristics, such as gender and ethnicity as well as whether the people arrived on foot or by car. A quickly growing field of quantitative research analyses social media and the internet. One way it does this is by counting the occurrence of certain words, identifying whether they frequently occur near other words, and studying networks of people who know each other and their common characteristics. However, closed questionnaires remain the most well-known form of quantitative data collection.

Closed questionnaires – frequently referred to as surveys – pose a question and give a limited number of possible responses, though they may include a qualitative 'other' field that respondents can fill in if they feel none of the options is adequate. Some of these questions can clearly be answered with a number, such as age, number of years of education completed, and year in which the respondent left full-time education. The answers to other questions have a number applied to them after the fact in order for the researcher to make sense of them, such as sex, marital status, ethnicity and educational qualifications. This process, called coding, is discussed in greater detail in Chapter 3.

Whatever the methods used to collect the data, quantitative data is analysed using statistical methods. If using documents, this is likely to take the form of content analysis, which is sometimes carried out using specialist software, while surveys will generally be analysed using a dedicated statistical program. The most common programs are IBM SPSS Statistics ('SPSS'), Stata, SAS, Mini-Tab and R. You can conduct a lot of research by performing statistical analysis on data that others have already collected. This is called secondary data, while data that you yourself collect is called primary data.

While some research projects do call for doing your own survey research, you should always check what data is already available to you. A wealth of secondary data can be found that has been collected using professional sampling and contains a lot of interesting findings. While the main disadvantage is that you do not have the option to influence the choice and phrasing of the questions asked, it gives most researchers access to a quality of data that few would have the time and resources to collect themselves. Doing research does not mean you have to do everything from scratch! It is perfectly valid and interesting to trawl through data that someone else has gathered to find interesting things.

This section gives an overview of some of the most common secondary data sources that are freely available. This selection is focused on European and worldwide data but includes some examples that are specific to the UK and the United States. Sources are listed in alphabetical order.

Afrobarometer

Afrobarometer covers 37 African countries, with data collected in seven waves since 1999. The data is publicly available and covers countries across Africa, though coverage of central Africa is more limited. The survey countries represent around three-quarters of the African population. This underutilized data is publicly available and includes topics such as democracy and politics, citizenship and identity, gender, security, corruption and international relations. The website includes an online data analysis tool, and the datasets can be downloaded in SPSS format.

http://afrobarometer.org/

American National Election Study (ANES)

The ANES is one of the most well-known election studies in the world because of the wealth of data it gathers about voters, identifiable down to the precinct level. Themes include voting behaviour and public opinion on a variety of topics. The study includes some panel studies, which follow the same respondents over a period of time to track changes in opinions and measure the effects of campaigns and events that occur over the period monitored. Data is available in a variety of formats for free download after registration.

https://electionstudies.org/

Arab Barometer

The Arab Barometer has covered the Middle East and North Africa (MENA) in four waves since 2006. The data is publicly available and asks a range of questions on topics including corruption, extremism, gender, political institutions and international relations. This is an underutilized resource for providing insights into public opinion in the MENA region. The website has a basic online analysis tool and data downloads in SPSS and comma-separated values formats.

https://www.arabbarometer.org

British Election Study (BES)

The BES includes survey data for every UK general election since 1964. More recently, the study has incorporated online panels and experimental surveys to supplement the face-to-face data. Each post-election survey contains a set of questions that is standard for all participants in the Comparative Study of Electoral Systems (hosted on GESIS; see below), allowing comparison across countries. The website includes some basic online analysis tools for the most recent data. Data is normally available for download in SPSS and Stata formats.

https://www.britishelectionstudy.com/

Eurostat

Eurostat is the official statistics database maintained by the EU. It contains information about EU and European Economic Area countries on many different themes, including population and social conditions, economy and finance, the environment and regional statistics. Eurostat aims to provide cross-national data that is comparable. For example, even something that seems straightforward, like unemployment, may be measured differently in different countries and is therefore not really comparable. Eurostat data is collected using the same measurements and methodology across all participating countries in order to allow researchers to make meaningful comparisons. Users do not need to register in order to access most of the data. Some tools allow you to explore and manipulate the data online, and you can download the desired information in a variety of file formats.

https://ec.europa.eu/eurostat

GESIS

GESIS is a German repository of survey data which also hosts several European-level surveys, such as the Eurobarometer and the European Values Survey (EVS). Both the Eurobarometer and the EVS are influential pan-European public opinion polls. While the EVS is only run slightly more than once per decade, the standard Eurobarometer runs twice a year, with standing questions on the EU, immigration, the environment, the economy and labour market, defence, health and culture. Standard Eurobarometer surveys are supplemented with special surveys, which focus more narrowly on a particular topic; flash surveys, which are requested by the European Commission and are more likely to be used in policymaking; and qualitative studies, which examine a topic in greater depth. GESIS also hosts the International Social Survey Programme, the Comparative Study of Electoral Systems, and the European Election Studies. Access to the data is normally free of charge but does require registration. Online tools include basic analysis and variable and questionnaire search facilities. The datasets are available in a variety of formats, usually for SPSS and Stata.

https://www.gesis.org/en/services/research

Several of the GESIS studies are available with online analysis, including keyword search facilities to identify suitable variables across a range of surveys. These can be found on ZACAT.

https://zacat.gesis.org/webview/index.jsp

Harvard Dataverse Network

Based at Harvard University, the Dataverse is a repository of data from researchers throughout the world who are willing to share the data they have collected in order to allow other researchers to test their findings and explore their data. Unlike most of the other resources listed in this section, the Dataverse is not specific to the social sciences, but it does contain contributions from social science researchers. Data can be found through keyword searches and is freely available after registration. Files are available for download in a variety of formats.

https://dataverse.harvard.edu

International Consortium for Political and Social Research (ICPSR)

Based at the University of Michigan, this repository contains a wealth of data. Though it has a bias towards the United States that is reflective of its hosts, it also contains the datasets for Afrobarometer, Eurobarometer, the Israeli Election Study and the China Multi-Generational Panel, to name but a few. You can browse by topic, search for variables and find publications based on the datasets. The ICPSR also has a YouTube channel with tutorials on using the resources and SPSS. Some datasets have online analysis tools to explore the data before deciding whether to download it.

https://www.icpsr.umich.edu/icpsrweb/ICPSR

Office for National Statistics (ONS)

The ONS is the UK government's official statistics repository. Perhaps its most famous survey is the Census, but it contains a wide array of other official statistics, including crime, education, economy and labour market, people and populations, and government. Statistics are gathered at local, regional and national levels, though some of the micro-level data is protected due to its sensitivity. Some of the data can be explored using online tools, with quite a variety of interactive maps. Most of the data is available to download as Excel spreadsheets, which require some manipulation to convert them for use in statistics programs like SPSS. While you can perform many basic statistical functions in Excel, the more advanced functions are much more straightforward in software packages designed for statistics.

https://www.ons.gov.uk

Organisation for Economic Co-operation and Development (OECD)

The OECD keeps statistics on more than just its member states and on a wide variety of social themes – not just the economy! It covers demography and population, development, education, environment and technology, to name but a few non-economic themes. It is also the repository for data from the Programme for International Student Assessment (PISA), among other international surveys. Core data can be explored on the website and can be downloaded in Excel formats. To gain access to the complete databases, you must have a subscription to the OECD's iLibrary. Many universities do subscribe to the database, so be sure to check whether you might have institutional access. The iLibrary includes extensive interactive tools and allows downloads of tables and charts.

https://stats.oecd.org

UK Data Service (UKDS)

The UKDS (formerly the Economic and Social Data Service) contains both qualitative and quantitative data from thousands of research projects as well as official government data. You can read interview transcripts and download survey results, and there are even multimedia projects. You can search for data by theme, country and keyword. Core themes include ageing, the labour market, housing and the local environment, crime and social control, and health and health behaviour. Some of the data held comes from long-running, government-sponsored surveys, such as the UK Census, the BES and the British Social Attitudes Survey. Other data is shared from specific research projects. The projects were not all undertaken in the UK, and some contain cross-national and foreign language data. Some of the data can be explored using online tools, but most of the datasets must be downloaded to explore them. You must register in order to use the service, and some datasets are protected and require a higher level of clearance due to the level of anonymity or sensitivity of the data.

https://ukdataservice.ac.uk

The UKDS also produces a series of guides, including a guide to navigating other platforms' online data services. This includes guides to a range of UN and OECD data. The UKDS has brought some World Bank, OECD, International Monetary Fund, UN, International Energy Agency and Human Rights Atlas data into its online analysis tool. The UKDS online tool is laid out using the same formatting and options as the OECD's own interface.

https://stats2.digitalresources.jisc.ac.uk

United Nations Statistics Division

The UN keeps statistics on population development worldwide, including demographics, fertility and mortality, and migration data. You can use the tools to explore individual indicators online or you can download the data in Excel format, which will require some tweaking to use in a dedicated statistics program. The UN Statistics Division is the core website for all data and will redirect you to appropriate divisions (such as the UN Development Programme, or the Population Division) based on the data you are looking for. Much of the data is collected annually. Accessing time series data is not always straightforward, and gaps in the data occur frequently, but the UN has a wealth of cross-national, comparative data. No registration is required to access the data.

https://unstats.un.org/home

World Bank

The World Bank also monitors a series of development indicators around the world, including additional topics not normally covered by the UN Development Programme, such as aid effectiveness, climate change and energy, in addition to general development indicators. Much of the data can be manipulated online in graphical and tabular format and is available freely for download in Excel formats. Excel data can be imported into SPSS to run more complex analysis. This is most easily done if the variable names occur in the first row of the spreadsheet. The data is generally available without requiring registration.

https://data.worldbank.org

DATASETS USED IN THIS BOOK

These are just a few of the resources available to researchers. This textbook uses one comparative politics dataset: the cross-national European Social Survey (ESS). It also uses one IR dataset compiled from UN Human Development data, paired with V-Dem and

Freedom House democracy data. Most of the chapters will use a single dataset for the whole chapter because the nature of the data in each of the sets is more suited to some statistical techniques than others and because each chapter is normally framed around answering a specific research question. The datasets are freely available for download, and I strongly recommend that you follow along with the examples in the book in order to practise for yourself as you learn about the tests. Each example is accompanied by the procedure for you to produce the same results, and the chapter ends with some exercises for further practice.

European Social Survey (ESS)

The ESS is a cross-national survey that has been conducted every two years in Europe since 2002. It includes 36 countries across a broad geographic definition of Europe (including Israel, the Russian Federation and Turkey, for example) and asks a variety of questions on politics, trust, media, well-being and society, values and socio-demographics. Each round also contains extra questions on a specific theme. Round 7, which was conducted in 2014 and is used for the examples in this textbook, includes extra questions on immigration. The ESS is used in many publications by researchers around the world, so you can always check your findings against other researchers by conducting a literature search. The ESS website also has a bibliography database, which indexes publications that use ESS data. The data used in this book is the ESS round 7 integrated file, edition 2.2. Please keep in mind that adjustments to the data may have occurred since the publication of this book, which means your results will not perfectly reflect the results in this book. You are strongly recommended to use the accompanying syntax documents to rerun the results using your version of the data file.

http://www.europeansocialsurvey.org

UN Human Development Data

The IR dataset is compiled from UN Human Development statistics. The UN Human Development data has been collected annually by the UNDP since 1990. It collects a wide variety of data to measure development and quality of life beyond economic indicators. It combines several variables to create a Human Development Index (HDI) each year, which ranks how countries are doing overall, including variables like literacy, health, poverty and employment. Data is also collected on gender and economic inequality, refugees and immigration, prison populations and some public opinion questions. Like the ESS, the UN data is used by many researchers each year in addition to the UN's own annual development reports.

The UN's human development data can be found on the UN Development Programme website. The data used for this textbook ends in 2015, but you can download more recent data from the UN. With some reformatting, you can integrate this into the textbook dataset.

http://hdr.undp.org/en/data

CONCLUSIONS

This chapter has introduced some of the core philosophical debates and assumptions that underpin approaches to research. As we have demonstrated, the position taken on ontology and epistemology has significant implications for the tools a researcher uses to collect and analyse data.

ACTIVITIES

1. Navigate to one of the websites with online analysis tools, such as ZACAT (https://zacat.gesis.org/webview/index.jsp). Search for a keyword or phrase of interest to you, such as immigration, political party or climate change. The search results, shown on the left-hand side of the screen, should come from a variety of different surveys. Try clicking on the most recent result you can see, such as a recent Eurobarometer poll. If you click on the survey name, you can download the data file for the survey, or you can browse through the variable descriptions to find a variable of interest to you. Switch the tab at the top from Description to Tabulation. Add the variable to the rows in the table by clicking on the variable name in the left-hand navigation frame and selecting 'Add to row'. You can add a second variable, such as the country, to the columns. Try changing the way it displays the results, such as switching between raw numbers and column percentages. You can also change the appearance to a chart or export your results to Excel using the icons across the top bar. Experiment with a few variable combinations and display options, such as displaying as a table or a chart.

2. Navigate to the United Nations Statistics Division (https://unstats.un.org/home/). In the Data tab, choose a data portal, such as UN Data. Browse through the databases listed to a topic of interest to you, such as gender, or enter some keywords into the Search bar. View data for a variable of interest to you, such as Adult literacy rate. You can then specify countries, years or sub-groups using the navigation tools on the left. Some databases will also link to more recent, separate websites in the Source information, such as the separate page for gender data post-2005. The UN's web pages can be frustrating to navigate, but they contain a wealth of information, some of it available for online analysis, and most of it available for download as spreadsheets. Try looking at the data for a few indicators, focusing on one or two countries.

(Continued)

3. Navigate to the ESS (http://www.europeansocialsurvey.org). In the Data and Documentation section, browse to the overview by themes. You should see a table that has the survey round in the columns and a variety of themes in the rows. You'll notice that some themes are covered every round - such as politics, gender and human values - while others are covered on a rotating basis - such as ageism, which was surveyed in round 3 (2006) and round 8 (2016). Click on a theme of interest to you to load a list of survey questions on that theme. Click the Info button next to a variable to find out the variable label, the full question text, answer options and how many survey answers are available on that question. Click on the question text itself to open the online analysis tool. The navigation on this tool is the same as with ZACAT, with study and variable information on the left, and options to toggle between Description, Tabulation and Analysis across the top. When using the Tabulation tool, you can display your results as a table or chart, or export the results in Excel format. Experiment with two variables, as in the first activity, adding one to rows and one to columns.
4. Navigate to the ESS website. In the Data and Documentation section, download the integrated data file for round 7 (2014). You may need to register for an account. The integrated (all countries) data file, round 7, is the file used for the examples in this book. There are other download options, including downloading all of the rounds in a single file, downloading all data for a specific country, or downloading data by a selection of specific themes, any of which you may find useful for your own research. Make sure that you download the SPSS file. It is also a good idea to download the questionnaire file(s) to use alongside the dataset, since this will give you the full question wording and answer options.

FURTHER READING

Many students encountering metaphysics or philosophy of research - including ontology, epistemology and methodology - for the first time can find the explanations of these complex concepts difficult to follow. Below are two suggestions for further reading on philosophy of research and one practical manual for getting started in applied research.

Grix, J. (2018) *The Foundations of Research*. London: Macmillan.
This book gives a background to the philosophy of research in straightforward language. See especially chapter 5 ('Introducing the key research paradigms') and chapter 6 ('The types and uses of theory in research').

Marsh, D., Ercan, S.A. and Furlong, P. (2018) 'A skin not a sweater: ontology and epistemology in political science', in V. Lowndes, D. Marsh and G. Stoker (eds), *Theory and Methods in Political Science*. London: Palgrave. pp. 177-98.
This book introduces many of the metaphysical debates and how they affect social research, particularly in political science.

Rich, R.C., Brians, C.L., Manheim, J.B. and Willnat, L. (2018) *Empirical Political Analysis*, 9th edn. Abingdon: Routledge.

This book covers the fundamentals of research design in a political science context. It includes both a discussion of philosophy of research and a discussion of techniques for collecting quantitative data.

REFERENCES

Bhaskar, R. (1978) *A Realist Theory of Science*. Hemel Hempstead: Harvester.

Blaikie, N. (2000) *Designing Social Research*. Cambridge: Polity.

Bryman, A. (2008) *Social Research Methods*. Oxford: Oxford University Press.

Comte, A. (1908) *A General View of Positivism*. Tr. J.H. Bridges. London: George Routledge and Sons.

Fogg, A. and Wallace, M. (2014, 13 Aug) 'Does everyone have a right to a summer holiday?' *Guardian*. (https://www.theguardian.com/commentisfree/2014/aug/13/katja-kipping-die-linke-holiday-vouchers-benefits-claimants).

Furlong, P. and Marsh, D. (2010) 'A skin not a sweater: ontology and epistemology in political science', in D. Marsh and G. Stoker (eds), *Theory and Methods in Political Science*. Basingstoke: Palgrave Macmillan. pp. 184–211.

Hay, C. (2002) *Political Analysis*. London: Palgrave Macmillan.

Halperin, S. and Heath, O. (2017) *Political Research: Methods and Practical Skills*, 2nd edn. Oxford: Oxford University Press.

Hopf, T. (2007) 'The limits of interpreting evidence', in R.N. Lebox and M.I. Lichbach (eds), *Theory and Evidence in Comparative Politics and International Relations*. Basingstoke: Palgrave Macmillan. pp. 55–84.

Hughes, J.A. (1980) *The Philosophy of Social Research*, 1st edn. London: Longman.

Hunt, E. (2017, 22 Jan) 'Trump's inauguration crowd: Sean Spicer's claims versus the evidence', *Guardian*. (https://www.theguardian.com/us-news/2017/jan/22/trump-inauguration-crowd-sean-spicers-claims-versus-the-evidence).

Khlentzos, D. (2016, 14 Jun) 'Metaphysical realism', *Stanford Encyclopedia of Philosophy*. (https://plato.stanford.edu/entries/realism-sem-challenge/).

Morris, W.E. and Brown, C.R. (2014) 'David Hume', *Stanford Encyclopedia of Philosophy*. (https://plato.stanford.edu/entries/hume/).

Moses, J.W. and Knutsen, T.L. (2012) *Ways of Knowing: Competing Methodologies in Social and Political Research*, 2nd edn. London: Sage.

NBC (2017, 22 Jan) *Meet the Press with Chuck Todd* [TV programme]. (video: https://www.nbcnews.com/meet-the-press/video/conway-press-secretary-gave-alternative-facts-860142147643; transcript: https://www.nbcnews.com/meet-the-press/meet-press-01-22-17-n710491).

ONS (2017, 27 Jun) 'Persistent poverty in the UK and EU: 2015'. (https://www.ons.gov.uk/peoplepopulationandcommunity/personalandhouseholdfinances/incomeandwealth/articles/persistentpovertyintheukandeu/2015).

Pope, C. and Mays, N. (1995) 'Researching the parts other methods cannot reach: an introduction to qualitative methods in health and health services research', *British Medical Journal*, 311: 42–5.

PSE (2013, 28 Mar) 'Going backwards: 1983–2012', *Poverty and Social Exclusion UK*. (http://www.poverty.ac.uk/pse-research/going-backwards-1983-2012).

UN (United Nations) (1995, 6–12 Mar) 'Report of the World summit for social development', A/CONF.166/9. (http://undocs.org/A/CONF.166/9).

Woodward, D. (2010, 4 Jul) 'How poor is "poor"? Towards a rights-based poverty line', *New Economics Foundation*. (http://neweconomics.org/2010/07/how-poor-is-poor).

3

GETTING STARTED WITH SPSS

CHAPTER SUMMARY

This chapter introduces the main windows of the SPSS software environment: the Data Editor, Output and Syntax Editor windows. We look at how concepts about particular cases (e.g. countries, individuals) may be represented in a form appropriate for statistical analysis and ways to handle missing information. This chapter gives key points to keep in mind when working with your data files and provides general instructions for inputting and importing data. The final section of this chapter introduces, and later critiques, a very common approach to classifying variables, also referred to as 'levels of measurement'. We discuss how variable classification may be used to help inform the kinds of analysis that are appropriate.

OBJECTIVES

In this chapter, you will learn:

- What primary data is and how to put it into SPSS
- The key functions of the Data Editor, Output and Syntax files
- How to use syntax to adhere to good statistical practice and save yourself future work
- The most common way of classifying variable types (levels of measurement) and its shortcomings.

INTRODUCTION

IBM SPSS Statistics ('SPSS') is a software program that is designed to analyse data. It has a long history, dating back to the 1960s, and has long been the most popular choice for academic researchers needing to analyse data and to teach students how to do so. There are alternatives, with other common packages including Stata and R. The latter is becoming more widespread because it is an open-source program, but it requires command-line input or an overlaid user interface, making it much less user-friendly for learners who are not confident in computer programming. SPSS requires a paid licence, but many universities and employers use it because of its relative ease of learning and menu-based 'point-and-click' interface. Some of these menus – such as File, Edit and View – will be familiar to users of other common software packages. This chapter provides you with a first introduction to the main files and windows used in SPSS and introduces the statistical concept of levels of measurement, a system for identifying the type of data you are working with.

Working with data in SPSS will normally require you to work with two or three files simultaneously. The main file will be the data file (file extension .sav), which contains all of the data and variable information. In addition, any outputs that you create – such as tables and charts – will appear in an output file (file extension .spv). The other main file type is the syntax file (file extension .sps), which keeps a record of the commands you use to manipulate the data. The syntax file is not essential for SPSS to function, but learning to use the syntax file, even at a very basic level, can save you a lot of time in the long run by allowing you to alter and reproduce your outputs very quickly. We will talk through the two default windows in SPSS in this chapter: the Data Editor and Output. We will talk through the Syntax window in the next chapter.

A note of caution: SPSS does not auto-save your work. Whenever you have made changes to a file, an asterisk (*) will appear at the top by the file name. If this change was unintentional, you can close the file without saving to erase the changes. Each window in SPSS represents a separate file, and each file must be saved manually. As we will emphasize throughout this book, you should save regularly, always have back-ups, and seek to create new variables rather than changing the original data. Conscientious use of the syntax document will also allow you to reproduce any changes or analysis very quickly if you do have to revert to a previous version of the file.

DATA EDITOR

The main window of SPSS is the Data Editor, which contains your data. The data file (.sav) is the main file where all of your data is saved. When you open a data file, it opens in the Data Editor window. If you close this file, it will exit SPSS. Most of the secondary data sources discussed in the previous chapter make datasets available that are already in SPSS format (file extension .sav), including all three datasets used as examples throughout this textbook. In this case, you simply need to open the secondary dataset and start working. You can open an SPSS data file by browsing to it on the start-up screen when you first open the program or File > Open > Data within the main program. For the rest of this chapter, you should download and open the ESS round 7 dataset so that you can follow along with the examples.

The Data Editor window has two viewing tabs: Data View and Variable View. You can toggle between these in the bottom left-hand corner of the data window. You will use the Variable View tab the majority of the time when working with your dataset. In Variable View, each row represents one *variable*. A variable is a characteristic of a case, such as marital status, income or age, if talking about individuals; or size of a country's economy, number of immigrants or unemployment levels, if talking about countries. Variables must have possible answers that can differ from each other (can vary). For example, if you are using data from the UK Census, all responses are from the UK, so having this as a variable would not make sense. However, you could have a variable representing the countries that constitute the UK (England, Scotland, Wales and Northern Ireland) because this does vary between different respondents. If using survey data, each variable normally represents the answer to one question. If, however, a question allows respondents to choose more than one category, the responses to a single question may be recorded as a series of variables, with one variable per response option. This is because it is not possible to record more than one value for a respondent in each variable. For example, if respondents are asked to indicate which newspapers they read at least once per week, they could tick more than one box. When this is turned into variables, it would be recorded as a series of yes/no responses, with one variable for each newspaper.

In Data View, each row represents one *case*. A case is the smallest unit of analysis in your dataset. If you are using data that came from a survey questionnaire administered to individuals, such as the ESS data, each case represents an individual's set of responses. This means that each row gives one respondent's answers to each of the survey questions. In some surveys, a case would be a household, with an entire household's responses recorded on a single questionnaire, such as census questionnaires. If you are using other data, such as the UN composite data, each case represents one country. Each case will normally have a variable with a unique identifier, such as a randomly assigned number, or the country name if countries are the unit of analysis. Although this is not strictly necessary for the file to function, it is good practice because it allows you to identify cases that might contain errors and re-examine the original questionnaire if you have input the data yourself.

Variable View

The Variable View tab gives you an overview of all of your variables, including their text labels and measurement type (discussed in more detail later in this chapter). Each column in Variable View gives you different information about a variable.

The variable *name* appears in the first column; this is the name that appears in the column headings in Data View. The names are usually kept short for ease of use in writing syntax, and they are governed by strict rules that require them to start with a letter and proscribe spaces, punctuation and many special characters (though $, # and @ are allowed if they are not the first character). The names cannot be more than 64 characters long, must each be unique and cannot be SPSS reserved keywords (ALL, AND, BY, EQ, GE, GT, LE, LT, NE, NOT, OR, TO and WITH). In some datasets, the name will represent a short form of the variable label, such as 'trstprl' as the variable name for 'Trust in country's parliament' in the ESS dataset. In other datasets, the variables are simply consecutively numbered, such as var001, var002, var003, etc. If you are inputting your own data, we would recommend creating names that are linked to the variable content, as this will make it much easier to work with the syntax. SPSS is not case sensitive for variable names, even though it will store any upper- and lowercase formatting applied by the user. However, other statistical packages – such as R and Stata – *are* case sensitive, so you should use caution in naming your variables. For example, in SPSS, Sex and sex would be interchangeable, but in other systems, they would operate as two separate pieces of information. Capitalization is also important when using string data.

The next column in Variable View is *Type*. This reflects whether the data takes the form of words or numbers. String means that the variable content in Data View is composed of words or letters. String format is more likely to apply to answers to open-ended questions in questionnaires (i.e. questions that do not have a set of answer choices but prompt respondents to write in a text box). String data should be used very carefully in SPSS and can present problems with auto-coding. Numeric means that the data has been entered as numbers. This can be because the data itself comprises a number, such as the number of children a respondent has or the year someone was born; but it can also be because numbers have been assigned to represent words to expand the possibilities for analysis in SPSS, such as 1=female, 2=male, 3=non-binary, etc. This is called *coding*, which we will look at in greater detail below.

The *Width* and *Decimals* columns provide information about how many characters are reported for those variables. The default width is 8 characters, which is sufficient for most numeric data, but this can be adjusted for string data or large numbers – for example, reporting the GDP for the United States would require 14 characters. The default number of decimal places is two, but this may be irrelevant depending on the units of a particular variable. For example, if you report the number of children in a household, children would be counted in whole numbers, so you would not need any decimal places. Decimal places are also unnecessary when the numeric coding represents word-based categories, such as political party preference.

The *Label* column gives a more detailed title for the variables. Unlike the variable name, the labels can contain spaces and are written in coherent prose. The label should give enough information about the variable such that you would not routinely have to consult the questionnaire to get an idea of the variable contents. For example, there is a variable in the ESS dataset with the name `etapapl`, which does not enlighten us about its contents; but its label is 'Easy to take part in politics', which makes it much clearer.

The *Values* column tells you what words are paired with the numbers recorded in the dataset. This pairing of numbers to represent words is known as *coding*. Coding is the process of attaching a combination of numbers or letters to represent each possible value for that variable to turn it into a numerical value for analysis. It is common for numbers to be attached to particular values of variables, even where the underlying data is not numeric. It is possible to leave the data as simple text (or 'strings'), but analysts tend to prefer variables to have an underlying numeric construction because it widens the possibilities of analysis. A common exception is the labelling of countries and regions. For example, in the ESS, the variable for the country where the respondent was interviewed [`cntry`] is formed in standardized two-letter abbreviations. In this system, AT means Austria, BE means Belgium, CH means Switzerland, etc. These codes are usually based on one of the international standards, such as ISO 3166-1 alpha-2 (two-letter country codes), alpha-3 (three-letter country codes) and numeric (three-digit country codes).

The majority of variables will be coded to use numbers to represent text. For example, in the ESS, there is a variable for how interested the respondent is in politics [`polintr`], where '1' means (is coded) 'Very interested', '2' means 'Quite interested', '3' means 'Hardly interested' and '4' means 'Not at all interested'. Sometimes there are labels for all numbers, such as the respondent's religious denomination, where all word-based categories have been coded with numbers for SPSS analysis. For variables where the responses run on a continuum, there are sometimes only labels for the two extremes of the continuum, such as How satisfied with life as a whole [stflife], where 0=extremely dissatisfied and 10=extremely satisfied, with no labels in between. Some variables, normally where the numbers reported actually represent numbers and not words, only report value labels for missing answers, such as Age when completed full-time education, United Kingdom [edagegb], where the only labels are for respondents still in full-time education, refusals, don't know and no answer. You can open the full list of value labels for any variable by clicking on the relevant cell in the Values column, then clicking the triple-dot button that appears on the right of the box. This is also the dialogue box you will need if you want to edit, add or delete value labels using the menu-driven approach.

The *Missing* column identifies which variables SPSS treats as missing in its analysis. This affects how it processes the data. Within a dataset there are often 'gaps' of various kinds, where we might expect there to be data on a particular case, but there is none. Missing values can arise for several reasons. First, data may be missing because that piece of information is simply not relevant or applicable. An individual who is not working will not have a current wage rate; an individual who was not old enough to vote in the last election will not have information about the party they voted for. This kind of information may be said to be structurally missing. An important type of missing data is found in datasets that track people over time (called panel studies), like Understanding Society, where people stop taking part over time. This is generally known as attrition and may arise because people no longer wish to take part (an active refusal) or have moved and cannot be located (non-contact). Such longitudinal datasets may lose a fair proportion of people to attrition at each wave, and judgement is needed about how to adjust for such losses in any analysis.

Where an entire case is missing, such as arises with attrition from longitudinal data, this is known as unit non-response. However, in most datasets the data collection is one-off (a cross-section) and missing data may arise as item non-response, or data that is missing for particular questions in the case of surveys. This kind of missing data may occur because people either do not want to answer the particular question (a refusal), or are unable to answer because they lack the relevant information (a 'don't know' response). There are also longitudinal datasets, such as the ESS cumulative datasets, where the data from several cross-sectional surveys asking a common core of questions has been combined into a single dataset to allow analysis of trends over time. In these cases, there will be variables with missing data because some questions were not asked in every round of the survey.

Missing responses are also likely to be higher for sensitive variables, such as on household savings or sex lives; in these cases, we would expect to encounter higher rates of respondents refusing to answer the question, especially if the survey was administered face to face. For this reason, sometimes such data is collected in less overt ways, such as using a self-completion questionnaire within an overall face-to-face interview. Questions about precise quantities or on topics not frequently considered may also lead to 'don't know' responses. This might occur, for example, when asking a respondent what their earnings were two years ago; trying to collect the incomes of those working as self-employed is particularly prone both to refusals and to 'don't knows'.

You may decide as you work with it to change whether an answer is treated as missing or not. For example, if you wanted to look at political party identification, you might be interested if a large proportion of respondents reported 'don't know', so you might decide that you wanted to include those answers in the main analysis, rather than excluding them as set by the missing values in the ESS. Missing values are normally coded as negative values (–1 through –5, for example) or high numbers (77, 88 and 99, for example) in order to avoid confusion with any of the 'real' responses. As with the value labels, you can open the full missing values dialogue box by clicking on the relevant row in the Missing column, then clicking the triple-dot button that appears on the right of the box. This allows you to see which values or value ranges are identified as missing and allows you to modify these, if needed.

The other main column of interest is *Measure*. This is where the variable type is classified. We will discuss more about type-casting variables and the potential pitfalls of following the classic approach used in SPSS later in this chapter, so here we will just look at how this column is laid out. If you click on one of the answers in the Measure column, you will notice that a drop-down menu appears with the options Nominal (symbolized by three circles), Ordinal (symbolized by three escalating bars) and Continuous (symbolized by a ruler). The measure recorded does matter, especially for the SPSS Chart Editor, so there may be cases when you need to alter the recorded type. You may also find that publicly available survey data does not record the variable type at all, leaving all variables as the default (nominal). This may cause problems in your analysis, so make sure that you check the measure if you receive an error message, or if your results do not look as you expected.

If you have too many columns to fit easily on your screen size and find that you do not frequently need to use some of them (such as Width, Decimals, Align or Role), you can choose not to display the unnecessary columns using View > Customize Variable View. Simply untick the columns you do not need to view. If you change your mind, you can return to that menu and click Restore Defaults.

Data View

The other view in the main Data Editor window is Data View. You will spend most of your time in Variable View, only entering Data View to input data or if your results are surprising, leading you to check whether there is an error in the data. You should be very careful in Data View, as it is very easy to accidentally change the results by typing in one of the cells. The Data View tab shows the data in a format similar to a spreadsheet. Each column in Data View represents one variable, while each row represents one *case*.

You can toggle the display of the variable responses to show either the alphanumeric coding or the value labels. You can do this by using the menu sequence View > Value Labels or by clicking on the icon with 1 and A in the icon ribbon at the top of the screen. Watch how the value labels appear and disappear as you toggle this on and off.

If you are starting from scratch to input your own data, say from a survey that you have conducted, there are good reasons to type this directly into SPSS. This can be more efficient because you can apply all of the appropriate labels and measures as you go. If you are entering your data manually into SPSS, you will need to create a new data file (File > New > Data). When inputting your data, you can take one of two approaches: you can either create a *codebook* before entering the data and then only enter the numbers representing the responses, or you can enter alphanumeric data (data composed of words and/or numbers) and automatically recode the text responses afterwards. A *codebook* contains information identifying each variable (such as a survey question) and possible values (such as response options to the question). When survey organizations provide datasets that are pre-formatted for statistics programs, this will normally be accompanied by a codebook, which shows you what numbers were applied to answer categories. It's also possible to produce a codebook from within SPSS for occasions when you want an overview of the coding of a variable.

The advantage of producing a coding scheme before you enter your data into SPSS, rather than entering text data and automatically recoding afterwards, is that it will ensure that the values appear in a logical order rather than an alphabetical order. To take the example of the political interest variable again, if you entered the data into the Data Editor in text form and automatically recoded it afterwards, SPSS would assign 1 to 'Hardly interested', 2 to 'Not at all interested', 3 to 'Quite interested' and 4 to 'Very interested', because this would be the alphabetized order of responses. This might not be what you would wish later when analysing your data, as responses to this question have a logical order that is not the same as alphabetical order. However, the advantage of entering the alphanumeric data and then automatically recoding afterwards is that it may be much quicker, and data entry can be much easier when you are not trying to remember the numeric values for each response to a survey.

If you decide to set up a coding scheme in advance, it may be helpful to write the response numbers onto your survey. If you have carried out your survey electronically and have the data as a spreadsheet, you may find it easier to set up your coding scheme, then use Find and Replace within each column to replace the text data with the chosen coding numbers. If taking either of these approaches, make sure that you have a back-up copy of your raw data that you can consult in case you think you have made errors in coding; and make sure that you take good notes of what numbers you have assigned to each set of values for a variable. If you decide to take the approach of starting with text data and then auto-recoding it, you will need to make sure that there are no errors or variations in spelling that would lead SPSS to separate the answers into different categories. For example, if you asked respondents which political party they voted for in the last election and allowed a free response, you would need to make sure that you didn't have some responses recorded as 'Conservatives' while others were 'Conservative Party'.

If your data is in spreadsheet or database format and you want to import this into SPSS, you can do this through File > Import Data > Choose the file type. SPSS can read many spreadsheet and database formats, such as text and comma-delimited documents (.csv, .dat, .txt, .tab), Microsoft Excel (.xls, .xlsx, .xlsm), Structured Query Language (.sql) and Microsoft Access (.accdb, .mdb). SPSS can also read other statistical software formats, such as Stata (.dta) and SAS (.sas7bdat, .sd7, .sd2, .ssd01, .ssd04, .xpt). If importing from a spreadsheet or delimited document, you should ensure that your data is laid out in a grid format, with variable names in the first row of the document and a separate column for each variable. Each row below the first row should represent a specific case. If your data is in this format, SPSS should be able to import it easily. You will probably need to do some work after importing data from other formats to attach appropriate labels to the variables and value labels, or to auto-recode string variables (also referred to as alphanumeric, which can be composed of any combination of letters, numbers and other characters) into numeric variables for analysis. The process of auto-recoding is covered in Chapter 4.

If not using auto-recode, the selection of labels may be mechanical, but it is worth reflecting upon. In practice it is most common to see people label gender as 1 being male, 2 being female – the 'second sex', as de Beauvoir put it; or marital status to have a set of codes, but with 1=Single, 2=Married, and cohabiting being lower down the list, either before or after divorce and separation. This is, of course, merely a convenient means of storing data rather than any kind of statement about the *kind* of data being represented, such as the index numbers sometimes used to classify books in libraries. However, it is still worth considering the kinds of underlying ideas that might be driving such coding, and the idea of '1' representing some kind of normality. Where data is only capable of having two values, it can be more meaningful (and perhaps progressive) to having a variable called by the name of the label attached to code '1', with others being zero – such as a variable called `female`, with 1=female and 0=male. The norm of only providing two answer options for sex is itself also something to consider if you are designing a questionnaire yourself, with estimates of 1 to 2 per cent of the population being intersex (Fausto-Sterling, 2000).

If you are inputting your own data for the first time, it is always worth looking at how other datasets have been set up to get an idea of how you might want to lay out the coding scheme as well as what sorts of variable names and labels seem to be the most helpful and intuitive. If you are new to data analysis, learning for the first time using your own dataset can be very challenging, and you will find it helpful to consult some of the many resources available online, including how-to videos, to walk you through the process.

OUTPUT

The other default window in SPSS is the output window. When you open a data file (.sav) in the Data Editor in SPSS, it will automatically create a new output file as well. The output file (.spv) opens in a separate window, usually with the default name Output1. This file provides a log of all of the actions you have taken and outputs you have produced.

Any tables and charts that you produce will appear here, along with the accompanying syntax and any error messages. The content in this file is interactive and can be edited. For example, you can activate tables to change the way the data is displayed, in terms of both layout formatting and content displayed. You can also activate charts to change their colours and other formatting. You can also use the output file to make notes to yourself, whether a note interpreting your results or reminding yourself how you went about producing that content. If you produce something that you want to discard, you can also delete any outputs that appear in the output file. All of these options make it a very powerful tool, and we would strongly recommend that you keep a copy of your outputs so that you do not have to reproduce content repeatedly.

SYNTAX

In the previous section, we looked at the default windows in SPSS: Data Editor and Outputs. The third main file type that you will encounter in SPSS is the syntax file (.sps). To open a new Syntax Editor window, click File > New > Syntax; to open an existing file, click File > Open > Syntax. The syntax file is a series of commands that tell SPSS what you want it to do. This can include everything from adjusting the labels on a variable to running complex analyses. Many introductions to SPSS skirt around the Syntax window, instead teaching an entirely menu-driven approach, but there are some very good reasons to engage early and often with the syntax file, even if you do not write the syntax yourself. You can keep a log of every menu command you perform by using the Paste button each time you carry out a task. This provides you with a record of what you have done and will allow you to replicate your previous work very quickly if needed. You can also write notes to yourself in the syntax file to remind yourself what you were doing, why you were doing it that way and what the results generally indicated. You will see, for example, that we have written some notes into the syntax files accompanying this textbook to indicate which examples and exercises each block of syntax pertains to.

Using the Paste button from the dialogue boxes will help build up familiarity with commands. As you grow more familiar with each command, producing new results with minor changes will get much faster. For example, you might use the menus to produce a table that shows respondents' UK political party affiliation [`prtclbgb`] against whether they voted in the last election [`vote`]. If you paste the syntax, then you could very quickly reproduce the same results for Austria by copying the command and replacing UK political party affiliation [`prtclbgb`] with Austrian political party affiliation [`prtclcat`]. But be aware that such pasted syntax is much longer than the minimum it needs to be, as sometimes elements are included which are the defaults, and the commands are not abbreviated in any way. For example, if you pasted the syntax for a basic frequency table for `prtclbgb`, which shows the number and proportion of respondents who selected each answer, the results would be:

```
FREQUENCIES VARIABLES=prtclbgb
  /ORDER=ANALYSIS.
```

However, not all of this information is necessary to produce the table. Writing the syntax directly, you could produce the same table by specifying:

```
FREQUENCIES VARIABLES=prtclbgb.
```

The syntax could be simplified even further with the same result by writing:

```
Freq prtclbgb.
```

However, too much shortening is not always a sensible idea and may make the syntax harder rather than simpler to read when revisiting it, and oversimplifying will also prevent helpful features like colour coding and auto-complete from activating. For example, if you start typing a command in the syntax window, SPSS will prompt you with available options using auto-complete. Using these prompts to guide you can help you to avoid error messages and will also colour code your syntax (see Table 3.1 and below for further discussion) to reflect the part of the syntax as well as highlighting commands in a navigation pane on the left-hand side of the window. If you shorten your syntax too much, this will not happen, though the syntax will still produce the desired result.

Table 3.1 SPSS syntax colour coding

Colour	**Meaning**
Dark blue	Main commands
Green	Subcommands
Red	Options
Grey	Comments
Black	Variable names; other text

Syntax must follow a number of key rules to work. Each block of syntax begins with a word that is the name of the command. If you start to type the name of a command, SPSS will prompt you with matches. For example, if you type Variable, SPSS will prompt you with a list of options, including variable alignment, variable attribute, variable labels and variable level. Using the command name prompted by SPSS will also cause SPSS to colour code the command in blue and bold. Main commands also appear in the left-hand navigation column of the Syntax window. In addition to starting each block with the name of the main command, there are two key items of punctuation in the syntax: the full stop (.) and the forward slash (/). Every command must end with a full stop. Full stops indicate the end of a command and are therefore very important for telling SPSS when to start and stop. When a block of syntax has failed to produce the desired result, the first error to check for is whether a full stop is missing.

The slash usually indicates a subcommand. Looking at the example above, the Frequencies subcommand identifies a series of output and formatting options (such as bar chart, format, grouped, statistics) that can be specified in addition to the main table. It is generally a good idea to use the slash with a subcommand, although it is not always needed for the syntax to function. Using a slash before the subcommand will change the colour of the subcommand to green, making it easier to differentiate from main commands. After choosing the subcommand, typing = will bring up the options for that subcommand. These are coded in red. The colours are not friendly to many forms of colour blindness, but the auto-complete feature is still useful, and the main commands also highlight in bold, making them more visible. It is good practice to start a new command (and subcommand) at the beginning of a new line. It can also be helpful to indent subcommands to create a clear visual distinction between main commands and subcommands. However, failing to observe these conventions will not usually stop SPSS from running simple syntax.

Good syntax style

Having good syntax 'style' can make it much easier for you to revisit the file later by keeping notes and maintaining good organization. It is a good idea to keep an annotated copy of everything you have done, including attempts that have not worked. One way of doing this would be to keep two separate syntax files for any piece of work: one containing all of the rough workings, including any failures and error-checking; and one containing only the final, 'clean' results. The latter is the style of syntax that we share in the materials accompanying this textbook.

You can annotate your syntax file by starting a new phrase with an asterisk (*). You will notice that the text after the asterisk, until you enter a full stop, will switch to grey. SPSS will continue to ignore the annotation as long as you do not finish a sentence with a full stop, then move to a new line. You might wish to make a note at the beginning of a syntax file that serves as an abstract of what the file contains. You might then add further information around certain commands to indicate why you were undertaking a certain test, or what part of your writing the results pertain to, such as: '* Results for Table 3.1'.

When working with longer syntax documents or blocks of several commands that you wish to run together, you might wish to add break points or bookmarks. Break points are helpful to establish a hard stop if you want SPSS to run several commands before stopping. Bookmarks can serve as break points but also for speedy navigation between sections. These are not essential and, with shorter syntax files, you can achieve the same effect by highlighting the section of commands you wish to run, then clicking Run > Selection.

If you don't start out with syntax but later want to start using it, you can extract the syntax from the Log sections in the Output window. You can find many useful guides to extend your knowledge of SPSS syntax. SPSS has its own Command Syntax Reference document, which is freely available from IBM's SPSS support website as well as within the program (Help > Command Syntax Reference). A quick web search for SPSS syntax cheat sheets will also turn up a wealth of user-created resources and video tutorials.

After the previous discussion, it may seem like the menus are easier to use than syntax. So why would anyone want to use syntax? There are two main reasons: it will benefit you as a researcher, and it will benefit the discipline.

Benefits for the researcher (you)

The greatest benefit of using SPSS syntax is pragmatic: it is far easier to 'retrace your steps' with syntax if you need to recall the modifications you have made to your dataset, or if you have to download your dataset again because the file corrupts, or you have introduced errors. For example, if you are using a secondary dataset, or have used an online survey method that allows you to export your 'raw' survey data in SPSS format, using syntax to modify variable labels or compute new variables means that you do not have to worry if you lose the SPSS data file you have been working on; you can just re-download the data and rerun your syntax to get your data back. It is also far easier to find and correct mistakes in your analysis if you have the syntax, as opposed to if you had used the menus.

If you are looking at longer term research, syntax can easily be modified and re-used on future projects, saving you time and effort in the long run. This means that you are unlikely to have to start from scratch the next time you carry out a research project. Syntax also remains relatively unchanged between different versions of SPSS (though there are a few notable exceptions), while the menus and dialogue windows have changed considerably, so syntax provides a longer term, more transferrable record of your work. If you are working in a team, it is much easier to communicate to others what actions you performed in SPSS by showing someone your syntax than it is to describe how you used the menus. In general, if you are working on a major project (like a thesis, dissertation or research for publication), or if you are collaborating with others on data analysis, we strongly recommend using SPSS syntax. An increasing number of teachers also require the submission of syntax and/or output files with data reports.

Benefits for the discipline

A number of concerns have been raised regarding the practice of quantitative research across a wide range of academic disciplines, including natural sciences (Fanelli, 2009), psychology (Stroebe et al., 2012), economics (Herndon et al., 2014) and health research (Ioannidis, 2005). In a famous article, Ioannidis (2005) suggested that most empirical findings within health research might well be false. Politics and international relations research in the UK has perhaps been less affected as it contains fewer quantitative studies, and many of the quantitative studies that exist are less likely to affect policymaking or personal safety. However, as an academic subject, it faces the same kinds of incentive structures and practices that may have negatively affected these other disciplines. The concerns about the quality of research publications centre on inadvertent errors and academic misconduct (including fabrication and falsification).

In the processes of creating new variables and conducting analysis, it is all too easy for mistakes to occur by accident. The history of computing contains a number of famous examples. In 1999 an expensive (USD 125 million) satellite designed to orbit Mars burned up in that planet's atmosphere because some of the software was using imperial measurements rather than the metric system, with the latter having been set out as a requirement throughout (Grossman, 2010). Software bugs have also been linked to unexpected acceleration in Toyota vehicles, which has been associated with a significant number of deaths (Dunn, 2013).

One might assume that errors in programming socio-economic research problems would have less drastic consequences, and mostly that is true. However, sometimes errors even in social science research can have widespread impact. In 2010, Reinhart and Rogoff 'showed' that the rate of economic growth in a country would slow when public debt exceeded 90 per cent of GDP. This was used as justification for implementing steep austerity measures in several countries on the grounds that austerity was necessary to avoid further economic damage. Their work was quoted by a range of politicians, including US House Budget Committee Chairman Paul Ryan, EU Commissioner Olli Rehn and UK Chancellor of the Exchequer George Osborne (Coy, 2013; Pollin, 2014). There are a number of important substantive and empirical critiques of this paper, but it is also clear that the spreadsheet used to calculate the main results was flawed and led to the exclusion of a number of countries at the top of the spreadsheet. This omission changed the median annual GDP growth for high-debt countries from –0.1 per cent to 2.2 per cent. The errors were discovered by a doctoral student running a replication exercise for a module he was taking (Herndon et al., 2014).

Another example from the social sciences concerns the effect of marital breakdown on divorce. Weitzman (1985) looked at a group of married couples who divorced, and measured the effects on their material resources. She wrote that women's living standards decreased by 73 per cent in the year following divorce, while men's living standards rose by some 43 per cent. This helped to set the tone for policies that would seek to better align their living standards. However, in a re-analysis, Peterson (1996) found a large number of errors and discrepancies. When these were corrected, the actual changes in income were around a 27 per cent reduction for women and a 10 per cent increase for men. Of course, these are still rather large changes and still show clear differentiated impact along gender lines, but they do cast a rather different perspective on the figures – and indeed are more in line with other studies of the same phenomenon.

Dewald et al. (1986) attempted to replicate the results of economics articles published in the early 1980s. They started by contacting the authors of those articles and requesting the data and programs needed to demonstrate the findings of their published work. Broadly speaking, one-third of authors did not respond, and another third responded to decline the request – sometimes because data had been lost or programs not preserved, or more rarely that the relevant data was confidential. Even where authors did respond in a helpful fashion, the researchers were often unable to precisely replicate the findings. To be fair, this was at a time when data was less often shared than today, and where the production of statistical results was a more complex undertaking, only really in the process of moving from remote access (mainframe) environments to desktop-based personal computers with more user-friendly features. The authors of this replication study concluded that, 'It is widely recognized that errors occur in empirical economic research and appear in published empirical articles. Our results...suggest that such errors may be quite common' (Dewald et al., 1986: 600).

The role that syntax plays in this is by simplifying the process of replication. The 'gold standard' for academic research is to share both the data (unless protected for reasons of safeguarding, anonymity or confidentiality of the participants) and the syntax used to analyse the data (Janz, 2016). This greater transparency allows other researchers – often students whose teachers have set them a replication exercise – to test out the analysis and identify potential errors (King, 1995). Replication exercises cannot, of course, reliably identify when a researcher has fabricated the data itself, though this is sometimes distinguishable by the lack of consistency with findings by other researchers. We would strongly recommend not only ensuring that your own work conforms to this gold standard but also that early-career researchers take the opportunity to try out replication using available data. You can get started with a repository like the Harvard Dataverse (for more about this, see Chapter 2).

LEVELS OF MEASUREMENT

Levels of measurement are a way of classifying the type of data we are looking at, which can help us to identify statistical tests that will be appropriate. If we do not think about the nature of the data we are analysing, we might summarize it in ways that do not help us to understand it and might even lead us to inaccurate conclusions. For example, it would not be meaningful to talk about having a mean sex of 1.2 or a median colour of car that is red. However, if you ask SPSS to produce these statistics, it will. We need to understand the nature of our data in order to make good choices about how to analyse it, and one of the most common ways of doing this is to classify variables by their level of measurement.

The most common system was devised by Stanley Smith Stevens, who noted that 'the statistical manipulations that can legitimately be applied to empirical data depend upon the type of scale against which the data are ordered' (Stevens, 1946: 677). The different scales against which data could be measured were described as being nominal, ordered, interval and ratio. Nominal data can be broken into discrete categories, but there is no inherent order to the categories. Sex, marital status and political party affiliation are all examples of nominal variables. Ordinal data is still measured in categories, but the categories can be placed in a logical order. Examples of ordinal data include age groups (18–24, 25–34, 35–44, etc.); spectrums of agreement, importance, etc. (strongly agree, agree, disagree, disagree strongly); and highest educational attainment (no qualifications, some secondary school, completed secondary school, some tertiary, tertiary degree, etc.). Interval data and ratio data are data that can be measured numerically. With interval data, the distance between the intervals is the same, but zero does not constitute the starting point. With ratio data, the distance between intervals is the same, but the scale starts with an absolute zero. For example, if we measure someone's height in centimetres, the distance between intervals is always 1 cm, and height starts at an absolute zero, making it ratio data. Other examples include age, income and years of education completed. There are examples of each type listed in Table 3.2.

Table 3.2 Examples of levels of measurement

Scale of measurement	SPSS name	Other names for concepts		Examples
Nominal	Nominal	Dichotomous / binary (if exactly two values); qualitative	Categorical	Political affiliation, religion, marital status, ethnic group
Ordinal	Ordinal	Ordered		Position (1st, 2nd, 3rd, etc.) in some kind of competition; preferences for one party over another; attitude scales (such as 'strongly agree, agree, disagree, strongly disagree')
Interval	Scale	Continuous; quantitative	Discrete	IQ, calendar years
Ratio			Continuous	Income, height, weight

There are other typologies that have arisen since Stevens'. In SPSS, there are three types used: nominal, ordinal and scale. In this typology, scale encompasses Stevens' interval and ratio. Other typologies use a dichotomy between categorical data (where the differences between categories cannot be meaningfully measured) and continuous (where it can). These classification systems form *typologies*, where each variable may be classified into only one of these categories, and the categories are mutually exclusive and exhaustive. Having established such a typology, in the past it was standard to use it to identify particular statistical approaches that were appropriate, both for simpler and for more advanced statistical concepts (Andrews et al., 1981). In Table 3.3 we set out a guide to the kind of simple statistics that seem to make most sense for data of different kinds. We will talk through more of the nuances of selecting the right kinds of data for various tests as we encounter each test in the later chapters.

Table 3.3 Examples of statistical tests by level of measurement

	Nominal	**Ordinal**	**Continuous**
Frequency	Yes	Yes (unless large number of categories)	No (or only if small-*N*)
Measures of central tendency	Mode	Mode, median	Mode, median, mean
Correlation and regression (linear)	No – but other statistics possible	No – but other statistics possible	Yes

In secondary datasets, the level of measurement will normally be set already. However, this has not always been done accurately, and there are also instances when you wish to manually change a level, such as changing how the data is treated to produce a chart. In Box 3.1 we show how to do this, first by using syntax, then using the graphical user interface. Because we want to encourage you to get comfortable with syntax, we will always provide the syntax instructions first, with a short explanation of the different components of the command, then the menu instructions.

BOX 3.1 SETTING OR CHANGING THE MEASUREMENT LEVEL

This box shows you how to set or change the level of measurement of a variable. This is appropriate for classifying variables after entering data and for reclassifying variables that have been incorrectly entered or for which you need to change the classification for analysis, such as producing charts that are dependent upon using specific types of variables.

Syntax

It is possible to set/change the measurement level for a list of variables using syntax. You simply need the VARIABLE LEVEL command, followed by a list of variables you wish to have the same level of measurement, then the level of measurement in parentheses. For example:

```
VARIABLE LEVEL gndr cntry (nominal).
```

You can change multiple levels of measurement in the same command by separating the levels with a slash (/). For example:

```
VARIABLE LEVEL

gndr (nominal)
```

(Continued)

```
/trstprl trstlgl (ordinal)

/height weight agea (scale).
```

Menu instructions

To change the measure, open the Data Editor window, Variable View tab. Within the Data Editor window, simply click the cell of the measure you want to change (such as clicking on Nominal), and select the measure from the drop-down menu. Taking this approach, you can only change one variable at a time.

A critique of levels of measurement

> My propositions are elucidatory in this way: he who understands me finally recognizes them as senseless, when he has climbed out through them, on them, over them. (He must so to speak throw away the ladder, after he has climbed up on it). He must surmount these propositions; then he sees the world rightly. (Wittgenstein, 1922: 6.54)

The approach of classifying variables in a hierarchy from ratio to nominal has been influential in the writing of statistical textbooks and probably to an even greater extent in the delivery of statistics teaching to students in the social sciences. This is not an issue without controversy, however, and there are several issues that come with this typology. Having established this classification system, it then can become a simple tick-box matter to rule that certain approaches are statistically legitimate, while others are not. Indeed, it may be used as a basis for a kind of expert system that diagnoses that kinds of tests and statistical approaches are relevant in different circumstances (Andrews et al., 1981). However, it is worth a caution that this typology has been strongly attacked by statisticians, and in particular the idea that such absolutes may be applied to data independently of the research questions that are being addressed. It is quite common to present averages of rankings, for instance (such as the changing average position of a country within the PISA league tables of educational performance; or of a sports team within a particular division). Some types of data are also hard to place on the scale. For instance, percentages or fractional amounts may look like standard ratio variables, but they are not because the data cannot go below 0 or above 100. This constraint can have important implications for different kinds of statistical methods (such as linear regression) that we discuss later. At a practical level, the apparently illegitimate use of data that is ordinal (such as attitude scales), treating it as being on an interval scale, is fairly routine in many disciplines and may not generate misleading information. Indeed Stevens (1951) recognized this issue in his later writings and saw pragmatic reasons for the apparent mistreatment of ordinal data as being of a more informative interval kind. There are also alternative taxonomies of variable types (Mosteller and Tukey, 1977: chapter 5).

This typology can also draw artificial distinctions between categories. For example, it is very straightforward to convert continuous data (such as age) into categorical data (such as age groups). Even ordinal categorical data is often combined in ways that create a continuous variable. For example, in the ESS, there is a bank of questions about views on immigration, such as Immigration bad or good for country's economy [imbgeco], Country's cultural life undermined or enriched by immigrants [imueclt] and Immigrants make country worse or better place to live [imwbcnt]. In such cases, researchers may combine the answers to a variety of questions to create an 'index' variable. Index variables can be useful analytical tools for creating greater variation between respondents by identifying respondents who consistently feel very strongly about a topic. These transformations can be achieved by recoding (changing the categories of the data, covered in Chapter 4) and computing (combining multiple variables or mathematically manipulating existing variables, covered in Chapters 7, 9 and 10).

For most purposes the attribution of measurement levels will not change the way that SPSS functions, but with three important exceptions – Chart Builder, custom Tables and the Tree approach to investigating data structures. For most users, it is when using Chart Builder (discussed in Chapters 5 and 8) that the setting of measurement levels will be important. In its default settings, SPSS will remind the user of the importance of setting appropriate measurement levels when using such commands, such as when starting Chart Builder. There is also a reminder to set value labels for categorical variables and for each category, as this information is used in labelling graphs.

CONCLUSIONS

This chapter has introduced you to the main windows of SPSS: the Data Editor, Output and Syntax windows. Each of these plays a different role in the function of the program and saves as a separate file. We have looked at some of the key elements within each file and have covered some initial adjustments you might want to make to the way variable information is stored. You have learned how to input your own data and how to keep a record of your work. From the next chapter, you will start producing and analysing your own statistics using the two key datasets for this book: the ESS (round 7) and the UN composite dataset.

ACTIVITIES

1. Open a new file in Data Editor. Create five new variables in Variable View using the information in Table 3.4. Then enter the data from Table 3.5 in the Data View tab, using a new row for each respondent. Check that you have entered the value labels correctly by toggling the Value Labels display in the Data View tab.

(Continued)

Table 3.4 Variable information

Name	Type	Label	Values	Missing	Measure
idno	Numeric	Respondent's ID number			
yrbrn	Numeric	Year of birth	-7 Refused -8 Don't know -9 No answer	Range Low: -99 High: -1	Scale
vote	Numeric	Voted last national election	1 Yes 2 No -7 Refused -8 Don't know -9 No answer	Range Low: -99 High: -1	Nominal
happy	Numeric	How happy are you	0 Extremely unhappy 10 Extremely happy -7 Refused -8 Don't know -9 No answer	Range Low: -99 High: -1	Ordinal
cntry	String	Country	AT Austria BE Belgium CH Switzerland CZ Czech Republic		Nominal

Table 3.5 Respondent information

idno	yrbrn	vote	happy	cntry
1001	1965	1	10	CH
1002	1972	1	-9	BE
1003	1989	2	3	AT
1004	-7	2	6	CZ

2. Open the ESS dataset and create a new data file. Choose three variables from the ESS and practise inputting the same information into the new data file to create three new variables. Then create responses for four respondents. Practise toggling the view in Data View so that you can see the codes or the labels.

FURTHER READING

Cunningham, J.B. and Aldrich, J.O. (2016) *Using IBM SPSS Statistics: An Interactive Hands-On Approach*. London: Sage.

See chapters 1 and 2 for getting to know the SPSS environment and chapter 3 for information on importing, inputting and exporting data. Gives step-by-step point-and-click instructions with screenshots but takes an entirely menu-driven approach; in other words, no discussion of syntax.

IBM SPSS Statistics Coach (https://www.ibm.com/support/knowledgecenter/en/SSLVMB_24.0.0/spss/statcoach/statcoach_main.html).
You can change version easily to the version of SPSS you are using. This will walk you through a series of questions to help you determine which function to carry out. Because it is based on a series of questions where you have to choose between options, this is useful when there is a clear-cut answer but will not highlight situations when there is more than one way that you might go about your analysis.

IBM SPSS Statistics Command Syntax Reference (https://www.ibm.com/support/knowledgecenter/en/SSLVMB_24.0.0/statistics_reference_project_ddita-gentopic2.html).
This is also accessible through Help > Command Syntax Reference within the software windows. Provides information about every syntax command, including the rules that must be followed for that command. Very useful as a reference guide but not straightforward for getting started.

Pallant, J. (2016) *SPSS Survival Manual*. London: McGraw-Hill Education.
See chapters 1 to 5 for content related to getting started and inputting or importing data. Provides more information than most texts about preparing and entering your own data into SPSS. Good for helping you to produce statistics but weaker on understanding what your outputs mean. Discusses syntax and provides the syntax for many of the tasks, though usually in Paste format rather than discussing shortened syntax or unnecessary commands.

Various (2016) 'Replication forum', *International Studies Perspectives*, 17 (4): 361–475. (https://academic.oup.com/isp/issue/17/4).
Discusses the importance of replication.

REFERENCES

Andrews, F.M., Klem, L., Davidson, T.N., O'Malley, P.M. and Rodgers, W.L. (1981) *A Guide for Selecting Statistical Techniques for Analysing Social Science Data*. Ann Arbor: Institute for Social Research, University of Michigan.

Coy, P. (2013, 18 Apr) 'FAQ: Reinhart, Rogoff, and the Excel Error That Changed History', *Bloomberg Businessweek*. (https://www.bloomberg.com/news/articles/2013-04-18/faq-reinhart-rogoff-and-the-excel-error-that-changed-history).

Dewald, W.G., Thursby, J.G. and Anderson, R.G. (1986) 'Replication in empirical economics: the journal of money, credit and banking project', *American Economic Review*, 73 (4): 587–603.

Dunn, M. (2013, 28 Oct) 'Toyota's killer firmware: bad design and its consequences', *EDN Network*. (www.edn.com/design/automotive/4423428/Toyota-s-killer-firmware--Bad-design-and-its-consequences).

Fanelli, D. (2009) 'How many scientists fabricate and falsify research? A systematic review and meta-analysis of survey data', *PLOS ONE*, 4 (5): e5738. (https://doi.org/10.1371/journal.pone.0005738).

Fausto-Sterling, A. (2000) *Sexing the Body: Gender Politics and the Construction of Sexuality*. New York: Basic Books.

Grossman, L. (2010, 10 Oct) 'Nov. 10, 1999: metric math mistake muffed Mars meteorology mission', *Wired*. (www.wired.com/2010/11/1110mars-climate-observer-report/).

Herndon, T., Ash, M. and Pollin, R. (2014) 'Does high public debt consistently stifle economic growth? A critique of Reinhart and Rogoff', *Cambridge Journal of Economics*, 38 (2), 257–79. (https://doi.org/10.1093/cje/bet075).

Ioannidis, J.P.A. (2005) 'Why most published research findings are false', *PLOS Medicine*, 2 (8): e124. (https://doi.org/10.1371/journal.pmed.0020124).

Janz, N. (2016) 'Bringing the gold standard into the classroom: replication in university teaching', *International Studies Perspectives*, 17 (4): 392–407. (https://doi.org/10.1111/insp.12104).

King, G. (1995) 'Replication, replication', *PS: Political Science & Politics*, 28 (3): 444–52. (https://doi.org/10.2307/420301).

Mosteller, F. and Tukey, J.W. (1977) *Data Analysis and Regression: A Second Course in Statistics*. Boston, MA: Addison-Wesley.

Peterson, R.R. (1996) 'A re-evaluation of the economic consequences of divorce', *American Sociological Review*, 61 (3): 528–36. (https://doi.org/10.2307/2096363).

Pollin, R. (2014, 3 Jan) 'Public debt, GDP growth, and austerity: why Reinhart and Rogoff are wrong', *OUPblog*. (https://blog.oup.com/2014/01/public-debt-gdp-growth-austerity-why-reinhart-and-rogoff-are-wrong/).

Reinhart, C.M. and Rogoff, K.S. (2010) 'Growth in a time of debt', *American Economic Review*, 100 (2): 573–78. (https://doi.org/10.1257/aer.100.2.573).

Stevens, S.S. (1946) 'On the theory of levels of measurement', *Science*, 103 (2684): 677–80.

Stevens, S.S. (1951) 'Mathematics, measurement, and psychophysics', in S.S. Stevens (ed.), *Handbook of Experimental Psychology*. New York: John Wiley. pp. 1–49.

Stroebe, W., Postmes, T. and Spears, R. (2012) 'Scientific misconduct and the myth of self-correction in science', *Perspectives on Psychological Science*, 7 (6): 670–88. (https://doi.org/10.1177%2F1745691612460687).

Weitzman, L.J. (1985) *The Divorce Revolution: The Unexpected Social and Economic Consequences for Women and Children in America*. New York: The Free Press.

Wittgenstein, L. (1922) *Tractatus Logico-Philosophicus*. London: Routledge.

4

DESCRIBING CATEGORICAL DATA

CHAPTER SUMMARY

This chapter introduces you to the production and interpretation of frequency tables and crosstabs using categorical data. Categorical data is some of the most common data in social statistics and is often used to describe populations. This can be done through simple frequencies of occurrences of a single variable or through bivariate tables that show us pairings of options between two variables. The results can be expressed through counts of the number of times an answer or pair of answers occur, or through percentages that represent this as a proportion. Each of the options conveys the same data differently and helps us to make different points, so it's very important to be able to produce and interpret the data correctly.

OBJECTIVES

In this chapter, you will learn:

- How to produce a table with one categorical variable
- How to produce a crosstabulation with two categorical variables
- How to produce and interpret a variety of percentages
- How to recode variables to create categorical variables or to combine into fewer categories
- How to customize the appearance of the output tables.

INTRODUCTION

Many politics datasets, like the ESS, are dominated by categorical variables and have very few continuous variables. Politics researchers frequently want to answer questions about voting intention, history and party identification; educational qualifications; religion; marital status; ethnicity and citizenship; and public opinion on a range of issues. All of these common variables are categorical. This chapter works through the most common ways of describing this data by producing univariate frequency tables and bivariate crosstabulations.

All examples in this chapter use the ESS round 7 dataset.

FREQUENCY TABLES

Frequencies are just about counting: how many people chose each of the answers to a specific question? How many countries have a certain characteristic? Univariate frequency tables answer the question, 'How many...?' about one variable at a time: uni=one, variate=variable. In the IBM SPSS Statistics ('SPSS') environment, the term 'frequency table' only refers to univariate tables; tables with frequencies of two variables (bivariate) or more (multivariate) are referred to as crosstabs. Frequency tables should normally only be used with categorical data, meaning variables that are nominal or ordinal, unless you are trying to check for outliers or specific values. We will see why frequency tables are not usually helpful for describing continuous variables later in this chapter. Common categorical variables include attributes like gender, ethnicity, marital status, occupation, educational qualifications, political party identification and religion. (For a reminder of the differences between categorical and continuous data, see the discussion of levels of measurement in Chapter 3.)

Frequency tables in SPSS will contain the different answer options in the rows and the frequency, per cent, valid per cent and cumulative per cent in the columns. Each of these columns displays the frequency information in slightly different ways. We will start with looking at the frequency of participation in the last national election [vote] in the ESS round 7 data. This is a categorical variable that asked respondents whether they voted in the last national election, with answer options of 'yes', 'no' or 'not eligible to vote'. Box 4.1 shows you how to produce this frequency table.

BOX 4.1 FREQUENCY TABLE

This box teaches you how to run a frequency table using Voted in the last national election [vote]. The results from this test can be seen in Table 4.1.

Syntax

```
FREQUENCIES VARIABLES=vote
  /ORDER=ANALYSIS.
```

You can run your command by highlighting the material and pressing the large, green Play button; or you can right click and choose one of the Run commands.

Menu instructions

Analyze > Descriptive Statistics > Frequencies

Find Voted in last national election [vote].

Move vote to the Variable(s) box either by double clicking the variable name or by clicking once and then clicking the arrow between the two boxes.

Make sure that the box for Display Frequency Tables in the bottom left-hand corner is ticked.

Press OK to run it or Paste to copy the command into the Syntax window, then run the syntax.

(Continued)

When you have successfully run your table, it will appear in the Output window. Remember: each window in SPSS represents a different file, and each of these files needs to be saved individually in order to keep the information in that window. You may not always feel the need to keep your outputs if you keep pasting your syntax, as this will allow you to rerun anything you wish to at any time.

Table 4.1 Frequency of voting in last national election

		Frequency	Per cent	Valid per cent	Cumulative per cent
Valid	Yes	27867	69.3	69.9	69.9
	No	8492	21.1	21.3	91.2
	Not eligible to vote	3498	8.7	8.8	100.0
	Total	39857	99.2	100.0	
Missing	Refusal	47	.1		
	Don't know	279	.7		
	No answer	2	.0		
	Total	328	.8		
Total		40185	100.0		

The frequency table contains four different statistics: frequency, per cent, valid per cent and cumulative per cent. In the rows, the answers are divided into Valid and Missing and Total as well as answer options within those headings. We will look at each of these elements in turn. In the leftmost column, you will notice the labels Valid, Missing and Total. Valid answers are those where the survey respondent answered the question or where the information was available to answer the question. Missing data is where the respondent did not answer the question or the information was not available. Data that is marked 'missing' can sometimes depend on what you, as a researcher, are looking for: sometimes it is important to know how many people refused to answer a question or said they did not know; other times, we are not interested in those people and decide to exclude them from our analysis. Total tells us the full number of people or cases in the dataset, whether the question was answered or left blank.

In the column to the right of Valid, Missing and Total, we can see all of the possible answers to the question. In this case, answers marked 'valid' were respondents who said 'yes' (they voted in the last national election), 'no' (they did not vote in the last national election), and 'not eligible to vote' (usually either too young or other reasons, such as immigration status). Responses marked as 'missing' were refusals to answer the question, those who said they didn't know and those who gave no answer. Now have a look at the column titled Frequency in Table 4.1. This shows us the simple count of each of the possible responses.

Looking at the answers within the Valid categories, we can see that 27,876 people said they voted in the last national election, 8,492 people said they didn't vote and 3,498 people said they were ineligible to vote. This gives us a total of 39,857 valid responses. Looking at the Missing categories, we see that 47 people refused to answer the question, 279 people didn't know whether they voted and 2 did not provide an answer, for a total of 328 answers marked as missing. Adding up all of the sub-totals should always equal the same number as the overall total. Thus, we can see that 39,857 people gave valid responses and 328 people gave invalid responses, bringing the overall total to 40,185 respondents. If there are no missing responses, the separate missing and overall total sections will disappear from the table. You can reclassify missing values. For example, you might decide that it is relevant to include 'don't know' as a valid response and reclassify the missing responses accordingly. This would trigger a recalculation in the table. We look at reclassifying missing values in Chapter 6.

Now turn to the next column, labelled Per cent. For this column, it does not matter whether an answer is classed as valid or missing; the percentages offered are based on all values recorded. In this case, 0.8 per cent of responses were marked as missing, with 99.2 per cent falling into one of the valid categories. In this, we can see that 69.3 per cent of respondents across all of the ESS countries reported having voted in the last election. This number shifts slightly if we look at the Valid per cent column. This column calculates the proportions based only on answers marked as valid. In this case, it means filtering out the refusals, don't knows and no answers. This means that 69.9 per cent of valid responses were that the respondent voted in the last national election. Finally, the Cumulative per cent column adds the valid per cent of each subsequent row until 100 per cent is reached. This is not terribly enlightening when looking at this variable, but the cumulative per cent can be useful when looking at ordinal variables, such as a question with strongly agree, agree, disagree, disagree strongly. The Cumulative per cent column would give you a quick overview of what proportion of responses overall agreed (agree plus strongly agree). However, in general, you are likely to use the Cumulative per cent column less than the others when producing frequency tables.

Practise running and interpreting a few more tables on some variables of interest to you until you feel comfortable with this process. You can find some suggestions at the end of the chapter. Remember only to use frequency tables for nominal or ordinal variables. To see why this is important, select a continuous (scale) variable like age [`agea`] or hours normally worked [`wkhtot`] and run a frequency table. What happened? You will find that you have created a ridiculously long table that, because of its length, is very difficult to interpret. Frequency tables are simply not the most accessible way to learn about continuous data. Instead, we use measures of central tendency (mean, median and mode) and dispersion (ranges, standard deviation) to learn about continuous variables. We will address these in Chapter 7.

For the next section of the chapter, we want to look at voting behaviour, but we want to filter the responses so that we are only looking at UK respondents. To do this, we need to select cases so that we only use cases where the country recorded is UK. First we need to auto-recode the country variable [`cntry`] from a string variable into a numeric variable. Then we need to consult the codebook to identify the value assigned to the UK. After this, we can use the Select Cases command to filter the results. To do this, see the instructions in Box 4.2.

BOX 4.2 AUTO-RECODE AND SELECT CASES

This box shows you how to auto-recode a string variable and how to select only (filter) responses collected in the UK. To do this, we need to start by auto-recoding country [cntry] into a numeric variable [country]. Then we need to consult the codebook to find out the numeric value assigned to the UK. The results for voting with only UK respondents are in Table 4.2.

Syntax

Auto-recoding the country variable from a string variable into a categorical variable.

```
AUTORECODE VARIABLES=cntry
  /INTO country
  /BLANK=MISSING
  /PRINT.
```

Select only UK cases (UK=11). Filter is renamed from default filter_$ to filter_country.

```
USE ALL.
COMPUTE filter_country=(country=11).
VARIABLE LABELS filter_country 'country=11 (FILTER)'.
VALUE LABELS filter_country 0 'Not Selected' 1
'Selected'.
FORMATS filter_country (f1.0).
FILTER BY filter_country.
EXECUTE.
```

To turn Select Cases off when you don't want to filter responses anymore.

```
USE ALL.
EXECUTE.
```

Menu instructions

Auto-recoding instructions

Transform > Automatic Recode

Move the original variable [cntry] from the variable list on the left to the box on the right (Variable > New Name).

Type the name of the output variable [`country`] into the New Name box, then click Add New Name.

Click Paste, then select the syntax and press the Play button in Syntax Editor.

Select Cases instructions

To find out which numbers represent the specific answers we are interested in for filtering cases, we need to look at the value labels for the variable. To find this out:

1. Go to the Variable View in the main data window.
2. Scroll down (or search) to find the variable 'Country (recoded)' (country).
3. Click on the triple dots in the Values column to open the Value Labels window, which shows us which number is applied to each of the different parties.
4. Note the relevant values: 11=United Kingdom.
5. Close the Value Label box. You are now ready to select your cases.

Data > Select Cases

In the Select options, choose 'If condition is satisfied', then click If to specify the conditions.

Move the filtering variable (country) from the list of variables on the left into the main box on the right.

1. To select a specific number, use =. For example: country=11.
2. To select a range of numbers, use greater than (>), greater than or equal to (>=), less than (<), less than or equal to (<=) and the ampersand (&) to connect the criteria. For example, country >= 1 & country <=3 would choose all cases where the value was between 1 and 3 for countries (in this case, Austria, Belgium and Switzerland).
3. When you have specified your cases, press Continue and OK/Paste.

In this case, make sure that the box reads: country=11.

Click Continue, then Paste.

Select the syntax and click the Play button in the Syntax Editor window.

To confirm that your filter has worked properly, run a frequency table on the variable you have filtered. Check that all of the cases you wanted, and only those cases, appear in the frequency table. You can also visually check that you've filtered cases by clicking the Data View tab in the Data Editor window. If a filter is active, you should see a diagonal line struck through the cases that are filtered out, looking at the row numbers on the left-hand side.

To turn Select Cases off again:

Data > Select Cases > All cases.

Click OK.

Table 4.2 Frequency of voting in the last national election, UK respondents

		Frequency	Per cent	Valid per cent	Cumulative per cent
Valid	Yes	1525	67.4	67.6	67.6
	No	608	26.9	27.0	94.6
	Not eligible to vote	122	5.4	5.4	100.0
	Total	2255	99.6	100.0	
Missing	Refusal	1	.0		
	Don't know	8	.4		
	Total	9	.4		
Total		2264	100.0		

In Table 4.2 we can see the filtered results for voting with only responses from the UK. From this, we can see that 1,525 respondents voted in the last national election, 608 did not, 122 were ineligible, 1 refused to answer the question and 8 didn't know whether they had voted. This means that 67.6 per cent of valid responses were that the respondent had voted. We can get an idea of how closely our respondents reflect the official turnout data by comparing our results to the official Electoral Commission turnout data. The majority of responses in this dataset refer to the 2010 general election in the UK (more on how we know this is in the next section). According to the Electoral Commission (2018), turnout in the 2010 general election was 65.1 per cent. In the survey, 67.4 per cent of respondents said they had voted in the last national election. From this we can see that there is a 2.3 per cent gap between the official turnout data and the survey data. Given the tendencies documented elsewhere of populations to over-report their participation in elections, this is remarkably close to the data.

Let's return to the difference between the Per cent and Valid per cent columns. It is easier to understand the key differences when examining data with a larger number of missing responses, so we will look at Party voted for in the last national election, United Kingdom [`prtvtbgb`] (see Table 4.3). In this case, we have 863 responses that have been marked missing, which equates to 38.1 per cent of all responses to the question. We can see that the percentages provided in the Per cent column include both valid and missing responses, with all responses combined equalling 100 per cent. The Valid per cent column, on the other hand, only takes into account valid answers and excludes the missing data from the calculation. Look at the Conservative row. We can see 488 respondents reported voting Conservative in the last general election. If we take 488 respondents divided by a total pool of 2,264 respondents, we get the answer in the Per cent column: 21.6 per cent of all respondents voted Conservative. If, however, we want to know what the share of votes cast that this represents, we turn to the Valid per cent column, which divides the Conservative votes by a total pool of 1,401 voters, equating to 34.8 per cent of the vote share.

Table 4.3 Party voted for in last national election, United Kingdom [`prtvtbgb`]

		Frequency	Per cent	Valid per cent	Cumulative per cent
Valid	Conservative	488	21.6	34.8	34.8
	Labour	461	20.4	32.9	67.7
	Liberal Democrat	210	9.3	15.0	82.7
	Scottish National Party	39	1.7	2.8	85.5
	Plaid Cymru	7	.3	.5	86.0
	Green Party	38	1.7	2.7	88.7
	UK Independence Party	104	4.6	7.4	96.1
	Other	20	.9	1.4	97.6
	Ulster Unionist Party (nir)	9	.4	.6	98.2
	Democratic Unionist Party (nir)	7	.3	.5	98.7
	Sinn Fein (nir)	4	.2	.3	99.0
	Social Democratic and Labour Party (nir)	6	.3	.4	99.4
	Alliance Party (nir)	4	.2	.3	99.7
	Independent(s) (nir)	3	.1	.2	99.9
	Other (nir)	1	.0	.1	100.0
	Total	1401	61.9	100.0	
Missing	Not applicable	739	32.6		
	Refusal	73	3.2		
	Don't know	51	2.3		
	Total	863	38.1		
Total		2264	100.0		

We can again check the validity of our data by comparing this to the actual election results (comparing the sample to the population). Records indicate that the Conservatives received 36.1 per cent of votes cast in the 2010 general election (BBC, 2010), so our sample again compares very closely to the recorded result. On the other hand, the comparison is not quite so consistent for support for Labour (sample: 32.9 per cent; actual: 29.0 per cent) or the Liberal Democrats (sample: 15.0 per cent; actual: 23.0 per cent), and UKIP supporters are distinctly overrepresented (sample: 7.4 per cent; actual: 3.1 per cent).

Now we will finally look at the Cumulative per cent column. This column simply adds up all of the valid percentages from that row and all rows above it. This means that the first row in the Cumulative per cent column will always be the same as the number in the Valid per cent column (in this example, 34.8 per cent). The second row adds on this 34.8 per cent to the next Valid per cent (32.9 per cent) to equal 67.7 per cent. This means that the third row (Liberal Democrat) cumulative per cent shows us what percentage of the valid respondents reported that they voted for one of the three main parties in the UK, indicating that the

Conservatives, Labour and the Liberal Democrats accounted for 82.7 per cent of all valid responses; in reality, votes for these three parties in 2010 represented 88.1 per cent of all valid votes cast.

CROSSTABS

These results only show how respondents voted in the last national election. Round 7 of the ESS was carried out in the UK during two periods between September 2014 and December 2015 (ESS, 2015), so the 'last national election' in this case could refer to either the 6 May 2010 general election, which resulted in a coalition government between the Conservatives and the Liberal Democrats, or the 7 May 2015 general election, which resulted in a Conservative majority. To find out how many responses applied to each of these elections, we need to produce a table with two variables: the month [inwmme] and year [inwyye] the interview ended. A table containing two or more categorical variables is referred to as a crosstabulation, or crosstab.

Crosstabs are also referred to as contingency tables, crosstabulations and two-way (or three-way or multi-way) tables. They allow us to look at two or more categorical variables at once, finding pairs of answers. Every time you look at a table that has information about one variable in the rows and another in the columns, you are looking at a crosstab. Crosstabs are standard fare for public opinion polls. For example, you might see a crosstab of voting intention that shows you party against sex, age group or ethnicity. Sometimes tables are expressed in counts, sometimes in percentages and sometimes in both.

To continue with the example in the previous section, we want to find out how many of the survey responses from the UK would be about the 2010 general election as opposed to the 2015 general election. If we ran separate frequency tables for the month and year, we would not be able to identify these pairings: we would know that there were 1,660 surveys completed in 2014 and 600 in 2015; we would know that October was the month in which the most surveys were completed (1,132) and August the least (2). But we would not know that, of the 1,132 surveys completed in the month of October, 863 of them were completed in 2014 and 269 of them were completed in 2015. To learn this, we need a crosstab. To find this out, we need to crosstabulate the month [inwmme] and year [inwyye] the interview ended. Box 4.3 shows how to produce a simple crosstab for these variables.

BOX 4.3 CROSSTAB WITH TWO VARIABLES, COUNTS ONLY

This box teaches you how to create a crosstab using two variables: the month [inwmme] and year [inwyye] the survey interview ended. The results are in Table 4.4.

Syntax

The main command for a crosstab is `CROSSTABS`. There are several other options regarding the statistics and formatting, which we will add in later instructions.

```
CROSSTABS inwmme by inwyye.
```

The variable that you write first in the syntax [`inwmme`] will appear in the rows; the one you write second [`inwyye`] will appear in the columns.

Menu instructions

Analyze > Descriptive Statistics > Crosstabs

Find End of interview, month [`inwmme`] and move to Rows box.

Find End of interview, year [`inwyye`] and move to Columns box.

Press OK to run it or Paste to copy the command into the Syntax window.

Table 4.4 Month and year survey was completed, UK respondents

Month/Year	2014	2015	Total
January	0	160	160
February	0	56	56
August	2	0	2
September	557	0	557
October	863	269	1132
November	213	115	328
December	25	0	25
Total	1660	600	2260

Our results indicate that 384 of the UK's 2,260 survey responses were collected after the 2015 general election took place (Table 4.4). This is calculated by adding up the cells for August, September, October, November and December 2015. (There were no interviews for either year that ended in March, April, May, June or July.) This means that the vast majority (1,876, or 83 per cent) of responses refer to the 2010 general election. (This could also explain why some respondents didn't remember whether they had voted.)

We will stay with the theme of voting, focusing on the UK results. We can test out some of the received wisdom about who votes and who is interested in politics, looking at some of the socio-economic drivers of voting, such as age and education level. For example, based on previous research, we would expect there to be an association between having higher educational qualifications and being more interested in politics. We can formulate this as a hypothesis to test:

H1. People with two or more A-levels will be more interested in politics than those with no formal qualifications.

To test this, we need to create a crosstab with highest level of education, United Kingdom respondents [edubgbl] and interest in politics [polintr]. Results are only displayed as counts. The results are in Table 4.5. To start with, we will produce a table that only has the counts. After interpreting this, we will learn how to insert percentages.

Table 4.5 Highest educational level completed [edubgbl] and interest in politics [polintr], UK respondents

	Very interested	Quite interested	Hardly interested	Not at all interested	Total
2 or more A-levels or equivalent	170	332	141	53	696
GNVQ Intermediate	9	31	29	13	82
Vocational GCSE or equivalent	15	56	40	18	129
5 or more GCSEs A*-C or equivalent	52	185	86	40	363
1-4 GCSEs A*-C or equivalent	26	98	76	61	261
Skills for Life	6	20	13	8	47
None of these	85	229	179	182	675
Total	363	951	564	375	2253

The row and column totals give us the same information as the frequency tables for the two variables. For example, from the column totals, we can see that the greatest number of respondents said they were quite interested in politics (951), followed by hardly interested (564), not at all interested (375) and very interested (363). These numbers are the same as those you would get from a frequency table for How interested in politics [polintr]. Looking at the row totals, we can see that the greatest number of respondents had two or more A-levels or equivalent (696), followed by none (675), five or more GCSEs A* to C or equivalent (363), 1 to 4 GCSEs A* to C or equivalent (261), vocational GCSE or equivalent (129), GNVQ Intermediate (82) and Skills for Life (47). This is the same data as we would get in a frequency table for 'Highest educational level completed, United Kingdom' (edubgbl). However, the rest of the table provides extra information that we can't glean from the univariate tables.

The crosstab that we have produced (Table 4.5) shows the number of people who selected each answer pairing, such as 2 or more A-levels or equivalent and Not at all interested (53 people), or None of these and Very interested (85 people). From the counts, we can get a rough idea of response patterns, though percentages will be more helpful for comparing groups to each other. We can see from the Case Processing Summary that there are nine missing cases. This means that nine people provided an answer marked as missing to one or both of the questions. If we look at other answer pairings, we can see that the most common is two or more A-levels or equivalent and quite interested in politics (332), followed by five or more GCSEs A* to C or equivalent and quite interested (185). The least common answer pairings were Skills for Life and very interested (6), followed by Skills for Life and not at all interested (8).

It's fine to interpret these numbers, but it becomes quite cumbersome to take all of the information in, which is where thinking in percentages can help instead. With crosstabs, we have different percentage options than frequency tables. The frequency tables gave us per cent, valid per cent and cumulative per cent. However, crosstabs only include valid answers to start with, so there is no equivalent to the valid or cumulative percentages. Instead, crosstabs have row, column and total percentages. Each of these helps us to look at the same data in a different way.

Total percentages present to us the proportion of all responses that a single answer pairing represents. For example, we can take the 332 people who had two or more A-levels or equivalent and were quite interested in politics as a proportion of the total number of respondents (2,253). Calculated by hand, this would be:

$$\frac{\text{Cell count}}{\text{Total valid responses}} \times 100 = \frac{332}{2{,}253} \times 100 = 14.74\%$$

We can, of course, calculate the percentage for each cell, but we can also simply ask for this data to be produced for us when running a crosstab (Box 4.4). When you create total percentages, the bottom rightmost cell in the table should be 100 per cent. Presenting data as total percentages means you are trying to make a point about the distribution of data overall. This is most pertinent when the responses are either very evenly distributed across most cells or very concentrated in relatively few cells: in other words, extremes. Otherwise, it can be quite difficult to digest the amount of information contained in a table with so many cells (Table 4.6).

Table 4.6 Highest educational level completed [edubgb1] and interest in politics [polintr], total percentages

		Very interested	Quite interested	Hardly interested	Not at all interested	Total
2 or more A-levels or equivalent	Count	170	332	141	53	696
	% of Total	7.5%	14.7%	6.3%	2.4%	30.9%
GNVQ Intermediate	Count	9	31	29	13	82
	% of Total	0.4%	1.4%	1.3%	0.6%	3.6%

(Continued)

Table 4.6 (Continued)

		Very interested	Quite interested	Hardly interested	Not at all interested	Total
Vocational GCSE or equivalent	Count	15	56	40	18	129
	% of Total	0.7%	2.5%	1.8%	0.8%	5.7%
5 or more GCSEs A*-C or equivalent	Count	52	185	86	40	363
	% of Total	2.3%	8.2%	3.8%	1.8%	16.1%
1-4 GCSEs A*-C or equivalent	Count	26	98	76	61	261
	% of Total	1.2%	4.3%	3.4%	2.7%	11.6%
Skills for Life (including Basic Skills, Key Skills, Entry Level Certificates)	Count	6	20	13	8	47
	% of Total	0.3%	0.9%	0.6%	0.4%	2.1%
None of these	Count	85	229	179	182	675
	% of Total	3.8%	10.2%	7.9%	8.1%	30.0%
	Count	363	951	564	375	2253
	% of Total	16.1%	42.2%	25.0%	16.6%	100.0%

We can reformat the table to make it easier to read using the Pivot Table editor. You can open this by double clicking on the table you want to edit; alternatively, you can right click on the table > Edit Content > In Separate Window; or left click to select the table, open the Edit menu > Edit Content > In Separate Window. This will open two windows, the Pivot Table and a window with Pivoting Trays. Try dragging the variables in the Pivoting Trays window to move them around. For example, you could move highest level of education to columns and interest in politics to rows. Try moving Statistics to columns instead of rows. This allows you to read the information in the columns more easily and more closely approximates the format used in academic journals, where percentages and counts are normally placed side by side instead of being arranged vertically. You can also reorder the statistics so that the percentage is displayed first. To do this, in the Pivot Table window, click once on Count. Click on Pivot in the menu bar > Reorder Categories > Swap > % of Total. To see how different this can look, compare Table 4.6 with Table 4.7.

Table 4.7 Highest education level completed and interest in politics, total percentages, rearranged

	Very interested		Quite interested		Hardly interested		Not at all interested		Total	
	%	N	%	N	%	N	%	N	%	N
2 or more A-levels or equivalent	7.5%	170	14.7%	332	6.3%	141	2.4%	53	30.9%	696
GNVQ Intermediate	0.4%	9	1.4%	31	1.3%	29	0.6%	13	3.6%	82

	Very interested		Quite interested		Hardly interested		Not at all interested		Total	
	%	N	%	N	%	N	%	N	%	N
Vocational GCSE or equivalent	0.7%	15	2.5%	56	1.8%	40	0.8%	18	5.7%	129
5 or more GCSEs A*-C or equivalent	2.3H%	52	8.2%	185	3.8%	86	1.8%	40	16.1%	363
1-4 GCSEs A*-C or equivalent	1.2%	26	4.3%	98	3.4%	76	2.7%	61	11.6%	261
Skills for Life	0.3%	6	0.9%	20	0.6%	13	0.4%	8	2.1%	47
None of these	3.8%	85	10.2%	229	7.9%	179	8.1%	182	30.0%	675
	16.1%	363	42.2%	951	25.0%	564	16.6%	375	100.0%	2253

BOX 4.4 CROSSTABS WITH TOTAL PERCENTAGES

This box teaches you how to make a crosstab with two variables, displaying the results as total percentages, with or without the counts displayed. This is appropriate for use with two categorical (nominal or ordinal) variables. The results are in Tables 4.5 and 4.6.

Syntax

```
CROSSTABS

  /TABLES=edubgbl BY polintr

  /FORMAT=AVALUE TABLES

  /CELLS=COUNT TOTAL

  /COUNT ROUND CELL.
```

This can be shortened to:

```
CROSSTABS edubgbl by polintr

/cells=count total.
```

The command in the syntax under `/CELLS=` tells you which frequencies or percentages the table will produce. The options are:

(Continued)

`COUNT`	observed frequencies
`ROW`	row percentages
`COLUMN`	column percentages
`TOTAL`	total percentages

If you want to produce a table that only has percentages in it and no counts, just omit 'count' from the /cells options:

```
CROSSTABS edubgbl by polintr
/cells=total.
```

Menu instructions

Analyze > Descriptive Statistics > Crosstabs

Find Highest level of education, United Kingdom: Up to 2 or more A-levels or equivalent [`edubgbl`] and move to Rows box.

Find How interested in politics [`polintr`] and move to Columns box.

> Cells > Percentages > Tick Total box.

Press Continue to exit Cells menu.

Press OK to run it or Paste to copy the command into the Syntax window.

If you want to produce a table that only has percentages in it and no counts, untick Observed in the Cells menu.

The total percentages don't really help us to test our hypothesis, however. For this, we need to compare proportions within our groups. We hypothesized that a higher proportion of people with A-levels would be very interested in politics than those with no qualifications. To test this, we need to calculate the levels of interest in politics for respondents within each educational qualification. This means that, if we have educational qualification in rows, we need row percentages. Again, this is something we can easily calculate by hand if we have the counts from the bivariate table. To show this, let's take again the count of people who had two or more A-levels or equivalent and were quite interested in politics (332). We also need the total number of people who had two or more A-levels or equivalent (696).

$$\frac{\text{Cell count}}{\text{Row total}} \times 100 = \frac{332}{696} \times 100 = 47.70\%$$

This shows us that slightly under half (47.7 per cent) of people who had two or more A-levels or equivalent were quite interested in politics. We can compare this to people who had no qualifications. The largest number of respondents with no qualifications said they were quite interested in politics: 229 out of a total of 675 people with no qualifications. We can again calculate this by hand:

$$\frac{\text{Cell count}}{\text{Row total}} \times 100 = \frac{229}{675} \times 100 = 33.93\%$$

This shows us that roughly one-third (33.9 per cent) of people with no qualifications were quite interested in politics. We can continue to calculate each of the values by hand, or we can use the option to produce row percentages when running the crosstab in order to finish testing our hypothesis (see Box 4.5 for instructions).

BOX 4.5 CROSSTABS WITH ROW PERCENTAGES

This box teaches you how to create a crosstab with two variables, displaying the results as row percentages. This test is appropriate for two categorical variables. To change the display options to exclude the counts, follow the instructions in Box 4.4. The results are in Table 4.8.

Table 4.8 Highest education level completed and interest in politics, row percentages

	Very interested	Quite interested	Hardly interested	Not at all interested	Total
2 or more A-levels or equivalent	24.4%	47.7%	20.3%	7.6%	100.0%
GNVQ Intermediate	11.0%	37.8%	35.4%	15.9%	100.0%
Vocational GCSE or equivalent	11.6%	43.4%	31.0%	14.0%	100.0%
5 or more GCSEs A*-C or equivalent	14.3%	51.0%	23.7%	11.0%	100.0%
1-4 GCSEs A*-C or equivalent	10.0%	37.5%	29.1%	23.4%	100.0%
Skills for Life	12.8%	42.6%	27.7%	17.0%	100.0%
None of these	12.6%	33.9%	26.5%	27.0%	100.0%
Total	16.1%	42.2%	25.0%	16.6%	100.0%

Syntax

```
CROSSTABS
  /TABLES=edubgb1 BY polintr
  /FORMAT=AVALUE TABLES
```

(Continued)

```
/CELLS=COUNT ROW
/COUNT ROUND CELL.
```

This can be shortened to:

```
CROSSTABS edubgbl by polintr
/cells=count row.
```

Menu instructions

Analyze > Descriptive Statistics > Crosstabs

Find Highest level of education, United Kingdom: Up to 2 or more A-levels or equivalent [edubgb1] and move to Rows box.

Find How interested in politics [polintr] and move to Columns box.

> Cells > Percentages > Tick Total box.

Press Continue to exit Cells menu.

Press OK to run it or Paste to copy the command into the Syntax window.

Table 4.8 displays the results with the counts excluded for ease of reading. We can check that our manual calculations tally with the results. We calculated that 33.93 per cent of people with no qualifications were quite interested in politics; the table is rounded to one decimal place and shows us 33.9 per cent, so our results do align. Now we can finally test our hypothesis about educational qualifications and interest in politics. The results indicate that our hypothesis is correct: a much higher proportion of people with two or more A-levels or equivalent were very interested in politics (24.4 per cent) than those with no qualifications (12.6 per cent); and a much higher proportion of people with no qualifications said they were not at all interested in politics (27.0 per cent) than people with A-levels (7.6 per cent). In fact, we can see that a much higher proportion of people with A-levels were very interested in politics than any other level of educational qualification, though those with one to four A* to C GCSEs had the second-highest proportion of respondents who were not at all interested in politics (23.4 per cent).

BOX 4.6 CROSSTABS WITH COLUMN PERCENTAGES

This box teaches you how to create a crosstab with two variables, displaying the results as column percentages. To change the display options to exclude the counts, follow the instructions in Box 4.4. The results are in Table 4.9.

Table 4.9 Highest education level completed and interest in politics, column percentages

	Very interested	Quite interested	Hardly interested	Not at all interested	Total
2 or more A-levels or equivalent	46.8%	34.9%	25.0%	14.1%	30.9%
GNVQ Intermediate	2.5%	3.3%	5.1%	3.5%	3.6%
Vocational GCSE or equivalent	4.1%	5.9%	7.1%	4.8%	5.7%
5 or more GCSEs A*-C or equivalent	14.3%	19.5%	15.2%	10.7%	16.1%
1-4 GCSEs A*-C or equivalent	7.2%	10.3%	13.5%	16.3%	11.6%
Skills for Life	1.7%	2.1%	2.3%	2.1%	2.1%
None of these	23.4%	24.1%	31.7%	48.5%	30.0%
Total	100.0%	100.0%	100.0%	100.0%	100.0%

Syntax

```
CROSSTABS
  /TABLES=edubgb1 BY polintr
  /FORMAT=AVALUE TABLES
  /CELLS=COUNT COLUMN
  /COUNT ROUND CELL.
```

This can be shortened to:

```
cross edubgb1 by polintr
/cells=count column.
```

Menu instructions

Analyze > Descriptive Statistics > Crosstabs

Find Highest level of education, United Kingdom: Up to 2 or more A-levels or equivalent [`edubgb1`] and move to Rows box.

Find How interested in politics [`polintr`] and move to Columns box.

> Cells > Percentages > Tick Total box.

Press Continue to exit Cells menu.

Press OK to run it or Paste to copy the command into the Syntax window.

Finally, let's run a crosstab with column percentages using the same variables. This time, we will interpret the outputs as a proportion of people who are very interested in politics rather than as a proportion of people with A-levels. It is again straightforward to calculate these percentages by hand. We can use one of the answer pairings from before: people with two or more A-levels or equivalent who are quite interested in politics (332). This time, we need the total number of people who are quite interested in politics (951).

$$\frac{\text{Cell count}}{\text{Column total}} \times 100 = \frac{332}{951} \times 100 = 34.91\%$$

Box 4.6 shows how to run crosstabs with column percentages. Table 4.9 shows the results with the counts omitted for simplicity. A very clear picture emerges when we look at the column for 'very interested', with nearly half (46.8 per cent) of respondents who are very interested in politics holding two or more A-levels or equivalent. However, we can also see that this group dominates every column except Not at all interested and represents nearly one-third (30.9 per cent) of the respondents. It is important when selecting appropriate percentages to be aware of the potential influence of such imbalances between respondent numbers, if it impacts the conclusions that you are drawing from your data. This is especially important to remember if one of the variables is a demographic variable (such as educational qualifications). For this example, it is more likely to answer interesting questions about the world to look at proportions within each educational qualification than to look at proportions within each level of political interest.

RECODING VARIABLES TO FEWER CATEGORIES

Sometimes we want to produce a crosstab in a way that simplifies the information by reducing the number of categories. For example, we might be interested in finding out whether older people really are more likely to vote. We can formulate this as a hypothesis:

H2. Older people are more likely to vote.

We can test this hypothesis by looking at patterns of voting [`vote`] across different age groups. However, the age variable in the dataset (Age of respondent, calculated, `agea`) is a scale variable. We don't want to produce a crosstab with one row for every age in the dataset; instead, we can recode the variable to make fewer categories. It is also possible to recode categorical variables into fewer categories, such as grouping ethnicities or combining agree/strongly agree into one category. Before recoding, you should check the codebook and statistics to find out what the low and high values are and what values are coded as missing in the original variable. When recoding, you should always recode into a new variable so that you keep the source variable data in its original form in case you need to return to it later.

After recoding, you should always crosstabulate the original variable and the new variable to check that your recoding worked as planned and that you didn't accidentally miss any values in the original data. Box 4.7 shows you how to recode a variable.

BOX 4.7 RECODING A VARIABLE

This box teaches you how to recode the scale variable for the respondent's age [agea] into a categorical variable [agerecoded].

Syntax

The command for recoding is RECODE. This is followed by the name of the variable to be recoded, then the values to be combined, with each combination in parentheses. For example, if you want to combine ages 1 through 17 into the first category, the syntax would be (1 thru 17=1). The command ELSE tells SPSS what to do with any values not specified in the recoding scheme. At the end, make sure you include 'into' followed by the name of the new variable you want to create. Type EXECUTE at the end to ensure that SPSS does not leave the transformation as pending. You will then need to apply the variable label (the label for the new variable) and value labels (labels for each of the categories).

```
*Recode agea.
RECODE agea
  (1 thru 17=1)
  (18 thru 24=2)
  (25 thru 34=3)
  (35 thru 44=4)
  (45 thru 54=5)
  (55 thru 64=6)
  (65 thru 114=7)
  (else=copy)
  into agerecoded.
  EXECUTE.
```

Apply variable and value labels to agerecoded.

```
VARIABLE LABELS agerecoded 'Age group'.
VALUE LABELS agerecoded
  1 'Under 18'
  2 '18-24'
```

(Continued)

```
3 '25-34'
4 '35-44'
5 '45-54'
6 '55-64'
7 '65+'
999 'Not available'.
```

Set missing values.

```
MISSING VALUES agerecoded (999).
```

Check that the recoding worked.

```
CROSSTABS agea by agerecoded.
```

Menu instructions

Transform > Recode into Different Variables

Move the original variable (Age of respondent, calculated, `agea`) into the middle box (labelled Numeric Variable -> Output Variable).

In the Output Variable section on the right, fill in the Name of the new variable [`agerecoded`] and the Label (Age group).

Click Change. (This should replace the ? in the middle box with the name of the new variable.)

> Old and New Values.

Old Value: Range. (You can choose individual pairings for recoding specific values, but range is the preferred option for recoding age.)

Fill in one of the ranges specified above (such as 1 through 17), then put the new category value (such as 1 for the range 1-17) in the New Value box on the left.

Each time you fill in the Old and New Values, you must press Add so that the transformation appears in the Old -> New box on the right.

After filling in all of the Old and New Values to create 7 new categories, select All other values and Copy old values, then Add.

Click Continue.

Click Paste to keep a copy in syntax. Then, in the syntax window, select the block of text you have produced and press the green play triangle.

Or, press OK without pasting.

In the Variable View of the Data Editor window, scroll to the bottom of the variable list to find your new variable. The Name and Label columns should be complete, but you still need to fill in the information for Values and Missing. Apply the value labels specified in the syntax instructions (such as 1=Under 18). Specify 999 as a discrete missing value.

Run a crosstab to check your recoding.

Analyze > Descriptive Statistics > Crosstabs

Put the original age variable [agea] into Rows.

Put the new age variable [agerecoded] into Columns.

Press Paste, then run the syntax.

Once you have produced your categorical age variable, produce a crosstab with age recoded and vote. You will need to identify the appropriate percentages to see which age group has the highest voting activity. In this case, we want to know the split within age groups, so if we put age groups into rows, we want the row percentages; if we put age groups into columns, we want the column percentages. The results are in Table 4.10. As we can see, nearly a third of the 18- to 24-year-olds were ineligible to vote in the last election, which makes it hard to draw conclusions from the percentages; but looking at the older age groups, there is a clear progression of higher levels of voting as respondents age, supporting the hypothesis that older people are more likely to vote.

Table 4.10 Voting activity by age group

Age group	Voted	Didn't vote	Not eligible to vote	Total
Under 18	0.9%	9.3%	89.8%	100.0%
18–24	42.6%	27.6%	29.8%	100.0%
25–34	63.4%	29.8%	6.8%	100.0%
35–44	70.2%	24.3%	5.5%	100.0%
45–54	75.1%	20.6%	4.3%	100.0%
55–64	79.8%	17.5%	2.7%	100.0%
65+	81.3%	16.8%	2.0%	100.0%
Total	69.9%	21.3%	8.8%	100.0%

ADJUSTING TABLE APPEARANCE

It is helpful to be inducted into professional standards for table formatting as soon as you start producing your own data. There are very clear conventions in the social sciences for formatting data tables, and knowing how to change the appearance of tables in SPSS from the outset will save you a lot of time and effort later.

Tables in social sciences publications normally have a solid line across the top and bottom of the table, and a line that runs across the bottom of the column headings. You will notice that this is the convention followed in this book. In longer, more complex tables, there may be additional, thin lines added within the table to make it as easily comprehensible as possible. This can take a great deal of formatting after you produce the tables if you use the SPSS defaults. However, there are inbuilt templates that you can use to produce tables that are already professionally formatted, and you can adjust the default fonts used to match the font that you intend to use in the rest of your write-up to create a uniform, professional appearance.

To change the table default appearance, open Edit > Options > Pivot Tables. As a starting point, choose one of the APA options from TableLook. This will ensure that the lines are placed appropriately. Click Apply and close the Options window, then reproduce one of the tables from earlier in the chapter. You should notice that the appearance is different this time.

To change the default font, right click on your table in the Output window > Edit Content > In Separate Window. In the Pivot Table window, choose the Format > Table Properties > Cell Formats. If you can't see the Format menu, you may need to move the Formatting Toolbar out of the way; it has a tendency to overlay the table so that you cannot see the menu options in the Pivot Table window. In the Cell Formats tab, change the font face and size to match the font you will use in your writing. You will need to change each element individually, using the drop-down menu next to Area (above the sample table). When you have finished, click OK. When you are sure the table looks how you want to keep it, click Format > TableLooks > Save Look. If you are working on a shared computer, you may not be able to save your template in the SPSS directory but will need to save it to your personal files and take note of where you saved it.

Once you have created your custom table 'look', close your Pivot Table. In the main program window, return to Edit > Options > Pivot Tables. Choose your custom template. You may need to click Browse if you had to save the template to your personal files. When you have located your template, choose it and click OK to close the Options window. Try rerunning some of your syntax from earlier in the chapter. You should find that your outputs are now formatted according to your template.

CONCLUSIONS

This chapter has introduced you to techniques to run univariate and bivariate tables using categorical variables. You should be able to understand the difference between Per cent and Valid per cent when interpreting a frequency table. You have created crosstabs that are displayed as counts, row percentages, column percentages and total percentages. You have also learned how to select specific cases so that you can isolate specific sets of answers for analysis. Finally, you have learned how to create a custom table layout to save you time in formatting your tables in the future. In the next chapter, we will look at ways of visualizing this information.

Chapter 6 will explore more advanced techniques with crosstabs, learning how to work with missing data and how to incorporate more than two categorical variables in a single table.

ACTIVITIES

Activities 4.1 and 4.2 Frequency tables

Create a frequency table for the variables identified below. Answer the questions below about each of the variables. You can check your answers at the end of the book.

1. How many valid responses are there? How many missing responses?
2. How many respondents selected each of the different answer possibilities for UK-wide political parties (Conservative, Labour, Liberal Democrat, Green Party, UKIP)? Which was the most common response? Which was the least common?
3. Is there a very big difference between the values in the Per cent and Valid per cent columns? Why or why not?
4. What do your results mean for respondents' level of support for political parties? Practise writing a few sentences about what you see.

Variables:

1. Which party feel closer to, United Kingdom [`prtclbgb`]
2. How interested in politics [`polintr`], UK respondents

Activity 4.3 Crosstab of Austrian party affiliation and party closeness

Create a crosstab for Which party feel closer to, Austria [`prtclcat`] and How close to party [`prtdgcl`]. Choose the appropriate percentages to show how close people feel within each party affiliation.

1. What are the four parties with the most respondents?
2. Which of these party's supporters feel closest to the party (the greatest proportion who feel 'very close')?
3. Look up these parties to find out where they are placed on the left-right political spectrum. Is there any pattern between placement on the left-right spectrum and how close supporters feel to the party?

Activity 4.4 Crosstab of unemployment and voting

Select only responses from Germany. Create a crosstab for Ever unemployed and seeking work for a period more than three months [`uemp3m`] and Voted in the last national election [`vote`]. Produce counts and appropriate percentages for showing voting patterns within different categories of experience of unemployment.

(Continued)

1. How many responses in total are there for Germany?
2. What proportion of people who haven't experienced long-term unemployment voted in the last national election? What proportion of those who have experienced long-term unemployment voted in the last national election?

FURTHER READING

Frequency tables and crosstabs for categorical data are taught as an afterthought in most statistics books because of the type of data more frequently encountered in disciplines like psychology and the natural sciences. For this reason, it can be difficult to find extensive discussions of descriptive statistics for categorical data.

Halperin, S. and Heath, O. (2017) *Political Research: Methods and Practical Skills*, 2nd edn. Oxford: Oxford University Press.
For a discussion of the difference between descriptive and inferential statistics, see chapter 15 ('Quantitative analysis: Description and inference').

Marchant-Shapiro, T. (2015) *Statistics for Political Analysis: Understanding the Numbers*. London: Sage/CQ Press.
This book includes some basic instructions for using SPSS to conduct data analysis, and the examples are from political science. There is a discussion of crosstabs ('contingency tables') in chapter 8 ('Describing the pattern: what do you see?').

Pallant, J. (2016) *SPSS Survival Manual*. Maidenhead: Open University Press/McGraw-Hill Education.
This book provides a functional overview of how to produce statistics in SPSS. See chapter 6 ('Descriptive statistics') for an overview of how to produce frequency tables. For the content associated with categorical descriptive statistics, focus on the section 'Categorical variables'. For further information on producing crosstabs, see the section on chi squared tests in chapter 16 ('Non-parametric statistics').

REFERENCES

BBC (2010) 'Election 2010: National results', *BBC News*. (http://news.bbc.co.uk/1/shared/election2010/results).

Electoral Commission (2018) 'Electoral data', *The Electoral Commission*. (https://www.electoralcommission.org.uk/our-work/our-research/electoral-data).

ESS(2015) 'ESS 7 – 2014 Fieldwork Summary and Deviations', *European Social Survey*. (http://www.europeansocialsurvey.org/data/deviations_7.html).

5

VISUALIZING CATEGORICAL DATA

CHAPTER SUMMARY

In the previous chapter, you learned how to create some simple uni- and bivariate tables using categorical data. Data visualization can be used as another way of conveying the same information, whether to explore your data or to present your results. This chapter shows you how to create some of the most common data visualizations using categorical data. You will be introduced to the main types of charts and learn how to match them with appropriate variables. The final section of the chapter shows you some techniques for customizing the appearance of your results to make your visualizations look more professional.

OBJECTIVES

In this chapter, you will learn:

- How to produce some of the most common types of charts and when to use them
- How to use data visualization to explore your data
- How to present your visualizations professionally.

INTRODUCTION

Many readers will be familiar with the expression 'A picture is worth a thousand words', a phrase that exists in various forms in many cultures. This makes the point that when data can be presented in the form of a graphic or chart, the message is often more quickly understood than in the form of a narrative or a dense-looking table of results. However, a poorly designed visualization may confuse or distort the meaning of data. Increasingly there is something of a divide between statistical graphics and information visualization or 'infoviz' (see Gelman and Unwin, 2013).

Data visualization can play an important role at many points in the process of analysis. It can provide a quick overview for a researcher to get to know the distribution of answers; it can help to identify potential outliers and distortions; and it can provide a summary that makes trends easier to identify than tabular formatting of data. The most famous example of the last point is Anscombe's quartet (Figure 5.1; Table 5.1). In his highly influential article, Anscombe (1973) made a clear case for the contribution of data visualization to our understanding of data. The point he made still stands: graphing our data can highlight possible underlying shapes, trends and outliers that influence the way that we then choose to analyse data; thus, data visualization should be an integral part of the data analysis process.

Table 5.1 Anscombe's quartet

I		II		III		IV	
x	y	x	y	x	y	x	y
10.0	8.04	10.0	9.14	10.0	7.46	8.0	6.58
8.0	6.95	8.0	8.14	8.0	6.77	8.0	5.76
13.0	7.58	13.0	8.74	13.0	12.74	8.0	7.71
9.0	8.81	9.0	8.77	9.0	7.11	8.0	8.84
11.0	8.33	11.0	9.26	11.0	7.81	8.0	8.47
14.0	9.96	14.0	8.10	14.0	8.84	8.0	7.04
6.0	7.24	6.0	6.13	6.0	6.08	8.0	5.25
4.0	4.26	4.0	3.10	4.0	5.39	19.0	12.50
12.0	10.84	12.0	9.13	12.0	8.15	8.0	5.56
7.0	4.82	7.0	7.26	7.0	6.42	8.0	7.91
5.0	5.68	5.0	4.74	5.0	5.73	8.0	6.89

Source: Anscombe (1973)

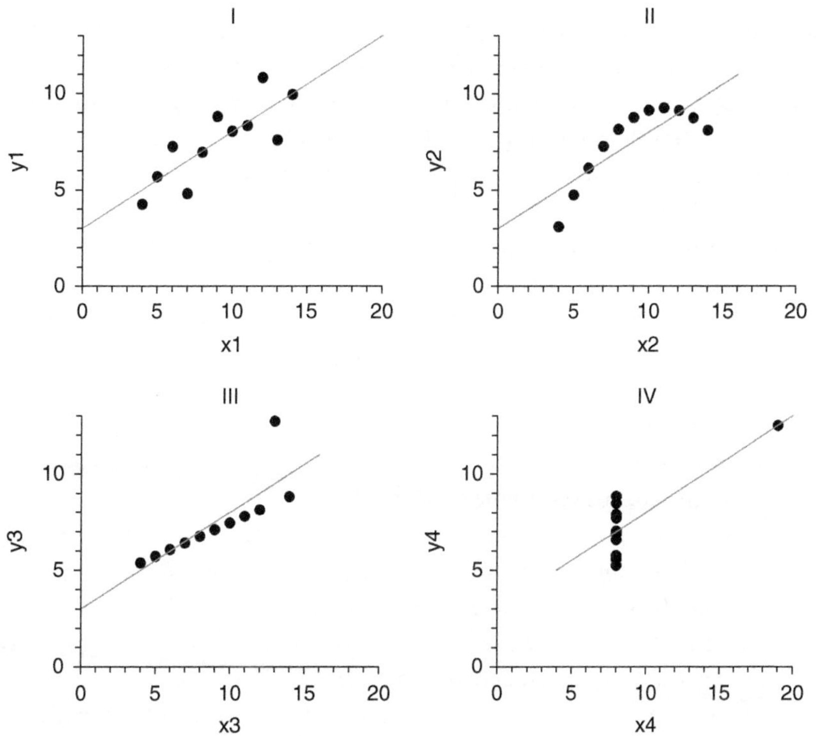

Figure 5.1 Anscombe's quartet visualized

The rest of this chapter focuses on how to visualize data in IBM SPSS Statistics ('SPSS'). We will start with an overview of the many ways to create charts in SPSS, giving an outline of the reasons why you might wish to choose each of these. The rest of this chapter walks through some of the most common types of charts, working through the types of data each is appropriate for and how to create them in SPSS. The chapter will walk you through how to produce each type of chart using syntax and menus. All of the worked examples in this chapter use the ESS, round 7 (2012–14). For more information about the ESS and where to find it, see Chapter 2.

There are at least five different ways of using SPSS to generate attractive plots or charts. We will look at each of these in turn.

1. Export results to another package, such as in spreadsheet format.
2. Add graphing options within statistical commands.
3. Use the legacy dialogues stemming from more rudimentary graphing capabilities.
4. Use the Graphboard Template Chooser.
5. Use Chart Builder and the underlying Graphics Production Language (GPL).

Exporting SPSS data for external visualization

For those just starting out it can be helpful to export the statistical summary tables from SPSS, then graph them with other software, such as using spreadsheets. Some presentation-style charts are easily accessed in spreadsheet and presentation packages, such as Microsoft's Excel and PowerPoint, Apple's Numbers, OpenOffice and LibreOffice Calc, or Google Sheets. There are an ever-increasing range of free online systems that allow you to create charts, such as Google Charts. The interactive features in these packages may make for ease of labelling and changes of format, but you will normally have to repeat the same step for customization for each subsequent chart, rather than being able to replicate your formatting in a couple of clicks.

In addition to allowing you to graph your data with a more familiar program, exporting your data can also enable you to combine the outputs from multiple datasets in a quick, relatively easy manner. For example, you might be working with different waves of the same survey that are not available as a longitudinal dataset, such as the Eurobarometer data for more recent years, and exporting your data from multiple analyses would allow you to create a chart over time of answers to the same question.

SPSS makes exporting your results straightforward, as statistical output, such as tables, may be exported into common data formats, such as .xls and .xlsx. You can copy individual table results from the Output window by right clicking on the table or selecting the table and using the Edit menu > Copy Special > Excel Worksheet (BIFF). This content will then paste seamlessly into a spreadsheet. Alternatively, if you want to export all or a selection of your outputs, you can do this through File > Export > Objects to Export (select All, All visible or Selected). Choose your desired export format (such as Excel) under Type. Indicate where you want the exported file to be located in the File Name options, then press OK.

Adding charts to a statistical command

The most straightforward way to create a simple chart is to add it to your statistical output when producing a table. Some of the standard statistical commands allow for further output in the form of charts. For example, if you are producing a univariate frequency table, the `FREQUENCIES` command has a sub-menu called Charts, which allows specification of bar charts, pie charts or histograms (Box 5.1). Histograms may be overlaid with a normal curve for visual inspection of how far the sample distribution departs from normality. The menu system also allows for specifying that the charts contain either frequencies (counts of numbers of cases) or percentages.

BOX 5.1 PRODUCING A FREQUENCY TABLE WITH A BAR CHART SHOWING PERCENTAGES

This box teaches you how to produce a simple bar chart displaying percentages at the same time as a frequency table using the variable How interested in politics [`polintr`]. The results are shown in Table 5.2 and Figure 5.2.

Syntax

```
FREQUENCIES VARIABLES=polintr

  /BARCHART PERCENT.
```

You will see that the syntax is the same as a standard frequency table, with the addition of the `/barchart` command. When you type / under a frequency table, the chart options are:

`BARCHART`	A simple bar chart for use with one categorical variable
`HISTOGRAM`	A complex bar chart for portraying one continuous variable
`PIECHART`	A simple pie chart for use with one categorical variable, preferably with no more than five categories

For bar charts and pie charts, you can show the chart results as a count (frequency) or per cent. If you want to display the frequencies in the bar chart, you can replace 'percent' with 'count' in the syntax above. To create a pie chart, replace 'barchart' with 'piechart' in the syntax above. We will look at histograms separately in Chapter 8 'Visualizing continuous data'.

Menu instructions

Analyze > Descriptive Statistics > Frequencies

Find How interested in politics [`polintr`].

(Continued)

Move to Variable(s) box either by double clicking the variable name or by clicking once and then clicking the arrow between the two boxes.

Make sure that the box for Display Frequency Tables in the bottom left-hand corner is ticked.

Open the Charts options.

Chart Type: Bar charts.

Chart Values: Percentages.

Continue.

Press OK to run it or Paste to copy the command into the Syntax window, then run the syntax.

Table 5.2 Frequency of interest in politics

		Frequency	Per cent	Valid per cent	Cumulative per cent
Valid	Very interested	4834	12.0	12.1	12.1
	Quite interested	14751	36.7	36.8	48.9
	Hardly interested	13102	32.6	32.7	81.6
	Not at all interested	7391	18.4	18.4	100.0
	Total	40078	99.7	100.0	
Missing	Refusal	18	.0		
	Don't know	77	.2		
	No answer	12	.0		
	Total	107	.3		
Total		40185	40185	100.0	

When producing a crosstab with two or more variables, 'Display clustered bar charts' is available on the front page of the CROSSTABS menu dialogue box (Box 5.2). These add-ons to statistical commands may give some idea to the underlying patterns of interest but tend to be relatively unsophisticated. When using some of the more advanced commands, and particularly regression, these kinds of charts are particularly important to scrutinize for diagnostic and model evaluation reasons. We will look in more detail at these sophisticated plots in later chapters. They are generally reserved for analyses involving continuous data.

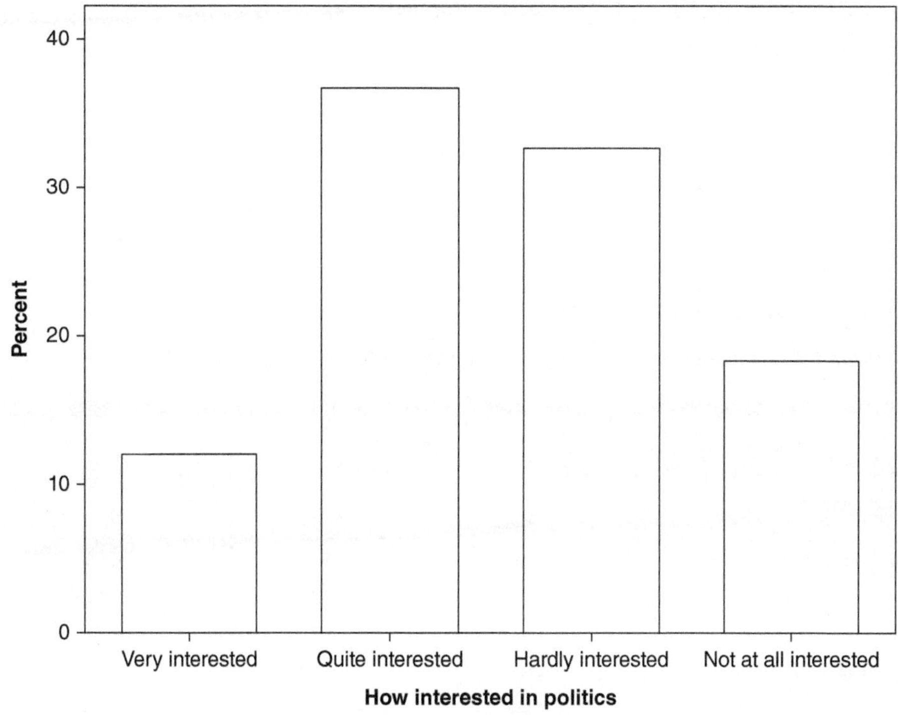

Figure 5.2 Simple bar chart of interest in politics

BOX 5.2 PRODUCING A CROSSTAB WITH A CLUSTERED BAR CHART

This box teaches you how to produce a clustered bar chart at the same time as a crosstab using the variables Gender [gndr] and How interested in politics [polintr]. Results are in Table 5.3 and Figure 5.3.

Syntax

```
CROSSTABS
  /TABLES=polintr BY gndr
  /FORMAT=AVALUE TABLES
  /CELLS=COUNT
  /COUNT ROUND CELL
  /BARCHART.
```

(Continued)

You should notice that the only difference in the syntax above to a routine crosstab is the final line of the command `/barchart`.

Menu instructions

Analyze > Descriptive Statistics > Crosstabs

Find How interested in politics [`polintr`] and move to Rows box.

Find Gender [`gndr`] and move to Columns box.

Tick Display clustered bar charts.

Press OK to run it or Paste to copy the command into the Syntax window.

Table 5.3 Interest in politics by sex

	Male	Female	Total
Very interested	3013	1821	4834
Quite interested	7518	7232	14750
Hardly interested	5443	7646	13089
Not at all interested	2848	4535	7383
Total	18822	21234	40056

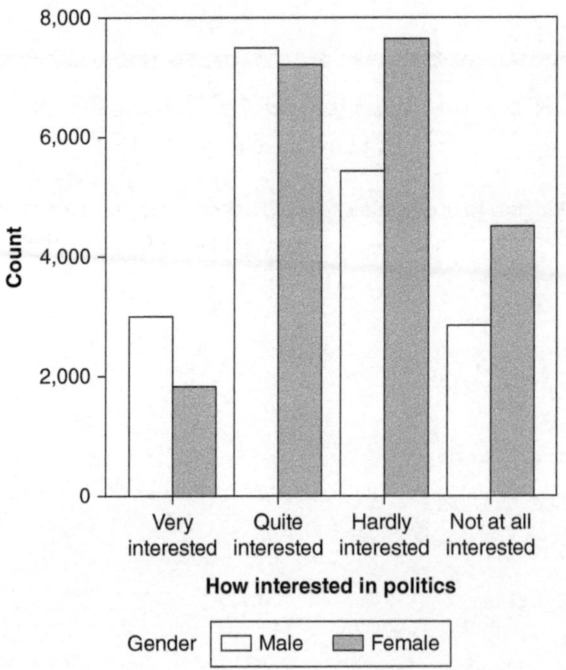

Figure 5.3 Clustered bar chart of interest in politics by sex

Legacy Dialogs

The third way, which is used occasionally in this book, is named Legacy Dialogs. The Legacy Dialogs are named that for a reason: they are a legacy from earlier versions of SPSS, when the graphing capability was much more limited. The Legacy Dialogs use the standard SPSS syntax format and are a straightforward way of creating basic charts. It may be worth sticking with this approach if you are already quite familiar with it, but if you are newer to SPSS it is better to avoid this step in favour of the Graphboard Template Chooser or Chart Builder, which are driven by graphics engines and are much more sophisticated. The syntax of the Legacy Dialogs is very straightforward, but because the Graphboard Template Chooser and Chart Builder can do everything the Legacy Dialogs can do, and more, we will not provide instruction on using this function.

Graphboard Template Chooser (GTC)

The GTC is most useful for advanced users who want a greater degree of control over the visualizations they produce. The greatest advantage of using the GTC over other approaches is that it allows you to make maps that use colours and shading to represent underlying data (referred to as 'choropleths'), which you cannot do through any of SPSS's other graphing functions. For other visualizations, the GTC works best with the software add-on program Visualization Designer, which requires a separate licence. However, if you do not need to create maps or custom visualizations, Chart Builder should be your default choice for graphing your data.

Chart Builder

Chart Builder uses an underlying language of GPL – the Graphics Production Language. If there are very detailed aspects of producing charts and figures that you need to customize, then Chart Builder (and GPL in particular) provide almost unrivalled control over what is produced. The Chart Builder interface is fairly straightforward to get started with, allowing you to drag and drop different variables and elements onto the chart area. The chart area also updates with random-generated data so that you can get a rough idea of how the chart will look.

However, because Chart Builder uses a different language, its syntax works differently from the statistical syntax you will learn elsewhere, and it is less straightforward than other aspects of SPSS syntax because it can specify a wider range of options. If you are just getting started with syntax, do not worry too much about the syntax for these charts, as it is produced using a much more complicated language. Working with charts in SPSS is one of the few times that using the user interface instead of the syntax is advisable. However, as we noted in the previous chapter, it is still important to keep a record of what you have done in a syntax file, as this will allow you to reproduce your outputs quickly and easily. Pasting will also allow you to compare your settings to ours to try to identify if you have entered anything differently, if your results are not the same as ours.

The rest of this chapter and Chapter 8 show you how to produce some of the most common chart types in political science and international relations research using Chart Builder. The charts covered in this book are:

- pie charts
- bar/column charts (simple bar charts, stacked bar charts and clustered bar charts)
- histograms (simple histograms and population pyramids)
- population pyramids
- line charts (simple line charts and multiple line charts)
- scatterplots
- boxplots.

Other less common and/or more advanced chart types not covered in this book are:

- donut charts
- maps, including choropleths
- area charts
- hybrid/dual axis charts.

Before learning how to produce each of these charts, you need to understand that different charts are suitable for different types of data. You need to be able to distinguish between nominal, ordinal and continuous data to choose an appropriate chart to visualize it. As we discussed in Chapter 3, these typologies are flawed, and continuous data can easily be converted into categorical data. However, you do need to understand your variable type – and check that it is classified correctly in SPSS – before you can produce a suitable chart. Table 5.4 provides an overview of the main chart types, what type of variable(s) they are suited to and the number of variables you can display in each chart type.

Table 5.4 Overview of chart types

Chart type	**Variable type**	**Sub-types**	**Number of variables**
Pie chart	Categorical	3D pie, donut chart	1 (simple), >1 (donut)
Bar/column chart	Categorical	Stacked column, clustered column	1 (simple), >1 (stacked, clustered)
Histogram	Continuous	Stacked histogram, population pyramid, frequency polygon	1 (histogram, frequency polygon), >1 (stacked histogram, population pyramid)
Line graph	Continuous preferable, minimum ordinal	Multiple line graph, area graph	>1
Scatterplot	Continuous	Grouped scatterplot	2 (simple), >2 (grouped)
Boxplot	Continuous	Clustered boxplot, high-low graphs	

PIE CHARTS

Our advice on pie charts is simple: don't use them. Our advice on 3D pie charts is similar: never use them. There are two key reasons for this advice:

1. Unless you are working with five or fewer categories, pie charts (and their derivatives, such as donut charts and 3D pie charts) very quickly become visually confusing.
2. They are often misleading in what they represent.

To illustrate this, look at Figure 5.4. It is quite hard to be see that the Conservative share of the vote was considerably larger than that of Labour (42.4 per cent to 27.6 per cent), and that Labour's share was not all that much greater than that of the SDP–Liberal Alliance (25.4 per cent). The effect is pronounced in a three-dimensional pie chart but still exists in a two-dimensional version. You might also notice that the numbers do not add up to

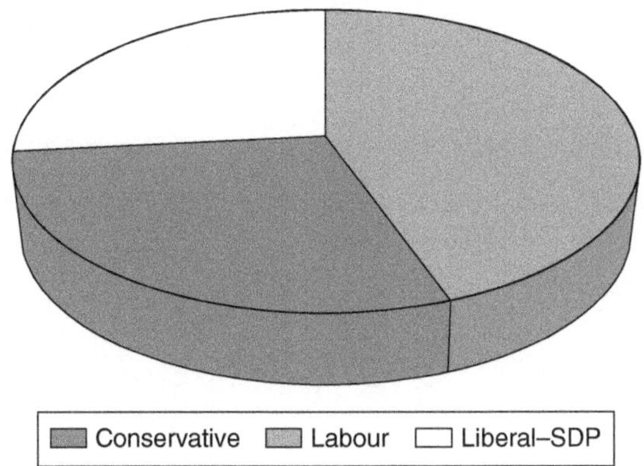

Figure 5.4 Pie chart of 1983 UK general election results

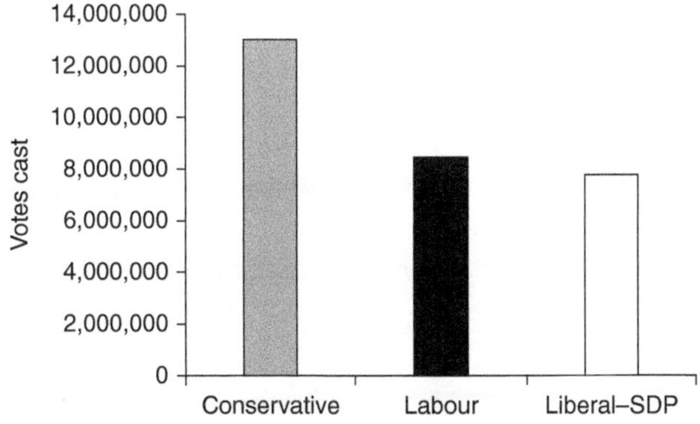

Figure 5.5 Column chart of 1983 UK general election results

100 per cent, even though it fills the pie. This is because 4.6 per cent of votes were cast for other parties; but pie charts will fill the pie with the available information, regardless of whether it actually equals a whole pie (100 per cent). A simple column or bar chart (see Figure 5.5) does a better job of showing the differences between the three main parties. There may be occasions where a very simple pie chart may have rhetorical effect, perhaps even ironic effect, but pie charts are generally better avoided. If you do require a pie chart, Box 5.3 will show you how to produce one.

BOX 5.3 PRODUCING A SIMPLE PIE CHART

This box teaches you how to produce a pie chart using the variable How interested in politics [`polintr`]. The results are in Figure 5.6.

Menu instructions

Graphs > Chart Builder

Confirm that your variables have been set to the appropriate measurement level.

Press OK when you're sure, for example, that your variable is set as nominal or ordinal to produce a pie chart.

> Gallery tab > Pie/Polar

Drag pie chart icon onto the chart area.

> Variables

Drag How interested in politics [`polintr`] onto the Slice by? box in the chart area.

Click Paste to keep a copy in syntax. Then, in the syntax window, select the block of text you have produced (starting with GGRAPH and ending with END GPL.) and press the green play triangle.

Or, press OK without pasting.

Syntax

```
GGRAPH
  /GRAPHDATASET NAME='graphdataset' VARIABLES=polintr COUNT() [name='COUNT']
MISSING=LISTWISE
  REPORTMISSING=NO
  /GRAPHSPEC SOURCE=INLINE.
```

```
BEGIN GPL
  SOURCE: s=userSource(id('graphdataset'))
  DATA: polintr=col(source(s), name('polintr'), unit.category())
  DATA: COUNT=col(source(s), name('COUNT'))
  COORD: polar.theta(startAngle(0))
  GUIDE: axis(dim(1), null())
  GUIDE: legend(aesthetic(aesthetic.color.interior), label('How interested
in politics'))
  SCALE: linear(dim(1), dataMinimum(), dataMaximum())
  SCALE: cat(aesthetic(aesthetic.color.interior), include('1', '2',
'3', '4'))
  ELEMENT: interval.stack(position(summary.percent(COUNT))), color.
interior(polintr))
END GPL.
```

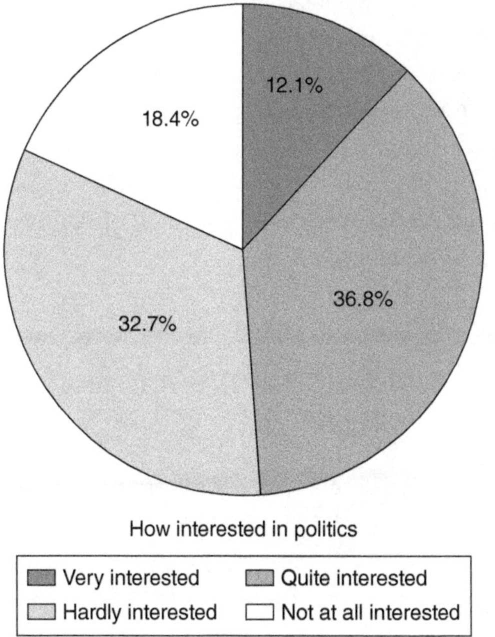

Figure 5.6 Pie chart of interest in politics [`polintr`]

BAR/COLUMN CHARTS

Bar and column charts display frequencies (counts and percentages) of categorical data. For example, counts for the variable How interested in politics [`polintr`] will show the number of people who said they were 'very interested', the number who said, 'quite interested', the number who said, 'hardly interested', and the number who said, 'not at all interested'. Percentages will show the proportion of respondents in a certain category, such as the proportion of respondents who were not at all interested in politics. Or, to return to our example of the 1983 UK general election results from the previous section, counts would show the number of votes for each party, while percentages would show the proportion of votes for each. With a bar or column chart, the numbers do not need to add up to 100 per cent, as in our example, where we have not reported the votes for many smaller parties.

Although commonly referred to as bar charts, strictly speaking a bar chart has horizontal bars, while a column chart has vertical columns. However, to avoid confusion, we will adopt the terminology used in SPSS, which refers to all of these as bar charts. Clustered and stacked charts allow you to add a second – or even third variable – to further break down the data. For example, you could show political party support broken down by sex, or support for female political leaders by country.

In this section, we will start with a simple bar chart containing one variable (How interested in politics [`polintr`]) (Box 5.4). Then we will create a clustered chart and a stacked chart using this variable and Gender [`gndr`]. As a side note, gender is not an accurate label for this variable, given that Male and Female were the only answer choices. There are, of course, far more than two expressions of gender, and gender should not be used interchangeably with sex. For this reason, the tables and charts produced using this variable are labelled 'sex'. Even this is, of course, inadequate, since there are more than two biological sexes. However, most social surveys still reflect dated understandings of gender and sex and offer only binary (male vs female) choices.

BOX 5.4 PRODUCING A SIMPLE BAR CHART WITH COUNTS

This box teaches you how to produce a simple bar chart with counts using the variable How interested in politics [`polintr`]. The results are in Figure 5.7.

Menu instructions

Graphs > Chart Builder

Confirm that your variables have been set to the appropriate measurement level.

Press OK when you're sure, for example, that your variable is set as nominal or ordinal to produce a simple bar chart.

> Gallery tab > Bar

Drag the first bar chart option (Simple Bar), with three beige columns, onto the chart area. (If you have trouble distinguishing colours or are not sure which one is the simple bar chart, SPSS will show you the label if you hover over the picture.)

> Variables

Drag How interested in politics [`polintr`] onto the X-Axis? box in the chart area.

Click Paste to keep a copy in syntax. Then, in the Syntax window, select the block of text you have produced (starting with GGRAPH and ending with END GPL.) and press the green play triangle.

Or, press OK without pasting.

Syntax

```
GGRAPH
  /GRAPHDATASET NAME='graphdataset' VARIABLES=polintr COUNT()[name='COUNT']
MISSING=LISTWISE
    REPORTMISSING=NO
  /GRAPHSPEC SOURCE=INLINE.
BEGIN GPL
  SOURCE: s=userSource(id('graphdataset'))
  DATA: polintr=col(source(s), name('polintr'), unit.category())
  DATA: COUNT=col(source(s), name('COUNT'))
  GUIDE: axis(dim(1), label('How interested in politics'))
  GUIDE: axis(dim(2), label('Count'))
  SCALE: cat(dim(1), include('1', '2', '3', '4'))
  SCALE: linear(dim(2), include(0))
  ELEMENT: interval(position(polintr*COUNT), shape.interior(shape.
square))
 END GPL.
```

Figure 5.7 shows the results as counts. We can see that roughly 5,000 respondents reported that they were 'very interested' in politics; about 15,000 said they were 'quite interested'; about 13,000 said they were 'hardly interested'; and about 7,000 were 'not at all interested'.

At the end of the chapter, in the section 'Adjusting chart appearance', you can find out how to turn on data labels so that you can see exact values for the bars. However, if we are interested in percentages instead of counts, we can change the Chart Builder options when we produce the chart so that it shows us percentage instead of counts. Instructions for doing this are in Box 5.5.

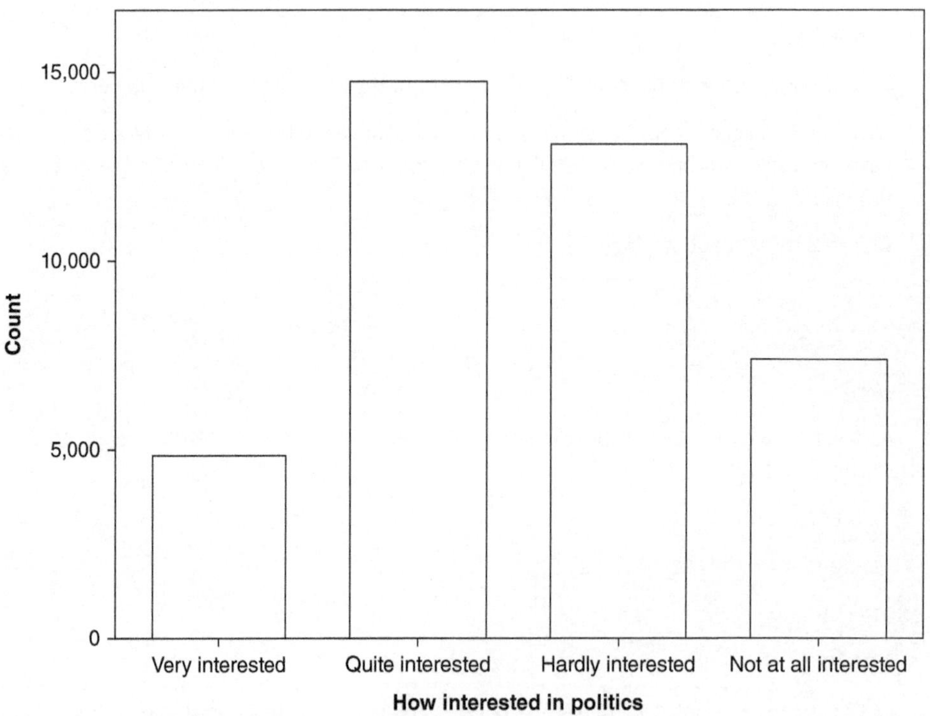

Figure 5.7 Simple bar chart of interest in politics, counts

BOX 5.5 PRODUCING A SIMPLE BAR CHART WITH PERCENTAGES

This box teaches you how to produce a simple bar chart with percentages using the variable How interested in politics [`polintr`]. The results are in Figure 5.8.

Menu instructions

Graphs > Chart Builder

Confirm that your variables have been set to the appropriate measurement level.

Press OK when you're sure, for example, that your variable is set as nominal or ordinal to produce a simple bar chart.

If you want to clear the settings from a previous chart, press Reset.

> Gallery tab > Bar

Drag the first bar chart option (Simple Bar), with three beige columns, onto the chart area. (If you have trouble distinguishing colours or are not sure which one is the simple bar chart, SPSS will show you the label if you hover over the picture.)

> Variables

Drag How interested in politics [`polintr`] onto the X-Axis? box in the chart area.

> Element Properties > Statistics

Under Statistic, change the drop-down menu from Count to Percentage.

Click Set Parameters.

Choose Grand Total from the drop-down menu for Denominator for Computing Percentages.

Click Continue.

Click Apply at the bottom of the Element Properties window.

Click Paste to keep a copy in syntax. Then, in the Syntax window, select the block of text you have produced (starting with GGRAPH and ending with END GPL.) and press the green play triangle.

Or, press OK without pasting.

Syntax

```
GGRAPH

  /GRAPHDATASET NAME='graphdataset' VARIABLES=polintr COUNT()[name='COUNT']
MISSING=LISTWISE

  REPORTMISSING=NO

  /GRAPHSPEC SOURCE=INLINE.

BEGIN GPL

  SOURCE: s=userSource(id('graphdataset'))

  DATA: polintr=col(source(s), name('polintr'), unit.category())

  DATA: COUNT=col(source(s), name('COUNT'))

  GUIDE: axis(dim(1), label('How interested in politics'))

  GUIDE: axis(dim(2), label('Percent'))

  SCALE: cat(dim(1), include('1', '2', '3', '4'))
```

(Continued)

```
  SCALE: linear(dim(2), include(0))

  ELEMENT: interval(position(summary.percent(polintr*COUNT, base.all
(acrossPanels()))),

    shape.interior(shape.square))

END GPL.
```

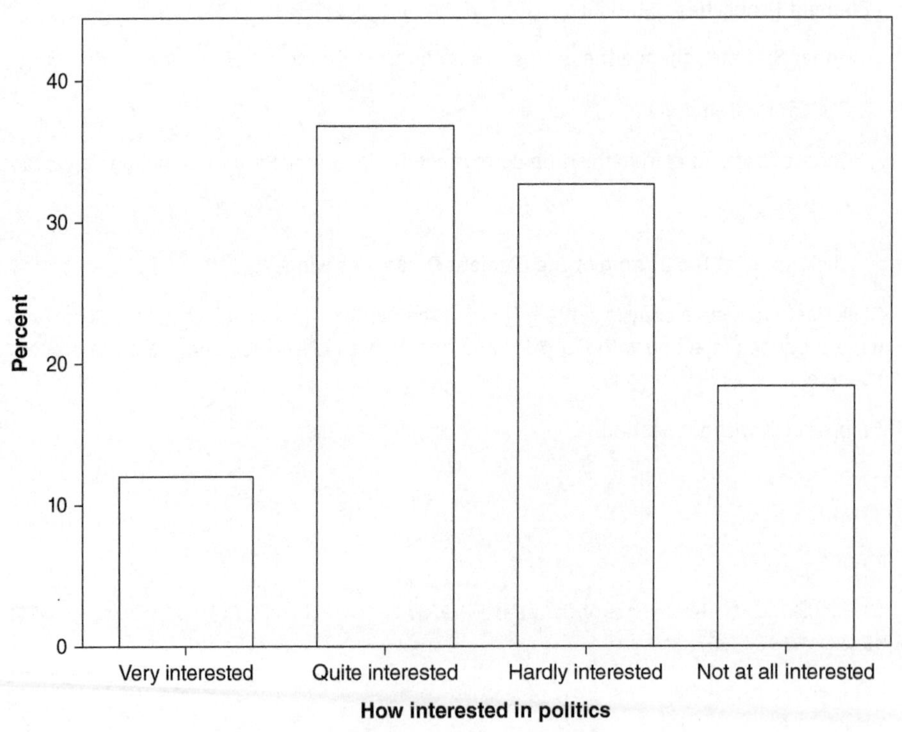

Figure 5.8 Simple bar chart of interest in politics [`polintr`], percentages

Figure 5.8 shows respondents' interest in politics by percentages instead of counts. You should notice that the bars are in the same proportion to each other as the chart we produced with counts, but this time the y-axis shows the results in percentage terms. This shows us that somewhat more than 10 per cent of respondents were 'very interested' in politics, about 35 per cent 'quite interested', about 33 per cent 'hardly interested', and a bit less than 20 per cent 'not at all interested'. We could, of course, easily calculate these percentages by hand using the counts, but doing this through Chart Builder gives us the option of adding data labels that show the exact value with the click of a button (covered at the end of the chapter, under 'Adjusting chart appearance').

We can add some extra information to this chart by creating a clustered or stacked column chart, which will allow us to compare responses based on another variable. In this case, we will compare men's versus women's interest in politics using Gender [gndr] (Box 5.6).

BOX 5.6 PRODUCING A CLUSTERED BAR CHART WITH PERCENTAGES

This box teaches you how to produce a clustered bar chart with percentages using the variables How interested in politics [polintr] and Gender [gndr]. The results are in Figure 5.9.

We will produce the percentages within groups. This means producing the proportion *of men* who are very interested, quite interested, etc., and the proportion *of women* who are very interested, quite interested, etc. If we instead produced total percentages, we would be showing the proportion of respondents who were male *and* very interested in politics, female *and* very interested in politics, etc. Producing the group percentages mean that the women's responses will add up to 100 per cent *and* the men's responses will add up to 100 per cent. If we produced the total percentages, all of the bars together would add up to 100 per cent.

Menu instructions

Graphs > Chart Builder

Confirm that your variables have been set to the appropriate measurement level.

Press OK when you're sure, for example, that your variable is set as nominal or ordinal to produce a clustered bar chart.

If you want to clear the settings from a previous chart, press Reset.

> Gallery tab > Bar

Drag the second bar chart option (Clustered Bar), with six columns in blue and green, onto the chart area. (If you have trouble distinguishing colours or are not sure which one is the clustered bar chart, SPSS will show you the label if you hover over the picture.)

> Variables

Drag How interested in politics [polintr] onto the X-Axis? box in the chart area.

Drag Gender [gndr] onto the Cluster on X: set color box in the chart area.

> Element Properties > Statistics

Under Statistic, change the drop-down menu from Count to Percentage.

Click Set Parameters.

Choose Total for Each Legend Variable Category (same fill color) from the drop-down menu for Denominator for Computing Percentages.

(Continued)

Click Continue.

Click Apply at the bottom of the Element Properties window.

Click Paste to keep a copy in syntax. Then, in the Syntax window, select the block of text you have produced (starting with GGRAPH and ending with END GPL.) and press the green play triangle. Or, press OK without pasting.

Syntax

```
GGRAPH
  /GRAPHDATASET NAME='graphdataset' VARIABLES=polintr COUNT()[name='COUNT']
gndr MISSING=LISTWISE
    REPORTMISSING=NO
  /GRAPHSPEC SOURCE=INLINE.
BEGIN GPL
  SOURCE: s=userSource(id('graphdataset'))
  DATA: polintr=col(source(s), name('polintr'), unit.category())
  DATA: COUNT=col(source(s), name('COUNT'))
  DATA: gndr=col(source(s), name('gndr'), unit.category())
  COORD: rect(dim(1,2), cluster(3,0))
  GUIDE: axis(dim(3), label('How interested in politics'))
  GUIDE: axis(dim(2), label('Percent'))
  GUIDE: legend(aesthetic(aesthetic.color.interior), label('Gender'))
  SCALE: cat(dim(3), include('1', '2', '3', '4'))
  SCALE: linear(dim(2), include(0))
  SCALE: cat(aesthetic(aesthetic.color.interior), include('1', '2'))
  SCALE: cat(dim(1), include('1', '2'))
  ELEMENT:
interval(position(summary.percent(gndr*COUNT*polintr,
  base.aesthetic (aesthetic(aesthetic.color.interior)))), color.interior
(gndr),
    shape.interior(shape.square))
END GPL.
```

Figure 5.9 shows the breakdown of interest in politics by gender. By using a clustered bar chart, we can compare our two groups (male and female). These results show that the distribution of male responses is more skewed towards being interested in politics, indicated by the male response bars being higher than the female response bars for 'very interested' and 'quite interested'; while the female responses are more skewed towards disinterest, with the female response bars being higher than the male response bars for 'hardly interested' and 'not interested at all'.

We might want to explore other possible demographics related to political interest, such as income groups. We could produce this as a clustered bar chart, but as you can see in Figure 5.10, this creates a very busy chart with far too much information to take in.

Instead, we can convey this information more succinctly using a stacked bar chart (Box 5.7). What this does is sub-divide each column according to the chosen categories so that each cluster in a clustered bar chart becomes a single column in the stacked bar chart. We also change this chart so that the income deciles run along the x-axis, and we use interest in politics to sub-divide each column's results.

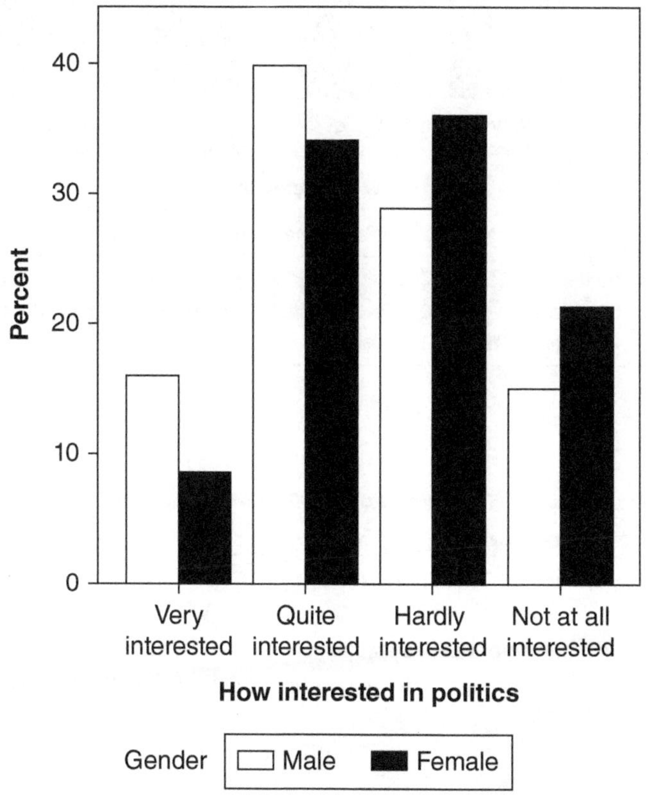

Figure 5.9 Clustered bar chart of interest in politics [`polintr`] by gender [`gndr`]

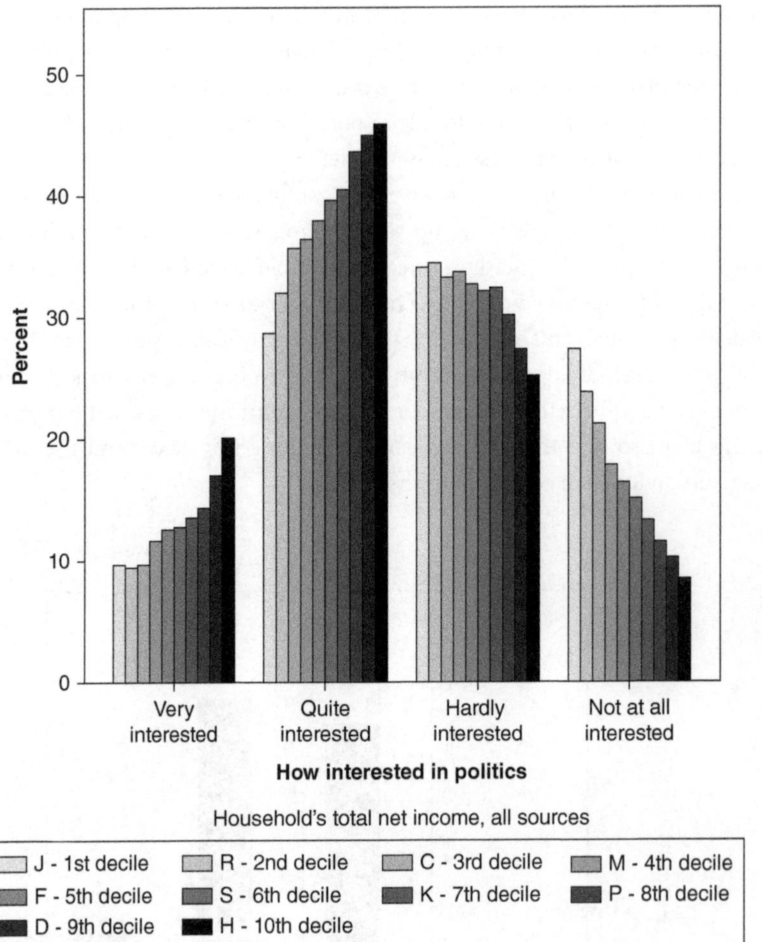

Figure 5.10 Clustered bar chart of interest in politics [`polintr`] by income deciles [`hinctnta`]

BOX 5.7 PRODUCING A STACKED BAR CHART WITH PERCENTAGES

This box teaches you how to produce a stacked bar chart with percentages using the variables How interested in politics [`polintr`] and Household's total net income, all sources [`hinctnta`]. The results are in Figure 5.11.

Menu instructions

Graphs > Chart Builder

Confirm that your variables have been set to the appropriate measurement level.

Press OK when you're sure, for example, that your variable is set as nominal or ordinal to produce a stacked bar chart.

If you want to clear the settings from a previous chart, press Reset.

> Gallery tab > Bar

Drag the third bar chart option (Stacked Bar), with three columns sub-divided in blue and green, onto the chart area. (If you have trouble distinguishing colours or are not sure which one is the stacked bar chart, SPSS will show you the label if you hover over the picture.)

> Variables

Drag Household's total net income, all sources [`hinctnta`] onto the X-Axis? box in the chart area.

Drag How interested in politics [`polintr`] onto the Stack: set color box in the chart area.

> Element Properties > Statistics

Under Statistic, change the drop-down menu from Count to Percentage.

Click Set Parameters.

Choose Total for Each X-Axis Category from the drop-down menu for Denominator for Computing Percentages.

Click Continue.

Click Apply at the bottom of the Element Properties window.

Click Paste to keep a copy in syntax. Then, in the Syntax window, select the block of text you have produced (starting with GGRAPH and ending with END GPL.) and press the green play triangle.

Or, press OK without pasting.

Syntax

```
GGRAPH
  /GRAPHDATASET NAME='graphdataset' VARIABLES=hinctnta COUNT()[name='COUNT']
polintr
    MISSING=LISTWISE REPORTMISSING=NO
  /GRAPHSPEC SOURCE=INLINE.
BEGIN GPL
  SOURCE: s=userSource(id('graphdataset'))
  DATA: hinctnta=col(source(s), name('hinctnta'), unit.category())
  DATA: COUNT=col(source(s), name('COUNT'))
  DATA: polintr=col(source(s), name('polintr'), unit.category())
```

(Continued)

```
  GUIDE: axis(dim(1), label('Household's total net income, all sources'))
  GUIDE: axis(dim(2), label('Percent'))
  GUIDE: legend(aesthetic(aesthetic.color.interior), label('How interested
in politics'))
  SCALE: cat(dim(1), include('1', '2', '3', '4', '5', '6', '7', '8', '9',
'10'))
  SCALE: linear(dim(2), include(0))
  SCALE: cat(aesthetic(aesthetic.color.interior), include('1', '2', '3',
'4'))
  ELEMENT: interval.stack(position(summary.percent(hinctnta*COUNT, base.
coordinate(dim(1)))),
    color.interior(polintr), shape.interior(shape.square))
END GPL.
```

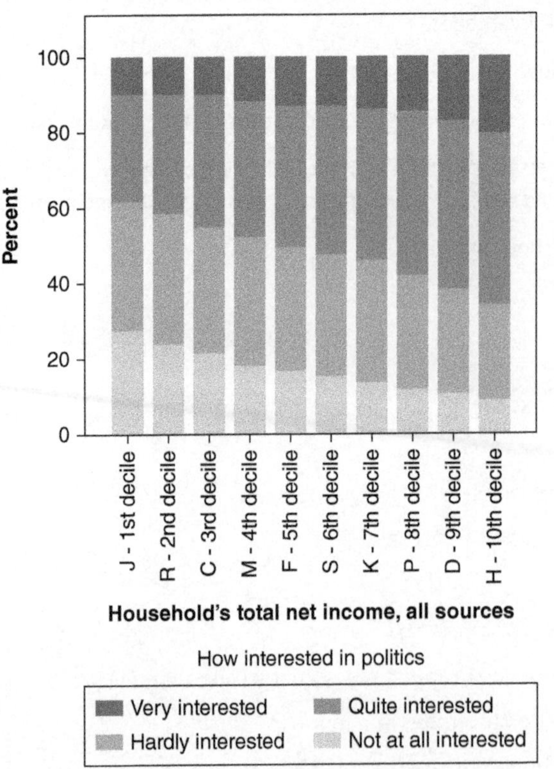

Figure 5.11 Stacked bar chart of interest in politics [`polintr`] by household income deciles [`hinctnta`], percentages

Figure 5.11 shows the breakdown of interest in politics by household income deciles. We have edited the x-axis labels to shorten the category names. You can find out how to perform this and other customizations at the end of this chapter, in the section 'Adjusting chart appearance'. Not only is the stacked bar chart a much simpler way of conveying this information than a clustered bar chart, but it also shows a very clear trend of increasing political interest as the household income decile increases, as you would expect from general political participation data, which consistently indicates that wealthier people are more engaged in politics. We can see, for example, that more than 60 per cent of people in the first (lowest) income decile reported that they were 'hardly' or 'not at all interested' in politics, compared to less than 40 per cent of those in the tenth (highest) income decile.

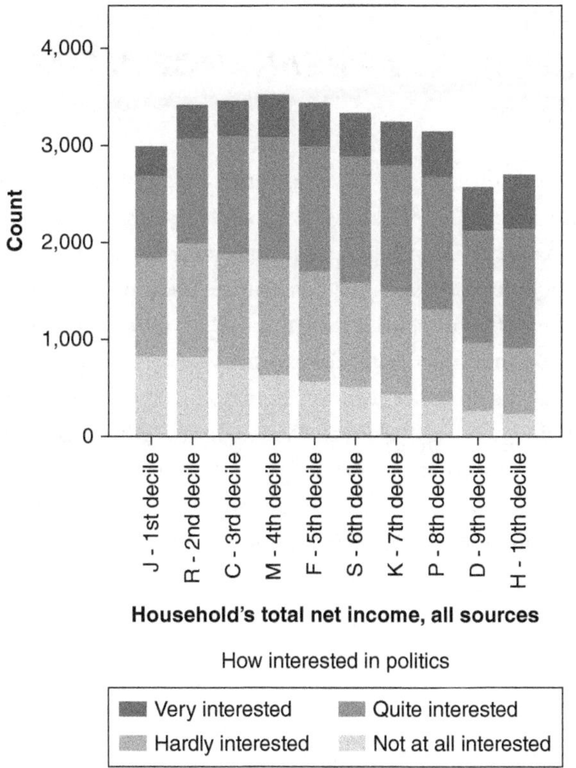

Figure 5.12 Stacked bar chart of interest in politics [polintr] by household income deciles [hinctnta], counts

To illustrate the difference between producing a stacked bar chart with percentages and one with counts, compare Figure 5.11 to Figure 5.12. Figure 5.11 shows the percentages within income groups. This means the proportion *of 1st decile income households* who are very interested, quite interested, etc., and the proportion *of 10th income decile households* who are very interested, quite interested, etc. If we instead produce counts (Figure 5.12), we are showing the number of respondents who fall into each category as well as how many of them expressed the different levels of interest in politics. This would show us more about the distribution of incomes across the income groups but is less clear on how to interpret their level of interest in politics. We can still see a clear downward trend in answers of 'not at all interested' across the household income deciles in Figure 5.12, but it is much harder to interpret the proportions of the categories at the top of the stack ('very' and 'quite interested'). This is because we have different numbers of respondents in each income decile, indicated by the total height of the stack. For example, we have about 3,000 respondents in the first income decile; the smallest group of respondents is the ninth income decile; and the largest group of respondents, by a small margin, is the fourth income decile.

ADJUSTING CHART APPEARANCE IN THE CHART EDITOR

You should not be put off using SPSS's own internal graphing capabilities by the default looks of the charts produced. While these may look fairly basic, with unappealing fonts and colours, these are easily customizable. You can transform the appearance of your chart using the Chart Editor, including adjusting colours, patterns, adding labels and changing the font face to match the text of your report. To open the Chart Editor, double click on the chart in the Output window. When the Chart Editor window opens, click on the chart to open the Properties window. If the Properties window does not open automatically, or you close it by accident, you can always open it again in Chart Editor > Edit > Properties. You will notice that different customizations are available to you depending on the type of chart you are editing. Chart Editor will only show the options suitable for your current chart.

Below we walk through some of the most common adjustments you might want to make. At the end, you can save your customization as a new template that you can apply to all future charts to give them a uniform, professional appearance that matches the formatting you use in your write-up of your findings.

Changing colours and fonts

By default, SPSS will produce your charts either in beige, or in a series of colours. To adjust the colours, open the Chart Editor by double clicking on a chart you have produced in your Output window. In the Properties window, open the Fill & Border tab. Click on a slice (in a pie) or bar (in a bar chart). Click the box of colour you want to change next to Fill or Border in Properties > Fill & Border. Choose a different colour, then click Apply to update the chart.

Keep in mind the consumers of your chart when you alter colours. For example, if you plan to submit the data visualization as part of a data report, you should take into account whether the submission will be viewed in colour or black and white, and if it is viewed in colour, whether the differences between colours will be visible to someone who has a form of colour blindness, which affects approximately 1 in 12 men and 1 in 200 women of European descent; prevalence in other populations around the world indicates similar, and sometimes higher, proportions. If the colours are important for conveying meaning, you should confirm that there is enough contrast between the colours, use colour schemes that are suitable for colour blindness (see, for example, Wilson, 2009), or use pattern fills (with bar and pie charts) or symbols (with line charts and scatterplots) to help differentiate between categories.

To change the font of an element, click on the item (such as the legend for How interested in politics in the pie chart), then make the adjustments in the Text Style tab of the Properties window. There are also some basic text adjustment tools that will appear in the second row of navigation tools on the main Chart Editor window.

Adding data labels and titles

To add labels to the bars or slices, click on the body of the pie chart or one of the bars, then toggle on Show Data Labels in the icon menus, or turn it on in the Elements menu > Show Data Labels. You can alter the font, background fill, border, etc. of the data labels by clicking on them to activate their options in the Properties window, then exploring options in Text Style (font face, size and colour of the labels), Fill & Border (for the labels) and Number Format (to change the number of decimal places, or decide whether to display the % symbol). In the Options menu, you can variously add a chart title, toggle the legend on and off, and add a variety of annotations and reference lines.

Saving as a template

The easiest way to produce consistently formatted charts the way that you want them to appear is to use or create a chart template. SPSS has a very limited range of templates that come with the program, so you are likely to be better off customizing your chart and saving your design as a custom template. Apply formatting changes that you want to save in Chart Editor, then go to File > Save Chart Template in the Chart Editor window. Select the formatting changes that you want it to pay attention to. You will probably want to tick all of the boxes for Styles, which includes text formatting, such as the font face and size, as well as fill, border and line styles. You are unlikely to want to save any of the Text content, as this will save the actual labels, which may not be applicable when working with other variables. You may want to experiment with saving Layout and Axes options to determine whether you want to save this information. If you are using a computer where you are not the administrator, you may need to save your template in an alternative location to the one where SPSS stores its built-in templates.

Once you have saved a template, you can apply it individually to charts by opening the Chart Editor, then File > Apply Chart Template. If you consistently want to use the same formatting, you can apply it universally by going to the main SPSS Edit menu (accessible through the Data Editor, Output or Syntax windows) > Charts tab > Chart template > switch to Use chart template file. Browse for your saved template, then press OK. This will produce all future charts using your customized template.

ACTIVITIES

Activity 5.1

Create a simple bar chart for Better for a country if almost everyone shares customs and traditions [`pplstrd`] with percentages.

1. Add Data Labels to the bars.
2. Change the Number Format (Properties > Number Format) for the data labels to show one decimal place and apply the change.
3. Change the Label Position (Properties > Data Value Labels > Label Position) to Custom. Select the option with the labels at the tops of the bars and apply the change.
4. What is the most popular answer? What is the least popular answer?

Activity 5.2

Select only responses from Spain. Create another bar chart for Better for a country if almost everyone shares customs and traditions [`pplstrd`] with percentages.

1. Add Data Labels to the bars.
2. Change the Number Format (Properties > Number Format) for the data labels to show one decimal place and apply the change.
3. Change the Label Position (Properties > Data Value Labels > Label Position) to Custom. Select the option with the labels at the tops of the bars and apply the change.
4. What is the most popular answer? What is the least popular answer?
5. How do Spain's answers compare to the survey as a whole?

Activity 5.3

Create a clustered bar chart for Were happy, how often past week [`wrhpp`] with country as the clustering variable. Show the results as a percentage. Remove all of the countries from the chart except Denmark and Sweden.

1. Which country's residents are happier?

2. What is the difference in the proportion of respondents reporting they were happy 'all or almost all of the time' between the two countries?

Activity 5.4

Create a stacked bar chart with Which party feel closer to, France [prtcldfr] on the x-axis and Important to care for nature and the environment [impenv] as the stack colour. Limit the parties to the UMP (Union pour un Mouvement Populaire, centre-right), PS (Parti Socialiste, centre-left) and FN (Front National, right-wing). Run the chart once with counts and once with percentages. For the percentages, set the parameters for the percentage to Total for Each X-Axis Category. (This is the equivalent of using column percentages so that each column will add up to 100 per cent.)

1. Before looking at your results, write a hypothesis about what you expect to find.
2. Which party's supporters show the greatest interest in the environment? Which show the least?
3. Does this confirm your hypothesis, refute it, or offer no evidence either way?

FURTHER READING

Many people like the works of Edward Tufte on the 'visual display of quantitative information'.
Tufte, E.R. (2001) *The Visual Display of Quantitative Information*. Cheshire, CT: Graphics Press.

More recently David McCandless has written about the design of more 'infographic' creations.
McCandless, D. (2012) *Information Is Beautiful*, 2nd edn. London: Collins.

A comprehensive book on data visualization in SPSS is:
Aldrich, J.O. and Rodriguez, H.M. (2013) *Building SPSS Graphs to Understand Data*. London: Sage.

And for a quick overview of what *not* to do with charts, see:

Full Fact (2013, 25 Jul) 'How to make bad charts in 7 simple rules', *Full Fact*. (https://fullfact.org/news/how-make-bad-charts-7-simple-rules/).

Hickly, W. (2013, 26 Jun) 'The 27 worst charts of all time', *Business Insider*. (https://www.businessinsider.com/the-27-worst-charts-of-all-time-2013-6?IR=T).

Schwarz, C.J. (n.d.) 'A short tour of bad graphs'. British Columbia: Simon Fraser University. (http://people.stat.sfu.ca/~cschwarz/Stat-650/Notes/PDF/ChapterBadgraphs.pdf).

REFERENCES

Anscombe, F.J. (1973) 'Graphs in statistical analysis', *American Statistician*, 27 (1): 17-21). (https://doi.org/10.1080/00031305.1973.10478966).

Gelman, A. and Unwin, A. (2013) 'Infovis and statistical graphics: different goals, different looks', *Journal of Computational and Graphical Statistics*, 22 (1), 2-28. (https://doi.org/10.1080/10618600.2012.761137).

Wilson, T. (2009, 18 Jun) 'Data visualization that is colorblind-friendly - Excel 2007?', *Analytics Demystified*. (https://analyticsdemystified.com/excel-tips/data-visualization-that-is-color-blind-friendly-excel-2007).

6

INFERENCE WITH CATEGORICAL DATA

CHAPTER SUMMARY

This chapter continues with Chapter 4's introduction to crosstabs using categorical data, expanding to creating tables with more than two variables and providing some techniques for working with missing data with crosstabs. The rest of the chapter is focused on statistical inference with categorical data, moving from describing what is, to assessing the strength of, the relationship between two or more variables. We look at a range of inferential statistics, starting with statistical significance (p-values) and chi squared tests, then looking at measures of strength of association (Cramer's V and adjusted standardized residuals).

OBJECTIVES

In this chapter, you will learn:

- How to work with missing data when using crosstabs
- How to produce a crosstabulation with more than two categorical variables
- How to produce and interpret measures of statistical significance
- How to produce and interpret measures of strength of association for relationships between categorical variables.

INTRODUCTION

This chapter uses advanced crosstab techniques to explore research questions about voter behaviour such as: Do Conservatives really have a higher voter turnout rate? Do Conservative voters have higher incomes? Do people with higher incomes turn out to vote more? This chapter starts by using some familiar variables from the previous chapter to illustrate why and how we might need to change the way that our missing data is classified when using crosstabs. The second part of the chapter shows how to produce and interpret a multivariate crosstab to test three hypotheses about voter behaviour drawn from the political science literature. The third part of the chapter introduces the concept of statistical significance and looks at the most commonly used test for statistical significance using categorical variables, the chi squared test. The final part of the chapter looks at measures of the strength of association, first looking at a measure of association between the two variables (Cramer's V), then at a measure of association between individual categories (adjusted standardized residuals). Understanding these measures will make your interpretation of categorical data much more meaningful and will make your analysis more convincing.

Missing data and crosstabs

One of the biggest problems working with data is dealing with missing data. Deciding what counts as 'missing' is actually far more subjective than researchers often realize, and it is sometimes necessary to classify the same answer as missing when carrying out one test but as valid when carrying out another test. Thus, the answer to the question 'What counts as missing?' is always, 'It depends.'

To illustrate this, we can start with two variables: interest in politics [`polintr`] and which party the respondent feels closest to [`prtclbgb`]. The second variable raises a very important note about crosstabs: they automatically exclude answers marked missing. This means, for example, that if we ran a crosstab between party identification [`prtclbgb`] and interest in politics [`polintr`], we would lose the level of interest in politics for all respondents who did not choose a political party [`prtclbgb` = 'not applicable']. This isn't a problem if we just want to know about people who identified with a political party; but nearly half of respondents (47.6 per cent) chose 'not applicable', which is coded as missing. Thus, if we leave all 'not applicable' answers coded as missing, we will exclude half of our sample. If we want to make sure that such a group is included in our analysis, then we need to make sure that we change the variables marked as missing before running the crosstab. This is also why it is important to check the frequency tables and get to know our data so that we are aware of answers that might be accidentally excluded from our analysis. In this case, we need to change the way the 'not applicable' answers to this question are categorized so that they are no longer considered missing (Box 6.1).

BOX 6.1 RECLASSIFYING MISSING VALUES

This box shows you how to reclassify missing values to include or exclude specific values from your analysis. The box uses the reclassification of 'not applicable' answers to Which party feel closer to, United Kingdom [`prtclbgb`] from a missing value to a valid value. To change missing values, we first need to know how 'not applicable' was coded by checking the value labels.

Syntax

```
CODEBOOK prtclbgb
  /VARINFO label valuelabels missing.
```

Table 6.1 Codebook results, which party feel closer to, United Kingdom [`prtclbgb`]; 'not applicable' marked as missing

		Value	Count	Per cent
Standard Attributes	**Label**	**Which party feel closer to, United Kingdom**		
Valid Values	1	Conservative	347	15.3%
	2	Labour	391	17.3%
	3	Liberal Democrat	56	2.5%

(Continued)

Table 6.1 (Continued)

		Value	Count	Per cent
	4	Scottish National Party	38	1.7%
	5	Plaid Cymru	3	0.1%
	6	Green Party	61	2.7%
	7	UK Independence Party	165	7.3%
	8	Other	14	0.6%
	9	Ulster Unionist Party (nir)	5	0.2%
	10	Democratic Unionist Party (nir)	8	0.3%
	11	Sinn Fein (nir)	7	0.3%
	12	Social Democratic and Labour Party (nir)	5	0.2%
	13	Alliance Party (nir)	3	0.1%
	14	Traditional Unionist Party (nir)	1	0.0%
	15	Green Party (nir)	0	0.0%
	16	Independent(s) (nir)	1	0.0%
	17	People Before Profit Alliance (nir)	0	0.0%
	18	Other (nir)	1	0.0%
Missing Values	66	Not applicable	1117	49.4%
	77	Refusal	30	1.3%
	88	Don't know	11	0.5%
	99	No answer	0	0.0%

The 'codebook' command provides you with contextual information about a variable, including information about how it has been coded. The output can include the statistics available when running a frequency table; here, we've only produced the information about the labels so that we can reclassify the 'not applicable' answers from missing to valid. We see that 'not applicable' is coded as 66; the other missing answer values are 77 (refusal), 88 (don't know) and 99 (no answer) (Table 6.1). We need to change the range of missing values, which is currently 66 through 99, to 77 through 99.

```
MISSING VALUES prtclbgb (77 thru 99).
```

Run the codebook command again or a frequency table with `prtclbgb` to ensure that 'not applicable' has now moved into the Valid values. If you want to change back the user-defined missing values for other analyses, this is easily done using the following command:

```
MISSING VALUES prtclbgb (66 thru 99).
```

Menu instructions

There are two ways to access the information needed to reclassify the 'not applicable' answers: through the codebook and through the data window. The instructions below describe each of these in turn.

Codebook

Analyze > Reports > Codebook

Variables tab > Move Which party feel closer to, United Kingdom [`prtclbgb`] to the Codebook Variables box on the right.

Output tab > Variable Information > Tick Label, Values labels and Missing values.

Statistics tab > Select relevant options if you want to run a frequency table at the same time.

OK/Paste.

Data window

Open the main data window.

> Variable View (you can toggle between Data View and Variable View in the bottom left of the screen).

Find Which party feel closer to, United Kingdom [`prtclbgb`] in the Label column.

Click the Values cell for `prtclbgb`.

Click the triple dots to open the Value Labels window for `prtclbgb`.

Find the number corresponding to the label Not applicable (66).

Close the Value Labels window.

Changing the missing value range

Click the Missing cell for `prtclbgb`.

Click the triple dots to open the Missing Values window for `prtclbgb`.

Change the range to run from 77 (Low) to 99 (High).

Click OK.

Run a frequency table with `prtclbgb` to check that 'not applicable' answers are now included in Valid answers.

Before we run a crosstab, we can draft a hypothesis about the relationship between identification with a specific political party and level of interest in politics:

H1. People who identify with a political party are more interested in politics than those who do not.

Now that we have included those who don't identify with any of the political parties ('not applicable' answers), we can run a crosstab that shows us the level of interest in politics within each group of political party supporters. In other words, if `prtclbgb` is in rows, we should use row percentages. We can delete the rows with fewer than 20 respondents from our table (such as Plaid Cymru, 4; Ulster Unionist Party, 7), as this is too few respondents to be able to make any conclusions about, and these are all regional parties.

Table 6.2 Interest in politics and political party identification, row percentages and counts

	Very interested	Quite interested	Hardly interested	Not at all interested	Total
Conservative	103	190	62	18	373
	27.6%	50.9%	16.6%	4.8%	100.0%
Labour	82	182	103	48	415
	19.8%	43.9%	24.8%	11.6%	100.0%
Liberal Democrat	9	37	12	6	64
	14.1%	57.8%	18.8%	9.4%	100.0%
Scottish National Party	11	25	8	4	48
	22.9%	52.1%	16.7%	8.3%	100.0%
Green Party	13	25	16	2	56
	23.2%	44.6%	28.6%	3.6%	100.0%
UKIP	32	82	37	15	166
	19.3%	49.4%	22.3%	9.0%	100.0%
Not applicable	97	373	307	281	1058
	9.2%	35.3%	29.0%	26.6%	100.0%
Total	359	928	559	377	2223
	16.1%	41.7%	25.1%	17.0%	100.0%

Looking at Table 6.2, we can see a very clear pattern: only 9.2 per cent of people who do not feel close to any political party ('not applicable') are very interested in politics. The lowest value for any of the political parties was at 14.1 per cent for the Liberal Democrats; 26.6 per cent of those who don't identify with a political party are not at all interested in politics; the next closest is 11.6 per cent for Labour supporters, with under 5 per cent for Conservative (4.8 per cent) and Green (3.6 per cent) supporters. This is very much what we would expect, as simply identifying with a political party is likely to indicate at least a basic level of interest in politics. We can also see that Conservative supporters have the highest proportion of respondents saying they are very interested in politics (27.6 per cent), with an impressive 78.5 per cent of Conservative supporters claiming they are very or somewhat interested in politics.

MULTIVARIATE CROSSTABS

Now that you know how to handle missing data with crosstabs, we can move on to building crosstabs that have more than two variables. There are many reasons why we might want to do this. For example, we might be interested in comparing answer pairings from different points in time; or we might want to add another variable to break down responses further. To illustrate this with an example, we will test the relationship between political party identification, turning out to vote and perceived income. This is grounded in political research that hypothesizes that:

H2. Conservatives have a higher voting turnout rate than liberals.

H3. People with higher subjective incomes have a higher voting turnout rate.

H4. Conservative voters have higher subjective incomes.

There is increasing evidence that subjective income measures and relative wealth are a better predictor of political views than objective measures (see, for example, Cruces et al., 2013; D'Ambrosio and Frick, 2007; Piketty, 1995). There is considerable variation in the degree to which someone's nominal income aligns with the perceived adequacy of their income, with other mitigating factors including the respondent's lifestyle as well as their relative deprivation compared to others who live near them. We can show some of this inconsistency with a crosstabulation of an objective measure of household income (Household's total net income, all sources `[hinctnta]`) with a subjective measure of household income (Feeling about household's income nowadays `[hincfel]`) (see Table 6.3). While we can see a broad trend of people identifying as 'living comfortably' as their household income decile increases, there is also considerable homogeneity of (dis)satisfaction between many of the objective income levels.

People's feeling of having enough can be a better predictor of voting patterns than their objective income. For this reason, we will use the subjective income measure [`hincfel`] to test out whether Conservatives in the UK have higher voter turnout and higher subjective income satisfaction. To create a three-way table, we need to think very carefully about the placement of variables and the type of percentages we choose for displaying our findings. We can move variables around using the pivot trays to experiment with different ways of organizing the information after producing the initial table, but we have to make sure that we produce the correct form of percentages before we do this. Box 6.2 teaches you how to create a multivariate crosstab.

Table 6.3 Objective [hinctnta] vs subjective [hincfel] income, UK respondents

	Living comfortably	Coping	Difficult	Very difficult	Total
1st decile	9.6%	34.5%	32.1%	23.9%	100.0%
2nd decile	14.1%	45.7%	29.5%	10.7%	100.0%
3rd decile	17.6%	50.3%	24.5%	7.7%	100.0%
4th decile	23.2%	53.6%	18.8%	4.4%	100.0%
5th decile	29.2%	53.2%	14.6%	3.0%	100.0%
6th decile	34.3%	52.2%	12.1%	1.4%	100.0%
7th decile	41.6%	48.4%	8.9%	1.2%	100.0%
8th decile	48.8%	43.9%	6.4%	0.9%	100.0%
9th decile	58.2%	36.4%	4.8%	0.5%	100.0%
10th decile	74.0%	23.4%	2.5%	0.1%	100.0%
Total	33.7%	45.0%	15.9%	5.4%	100.0%

BOX 6.2 MULTIVARIATE CROSSTABS

This box shows you how to create a crosstab with three variables: voting patterns [vote], subjective income [hincfel] and party identification [prtclbgb]. The results will be given in counts and row percentages. Selected results can be found in Table 6.4.

Syntax

The syntax is the same, whether you are creating a bivariate or multivariate crosstab: you simply need to add 'by [variable name]' for each additional variable. The order in which you enter the variables determines whether they are placed in the rows or columns, though you can always edit this afterwards with the pivot trays. The first variable you type [vote] will be placed in the rows; the second [hincfel] will appear in columns; and any subsequent variables [prtclbgb] will be added as an extra layer of rows. In other words, by default, only the second variable you type will be placed in columns; all others will appear in the rows, unless you edit the table afterwards. Keep this in mind when using row or column percentages.

```
CROSS vote by hincfel by prtclbgb

/cells=row count.
```

Menu instructions

When using the menu approach to create a multivariate crosstab, you should add the extra variable(s) to the Layer box. You can add more than one layer, if necessary, by pressing Next and inserting another variable.

Analyze > Descriptive Statistics > Crosstabs

Voted last national election [vote] > Rows.

Feeling about household's income nowadays [hincfel] > Columns.

Which party feel closer to, United Kingdom [prtclbgb] > Layer.

> Cells

> Percentages: Rows.

> Counts: Choose Observed or None based on preference.

OK/Paste.

Table 6.4 Voting patterns [vote] and subjective income [hincfel] by party identification [prtclbgb], selected results

Party	Voted in last national election	Living comfortably on present income		Coping on present income		Difficult on present income		Very difficult on present income		Total	
		N	%	N	%	N	%	N	%	N	%
Conservative	Yes	188	59.7%	107	34.0%	17	5.4%	3	1.0%	315	100.0%
	No	24	47.1%	20	39.2%	7	13.7%	0	0.0%	51	100.0%
	Not eligible to vote	4	57.1%	3	42.9%	0	0.0%	0	0.0%	7	100.0%
	Total	216	57.9%	130	34.9%	24	6.4%	3	0.8%	373	100.0%
Labour	Yes	113	35.0%	147	45.5%	50	15.5%	13	4.0%	323	100.0%
	No	16	22.9%	33	47.1%	10	14.3%	11	15.7%	70	100.0%
	Not eligible to vote	2	12.5%	10	62.5%	3	18.8%	1	6.3%	16	100.0%
	Total	131	32.0%	190	46.5%	63	15.4%	25	6.1%	409	100.0%
UKIP	Yes	49	37.7%	60	46.2%	16	12.3%	5	3.8%	130	100.0%
	No	7	22.6%	13	41.9%	8	25.8%	3	9.7%	31	100.0%
	Not eligible to vote	2	50.0%	1	25.0%	1	25.0%	0	0.0%	4	100.0%
	Total	58	35.2%	74	44.8%	25	15.2%	8	4.8%	165	100.0%
No party	Yes	227	40.9%	253	45.6%	64	11.5%	11	2.0%	555	100.0%
	No	105	25.5%	190	46.1%	85	20.6%	32	7.8%	412	100.0%
	Not eligible to vote	36	45.6%	27	34.2%	13	16.5%	3	3.8%	79	100.0%
	Total	368	35.2%	470	44.9%	162	15.5%	46	4.4%	1046	100.0%
Total	Yes	647	43.6%	634	42.7%	164	11.1%	39	2.6%	1484	100.0%
	No	165	27.4%	271	45.0%	117	19.4%	49	8.1%	602	100.0%
	Not eligible to vote	50	43.1%	43	37.1%	18	15.5%	5	4.3%	116	100.0%
	Total	862	39.1%	948	43.1%	299	13.6%	93	4.2%	2202	100.0%

The added complication of multivariate crosstabs mean that you must take extra care when selecting and interpreting any percentage-based statistics. In Table 6.4 Voting patterns [`vote`] and subjective income [`hincfel`] by party identification [`prtclbgb`] display row percentages because the variable of greatest interest is subjective income; row percentages with the variables entered in this order show us the distribution of answers across different subjective income levels. The regional parties (N=81), Liberal Democrats (N=63), Greens (N=55) and Other (N=10) have been removed from the reported result in order to make the data manageable and to exclude answers with very few respondents. Here we will walk through some interpretations to ensure that the meaning of this data is clear.

We can read the overall subjective income distribution by political party identification by reading the Total row within each political party. For example, we find that 59.7 per cent of respondents who identify with the Conservatives reported that they were living comfortably on their present income, which is considerably higher than supporters of Labour (35.0 per cent), UKIP (37.7 per cent) and none ('Not applicable') (40.9 per cent). There is a clear difference in subjective income between voters and non-voters, with a much higher proportion of voters reporting that they were living comfortably (43.6 per cent overall) than non-voters (27.4 per cent overall). This holds up within each of the party results: 12.6 per cent more Conservative voters living comfortably than Conservative non-voters (59.7 per cent versus 47.1 per cent); the gap is 12.1 per cent for Labour supporters (35.0 per cent versus 22.9 per cent) and 15.1 per cent for UKIP supporters (37.7 per cent versus 22.6 per cent).

Now we return to our original hypotheses:

H2. Conservatives have a higher voting rate than liberals.

H3. People with higher subjective incomes have a higher voting turnout rate.

H4. Conservative voters have higher subjective incomes.

We have confirmed both H3 and H4. However, our table has not allowed us to test H2 using row percentages with the variables in the present order. To test this hypothesis, we can swap subjective income and voting (Table 6.5), or we can run a simple bivariate crosstab with party identification and subjective income, as we don't need the variable for subjective income to test this hypothesis. This shows us that Conservative supporters had the highest reported rate of voting in the last national election (84.5 per cent). UKIP (78.8 per cent) and Labour (79.0 per cent) reported turnouts are very close to each other. Those who did not identify with one of the parties had the lowest turnout (53.1 per cent). We can also see within each of the groups of supporters that voting rates are highest among those who were 'living comfortably' (75.1 per cent overall) and lowest among those finding it 'very difficult' (41.9 per cent overall), with exceptions arising from answer pairings with very few respondents: there were only three Conservatives who were finding it very difficult to live on their present income, skewing the result. Our results have therefore confirmed all of our hypotheses and reinforced the existing findings in political science literature.

Table 6.5 Voter turnout [`vote`] by party identification [`prtclbgb`] and subjective income [`hincfel`], selected results

Party	Subjective income	Yes	No	Not eligible to vote	Total
Conservative	Living comfortably	87.0%	11.1%	1.9%	100.0%
	Coping	82.3%	15.4%	2.3%	100.0%
	Difficult	70.8%	29.2%	0.0%	100.0%
	Very difficult	100.0%	0.0%	0.0%	100.0%
	Total	84.5%	13.7%	1.9%	100.0%
Labour	Living comfortably	86.3%	12.2%	1.5%	100.0%
	Coping	77.4%	17.4%	5.3%	100.0%
	Difficult	79.4%	15.9%	4.8%	100.0%
	Very difficult	52.0%	44.0%	4.0%	100.0%
	Total	79.0%	17.1%	3.9%	100.0%
UKIP	Living comfortably	84.5%	12.1%	3.4%	100.0%
	Coping	81.1%	17.6%	1.4%	100.0%
	Difficult	64.0%	32.0%	4.0%	100.0%
	Very difficult	62.5%	37.5%	0.0%	100.0%
	Total	78.8%	18.8%	2.4%	100.0%
Not applicable	Living comfortably	61.7%	28.5%	9.8%	100.0%
	Coping	53.8%	40.4%	5.7%	100.0%
	Difficult	39.5%	52.5%	8.0%	100.0%
	Very difficult	23.9%	69.6%	6.5%	100.0%
	Total	53.1%	39.4%	7.6%	100.0%
Total	Living comfortably	75.1%	19.1%	5.8%	100.0%
	Coping	66.9%	28.6%	4.5%	100.0%
	Difficult	54.8%	39.1%	6.0%	100.0%
	Very difficult	41.9%	52.7%	5.4%	100.0%
	Total	67.4%	27.3%	5.3%	100.0%

STATISTICAL SIGNIFICANCE

We now move to our first inferential statistics test to determine statistical significance. In this section, we will focus our analysis on answering the question. 'What are the characteristics of people most hostile to immigration?' With most research questions like this one, researchers will begin by exploring a standard set of demographic characteristics, including:

- Sex
- Education
- Ethnicity
- Marital status
- Religion
- Political party identification
- Citizenship and immigration history.

We will not look at all of these characteristics in this section, but you can practise by exploring other variables using the same techniques. In this section, we will focus on different levels of support for immigration based on the respondent's own status as an immigrant.

The ESS has a series of questions about people's perceptions of immigration and immigrants. All of the variable names contain 'im', such as Allow many/few immigrants of same race/ethnic group as majority [`imsmetn`] and Immigration bad or good for country's economy [`imbgeco`]. Some of the variables are based on a scale from 'allow many' to 'allow none' (such as `imsmetn, imdfetn, eimpcnt, impcntr`), while others are measured on a 1–10 scale (such as `imbgeco, imueclt, imwbcnt`). We will look at the variables with a 1–10 scale in Chapter 7 onwards, as we will treat them as continuous for our analysis. In this chapter, we will focus on the categorical variables related to immigration, that is on how many immigrants people think should be allowed to come to their country. We will start with a crosstab of whether the respondent was born in the country [`brncntr`] with how many immigrants people would allow from the same race/ethnic group as the majority in their country [`imsmetn`]. Create a crosstab with birthplace [`brncntr`] in the columns and support for majority race/ethnic group immigration [`imsmetn`] in the rows, including observed counts and column percentages (Table 6.6).

Table 6.6 Support for immigration from majority race/ethnic group [`imsmetn`] by birthplace [`brncntr`]

	Yes		No		Total	
	N	**%**	**N**	**%**	**N**	**%**
Allow many to come and live here	8156	23.5%	1643	37.4%	9799	25.0%
Allow some	16120	46.3%	1947	44.4%	18067	46.1%

	Yes		No		Total	
	N	%	N	%	N	%
Allow a few	7997	23.0%	673	15.3%	8670	22.1%
Allow none	2507	7.2%	126	2.9%	2633	6.7%
Total	34780	100.0%	4389	100.0%	39169	100.0%

Take a moment to interpret the results. There seems to be a consistent pattern, with people who were born outside the country (i.e. immigrants) less supportive of immigration by the majority race/ethnicity than those born in the country. This seems to be a puzzling result: why would immigrants be more anti-immigration than natives? Is this result accurate? To answer the latter question, we can run tests that attempt to verify how likely this result is to be a chance occurrence.

One way to check for errors is by verifying a result using other variables that ask about similar phenomena. This checks for problems that arise from question wording, answer options or inconsistent views on the topic. In this case, we can do this by running further crosstabs with support for immigration from other ethnic groups [`imdfetn`] and immigration from poorer, non-European countries [`impcntr`] in the place of immigration from the majority ethnic group [`imsmetn`]. The combined results can be seen in Table 6.7. The results to all three questions follow the same pattern: respondents who were born outside of the country are less in favour of all of the immigrant groups than those born within the country. This seems to rule out the result being achieved by chance, but we can further verify this by testing for statistical significance.

Table 6.7 Support for immigration [`imsmetn, imdfetn, impcntr`] by birthplace [`brncntr`]

	Born in country		
	Yes	No	Total
Majority race/ethnic group			
Allow many	23.5%	37.4%	25.0%
Allow some	46.3%	44.4%	46.1%
Allow a few	23.0%	15.3%	22.1%
Allow none	7.2%	2.9%	6.7%
Total	100.0%	100.0%	100.0%
Different race/ethnic group			
Allow many	13.6%	16.8%	13.9%
Allow some	41.1%	44.0%	41.4%
Allow a few	31.9%	28.1%	31.5%

(Continued)

Table 6.7 (Continued)

	Born in country		
	Yes	**No**	**Total**
Allow none	13.4%	11.0%	13.1%
Total	100.0%	100.0%	100.0%
Poorer, non-European			
Allow many	11.2%	13.7%	11.5%
Allow some	34.4%	35.8%	34.5%
Allow a few	34.4%	31.6%	34.0%
Allow none	20.1%	19.0%	20.0%
Total	100.0%	100.0%	100.0%

A statistical significance test provides us with the probability that our result is not a chance occurrence arising from sampling error. Significance tests are only relevant when we are trying to make an inference about the general population based on a sample. This is generally the case with public opinion surveys, for example, where a sample of 1,000–2,000 people is used to make conclusions about the population as a whole. This is not relevant when using a dataset that is based on the whole population, like a census or a collection including all countries relevant to the topic of analysis. For example, the Correlates of War project is a census of all known wars since 1816. Although researchers may disagree about the measures used and the quality of data, it is not a sample: researchers who analyse the whole database are not extrapolating the findings from a sample (selected wars) to make conclusions about the population (wars).

Equally, national census data is not based on sampling: it is supposed to include all people living in a country. In practice, we know that there are people who are missing from census data, such as people without a fixed address, but the data includes almost everyone in a given country during the survey period. In these cases, tests for statistical significance are irrelevant. However, if we analyse a sample of census data – which is commonly done because a database of tens of millions of people is difficult to manage, and the need to protect the identities of respondents means that some of the variables are not publicly available – then tests of statistical significance are relevant because we are looking at a sample rather than the whole population.

It is also important to note that statistical significance only tells us whether our result is likely to be a real result or a fluke: it tells us nothing about the strength of the relationship between the variables. Because the calculation for statistical significance is sensitive to the sample size, small samples are much less likely to achieve a statistically significant result than large samples. For example, the ESS wave 7 dataset contains more than 40,000 respondents between all of the countries. The sheer number of people in the dataset make it much more likely to give a statistically significant result than a pilot survey of 100 people. Yet just because the ESS is much more likely to give a significant result does not mean that the relationship between the variables tested is actually strong. That is why tests of strength of association are generally more helpful than statistical significance. In fact, the calculations for strength of association usually incorporate calculations of statistical significance, making it impossible to get a strong result that is also statistically insignificant.

When reporting statistical significance, social scientists will normally use a series of thresholds to identify how confident we can be that we have a real result. The results are normally reported according to a series of thresholds rather than the exact significance given from the test. These thresholds represent the probability that this relationship is due to sampling error and would not be found in the wider population. They are expressed using p (for probability) < threshold, for example $p < 0.01$. Because smaller is better, you would report the lowest threshold that is still true for your significance. This may all sound a bit confusing at the moment, but it will become clearer when we look at some examples. Table 6.8 gives an overview of the thresholds and their interpretation.

Table 6.8 Common thresholds for statistical significance

Threshold	Interpretation
$p < 0.10$	Probability the finding is not repeated in the population is less than 10%
$p < 0.05$	Probability the finding is not repeated in the population is less than 5%
$p < 0.01$	Probability the finding is not repeated in the population is less than 1%
$p < 0.001$	Probability the finding is not repeated in the population is less than 0.1%

Because these thresholds are chosen by the author and vary between publications, you must be careful when reading publications that report statistical significance, as authors will accept any values under 0.1 as a significant finding, while others will set an upper threshold of 0.05. Publications with an upper threshold of 0.1 will normally use 0.05 and 0.01 as their second and third thresholds. Publications with an upper threshold of 0.05 will normally use 0.01 and 0.001 as their second and third thresholds. In practice, these thresholds are fairly arbitrary, as there is very little difference between the validity of results with a significance of $p = 0.049$ compared to $p = 0.051$, despite this resulting in some academic research being refused for publication for having exceeded the arbitrary threshold. For these reasons and others, there are increasing debates between researchers about the usefulness of tests of statistical significance. However, because they are still standard fare in publications, it is still important for students to learn how to carry out and interpret a test of statistical significance.

Chi squared

Chi squared is the most commonly quoted statistic when testing whether the patterns we think we see in crosstabs are real or not. Chi squared is based on calculated probabilities.

It compares the frequency of answer pairings to the frequency of pairings we would expect if the answers were allocated by chance. The greater the difference between what we would expect to see and what we actually see, the more confident we are that we have found a real pattern. The most important thing to remember with this test is that it is very sensitive to the number of responses, including the number of different possible answer pairings. This means that, if you have a small survey of 50 people but are testing two variables that had seven options each, the chi squared test is unlikely to work effectively. The rule of thumb here is that the expected frequency (the one predicted by chance, not the frequency we actually got) needs to be at least five for the equation to work properly. This means that we need to have enough survey respondents that we could allot five to every possible answer pairing in the test we are running. Thus, if we have two variables with seven options each, that means 49 possible answer pairings. If we allocate five respondents to each of those, that would mean we would need at least 245 respondents (49 × 5) to run a chi squared test on the results. Therefore, if you have variables with large numbers of categories, you may want to think about filtering them to exclude some of the smaller categories (such as excluding some of the political parties from analysis in the previous section) or logically amalgamating categories to create fewer, larger categories (such as grouping religious denominations or educational qualifications).

Chi squared statistics contain three main components: significance, value and degrees of freedom. The degrees of freedom simply tell us how large the crosstab table is, and the degrees of freedom and value are used to calculate the significance. The degrees of freedom will also be relevant when we look at strength of association using Cramer's V in the next section. The possible significance results from a chi squared test run from 0 to 1, and you are looking for numbers as close to 0 as possible, using the significance thresholds from Table 6.8. We will look at the value and degrees of freedom results that accompany the chi squared output as well.

We will start by using the same crosstab as we did at the start of this section, using whether the respondent was born in the country [`brncntr`] and their support for immigration from the majority ethnic group [`imsmetn`]. Follow the instructions in Box 6.3 to produce the chi squared result with your crosstab. The IBM SPSS Statistics ('SPSS') output for chi squared tests is particularly ugly and gives you lots of extra information, but do not let this put you off: we only really care about the first row of the table. We want to find out how likely it is that the pattern we think we saw is actually replicated in the population.

BOX 6.3 CHI SQUARED TEST FOR STATISTICAL SIGNIFICANCE

This box shows you how to produce a crosstab with chi squared (a measure of statistical significance). This test is appropriate for two categorical variables. The results can be found in Table 6.9.

Syntax

```
CROSSTABS
  /TABLES=imsmetn BY brncntr
  /FORMAT=AVALUE TABLES
  /STATISTICS=CHISQ
  /CELLS=COUNT EXPECTED COLUMN
  /COUNT ROUND CELL.
```

This can be simplified to:

```
CROSS imsmetn by brncntr
/statistics=chisq
/cells=count expected column.
```

The command in the syntax under `/STATISTICS=` tells you which statistical tests it will run alongside the crosstab. The options include:

`CHISQ`	Chi squared test
`PHI`	Phi and Cramer's V (for two nominal variables)
`LAMBDA`	Lambda (for two nominal variables)
`GAMMA`	Gamma (for two ordinal variables)
`BTAU/CTAU`	Kendall's tau, B and C (for two ordinal variables)

The `/CELLS=` menu gives options for which statistics you include within the body of the table. In Chapter 4, we used the options relating to counts and percentages. New options used in this chapter include:

`EXPECTED` Expected count; used for determining statistical significance

`ASRESID` Adjusted standardized residual, used for determining the strength of association between individual answer pairings

Menu instructions

Analyze > Descriptive Statistics > Crosstabs

Allow many/few immigrants of same race/ethnic group as majority [`imsmetn`]. > Rows

Born in country [`brncntr`] > Columns.

(Continued)

> Statistics

Tick Chi squared (if desired).

> Cells

Counts: tick Observed and Expected.

Percentages: tick Column.

OK/Paste.

Table 6.9 Support for majority ethnicity immigration [`imsmetn`] by respondent's country of birth [`brncntr`], including chi squared

		Born in country		Total
		Yes	No	
Allow many to come and live here	Count	8156	1643	9799
	Expected count	8701.0	1098.0	9799.0
	% within born in country	23.5%	37.4%	25.0%
Allow some	Count	16120	1947	18067
	Expected count	16042.5	2024.5	18067.0
	% within born in country	46.3%	44.4%	46.1%
Allow a few	Count	7997	673	8670
	Expected count	7698.5	971.5	8670.0
	% within born in country	23.0%	15.3%	22.1%
Allow none	Count	2507	126	2633
	Expected count	2338.0	295.0	2633.0
	% within born in country	7.2%	2.9%	6.7%
Total	Count	34780	4389	39169
	Expected count	34780.0	4389.0	39169.0
	% within born in country	100.0%	100.0%	100.0%

Chi squared tests

	Value	df	Asymptotic significance (2-sided)
Pearson chi squared	520.337[a]	3	.000
Likelihood ratio	522.527	3	.000
Linear-by-linear association	491.216	1	.000
N of valid cases	39169		

a. 0 cells (0.0%) have expected count less than 5. The minimum expected count is 295.04

Remember that we are looking for the probability that this is a random result and is not replicated in the wider population, which we can find out from looking at the asymptotic significance (2-sided) column for the Pearson chi squared row. The result is 0.000, which is excellent. This means that our result is unlikely to have occurred because of sampling error. We would report that the association between the birthplace of the respondent and their support for immigration of the same ethnicity as the majority is statistically significant at the level of $p < 0.001$, meaning that there is less than a 0.1 per cent chance that our result is not reflected in the wider population. This only tells us that there *is* a relationship, however, not how strong it is. Do not be tempted to claim that there is a strong relationship just because the significance is excellent. It is possible to have a statistically significant association between two variables that is so weak that it is almost negligible and therefore not terribly helpful for trying to explain a phenomenon. Nevertheless, a lot of publications still rely on chi squared as their main test, so it is important that you learn how to interpret it. If you do decide to use chi squared yourself, you would not normally include the chi squared tests table in your write-up; all you need to report is the p-value in the body of your analysis.

STRENGTH OF ASSOCIATION

Before testing for associations between two variables, you need to understand what an association is and what it is not. The most important thing to remember is that association does not imply causality: that is, just because two variables change in tandem with each other does not mean that one caused the other, nor even that their change is related through more than chance. In addition, although we commonly use the word 'correlation' to mean an association, in statistics a correlation is one specific type of association. Association can refer to three different ways that variables can be linked:

1. Covariance – two variables change together but may or may not actually be linked to each other. Although one might increase when the other increases/decreases, this may actually be a spurious relationship.
2. Association – one variable is linked to another in some way, with a variety of possible relationships between the two variables.
3. Correlation – two variables change together in a linear fashion and are related to each other (discussed more in Chapter 10).

There are five possible relationships between the associated variables:

1. The seeming pattern is spurious: there is not real relationship between A and B.
2. A causes B.
3. B causes A.
4. A and B are both caused by C; A and B do not cause each other.

5. A causes B and B causes A in a self-reinforcing relationship. This is the hardest to identify and explain.

Associations can be positive or negative. If the association is positive, when A increases, B will also increase. When portrayed graphically, a positive relationship looks like an uphill line with the peak of the hill on the right. If the association is negative, when A increases, B decreases. Portrayed graphically, a negative relationship looks like a downhill line with the peak of the line on the left. To test for association between categorical variables, we will use Cramer's V and adjusted standardized residuals. These might sound scary, but they are actually very straightforward once you understand what each of them does.

Phi/Cramer's V

Phi and Cramer's V are measures of strength of association between two categorical variables. If you are using two variables that only have two answer options (a 2 × 2 table), the values for phi and Cramer's V are identical, but phi is inconsistent when used on any larger tables. This means you can focus your interpretation on Cramer's V. The calculation of Cramer's V incorporates chi squared but takes it another step to tell us how strong the relationship is. Cramer's V comes with two elements: the significance and the value. The significance statistic tells you how likely it is that your result occurred from chance. You interpret the significance score the same way as you interpret significance for chi squared and every other statistical test: the closer to 0, the better, and it should generally be below either a 0.1 or 0.05 threshold. The Value statistic tells you how strong the association between the two variables is. The value also runs between 0 and 1. Unlike significance, with the value, the closer the number is to 1, the better. Interpreting this value depends on the size of the table you have produced. This means that a smaller Cramer's V indicates a strong result, the more categories you have for each variable. Table 6.10 shows some thresholds you can use to help you interpret the results.

Table 6.10 Thresholds for interpreting Cramer's V

df*	No effect	Small effect	Medium effect	Large effect
1	<0.10	0.10	0.30	0.50
2	<0.07	0.07	0.21	0.35
3	<0.06	0.06	0.17	0.29
4	<0.05	0.05	0.15	0.25
5	<0.04	0.04	0.13	0.22

* This can be found in the Chi squared tests table > Pearson chi squared row > df column.

To produce Cramer's V, follow the instructions for crosstabs in Box 6.4, including the phi and Cramer's V option. This will produce an extra table titled Symmetric Measures. The Cramer's V asymptotic significance column gives us the statistical significance (whether the association is just chance), the same as the chi squared result. When interpreting the Cramer's V result, you should check your significance first, as there is no point in making claims about the strength of a relationship if it turns out it is unlikely to be reproduced in the wider population. The Cramer's V value column gives us the strength of the relationship.

BOX 6.4 CRAMER'S V TEST FOR ASSOCIATION BETWEEN CATEGORICAL VARIABLES

This box shows you how to produce a crosstab with Cramer's V (a measure of strength of association). The results can be found in Table 6.11.

Syntax

```
CROSSTABS
  /TABLES=imsmetn BY brncntr
  /FORMAT=AVALUE TABLES
  /STATISTICS=CHISQ PHI
  /CELLS=COUNT EXPECTED COLUMN
  /COUNT ROUND CELL.
```

This can be simplified to:

```
CROSS imsmetn by brncntr
/statistics=chisq phi
/cells=count expected column.
```

Menu instructions

Analyze > Descriptive Statistics > Crosstabs

Allow many/few immigrants of same race/ethnic group as majority [`imsmetn`]. > Rows

Born in country [`brncntr`] > Columns.

> Statistics

Tick Chi squared (if desired).

Tick Phi and Cramer's V.

(Continued)

> Cells

Counts: tick Observed and Expected.

Percentages: tick Column.

OK/Paste.

Table 6.11 Support for majority ethnicity immigration [imsmetn] by respondent's country of birth [brncntr], including chi squared and Cramer's V

		Born in country		
		Yes	**No**	**Total**
Allow many to come and live here	Count	8156	1643	9799
	Expected count	8701.0	1098.0	9799.0
	% within born in country	23.5%	37.4%	25.0%
Allow some	Count	16120	1947	18067
	Expected count	16042.5	2024.5	18067.0
	% within born in country	46.3%	44.4%	46.1%
Allow a few	Count	7997	673	8670
	Expected count	7698.5	971.5	8670.0
	% within born in country	23.0%	15.3%	22.1%
Allow none	Count	2507	126	2633
	Expected count	2338.0	295.0	2633.0
	% within born in country	7.2%	2.9%	6.7%
Total	Count	34780	4389	39169
	Expected count	34780.0	4389.0	39169.0
	% within born in country	100.0%	100.0%	100.0%

Chi squared tests

	Value	**df**	**Asymptotic significance (2-sided)**
Pearson chi squared	520.337[a]	3	.000
Likelihood ratio	522.527	3	.000
Linear-by-linear association	491.216	1	.000
N of valid cases	39169		

a. 0 cells (0.0%) have expected count less than 5. The minimum expected count is 295.04

Symmetric measures

		Value	**Approximate significance**
Nominal by nominal	Phi	.115	.000
	Cramer's V	.115	.000
N of valid cases		39169	

After that, use the degrees of freedom (df) to select the appropriate interpretation of the Cramer's V value to judge the strength of the relationship. The threshold for strong relationships decreases as you increase the table size, and the degrees of freedom are based on the table size. The degrees of freedom value is given to you in the Pearson chi squared row of the Chi Squared Tests table, under df. You do not need to produce a chi squared result as well if you are happy to calculate your degrees of freedom manually. The degrees of freedom are easy to figure out yourself: the number is (the number of rows – 1) × (the number of columns – 1). The number of rows and columns is determined by how many valid categories there are for a variable. For example, Born in country [`brncntr`] has two categories (2 rows): yes and no; Father born in country [`facntr`] also has two categories (2 columns): yes and no. This means that the degrees of freedom equal 1: (2 rows – 1) × (2 columns – 1) → 1 × 1 = 1. How interested in politics [`polintr`] has four categories (4 columns): very interested, quite interested, hardly interested, not at all interested. If we cross this with `brncntr`, the degrees of freedom equal 3: (2 rows – 1) × (4 columns – 1) → 1 × 3 = 3.

To choose the correct ranges for interpreting the strength of association, you will need to read the appropriate Cramer's V thresholds for the number of degrees of freedom in your data table. In the case of support for immigration [`imsemetn`] compared to the respondent's birth country [`brncntr`], p<0.001, df is 3 and Cramer's V is 0.115, which equates to a small effect. Cramer's V for the relationship with support for immigration from other race/ethnic groups to the majority [`imdfetn`] and respondent's birth country [`brncntr`] yields a df of 3, p<0.001 and Cramer's V of 0.043, classed as no effect (Cramer's V0.06 with 3 df). Support for immigration from poorer, non-European countries [`impcntr`] crossed with respondent's birth country [`brncntr`] has a df of 3, p<0.001 and Cramer's V 0.030, indicating no relationship (Cramer's V0.06 with 3 df).

For tables with more than five degrees of freedom, you can calculate the appropriate threshold for strength of relationship yourself by using the standard thresholds for one degree of freedom (0.10=small, 0.30=medium, 0.50=large) divided by the square root of the number of degrees of freedom. For example, if we have a table with six degrees of freedom and want the threshold for a medium relationship, we calculate 0.30 (medium threshold)/$\sqrt{6}$ (degrees of freedom) = 0.30/2.45 (rounded) = 0.12. If we want to test the effect of subjective income [`hincfel`] against support for majority ethnic group immigration [`imsmetn`], the result is a table with 9 df and Cramer's V0.120 (p<0.001). In this case, the threshold for a medium relationship would be 0.30/$\sqrt{9}$ = 0.1; the threshold for a strong relationship would be $0.50/\sqrt{9} = 0.167$. This indicates a medium relationship between the respondent's feelings about their income and their support for further immigration.

ADJUSTED STANDARDIZED RESIDUALS

The final statistic you can use for testing associations between categorical variables is the adjusted standardized residual. This test is useful for telling us the strength of association between individual answer pairings rather than between the two variables. This can find associations at times even when the relationship between the two variables is statistically insignificant, or is statistically significant but very weak, by showing us specific pairings that are worth looking at. To produce the residuals, follow the usual instructions in Box 6.3, being sure to include adjusted standardized residuals in your results.

Residuals look at the difference between the observed and expected counts, giving an indication of how different the actual observation is compared to what you would expect if all of the answer pairings were allocated by chance. Using *standardized* residuals means that you can make a meaningful comparison of your result between different tables. If you did not use standardized residuals, the results that you received from one pair of variables would not be comparable to the result from another pair of variables. Standardization allows us to use a rule of ±2 to interpret the results from any crosstab: if the standardized residual is greater than 2 or less than –2, then the relationship is strong. The underlying maths of this is based on standard deviations: ±2 represents two standard deviations from the mean, indicating that your result lies outside of 95 per cent of normally distributed results. In other words, it is an outlier. The farther from 0 your result is, the more of an outlier it is compared to the expected count, which is based on random allocation of results. The results are 'adjusted' to take into account the size of the table, compensating for the number of possible answer pairings.

The residuals are most useful when the table contains at least three rows and three columns; if you interpret them with two rows or two columns, you will notice that the cells mirror each other. For example, if one of your variables had 'yes' and 'no' as possible answers, the 'yes' column might show a residual of 2.2, while the 'no' column might show –2.2. This simply means that respondents were more likely to choose yes and less likely to choose no. With these guidelines for interpretation, follow the instructions in Box 6.5 to create a crosstab with adjusted residuals using support for immigration from the majority ethnic group [`imsmetn`] and respondent's birth country [`brncntr`].

BOX 6.5 ADJUSTED STANDARDIZED RESIDUALS

This box shows you how to produce a crosstab with adjusted standardized residuals to indicate the strength of relationship between individual categories rather than between variables as a whole. This example uses support for majority ethnicity immigration [imsmetn] and respondent's country of birth [brncntr]. The results can be found in Table 6.12.

Syntax

```
CROSSTABS
  /TABLES=imsmetn BY brncntr
  /FORMAT=AVALUE TABLES
  /STATISTICS=CHISQ PHI
  /CELLS=COUNT EXPECTED COLUMN ARESID
  /COUNT ROUND CELL.
```

This can be simplified to:

```
CROSSTABS imsmetn by brncntr
/cells=count column asresid
/statistics=chisq phi.
```

Menu instructions

Analyze > Descriptive Statistics > Crosstabs

Allow many/few immigrants of same race/ethnic group as majority [imsmetn]. > Rows

Born in country [brncntr] > Columns.

> Statistics

Tick chi squared (if desired).

Tick phi and Cramer's V.

> Cells

Counts: tick Observed and Expected.

Percentages: tick Column.

Residuals: click Adjusted standardized.

OK/Paste.

In our previous tests, we received a statistically significant but weak association between the two variables. We might simply have dismissed these findings altogether if we didn't examine the adjusted standardized residuals. Instead, what we see is a very strong relationship for all of the answers except 'allow some', where the difference between those born in the country and those born abroad is less strong but still significant (Table 6.12). This is a cautionary tale that underscores the importance of checking our results thoroughly before dismissing a possible relationship. If we produce the residuals for our other two immigration variables [`imdfetn`, `impcntr`], we find strong results, with the weakest results generally coming from 'allow some', although 'allow none' is slightly weaker than 'allow some' (Adj. std. res. 1.7 versus 1.8) for allowing immigrants from poorer countries outside Europe.

Table 6.12 Support for majority ethnicity immigration [`imsmetn`] by respondent's country of birth [`brncntr`], including adjusted standardized residuals

	Born in country						Total	
	Yes			No				
	N	%	Adj. res.	N	%	Adj. res.	N	%
Allow many	8156	23.5%	−20.2	1643	37.4%	20.2	9799	25.0%
Allow some	16120	46.3%	2.5	1947	44.4%	−2.5	18067	46.1%
Allow a few	7997	23.0%	11.5	673	15.3%	−11.5	8670	22.1%
Allow none	2507	7.2%	10.8	126	2.9%	−10.8	2633	6.7%
Total	34780	100.0%		4389	100.0%		39169	100.0%

Now we will look at some adjusted standardized residuals using UK political party identification [`prtclbgb`] and support for immigration from the majority ethnic group [`imsmetn`], seeking an answer to the question, 'How does political party identification affect support for immigration?' We will test the hypotheses:

> H5. People who identify with the Labour Party have higher support for immigration than those who identify with the Conservative Party.
>
> H6. People who identify with the UK Independence Party (UKIP) will have lower support for immigration than those who identify with any of the other parties.

Table 6.13 Political party identification, UK-wide parties [`prtclbgb`]

		Frequency	Per cent	Valid per cent	Cumulative per cent
Valid	Conservative	373	39.1	39.1	39.1
	Labour	415	43.5	43.5	82.6
	UKIP	166	17.4	17.4	100.0
	Total	954	100.0	100.0	

Before working with the political party, however, we need to filter our data on political party identification so that we exclude results from regional parties. We want to filter cases so that we only get results for Conservative, Labour and UKIP. After selecting your cases, produce a frequency table to check that you have the data you expect. If you select your cases correctly, your results should look like Table 6.13. (See Chapter 4 for a reminder of how to select cases.) Once you have successfully filtered your results, run a crosstab with support for ethnic majority immigration [`imsmetn`] in the rows and party identification [`prtclgb`] in the columns, with column percentages, adjusted standardized residuals and Cramer's V.

Table 6.14 Support for immigration [`imsmetn`] by party identification [`prtclbgb`]

		Conservative	Labour	UKIP	Total
Allow many to come and live here	N	38	67	6	111
	%	10.2%	16.3%	3.7%	11.7%
	Adj. Res.	−1.1	3.8	−3.5	
Allow some	N	202	214	54	470
	%	54.4%	51.9%	32.9%	49.6%
	Adj. Res.	2.4	1.2	−4.7	
Allow a few	N	114	98	67	279
	%	30.7%	23.8%	40.9%	29.5%
	Adj. Res.	.7	−3.4	3.5	
Allow none	N	17	33	37	87
	%	4.6%	8.0%	22.6%	9.2%
	Adj. Res.	−3.9	−1.1	6.5	
Total	N	371	412	164	947
	%	100.0%	100.0%	100.0%	100.0%

Chi squared tests

	Value	df	Asymptotic significance (2-sided)
Pearson chi squared	81.478[a]	6	.000
Likelihood ratio	77.495	6	.000
Linear-by-linear association	58.673	1	.000
N of valid cases	947		

a. 0 cells (0.0%) have expected count less than 5. The minimum expected count is 15.07

(Continued)

Table 6.14 (Continued)

Symmetric measures			
		Value	**Approximate significance**
Nominal by nominal	Phi	.293	.000
	Cramer's V	.207	.000
N of valid cases		947	

Starting our interpretation with Cramer's V and the statistical significance, we can see that we have found a strong, significant relationship (Cramer's V 0.207, df 6, $p<0.001$). Looking at the individual results in Table 6.14, our adjusted standardized residuals range from the weakest at 0.7 (Conservative, 'allow a few') to the strongest at 6.5 (UKIP, 'allow none'). We can see from the positive adjusted standardized residuals that are well in excess of ±2 that far more of those who identify with Labour (3.8) chose 'allow many' than we would expect from a random distribution of results; far fewer UKIP (–3.5) supporters chose 'allow many' than a random allocation would predict. These results are in line with our hypotheses: Labour supporters are more supportive of immigration than Conservatives; and UKIP supporters are the least supportive of immigration. This is also reflected in the percentages: a higher proportion of Labour supporters chose 'allow many' (16.3 per cent) compared to Conservative ones (10.2 per cent). Nearly a quarter of UKIP supporters (22.6 per cent) chose 'allow none', which is more than triple the proportion of the next closest group (Labour, 8.0 per cent).

These results are consistent with the other two immigration variables we have used in this chapter [`imdfetn`, `impcntr`]. As we would expect from our general knowledge of political parties, the most left-wing party (Labour) also has the most pro-immigration supporters, with the right-wing parties (Conservative and UKIP) having the most anti-immigration supporters. In fact, the responses align perfectly with the placement of these parties relative to each other on the left–right scale.

CONCLUSION

This chapter has introduced you to advanced techniques with crosstabs, showing you how to manage user missing data, produce and interpret three-way tables, and test for strength of association between categorical variables. We used the data to answer questions about political party identification, including levels of interest in politics, subjective income, voting and support for immigration. You should now feel comfortable manipulating the variables using the pivot trays and changing the way the data is portrayed using different percentages. You should be able to produce and analyse tests of the statistical significance (chi squared) and strength (Cramer's V) of relationship between two variables as well as the strength of the relationship between individual answer pairings (adjusted standardized residuals).

ACTIVITIES

Activity 6.1

Create a multivariate crosstab with Born in country [brncntr], Father born in country [facntr] and Mother born in country [mocntr]. Include observed counts.

1. How many respondents answered all three questions?
2. How many respondents were born in the response country to two parents who were also born in that country?
3. How many respondents were born in the response country to two parents, of whom neither was born in that country?
4. Is it more common for a native-born respondent with one immigrant parent to be born to a foreign-born father or a foreign-born mother?
5. How many respondents were born in the response country to at least one immigrant parent?
6. How many respondents are immigrants in this table? What proportion of the total respondents does this constitute?

Activity 6.2

RQ: Do supporters of the Front National hold more openly racist views than supporters of other French political parties?

Filter cases for the following parties for Which party feel closer to, France [prtclcfr]: UMP (Union pour un Mouvement Populaire, centre-right), PS (Parti Socialiste, centre-left) and FN (Front National, right-wing). Create a crosstab with Which party feel closer to, France [prtclcfr] and Some races or ethnic groups: born less intelligent [smegbli]. Choose the appropriate percentages to show results within each party affiliation. Include a chi squared test, Cramer's V and adjusted standardized residuals.

1. Is the relationship between these two variables statistically significant? What p-threshold would you use to report the results?
2. How strong is the relationship between the two variables?
3. Which party's supporters give the highest level of agreement with the statement? Which party's supporters reject the statement most strongly?
4. Which answer pairings indicate a strong relationship? Which ones have no relationship?
5. How would you answer the research question?

Activity 6.3

Try the same analysis as the previous exercise using another country's political parties. Start by running a frequency to identify the three to four parties with the largest number of respondents. Then look up some background information about these parties to identify their placement on

(Continued)

the left-right spectrum. Based on this, develop a hypothesis about what you expect to find. Run the same tests as before using this country, including filtering the results.

Activity 6.4

RQ: How does education affect national identity?

There is some evidence that people with higher levels of education identify less strongly with their country and have lower levels of ethnocentrism (see, for example, Coenders and Scheepers, 2003). Test this using Highest level of education, ES - ISCED [`eisced`] and Feel close to country [`fclcntr`]. Run a crosstab with counts, appropriate percentages, a chi squared test, Cramer's V and adjusted standardized residuals.

1. Is the relationship between these two variables statistically significant? What p-threshold would you use to report the results?
2. How strong is the relationship between the two variables?
3. Which level of education has the greatest feeling of closeness to the country? Which level of education feels the least close?
4. Which answer pairings indicate a strong relationship? Which ones have no relationship?
5. How would you answer the research question?

Activity 6.5

RQ: How does education affect national identity?

Repeat the analysis from Activity 6.4 for two countries, producing all of the results for one country at a time. Are the results more consistent when using a single country's results?

FURTHER READING

Chi squared tests and phi/Cramer's V are covered in most statistics books, but the bias against categorical data in these sources means there are very few that discuss adjusted standardized residuals (also sometimes referred to as standardized Pearson residuals).

Agresti, A., Franklin, C.A. and Klingenberg, B. (2017) *Statistics: The Art and Science of Learning from Data*, 4th edn. London: Pearson.

This is one of the few books that discusses the use of standardized residuals for testing the relationship between categorical variables. See chapter 11 ('Analyzing the association between categorical variables'), especially section 11.4 ('Using residuals to reveal the pattern of association') for a discussion of residuals.

Marchant-Shapiro, T. (2015) *Statistics for Political Analysis: Understanding the Numbers*. London: Sage/CQ Press.

This book includes some basic instructions for using SPSS to conduct data analysis, and the examples are from political science. See chapter 9 ('Chi-square and Cramer's V: What do you expect?') for chi squared and phi/Cramer's V. See chapter 11 ('Multivariate relationships: Taking control'), particularly the section 'Three-way contingency tables', for a discussion of crosstabs with more than two variables.

Pallant, J. (2016) *SPSS Survival Manual*. Maidenhead: Open University Press/McGraw-Hill Education.
This book provides a functional overview of how to produce statistics in SPSS. See chapter 16 ('Non-parametric statistics') for a guide to produce chi squared and phi/Cramer's V.

REFERENCES

Coenders, M. and Scheepers, P. (2003) 'The effect of education on nationalism and ethnic exclusionism: an international comparison', *Political Psychology*, 24 (2): 313–43.

Cruces, G., Perez-Truglia, R. and Tetaz, M. (2013) 'Biased perceptions of income distribution and preferences for redistribution: evidence from a survey experiment', *Journal of Public Economics*, 98 (Feb): 100–112.

D'Ambrosio, C. and Frick, J.R. (2007) 'Income satisfaction and relative deprivation: an empirical link', *Social Indicators Research*, 81 (3): 497–519.

Piketty, T. (1995) 'Social mobility and redistributive politics', *Quarterly Journal of Economics*, 110 (3): 551–84.

7

DESCRIBING CONTINUOUS DATA

CHAPTER SUMMARY

This chapter introduces you to the production and interpretation of descriptive statistical tables for continuous data. Continuous data is less common in survey data than categorical data, but you are likely to encounter it more widely when you are looking at country-level data, as you commonly will in international relations, or when summarizing information about populations. This can be done using measures of central tendency (mean, median and mode) and measures of dispersion (ranges, variance and standard deviation). This chapter covers these measures before moving into simple inferential statistics using continuous data, introducing correlation. The chapter finishes with some important ways of manipulating continuous data to deal with outlier cases that skew results. This is very important for producing meaningful analysis.

OBJECTIVES

In this chapter, you will learn:

- How to produce a table with one variable
- How to produce and interpret the mean, median and mode
- How to measure the amount that other values deviate from the mean
- How to produce and interpret the most common measure of correlation
- Techniques for handling outlier cases.

INTRODUCTION

In Chapter 4, we encountered descriptive statistics for categorical variables, learning how to work with frequencies and percentages using the ESS dataset. The majority of variables in public opinion data are categorical. However, there are some key variables measured continuously, such as age/year of birth, income, number of children, years of full-time education completed. There are also some survey questions that are asked on extended scales, such as a 1–10 scale response for questions about immigration or self-placement on a left–right political scale. Continuous data becomes much more common when looking at country-level data, such as in the UN dataset used in this book, the Correlates of War and Global Terrorism databases, and World Bank data, to name but a few. The first half of this chapter looks at measures of central tendency and dispersion, which are the most common descriptive statistics for continuous variables. The second half of the chapter introduces correlation to test for association between two continuous variables.

The first half of this chapter uses the ESS dataset. The second half uses the UN dataset.

MEASURES OF CENTRAL TENDENCY

Measures of central tendency tell us what the 'average' case looks like. We talk about measures of central tendency a lot in everyday life: average age, average income, average height and average weight. Measures of central tendency lead to our knowing that the 'average' British household has a mean (equivalized disposable) income of £34,200 per year (ONS, 2019), and British women have an average of 1.76 children (ONS, 2018). From the data about 'average' number of children, it should be apparent that averages are not as clear-cut as they often seem: an individual family cannot have 1.76 children, as children only come in whole numbers, not in nine-tenths of a child. However, averages help us to get a general picture, which in this example tells us that the average British family has fewer than two children.

Mean

When we talk about averages, we are most commonly referring to the arithmetical mean. The mean is only appropriate for use with continuous variables. The mean is calculated by adding up the values of all of the responses and dividing by the number of responses. Because of how it is calculated, means are sensitive to very high or very low numbers, called outliers. For example, say you polled five people aged 22, 23, 24, 25 and 96. This would give you an average respondent age of 38, but you should feel that this does not really reflect the 'average' respondent, as most of them were in their early to mid-20s, and the one geriatric respondent considerably skewed the mean. This is particularly the case when looking at measures like income, where the variation can be considerable. To return to the example of average income in the UK, while the mean equivalized disposable income in 2018 was £34,200, the median was £28,400 (ONS, 2019). This is because some of the very high earners have a disproportionate effect on the mean income. For this reason, the ONS tends to focus on reporting median income.

Median

The median is not calculated using any division and is not sensitive to outliers. The median can be used with ordinal or continuous variables. It should not be used with nominal data, as it requires the data to have a natural rank or order. Calculating the median simply requires sorting all of the numbers from smallest to largest and finding the number in the middle. Because the median value represents the mid-point, you know that half of responses fall above the median value and half fall below. If we take our age poll from above, the middle number of 22, 23, 24, 25 and 96 is 24. You might feel that this was a much better representation of your respondents' ages. The median is particularly helpful when looking at income because of its ability to represent the mid-point. For example, median household disposable income of £28,400 means than half of households in the UK had incomes lower than this, while half had higher. The emphasis on median, especially with measures of income, includes other related calculations, such as gender pay gaps, which are often reported for both mean and median gap (BBC, 2019); and calculations of poverty, where one of the most common calculations is based on income less than 60 per cent of the median (UK Government, 2016).

Mode

The final measure of central tendency is the mode. Think of mode like fashion: if something is in fashion, you see it a lot. The mode is the only measure of central tendency appropriate for use with nominal variables, but it can also be used for ordinal and continuous variables, when there is a reason for doing so. The mode is simply the most frequently occurring value. It again can give a slightly different picture of the data to the mean and median. Say we polled 1,000 people about their monthly income. A total of 400 people told us they were not earning anything; 599 people were earning between £1 and £5,000 per month; and 1 person was earning £1,000,000 per month. We find that our mean is £2,500 per month, and our median is £1,000 per month. Neither of these numbers makes us very happy, however, because we know that 40 per cent of our respondents were not actually earning anything at all. In this case, the mode helps us to express this, as including the information that the mode is £0 indicates what is happening with the largest single block of respondents. If we return to the example of number of children in UK families, the mean number of children per woman was 1.76 (ONS, 2018). There are noticeable variations in the mode between different household types: the mode for families comprising a married couple with dependant children is two children, with 44 per cent of these families having two children versus 40 per cent having one child. However, the mode for other family compositions is one child: 51 per cent of cohabiting couples with children have only one child, rising to 55 per cent of lone parents (ONS, 2017b).

Quartiles, quintiles, deciles

Another way that continuous data can be reported is by breaking it down into groups. This essentially breaks down continuous data into categories to make comparisons of frequencies easier. This is essentially what IBM SPSS Statistics ('SPSS') is doing when it creates a histogram (covered in greater detail in Chapter 8): it is automatically splitting continuous responses into groups, which are then represented as bars. Quartiles (quarto = four groups), quintiles (quinta = five groups) and deciles (deca = ten groups) are commonly used for measures relating to income. When dividing into groups, the division is based on having equal sizes of groups rather than equal spacing of the continuous variable.

For example, the ONS reported gross household income by income decile group for 2015–16, based on 27,220 households (ONS, 2017a). Each decile comprised 2,720 households; then the average income within each of those deciles was calculated. In this case, the lowest decile had an average gross weekly household income of £130, compared to £2,280 for the highest decile. The means that the highest decile's mean weekly income was 17.5 times higher than the lowest decile and 1.8 times that of the ninth decile (£1,280).

Several common calculations of income inequality are based on ratios between these income groups. For example, the Palma ratio [`palmaratio`] is the ratio of the richest 10 per cent of the population's share of gross national income divided by the poorest 40 per cent's share (Cobham, n.d.); the quintile ratio [`quintileratio`] is the ratio of the average income of the richest 20 per cent of the population to the average income of the poorest 20 per cent of the population (UNDP, 2013). Both of these measures are included in the UN dataset. Many governments use quartiles and quintiles when looking at measures of deprivation. For example, the UK government uses Participation of Local Areas (POLAR) quintiles to measure the proportion of young people who enter higher education aged 18 or 19 within each postcode (OfS, 2019). Boxplots (covered in Chapter 8) are based on quartiles.

BOX 7.1 MEASURES OF CENTRAL TENDENCY

This example produces a table with the mean, median and mode for Age of respondent, calculated [`agea`]. Data has been filtered for UK respondents only. Post-stratification weighting is applied. The results can be found in Table 7.1.

Syntax

```
FREQUENCIES VARIABLES=agea
  /FORMAT=NOTABLE
  /STATISTICS=MEAN MEDIAN MODE
  /ORDER=ANALYSIS.
```

This can be shortened to:

```
FREQ agea
/format=notable
/statistics=mean median mode.
```

The command in the syntax under `/STATISTICS=` tells you which measures of central tendency or dispersion it will produce. The options for measures of central tendency are:

(Continued)

```
MEAN
MEDIAN
MODE
```

Menu instructions

Analyze > Descriptive Statistics > Frequencies

Age of respondent, calculated [agea] > Variable(s).

Untick Display frequency tables.

> Statistics

Central tendency: tick Mean, Median, Mode.

OK/Paste.

With this general overview of measures of central tendency in mind, follow the instructions in Box 7.1 to create a table for respondents' ages, limited to UK respondents (Table 7.1). From the results, we can see that the mean and median ages in this data are very close: the mean age is 52.2 years; the median age is 52 years. The mode, however, is 40 years, which tells us that the greatest number of respondents were 40 years old. SPSS also notes that there are multiple modes in the data, meaning there is more than one age that occurs the same number of times. Try running some further tables for Years of full-time education completed [eduyrs] and Total hours normally worked per week in main job overtime included [wkhtot]. Unfortunately, the income data in the ESS has been divided into deciles, so we do not have a continuous variable for income in this dataset. You can also run tables for measures of central tendency for some of the variables that asked questions with 0–10 scales for answers, such as Immigration bad or good for country's economy [imbgeco] and Country's cultural life undermined or enriched by immigrants [imueclt], although the very short scale of these variables means the statistics have limited utility.

Table 7.1 Measures of central tendency for various variables, UK respondents

	N		**Mean**	**Median**	**Mode**
	Valid	**Missing**			
Age of respondent, calculated	2243	21	52.20	52.00	40[a]
Years of full-time education completed	2250	14	13.56	13.00	11
Total hours normally worked per week in main job, overtime included	2107	157	37.13	40.00	40
Immigration bad or good for country's economy	2232	32	4.80	5.00	5
Country's cultural life undermined or enriched by immigrants	2220	44	4.95	5.00	5

a. Multiple modes exist. The smallest value is shown

Measures of central tendency only show us part of the picture, however. As the name indicates, they give us an idea about where the middle of the data is, but they do not indicate anything about the spread of the data. For this, we need measures of dispersion.

MEASURES OF DISPERSION

Measures of dispersion tell us how much variation there is compared to the 'average' case. Averages can hide how much variation there actually is in the data and can be very sensitive to very large or very small values, so it is important to look at measures both of central tendency and of dispersion. Measures of dispersion are only appropriate for use with continuous variables. The most common measures are ranges and standard deviation.

Ranges

Ranges give us an idea of where our data starts and stops. The range subtracts the lowest value (the minimum) from the highest value (the maximum). This gives us an idea of how spread out the responses are, as the mean could be the same for very different spreads of numbers. For example, say you read in a report that a survey of 1,000 people found that the average monthly income was £1,099.99. In this case, the survey is reporting the arithmetical mean, which is what we usually mean when we say 'average'. There are many different combinations of responses that could achieve this result, however. If 999 people earned £10 per month but one person earned £1,000,000, we would get this result; but we could also get an average of £1,099.99 while having our respondents' incomes ranging from £1,000 to £1,200 per month. It would give us a very different understanding of the composition of society if we knew that the range was from £10 to £1,000,000 than if the range were £1,000 to £1,200. The former society would have a greater amount of income inequality, which in a democracy would probably reflect that there was a smaller state and less intervention in the economic markets. The latter society would be much more egalitarian and would be likely to have greater levels of state intervention in the functioning of the economy.

Standard deviation

Standard deviation tells us how much responses differ (deviate) from the mean (standard). What it tells us could be called the distance from the mean. It is not perfect and is based on a few assumptions, but it will give us a reasonable idea of how much variation there is in our data. Standard deviation is about as complicated as it gets with measures of central tendency and dispersion, but you can understand it with some statistical outputs and basic addition and subtraction. Once you master standard deviation, you will have a greater understanding of statistics than the majority of the population!

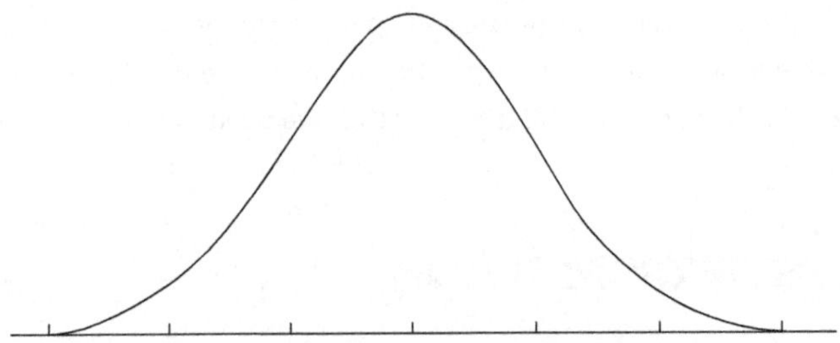

Figure 7.1 Bell curve

The major assumption that underlies the standard deviation calculation is that our data is normally distributed, meaning that it looks roughly like a bell curve (see the curve in Figure 7.1). It is called a bell curve because the shape looks quite a bit like an old-fashioned bell. When the data is normally distributed, 68.27 per cent of responses will fall within one standard deviation of the mean, 95.45 per cent of responses within two standard deviations, and 99.7 per cent within three standard deviations (Figure 7.2). This is also referred to as the 68–95–99.7 rule, or the empirical rule, and it is simply based on the area under a normal curve: the area contained between the lines of one standard deviation above and below the mean equals slightly over two-thirds of the total area under the curve.

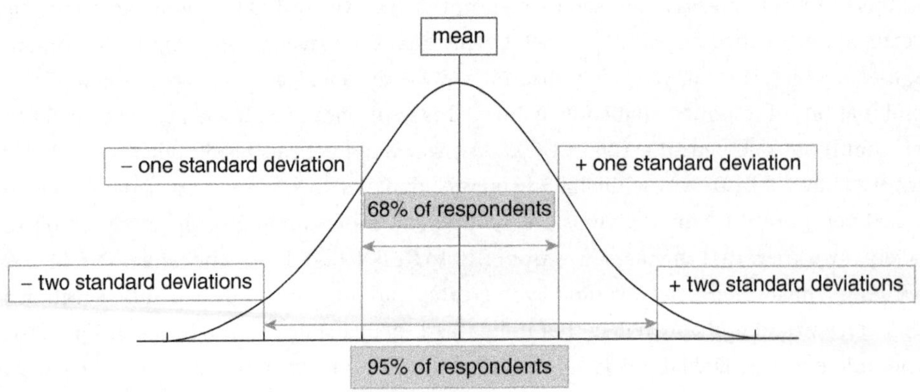

Figure 7.2 Standard deviation

To understand standard deviation as well as all of the measures we have learned about so far, we will work through an example using the number of years of full-time education completed [`eduyrs`] for all countries in the ESS. In Table 7.2, we see the number of valid and missing cases, mean, median, mode, standard deviation, range, minimum and maximum. We start with the number of cases, where we notice that there are 39,828 valid responses and 357 missing. The mean is 12.9. The unit of the mean reflects the unit of the variable, in this case years of full-time education completed. This means that the 'average' respondent has completed just under 13 years of full-time education. We notice that the median and the mode are both 12. The median indicates that the middle number of years is 12, while the mode indicates that 12 is the most common number of years. This is a fairly predictable result for a pan-European survey, as most countries require full-time education to the age of 18 and start somewhere around the age of 6. The fact that the mean, median and mode are all very close to each other gives us an early indication that our data is likely to have a normal distribution. We will look more at that in a moment when we explore standard deviation.

Skip over the standard deviation for a moment to look at the range, minimum and maximum. The range is 50 years, which reflects that the maximum in this case is 50, and the minimum is 0. This means that there is at least one respondent who reports having completed 50 years of full-time education, which is very unusual and seems likely to be a result of

Table 7.2 Years of full-time education completed

N	**Valid**	**39828**
	Missing	**357**
Mean		12.90
Median		12.00
Mode		12
Std. dev.		3.945
Range		50
Minimum		0
Maximum		50

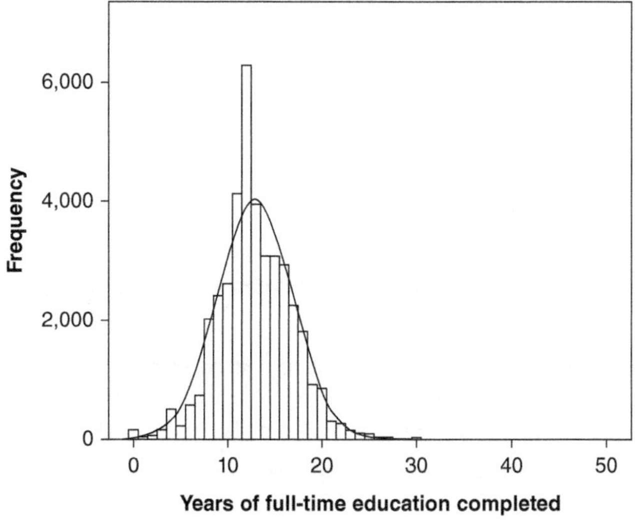

Figure 7.3 Histogram of years of full-time education completed [eduyrs]

misreporting or an error in recording the response; equally, there is at least one person who has completed no years of full-time education. Now that we have a general idea about what our data 'looks' like, we are ready to look at our histogram (Figure 7.3) and standard deviation.

First look at the histogram. The height of the bars reflects the frequency with which different answers were chosen (the mode). The high spike is 12 years, which we know from Table 7.2, which identified 12 as the mode. Sometimes we talk about data having a bimodal distribution. This happens when there are two spikes (modes) with a dip in between. This causes problems for analysis using measures of central tendency and distribution, which is why it is always important to check your data visually with a histogram alongside the statistical tables. If you look at the normal curve (the black curve overlaid on the bars), you should notice that the peak of the normal curve is just slightly to the right of the bar for 12 years; this is because the peak of the normal curve sits on the mean, in this case 12.9 years. Our x-axis goes out to 50 because of our outliers, even though there are so few of them that we cannot see even a blip on the axis where they occur. Nearly all responses fall below 30 years.

Now we are ready to talk about standard deviation. We said earlier that, when normally distributed (which our data very nearly is), about 68 per cent of responses will fall within one standard deviation of the mean. To understand this in practice, we need the mean (12.9) and the standard deviation (3.945). To get one standard deviation, it is the mean plus or minus the standard deviation, so 12.9 ± 3.945. We will start with the lower number: 12.9 – 3.945 = 8.955 years. Now the upper boundary: 12.9 + 3.945 = 16.845. This means that about two-thirds of respondents fall between 8.96 and 16.85 years of full-time education completed.

We also know from before that 95 per cent of responses fall within two standard deviations. This simply means doing the same thing while doubling the standard deviation value: 3.945 × 2 = 7.890. Again, we add and subtract this from the mean, which tells us that 95 per cent of responses fall between 5.010 and 20.790 years. Finally, we do the same thing for three standard deviations, which means that about 99.7 per cent of responses fall between 1.065 and 24.735 years. This makes sense when we look again at the histogram, as the bars virtually disappear after 25 years.

Now that you understand the main measures of central tendency and dispersion, you are ready to try it for yourself. Follow the instructions in Box 7.2 to recreate the statistics for years of full-time education completed.

BOX 7.2 FREQUENCIES FOR CONTINUOUS VARIABLES

This example produces a table with the mean, median, mode, standard deviation, range, minimum and maximum for Years of full-time education completed [eduyrs]. It also produces a histogram. Post-stratification weighting is applied. The results can be found in Table 7.2 and Figure 7.3.

Syntax

```
FREQUENCIES VARIABLES=eduyrs
```

```
/FORMAT=NOTABLE
/STATISTICS=STDDEV RANGE MINIMUM MAXIMUM MEAN MEDIAN MODE
/HISTOGRAM NORMAL.
```

The options for measures of dispersion under `/STATISTICS=` are:

`STDDEV`	standard deviation
`RANGE`	spread of data, calculated by subtracting the minimum from the maximum
`MINIMUM`	lowest answer given
`MAXIMUM`	highest answer given

Adding `/HISTOGRAM` will produce a histogram with the statistics. Adding `NORMAL` after `/HISTOGRAM` adds a normal curve to the histogram. Histograms by default will produce the mean, standard deviation and N in a box to the right of the chart.

Menu instructions

Analyze > Descriptive Statistics > Frequencies

Years of full-time education completed `[eduyrs]` > Variable(s).

Untick Display frequency tables.

> Statistics

Central tendency: select Mean, Median, Mode.

Dispersion: select Std. deviation, Range, Minimum, Maximum.

> Charts

Chart type: select Histograms, Show normal curve on histogram.

OK/Paste.

Editing the histogram output

The histogram in Figure 7.3 has been edited to adjust the x-axis range to run from 0 to 50 instead of -10 to 60. To do this:

Open Chart Editor: double click on the chart or right click > Edit Content > In Separate Window.

Click the numbers on the x-axis to reveal the relevant Properties window. (If this doesn't show automatically, right click on the x-axis numbers > Properties Window.)

> Scale

(Continued)

Minimum: change free-text box to 0.

Maximum: change free-text box to 50.

Apply.

Close the Chart Editor.

When editing the axis, SPSS will show a Data column that indicates the actual lowest and highest values. You can use this to prevent your accidentally excluding cases.

Now produce a table with median, mode, range, minimum and maximum, and histograms for the immigration-related variables measured on a 0–10 scale [`imbgeco`, `imueclt`, `imwbcnt`] (Table 7.3). What we notice about the mode of all three questions is that it falls directly in the middle of the scale: on an 11-point scale, 5 represents a neutral answer. If you also create histograms, it is clear that neutral is by far the most chosen point on the answer scale, although there is more variation on the question about immigrants' contribution to culture [`imueclt`] than the other two questions. As the higher median for the culture question indicates, we can see from the histograms that more responses to this question fall into the upper half of the scale than for the other two questions.

Table 7.3 Descriptive statistics: 0–10 scale questions about immigration [`imbgeco`, `imueclt`, `imwbcnt`]

	Economy [imbgeco]	Cultural life [imueclt]	Place to live [imwbcnt]
Valid	38789	38833	38664
Missing	1396	1352	1521
Mean	4.94	5.61	5.04
Median	5.00	6.00	5.00
Mode	5	5	5
Std. deviation	2.425	2.487	2.266
Range	10	10	10
Minimum	0	0	0
Maximum	10	10	10

However, all of this information only provides us with univariate descriptive statistics. In other words, this information only tells us about the characteristics of one variable at a time. We cannot use the data we have produced thus far to make claims about associations between variables. For example, we might want to know whether people who felt negatively about one question about immigration also felt negatively about the other two.

Other questions we might be interested in could include: do people with more years of education have more positive views of immigrants? Do people with higher incomes have more positive views of immigrants? To find out the answers to these questions, we need to run a correlation.

CORRELATION

A correlation test is a measure of association that uses two continuous variables. We used Cramer's V to test for association between two categorical variables; we use Pearson's r to test for association between two continuous variables. There are other types of correlation coefficients, but Pearson's r – also known as the Pearson product-moment correlation coefficient – is the most common in the social sciences. For a simple correlation, we can only test for association between two variables at a time; to run a correlation that incorporates more than two continuous variables, you need a partial correlation, which is part of a regression test (covered in Chapter 10). Although we can produce correlation coefficients as part of a much larger table with several variables, we have to interpret each variable pairing separately.

We will look at the key assumptions underlying Pearson's r correlations before moving on to the test itself. Pearson's correlation coefficients rely on five important characteristics of the data being tested:

1. Both variables are continuous.
2. The relationship is linear.
3. There are pairs of observations.
4. Extreme outliers are excluded.
5. The data is homoscedastic.

Let's look at each of these in greater detail.

Continuous data

Pearson's r will not work properly with categorical data. In practice, this is not quite as straightforward as it sounds. For example, in the ESS dataset, we have worked with some variables about immigration that run on a 0–10 scale. Researchers disagree among themselves whether such variables should be treated as continuous or categorical. Researchers who would treat such variables as continuous normally insist that the scale be at least 7 points – in this case it is 11 – and that the underlying concept behind the variable is continuous. This is easier to defend with the 0–10 scale variables in the ESS because the survey creators have not placed category names between the two extremes of the scale and instead have asked respondents to place themselves on a relatively continuous scale. With other variables, there is much less confusion about whether we can classify them as continuous. This includes the majority of the variables in the UN dataset, such as life expectancy, mean years of schooling and gross national income.

Linearity

The relationship between the two variables is linear: a scatterplot of the two variables should hint at a straight line. This is very important: there might be a strong relationship, but if it is a curve, Pearson's r cannot provide an accurate correlation. The more data points you have, the more easily you can discern whether you have a linear trend, a non-linear trend, or no trend at all. If you are working at a country level, for example, and you only have four countries, your trend may look linear in a way that it would not if you added more cases. For this reason, you should be careful about making conclusions about linearity with few data points. If there is an identifiable trend, but it is curved, there are several choices to straighten out a curvilinear relationship, including logging variables, which we will look at later in the chapter.

Pairs

Each respondent or observation (each row in the Data View in SPSS or each survey questionnaire when collecting the data) should have values for both of the variables being tested. For example, if female respondents were asked about their views of immigrants but not about education, while male respondents were asked about education but not about their views of immigrants, this would not be met. Without pairs of answers, correlation is not an appropriate test. In the UN dataset, the pairs assumptions are often violated if you are looking for data measured annually. Because of the amount of labour and expense involved in collecting even basic data in many countries, UN data is often collected every five years, or the data provided is for one point during a five-year period. However, if you are not necessarily looking for a continuous relationship with time, then there will be answer pairs available for most variables and most countries in the UN dataset.

Outliers

Extreme outliers should be excluded. They can affect the result returned just as they do when calculating a mean. One suggested cut-off is to exclude values that lie outside of ±3.29 standard deviations from the mean. This will require some manual calculations and is also an advanced technique but one that will really improve your results. We look at some of the other definitions of outliers in the discussion of boxplots in Chapter 8. The main thing to keep in mind is that outliers with continuous data can really skew some of the measures, such as the mean. They can also skew correlations by shifting the approximation of best fit for the distribution of the answer pairings.

Homoscedasticity

Homoscedastic (homo = same, scedasticity = variance; homoscedasticity = same variance) means that the shape formed by all of the dots in the scatterplot is closer to a tube or rectangle rather than a cone. If it is shaped like a cone, with dots considerably farther away from the trend line at one end of the scatterplot than at the other end, Pearson's r again will not return the best result.

Now we can look at what correlation tests can tell us. A correlation tests for a linear relationship between two variables with a consistent direction of change. The direction of change can be positive or negative. If it is positive, we expect that, as one variable increases, the other one does, too. For example, we would expect a positive correlation between hours spent revising and exam mark: as the number of hours spent revising increases, we would expect the exam mark (on average) to increase. The correlation coefficient tells us how consistently this happens: if it is very weakly positive, then we would expect that there would be quite a lot of students for whom this relationship is not true. If it is very strongly positive, then we would expect this to be true for the majority of our results, with relatively few students not seeing a payoff from extra hours of revision.

On the other hand, a correlation can also be negative. This means that, as one variable increases, the other decreases. If we take the example of exam revision again, as teachers, we would be very disheartened if students' exam scores actually went down with more hours spent revising, and we would have to question our teaching, the content of the exam, or both. But there are other relationships that we would expect to be negative. For example, based on our general knowledge about public opinion on immigration, we would expect hostility to immigration to decrease as the number of years of education increases.

The ESS dataset has a very limited number of continuous variables we can explore, however, with even income being recorded as a categorical variable. Instead, we will use the UN dataset for the rest of this chapter. The research question we will start with is, What is the relationship between gender inequality and development? We will use the UN's Gender Inequality Index (GII) [`gii`] to measure gender inequality. The GII combines three dimensions: reproductive health (maternal mortality ratio and adolescent fertility rate), empowerment (share of parliamentary seats held by each sex and higher education attainment levels) and labour market participation (women's participation in the workforce). These indicators are combined to create a single score from 0 to 1, with 0 being perfect gender equality.

We will measure development using a range of measures: exports and imports as a proportion of GDP [`trade`], foreign direct investment net inflows as a proportion of GDP [fdiinflow], gross national income per capita purchasing power parity (in 2011 USD) [gnipcppp], income inequality [incomeineq] and mean years of schooling [meanschyrs]. We can formulate several hypotheses to explore here, one for each of the variable pairs.

H1. International trade [trade] will be negatively correlated with gender inequality [gii].

H2. Foreign direct investment [fdiinflow] will be negatively correlated with gender inequality [gii].

H3. Gross national income per capita [gnipcppp] will be negatively correlated with gender inequality [gii].

H4. Income inequality [incomeineq] will be positively correlated with gender inequality [gii].

H5. Mean years of schooling [meanschyrs] will be negatively correlated with gender inequality [gii].

The first three hypotheses are based on the expectation that higher levels of economic development will be associated with lower gender inequality. The last two hypotheses are based on the expectation that high levels of income inequality and low levels education are more likely to result in worse outcomes for women.

We can check correlations in two ways: using a correlation test and running scatterplots. Scatterplots give us a visual representation of the statistics we read in the correlation test, but they also allow us to check for curvilinearity and homoscedasticity, neither of which is visible if we only run a correlation. Because of this, it is always a good idea to do a visual check before running the correlation test.

BOX 7.3 SCATTERPLOTS

You can only run a scatterplot for two variables at a time. Thus, for testing our hypotheses, you will need to run five separate scatterplots, one for each hypothesis. Results can be found in Figures 7.4 to 7.8.

Syntax

```
GRAPH
  /scatterplot(bivar)=gii with trade
  /missing=listwise.
```

The first variable that you include will be placed on the x-axis; the second will be placed on the y-axis.

Menu instructions

There are two ways to create scatterplots through the menus: using Chart Builder and using Legacy Dialogs. Legacy Dialogs was the route used for the syntax above and is simpler than using Chart Builder. However, Chart Builder provides some useful visual cues and is a more powerful tool.

Legacy Dialog instructions

Graphs > Legacy Dialogs > Scatter/Dot

Simple Scatter > Define.

Gender Inequality Index [`gii`] > X Axis.

Exports and imports (% of GDP) [`trade`] > Y Axis.

OK/Paste.

Chart Builder instructions

Graphs > Chart Builder

Gallery > Scatter/Dot > Click and drag Simple Scatter (first option) onto Chart Preview area (main box).

Variables > Gender Inequality Index [`gii`] > Click and drag to x-axis.

Variables > Exports and imports (% of GDP) [`trade`] > Click and drag to y-axis.

OK/Paste.

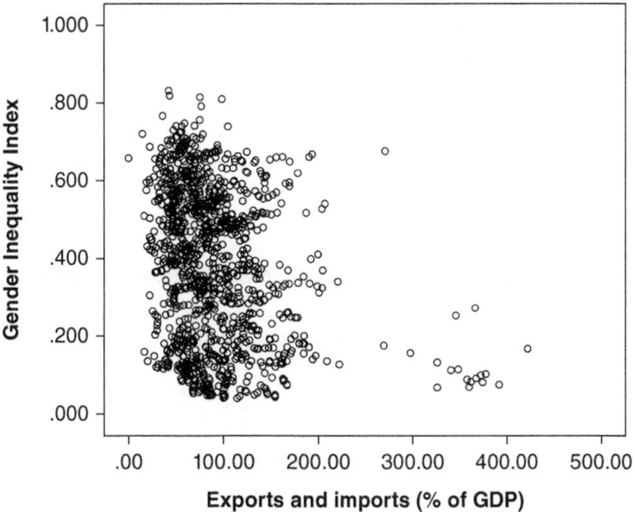

Figure 7.4 Scatterplot of gender inequality [`gii`] and international trade [`trade`]

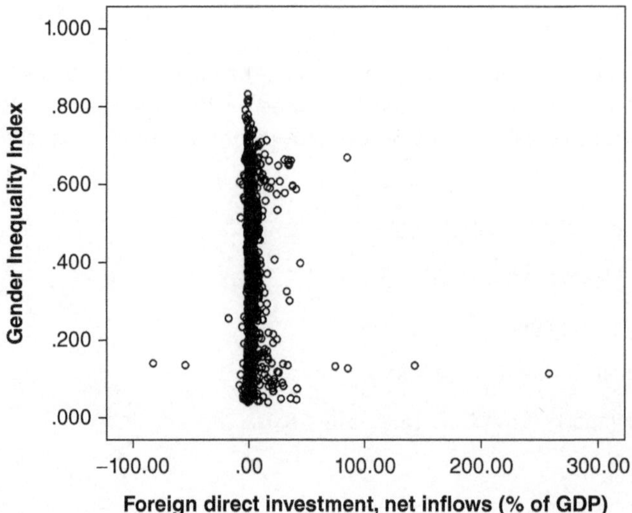

Figure 7.5 Scatterplot of gender inequality [gii] and foreign direct investment inflows [fdiinflow]

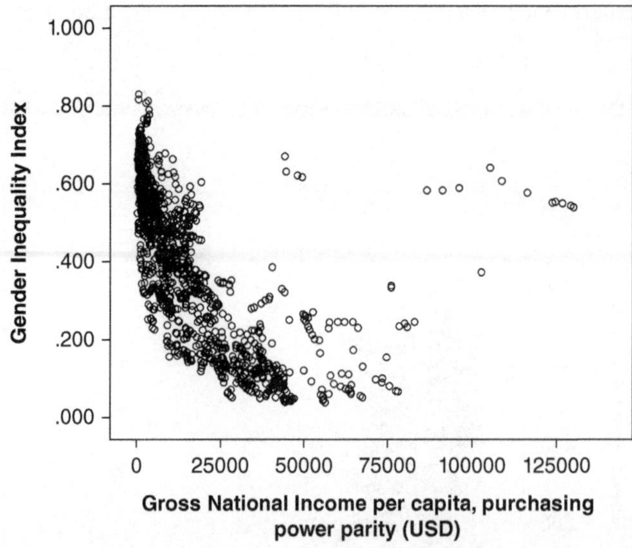

Figure 7.6 Scatterplot of gender inequality [gii] and gross national income, per capita [gnipcppp]

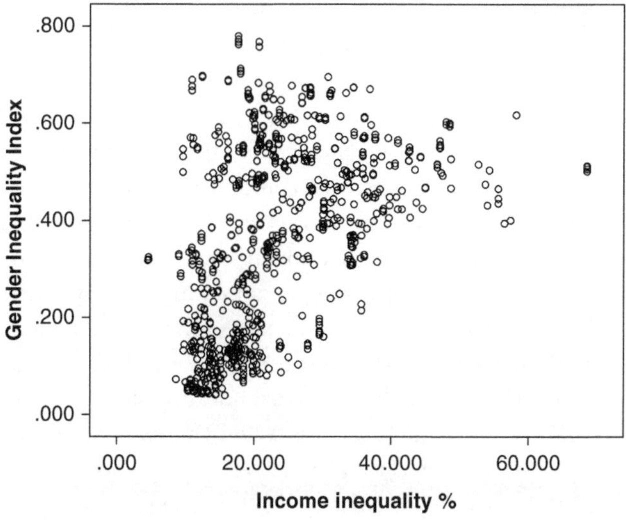

Figure 7.7 Scatterplot of gender inequality [gii] and income inequality [incomeineq]

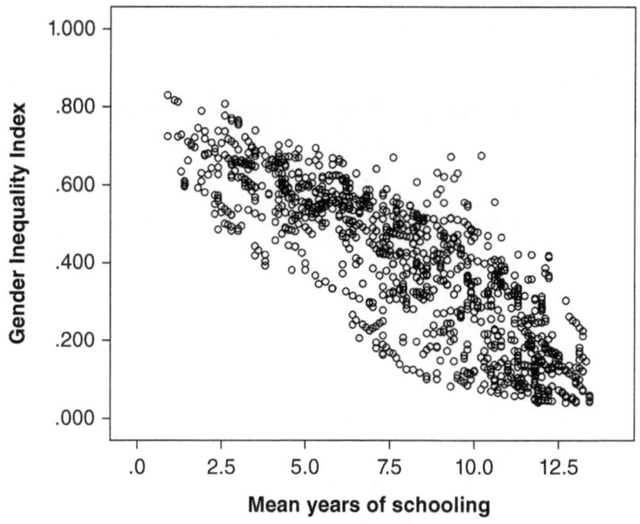

Figure 7.8 Scatterplot of gender inequality [gii] and mean years of schooling [meanschyrs]

The results of our scatterplots reveal quite a lot about our data and allow us to check for fulfilment of the four key assumptions we identified earlier. Table 7.4 summarizes whether the variable pairs have met each of the assumptions required for a correlation. All of the pairs meet the requirement for continuous data, as we selected continuous variables to start with. There are answer pairs available for all variable sets. If there were any without answer pairs, we would have received an error message when we tried to run a scatterplot. You might receive this error, for example, if you are using a dataset that contains several waves of data (such as the ESS waves 1 through 7 combined dataset), and you are trying to pair questions that were not asked in the same survey round, or were not asked in the same countries.

All of the variables except income inequality appear to have roughly linear trends. The easiest way to check for linearity after producing a scatterplot is to open the Chart Editor and select Fit line at total from the Elements menu. This will initially add a linear fit line. Check the r squared linear result number that appears in the top right corner of the graph. Then click the fit line to open the Fit Line Properties window. Try changing it to Quadratic if you think there is a u-shaped trend, or Cubic if you think there is an s-shaped trend. (Make sure you click Apply after making changes so that the chart updates.) If the r squared quadratic/cubic is noticeably higher than the r squared linear, then the data does not meet the linearity assumption. Try this with the scatterplot for gender inequality and income inequality, for example. In this case, the r squared linear result is 0.206, but the r squared quadratic result is 0.270, and the cubic result is 0.299. This clearly indicates that it is a curvilinear trend. If we do this for the scatterplot between gender inequality and international trade, on the other hand, the difference is very small: r squared linear is 0.071 and r squared quadratic is 0.072. Income inequality and gross national income also appear to violate the requirement of homoscedasticity: the results form a cone-like shape instead of a rectangle.

Table 7.4 Summary of assumptions met by variable pair

Variable paired with gender inequality	Continuous	Pairs	Linearity	Outliers	Homoscedasticity
International trade	Met	Met	Met	Not met	Met
Foreign direct investment	Met	Met	Met	Not met	Met
Gross national income	Met	Met	Not met	Not met	Met
Income inequality	Met	Met	Not met	Not met	Not met
Mean years of schooling	Met	Met	Met	Met	Met

To check for outliers, we will need to do some quick calculations. When discussing the assumptions regarding outliers earlier, we mentioned that 3.29 standard deviations is a rule of thumb for defining what results are outliers. This means that to check whether any of our variables violate this assumption, we need to find out what the standard deviation is for each one; then calculate 3.29 standard deviations in each direction; and exclude any outliers that fall outside of this range. To do this, we need to run a frequency table for our variables, ensuring that we include mean, standard deviation, minimum and maximum, as these are the four numbers we need to calculate thresholds for excluding outliers (Table 7.5).

Table 7.5 Summary statistics for calculating outliers

	N		Mean	Std. dev.	Min.	Max.
	Valid	Missing				
Gender Inequality Index	1246	3216	.39056	.194782	.040	.831
Trade (% of GDP)	1573	2889	88.7395	54.88540	.00	455.30

	N		Mean	Std. dev.	Min.	Max.
	Valid	**Missing**				
FDI inflows (% of GDP)	1605	2857	4.6406	10.81724	-79.70	255.40
GNI (per capita, PPP)	4436	26	14053.69	17541.283	178	129916
Income inequality %	847	3615	23.86564	10.734739	4.400	68.300
Mean years of schooling	3905	557	7.147	3.1916	.3	13.4

We will start with outliers for the GII. We need to start by calculating 3.29 standard deviations. We take the standard deviation (0.195) multiplied by 3.29, which equals 0.642. This means that our barrier for outliers is the mean (0.391) ± 3.29 standard deviations (0.642):

$$0.391 \pm 0.642 = -0.251,\ 1.033$$

This means that we should exclude any GII values that are lower than –0.251 or higher than 1.033. In fact, the GII as a measure only runs from 0 to 1. Given that the table shows us that the minimum observed value for this variable is 0.040 and the maximum observed value is 0.831, the GII meets the assumptions for outliers. If you carry out the same process for all of the other variables, you should find that the assumption about outliers is violated by international trade, gross national income and income inequality at the high values, and by foreign direct investment for both high and low values. Because this is the only condition that international trade and foreign direct investment violate, we can select our responses to exclude outliers before running a correlation test. For international trade, this means excluding values over 276.064. For foreign direct investment, this means excluding values over 34.754.

The only variable pairing that fits all of the assumptions without any adjustments is gender inequality and mean years of schooling (Figure 7.8). Here, we have a clear negative relationship: as the average number of years of education increases, gender inequality decreases. In the case of the GII, 0 equates to perfect gender equality, and 1 equates to perfect gender inequality. This result is therefore what we would expect: the highest levels of education are correlated with the highest level of gender equality. Now we can find out how strong this relationship is by running a correlation (Box 7.4).

BOX 7.4 PEARSON'S CORRELATION

This box shows you how to run the most common correlation calculation, Pearson's r, using mean years of schooling [meanschyrs] and the Gender Inequality Index [gii] from the UN dataset. The results can be found in Table 7.6.

(Continued)

Syntax

```
CORRELATIONS
  /VARIABLES=meanschyrs gii
  /PRINT=TWOTAIL NOSIG
  /MISSING=PAIRWISE.
```

Menu instructions

Analyze > Correlate > Bivariate

Mean years of schooling [meanschyrs] > Variables.

Gender Inequality Index [gii] > Variables.

Correlation Coefficients > Ensure Pearson is ticked.

Test of significance > Ensure Two-tailed is selected.

Flag significant correlations: if ticked, SPSS will add stars indicating the significance scores to the correlation coefficient. Select if desired.

Table 7.6 Correlation between mean years of schooling [meanschyrs] and Gender Inequality Index [gii]

		Mean years of schooling	Gender Inequality Index
Mean years of schooling	Pearson correlation	1	-.835*
	Sig. (2-tailed)		.000
	N	3905	1094
Gender Inequality Index	Pearson correlation	-.835*	1
	Sig. (2-tailed)	.000	
	N	1094	1246

* Correlation is significant at the 0.01 level (2-tailed).

We can see the results of our correlation in Table 7.6. Correlation coefficients, like Cramer's V, run from 0 (no association) to ±1 (perfect association). We use the thresholds for interpreting correlation coefficients in Table 7.7. These ranges were proposed by Cohen (1992) on the basis of how much variance in the second variable can be explained by the first variable. With Cohen's thresholds, r=0.10 would explain 1 per cent of total variance; r=0.30 would explain 9 per cent of total variance; and r=0.50 would explain 25 per cent of total variance.

Table 7.7 Ranges for interpreting correlation coefficients

Range	Interpretation
0–0.09	Very weak/no association
0.10–0.29	Small association
0.30–0.49	Moderate association
0.5–1.0	Strong association

The correlation table is symmetrical along a dividing line that runs from top left to bottom right. This means that we only need to interpret half the table to find all of the results. First, we can ignore the cells that pair the same variable with itself. For example, the top left result pairs education with education. Instead, we are interested in the pair of education and gender inequality. The N tells us that we have 3,905 cases with results for both education and gender inequality. The significance is 0.000, so we would report it using the significance threshold of $p<0.001$. As with Cramer's V, it is possible to have a statistically significant result with a very weak relationship, but it is not possible to have a strong relationship that is not statistically significant. Also, like Cramer's V, the focus should be on interpreting the strength of the relationship because the existence of statistical significance alone does not tell us anything beyond confirming whether our result is likely to arise from random error or is reflective of a consistent pattern, and this is very sensitive to the size of N.

Finally, we can look at the Pearson correlation result, which is –0.835. As we already saw from the scatterplot, the minus indicates a negative relationship. The number itself reports the strength of relationship, running from 0 (no relationship) to ±1 (perfect relationship). We will use the same strength thresholds as we used to interpret Cramer's V, so anything from 0.30 equates to a strong relationship. With a result of –0.835, we have a very strong relationship. For a single variable pairing, there is no need to include a table for the correlation. Instead, we would simply report the relevant numbers in our write-up. We might write about this result, 'Results of a Pearson correlation indicate a strong negative relationship between mean years of schooling and gender inequality ($r=-0.835$, $p<0.001$). This confirms H5.'

ADVANCED HANDLING OF DATA FOR CORRELATIONS

We mentioned earlier that there are ways that we can manipulate the data to work with curvilinear relationships and to exclude outliers. It is worth learning these techniques, as it means that we do not have to exclude a hypothesis from testing because it fails one of these assumptions and therefore is inappropriate for running a correlation.

When we looked at the thresholds for outliers, based on 3.29 standard deviations, we found that international trade, foreign direct investment, gross national income and income inequality all violated the assumption about outliers. When we exclude outliers, we should make sure that we only exclude them for the variables we are actually using at any given time, as we might otherwise exclude cases that we should not. For example, if we are working with GII and trade, we need to exclude the outliers for trade. However, if we move on to look at foreign direct investment, we need to make sure that we include the trade outliers again, as the cases that are outliers for trade might not be outliers for foreign direct investment. With that in mind, let's work first with trade. We can see from our summary statistics and calculated thresholds (Table 7.5) that we need to exclude values over 269.311, which represents the mean (88.739) + 3.29 standard deviations (180.572). We can do this by selecting cases (Box 7.5).

BOX 7.5 EXCLUDING OUTLIERS

This box shows you how to exclude outliers from the international trade variable [`trade`].

Syntax

```
USE ALL.

COMPUTE filter_$=(trade <= 269.311).

VARIABLE LABELS filter_$ 'trade <= 269.311 (FILTER)'.

VALUE LABELS filter_$ 0 'Not Selected' 1 'Selected'.

FORMATS filter_$ (f1.0).

FILTER BY filter_$.

EXECUTE.
```

To check that your filter has been implemented properly, run a frequency table. The maximum should not exceed 269.311. In this case, no case has exactly that value, so the maximum becomes 269.20.

```
FREQUENCIES trade

/format=notable

/statistics=stddev range minimum maximum mean median mode.
```

Menu instructions

Data > Select Cases > If condition is satisfied > If

Exports and imports (% of GDP) [`trade`] > equation box.

<=269.311

Continue.

OK/Paste.

Check that the filter has been applied correctly by creating a frequency table.

Analyze > Descriptive Statistics > Frequencies

Exports and imports (% of GDP) [trade] > Variable(s).

Untick Display frequency tables.

> Statistics

Central Tendency: select Mean, Median, Mode.

Dispersion: select Std. deviation, Range, Minimum, Maximum.

OK/Paste.

You should always check that your filter has worked correctly by running a summary statistics table to make sure that your maximum observed value is now the same as your calculated outlier maximum threshold. It may not equal precisely the value of your threshold, as it is very possible that none of the observed values happens to be exactly what you calculated the maximum would be. In this case, our new maximum value is 252.80 when the filter is applied. Because this was the only assumption that was violated, we can now run a correlation between GII and international trade. This returns a strong moderate correlation ($r=-0.227$, $p<0.001$), which means that, as gender inequality rises, international trade decreases. This supports H1.

If we follow the same process for foreign direct investment (first ensuring that we have turned off the filter for international trade), we should exclude all values below –30.947 and above 40.229 before running our correlation. This returns a very weak relationship with weak statistical significance ($r=-0.055$, $p<0.1$). This should not be a surprise, as the scatterplot (Figure 7.5) basically looked like a flat line. This means that, while international trade does correlate with gender equality, foreign direct investment does not, which aligns with findings from authors like Nicole Janz (2018), who has found a very mixed impact of FDI on repression in developing countries.

Finally, we had to exclude gross national income from our correlation both because of outliers and because it had a curvilinear relationship with gender inequality. We can straighten out this curve by creating a logged variable (Box 7.6). Once we have created a logged variable for gross national income, we get a negative linear relationship between logged gross national income and the GII (Figure 7.9), and it now meets the assumption of linearity required to run a correlation. However, we still need to check for outliers. We can do this by calculating the maximum for 3.29 standard deviations using the mean for the logged variable: 3.835 (mean) ± 1.830 (3.29 × standard deviation (0.556)) = 2.006, 5.665.

In this case, both the minimum (2.25) and maximum (5.11) fall within the outlier thresholds, so we do not need to exclude any outliers for the logged gross national income variable.

BOX 7.6 CREATING A LOGGED VARIABLE

This box shows you how to create a logged variable using gross national income [gni] to address violations of the assumption of linearity. Creating a logged variable involves computing a new variable based on the values of the original variable.

Syntax

```
COMPUTE loggni=LG10(gnipcppp).

VARIABLE LABELS loggni 'GNI, logged'.

EXECUTE.
```

Menu instructions

Transform > Compute Variable

Target Variable: choose a name for the new variable. We will use loggni.

> Type and Label

Label: add a descriptive name for the new variable, e.g. GNI, logged.

Function group: click Arithmetic

Double click Lg10 or select Lg10 and press the up arrow to move it into the Numeric Expression field.

Double click the variable [gnipcppp] while the ? in LG10(?) is highlighted in the Numeric Expression box.

Numeric Expression should now read: LG10(gnipcppp).

OK/Paste.

Run a new scatterplot with the Gender Inequality Index [gii] and logged GNI [loggni] to check that the relationship is now linear. The results can be found in Figure 7.9.

Now we are ready to run a correlation between logged GNI and gender inequality. The correlation result returned indicates a very strong relationship between gross national income and gender equality ($r=-0.785$, $p<0.001$). Because 1 indicates perfect inequality, while 0 indicates perfect equality, this is what we would expect: as gross national income increases, gender inequality decreases. This would seem to support proponents of the modernization thesis, who posit that economic development will help countries to overcome cultural barriers, such as traditional gender roles that are oppressive towards women (Inglehart and Welzel, 2005; Lipset, 1959; Rostow, 1960). Of course, a correlation only indicates association, not causality. More recent scholarship seems to indicate that, if anything, causality runs in the other direction: empowering women results in higher levels of economic growth (Chaaban and Cunningham, 2011; Dreze and Sen, 1999; Yunus, 1998).

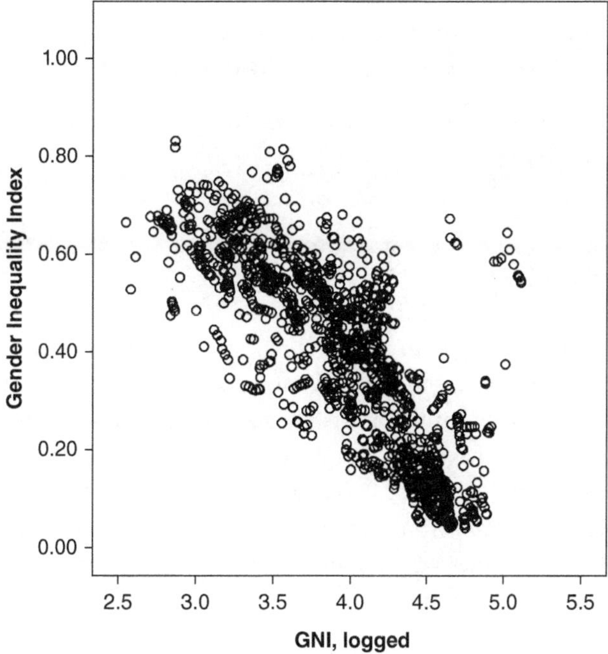

Figure 7.9 Scatterplot of gender inequality and GNI (logged)

We can now return to our five hypotheses to see what we have found. The statistical results are summarized in Table 7.8.

Table 7.8 Summary of correlations with gender inequality

Variable	R
International trade	−0.227***
Foreign direct investment	−0.055*
GNI (logged)	−0.785***
Income inequality	Assumptions violated
Mean years of schooling	−0.835***

*p<0.10, **p<0.01, ***p<0.001

H1. International trade [`trade`] will be negatively correlated with gender inequality [`gii`]. **True**

H2. Foreign direct investment [`fdiinflow`] will be negatively correlated with gender inequality [`gii`]. **False; no evidence**

H3. Gross national income per capita [`gnipcppp`] will be negatively correlated with gender inequality [`gii`]. **True**

H4. Income inequality [`incomeineq`] will be positively correlated with gender inequality [`gii`]. **Unknown; assumptions violated**

H5. Mean years of schooling [`meanschyrs`] will be negatively correlated with gender inequality [`gii`]. **True**

CONCLUSIONS

This chapter has introduced you to measures of central tendency (mean, median, mode), measures of dispersion (range, standard deviation) and Pearson's correlation. You should be comfortable now working with numbers like standard deviation to identify and exclude outliers from analysis. You have also learned more advanced techniques like logging data to create a linear relationship out of a curvilinear relationship. Having encountered tests of association between two categorical variables (Cramer's V) and two continuous variables (Pearson's r), the next chapter will introduce ways to test for relationships between one categorical and one continuous variable.

ACTIVITIES

Activity 7.1

Produce a table with appropriate measures of central tendency and dispersion for Net migration rate (per 1,000 people) [`netmig`].

1. How many valid observations are there? What unit does the N represent?
2. What is the lowest net migration rate? What does it mean when this number is negative?
3. Are the observations normally distributed?
4. Is there a noticeable difference between the mean and median? If so, what could explain this difference?

Activity 7.2

Complete the following table for testing the relationship between logged gross national income [`loggni`] and mean years of schooling [`meanschyrs`], female life expectancy [`femlifeexpect`] and total unemployment rate [unemprate], testing for violation of the assumptions for a correlation. For any variables where the only assumption violated is outliers, apply a filter and calculate the correlation coefficient for each answer pairing. Remember to remove the filter when testing other variables.

Table A.7.2 Summary of assumptions met by variable pair with logged GNI [loggni]

Variable paired with GNI pc, PPP	Continuous	Pairs	Linearity	Outliers	Homoscedasticity
Mean years of schooling [meanschyrs]	Met	Met	Met	Met	Met
Female life expectancy [femlifeexpect]	Met	Met	Met	Not met (minimum observation too low)	Met
Total unemployment rate [unemprate]	Met	Met	Not met (curvilinear)	Not met (maximum too high)	Not met

1. Which assumptions are violated? How could you try to manipulate the variables to meet the assumptions?
2. Which variables should have outliers excluded? What threshold should you use for exclusion?
3. Are the correlations statistically significant? Which correlation is the strongest?

Activity 7.3

Choose three to five variables you think might be correlated. Formulate hypotheses to match some of the variable pairings. Run a correlation.

1. Are the relationships statistically significant?
2. For statistically significant relationships, is the correlation positive or negative?
3. Were your hypotheses correct? Write up your results in a short paragraph.

FURTHER READING

Because continuous data is much more common outside of political science/international relations (IR), there are a wealth of resources for further reading.

Marchant-Shapiro, T. (2015) *Statistics for Political Analysis: Understanding the Numbers.* London: Sage/CQ Press.

This book includes some basic instructions for using SPSS to conduct data analysis, and the examples are from political science. See chapter 3 ('Measures of central tendency: That's some mean baseball') and chapter 4 ('Measures of dispersion: Missing the mark') for further reading on descriptive statistics for continuous variables. See chapter 10 ('Measures of association: Making connections') for correlation and Pearson's r.

Pallant, J. (2016) *SPSS Survival Manual*. Maidenhead: Open University Press/McGraw-Hill Education.
This book provides a functional overview of how to produce statistics in SPSS. See chapter 6 ('Descriptive statistics') for measures of central tendency and dispersion. See chapter 11 ('Correlation') for an overview of correlation and Pearson's r.

Urdan, T.C. (2017) *Statistics in Plain English*, 4th edn. Abingdon: Routledge.
This book discusses statistical concepts in much more accessible language than most. See especially chapter 2 ('Measures of central tendency') and chapter 3 ('Measures of variability') for further reading on descriptive statistics for continuous variables. See chapter 12 ('Correlation') for further discussion of correlation and Pearson's r.

REFERENCES

BBC (2019, 5 Apr) 'Gender pay: fewer than half of UK firms narrow gap', *BBC News*. (www.bbc.co.uk/news/business-47822291).

Chaaban, J. and Cunningham, W. (2011) 'Measuring the economic gain of investing in girls: the girl effect dividend', *World Bank Policy Research Working Papers*. Washington, DC: The World Bank. (https://doi.org/10.1596/1813-9450-5753).

Cobham, A. (n.d.) 'The Palma', *Uncounted*. (http://uncounted.org/palma/).

Cohen, J. (1992) 'A power primer', *Psychological Bulletin*, 112 (1): 155–9.

Dreze, J. and Sen, A. (1999) *India: Economic Development and Social Opportunity*. Oxford: Oxford University Press.

Inglehart, R. and Welzel, C. (2005) *Modernization, Cultural Change and Democracy: The Human Development Sequence*. Cambridge: Cambridge University Press.

Janz, N. (2018) 'Foreign direct investment and repression: An analysis across industry sectors', *Journal of Human Rights*, 17 (2): 163–83.

Lipset, S.M. (1959) 'Some social requisites of democracy: economic development and political legitimacy', *American Political Science Review*, 53 (Mar): 69–105.

OfS (2019) 'POLAR: Participation of Local Areas', *Office for Students*. (https://www.officeforstudents.org.uk/data-and-analysis/polar-participation-of-local-areas/).

ONS (2017a, 10 Mar) 'Gross household income by income decile group, UK, financial year ending 2016', *Office for National Statistics*. (https://www.ons.gov.uk/peoplepopulationandcommunity/

personalandhouseholdfinances/expenditure/adhocs/006770grosshouseholdincomebyincomedecilegroupukfinancialyearending2016).

ONS (2017b, 8 Nov) 'Families and households: 2017', *Office for National Statistics*. (https://www.ons.gov.uk/peoplepopulationandcommunity/birthsdeathsandmarriages/families/bulletins/familiesandhouseholds/2017).

ONS (2018, 18 Jul) 'Births in England and Wales: 2017', *Office for National Statistics*. (https://www.ons.gov.uk/peoplepopulationandcommunity/birthsdeathsandmarriageb/livebirths/bulletins/birthsummarytablesenglandandwales/2017).

ONS (2019, 26 Feb) 'Average household income, UK: Financial year ending 2018', *Office for National Statistics*. (https://www.ons.gov.uk/peoplepopulationandcommunity/personalandhouseholdfinances/incomeandwealth/bulletins/householddisposableincomeandinequality/yearending2018).

Rostow, W. (1960) *The Stages of Economic Growth: A Non-Communist Manifesto*. Cambridge: Cambridge University Press.

UK Government (2016, 26 Sept) 'How low income is measured in households below average income statistics', *Department for Work and Pensions*. (https://www.gov.uk/government/publications/how-low-income-is-measured).

UNDP (2013, 15 Nov) 'Income quintile ratio', *United Nations Development Programme Human Development Reports*. (http://hdr.undp.org/en/content/income-quintile-ratio).

Yunus, M. (1998) *Banker to the Poor: The Story of the Grameen Bank*. New Delhi: Penguin Books India.

8

VISUALIZING CONTINUOUS DATA

CHAPTER SUMMARY

In the previous chapter, you learned how to produce and interpret descriptive statistics for continuous data, including one inferential test. Through this process, you were introduced to histograms and scatterplots through the Legacy Dialogs. In this chapter, we look at ways of exploring and presenting continuous data using Chart Builder for data visualization. You will be introduced to the main types of charts appropriate for continuous variables. You will also learn options for customizing the appearance of these charts.

OBJECTIVES

In this chapter, you will learn:

- How to produce some of the most common types of charts for continuous data and when to use them
- How to use data visualization to check the distribution of responses and identify potential outliers
- How to present visualizations of continuous data professionally.

INTRODUCTION

In Chapter 5, you encountered some of the most common chart types for visualizing categorical data. This chapter introduces you to data visualization techniques for continuous variables and some options that combine categorical and continuous data. Data visualizations are especially important for getting to know your continuous data, checking for outliers and detecting violations of assumptions for inferential tests. The rest of this chapter covers some of the most common chart types in political science and international relations research. The charts covered in this chapter are:

- Histograms (simple histograms and population pyramids)
- Population pyramids
- Line charts (simple line charts and multiple line charts)
- Scatterplots
- Boxplots.

Other less common and/or more advanced chart types, not covered in this book, are:

- Area charts
- Hybrid/dual axis charts.

Before learning how to produce each of these charts, you need to understand that different charts are suitable for different types of data. This is why we covered levels of measurement in the same chapter: you need to be able to distinguish between nominal, ordinal and continuous data to choose an appropriate chart to visualize it. As we discussed earlier, these typologies are flawed, and continuous data can easily be converted into categorical data. However, you do need to understand your variable type – and check that it is classified correctly in IBM SPSS Statistics ('SPSS') – before you can produce a suitable chart. Table 8.1 provides an overview of the main chart types, what type of variable(s) they are suited to and the number of variables you can display in each chart type.

Table 8.1 Overview of chart types

Chart type	Variable type	Sub-types	Number of variables
Pie chart	Categorical	3D pie, donut chart	1 (simple), >1 (donut)
Bar/column chart	Categorical	Stacked column, clustered column	1 (simple), >1 (stacked, clustered)
Histogram	Continuous	Stacked histogram, population pyramid, frequency polygon	1 (histogram, frequency polygon), >1 (stacked histogram, population pyramid)
Line graph	Continuous preferable, minimum ordinal	Multiple line graph, area graph	>1
Scatterplot	Continuous	Grouped scatterplot	2 (simple), >2 (grouped)
Boxplot	Continuous	Clustered boxplot, high-low graphs	

The ESS dataset, like many public opinion surveys with political themes, overwhelmingly contains categorical data, with the only truly continuous variables being variables like hours worked, years in education and birth year/age. For this reason, all of the worked examples in this chapter use the UN composite dataset. The UN dataset is composed almost entirely of continuous variables.

HISTOGRAMS

A histogram may be thought of as a more sophisticated version of the bar chart, but it is used to show the distribution of continuous data rather than categorical data. Histograms are very useful for exploring continuous data because they can quickly identify whether the data has a normal distribution (symmetrical, with a peak in the middle where the mean is and dropping off fairly evenly to either side), bimodal distribution (with two peaks at different points and dropping off between and either side of these peaks), uniformly distributed (roughly even numbers all the way across, creating a rectangle effect), or skewed (with a peak that is not in the centre and with one side having a longer tail than the other), to name but a few of the possibilities. Box 8.1 shows how to produce a simple histogram. We also showed how to produce a simple histogram as part of a statistical command in Chapter 7.

BOX 8.1 PRODUCING A SIMPLE HISTOGRAM

This box teaches you how to produce a stacked bar chart with percentages using the variable Life expectancy [`lifeexpect`]. This chart is appropriate for one continuous variable. The results are in Figure 8.1.

Menu instructions

Graphs > Chart Builder

Confirm that your variables have been set to the appropriate measurement level.

Press OK when you're sure, for example, that your variable is set as nominal or ordinal to produce a simple histogram.

If you want to clear the settings from a previous chart, press Reset.

> Gallery tab > Histogram

Drag the first histogram option (Simple Histogram), with a series of beige columns, onto the chart area. (If you have trouble distinguishing colours or are not sure which one is the simple histogram, SPSS will show you the label if you hover over the picture.)

> Variables

Drag Life expectancy [`lifeexpect`] onto the X-Axis? box in the chart area.

> Element Properties

Tick the box for Display normal curve if desired.

Click Apply at the bottom of the Element Properties window.

Click Paste to keep a copy in syntax. Then, in the Syntax window, select the block of text you have produced (starting with `GGRAPH` and ending with `END GPL.`) and press the green play triangle.

Syntax

```
GGRAPH
  /GRAPHDATASET NAME='graphdataset' VARIABLES=lifeexpect MISSING=LIST-
WISE REPORTMISSING=NO
  /GRAPHSPEC SOURCE=INLINE.
BEGIN GPL
```

```
  SOURCE: s=userSource(id('graphdataset'))
  DATA: lifeexpect=col(source(s), name('lifeexpect'))
  GUIDE: axis(dim(1), label('Life expectancy'))
  GUIDE: axis(dim(2), label('Frequency'))
  ELEMENT: interval(position(summary.count(bin.rect(lifeexpect))), shape.
interior(shape.square))
  ELEMENT: line(position(density.normal(lifeexpect)), color('Normal'))
END GPL.
```

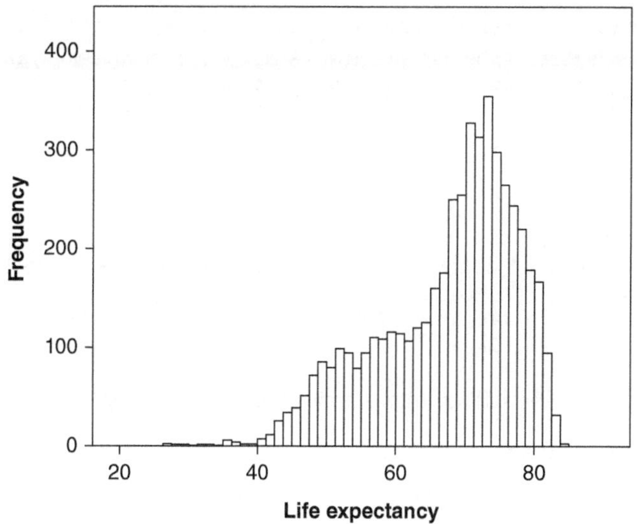

Figure 8.1 Histogram of life expectancy [lifeexpect] without normal curve

Figure 8.1 shows the distribution of life expectancy across all countries and all years of data. You can toggle the normal curve on and off using the Chart Editor. The x-axis of the histogram shows us the units of our chosen variable (life expectancy at birth), while the y-axis shows us the number of cases for each expected length of life. We can see from the shape of the histogram that the responses are not what we would call normally distributed. A normal distribution is symmetrical, with the greatest number of responses in the middle, decreasing to each side in a bell-shaped curve. This histogram has a peak at 74 years, drops off sharply to either side of the peak but then plateaus from about 50 to 65 before dropping off more steeply again. There are some barely visible blips above the x-axis between 25 and 40, indicating a handful of cases where the life expectancy at birth was below 40 years.

It is also possible, but fairly uncommon, to make a stacked histogram to which you add a categorical variable. This is uncommon because histograms tend to have the appearance of a densely populated bar chart, and the addition of stacks within the bars can be very visually confusing. Population pyramids, on the other hand, can be a very useful way of 'stacking' the information, but with the categories extending vertically to either side of the y-axis. This is most commonly done with binary gender (male/female). To create a population pyramid, you need one continuous and one categorical variable. If the categorical variable has more than two categories, you can only use two of them at a time. Box 8.2 shows how to make a population pyramid using life expectancy at birth [`lifeexpect`] and World Bank income groups [`wbincome`], comparing the highest and lowest income groups.

BOX 8.2 PRODUCING A POPULATION PYRAMID

This box shows you how to create a population pyramid using one continuous variable and a categorical variable that is either binomial (two categories) or for which only two categories are selected for comparison. The results are in Figure 8.2.

Menu instructions

Graphs > Chart Builder

Confirm that your variables have been set to the appropriate measurement level.

Press OK when you're sure, for example, that your variable is set as nominal or ordinal to produce a population pyramid.

If you want to clear the settings from a previous chart, press Reset.

> Gallery tab > Histogram

Drag the fourth histogram option (Population Pyramid), with a series of blue and green bars extending horizontally from the middle, onto the chart area. (If you have trouble distinguishing colours or are not sure which one is the simple histogram, SPSS will show you the label if you hover over the picture.)

> Variables

Drag Life expectancy [`lifeexpect`] onto the Distribution Variable? box in the chart area.

Drag World Bank income groups [`wbincome`] onto the Split Variable? box in the chart area.

> Element Properties > Edit Properties of

Select Split (Pyramid1). This should show the categories in the Order box.

Move Upper middle income and Lower middle income to the Excluded box.

Click Apply at the bottom of the Element Properties window.

Click Paste to keep a copy in syntax. Then, in the Syntax window, select the block of text you have produced (starting with `GGRAPH` and ending with `END GPL.`) and press the green play triangle.

Syntax

```
GGRAPH
  /GRAPHDATASET NAME='graphdataset' VARIABLES=lifeexpect wbincome
MISSING=LISTWISE REPORTMISSING=NO
  /GRAPHSPEC SOURCE=INLINE.
BEGIN GPL
  SOURCE: s=userSource(id('graphdataset'))
  DATA: lifeexpect=col(source(s), name('lifeexpect'))
  DATA: wbincome=col(source(s), name('wbincome'),
notIn('2', '3'), unit.category())
  COORD: transpose(mirror(rect(dim(1,2))))
  GUIDE: axis(dim(1), label('Life expectancy'))
  GUIDE: axis(dim(1), opposite(), label('Life expectancy'))
  GUIDE: axis(dim(2), label('Frequency'))
   GUIDE: axis(dim(3), label('World Bank income group'), opposite(),
gap(0px))
  GUIDE: legend(aesthetic(aesthetic.color), null())
  SCALE: cat(dim(3), include('1', '4'))
  ELEMENT:
interval(position(summary.count(bin.rect(lifeexpect*1*wbincome))),color.
interior(wbincome))
END GPL.
```

If the output creates two separate charts rather than one chart that looks like Figure 8.2:

Double click on the chart to open Chart Editor.

Options > Transpose Chart.

Figure 8.2 shows the distribution of cases by the life expectancy at birth, split between the highest and lowest income groups, with the highest income group to the left of the y-axis and the lowest income group to the right. This is produced with the counts, so it not only shows the distribution of life expectancies within the two groups but also demonstrates that there are far more cases in the high-income group with life expectancies around 80 years, while the greatest frequency for low-income cases is just below 60 years. The majority of cases in each income group do not overlap each other at all, showing a stark contrast in life expectancy between the richest and poorest countries. Figure 8.3 adds gridlines to make it easier to read the frequencies. (You can learn how to do this at the end of this chapter, in the section 'Adjusting chart appearance in the Chart Editor'.)

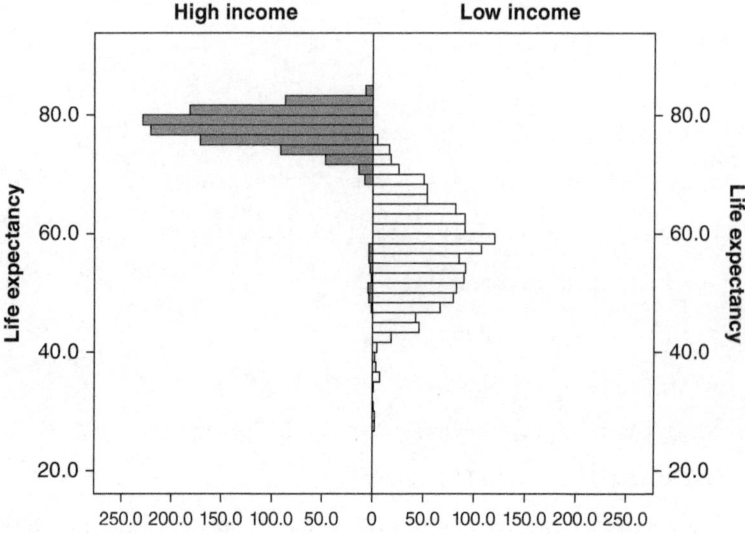

Figure 8.2 Population pyramid of life expectancy [lifeexpect] and World Bank income groups [wbincome]

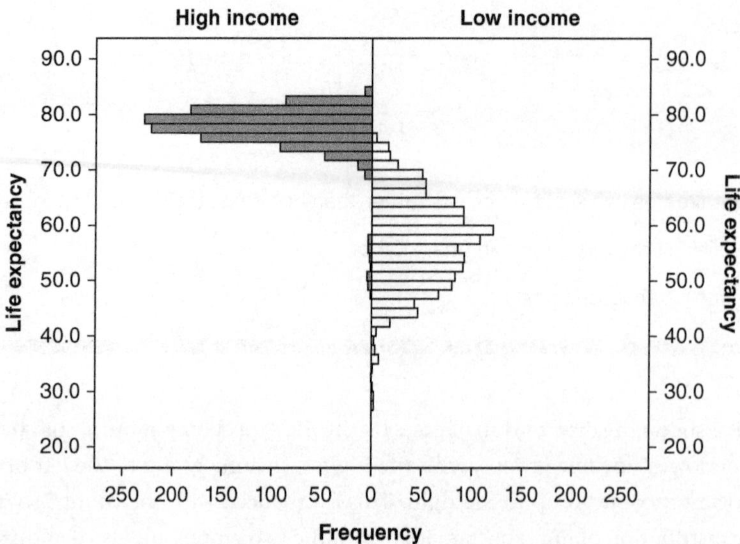

Figure 8.3 Population pyramid of life expectancy [lifeexpect] and World Bank income group [wbincome], gridlines added

If you focus on the cases with a life expectancy just below the 70-year gridline, you can see that there are about 50 cases in the low-income group with this life expectancy, compared to fewer than 5 in the high-income group. On the other hand, there are around 225 cases with a life expectancy just under 80 years in the high-income group, compared to no visible cases in the low-income group. Ignoring the values with only a handful of cases, both groups are normally distributed, with far less variation in the high-income group than the low-income group. Population pyramids highlight such differences in the distribution of cases very nicely.

LINE CHARTS

Line charts are used with two continuous variables. They are useful to track changes or trends over time and to illustrate the relationship between two or more variables. Simple line charts will plot one variable along the x-axis and one along the y-axis. Multiple line charts can create a series of lines that are broken up by categories, similar to the effect of a stacked bar chart. If you do not add a second variable to a simple line chart, it will plot what is essentially a histogram, simply displaying the data using lines instead of bars. Just as we learned how to produce bar charts with categorical variables that showed counts and percentages, we will show you how to produce line charts that show values, means and sums.

Box 8.3 explains how to create a simple line chart with means. We will look at the global trend in life expectancy at birth [`lifeexpect`] over time [`year`]. Because our dataset is composed of 190 countries, we use the mean to show what the global average is. You can look at the trend for individual countries by using 'Select Cases', covered in Chapter 4.

BOX 8.3 PRODUCING A SIMPLE LINE CHART WITH MEANS

This box shows you how to produce a simple line chart that plots the mean value rather than all values. The results are in Figure 8.4.

Menu instructions

Graphs > Chart Builder

Confirm that your variables have been set to the appropriate measurement level.

Press OK when you're sure, for example, that your two variables are set to scale to produce a simple line chart.

If you want to clear the settings from a previous chart, press Reset.

(Continued)

> Gallery tab > Line

Drag the first line chart option (Simple Line), with a single black line, onto the chart area. (If you have trouble distinguishing colours or are not sure which one is the simple line chart, SPSS will show you the label if you hover over the picture.)

> Variables

Drag Year [year] onto the X-Axis? box in the chart area.

Drag Life expectancy [lifeexpect] onto the Y-Axis? box in the chart area.

> Element Properties > Statistics

Under Statistic, change the drop-down menu to Mean.

Click Apply at the bottom of the Element Properties window.

Click Paste to keep a copy in syntax. Then, in the Syntax window, select the block of text you have produced (starting with GGRAPH and ending with END GPL.) and press the green play triangle.

Or, press OK without pasting.

Syntax

```
GGRAPH
  /GRAPHDATASET NAME='graphdataset' VARIABLES=Year MEAN(lifeexpect)
[name='MEAN_lifeexpect']
    MISSING=LISTWISE REPORTMISSING=NO
  /GRAPHSPEC SOURCE=INLINE.
BEGIN GPL
  SOURCE: s=userSource(id('graphdataset'))
  DATA: Year=col(source(s), name('Year'))
  DATA: MEAN_lifeexpect=col(source(s), name('MEAN_lifeexpect'))
  GUIDE: axis(dim(1), label('Year'))
  GUIDE: axis(dim(2), label('Mean Life expectancy'))
  ELEMENT: line(position(Year*MEAN_lifeexpect), missing.wings())
END GPL.
```

Figure 8.4 shows a simple line chart of the mean of all countries in the dataset for life expectancy at birth between 1990 and 2015. This shows a very clear upward trend, indicating that average life expectancy has increased from somewhat under 65 years to

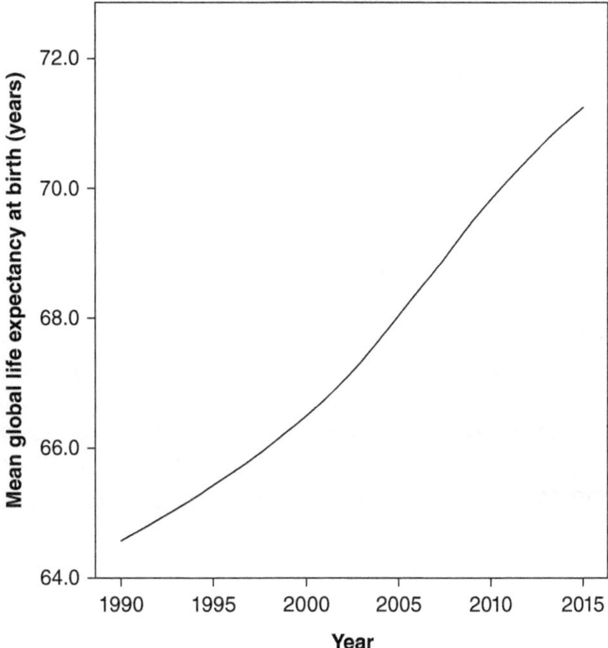

Figure 8.4 Line chart of mean life expectancy at birth [lifeexpect], 1990–2015

around 71 years over the course of 25 years. The chart is displayed here with the default axis scaling, which means that SPSS has selected 64 years as the lowest value on the y-axis. You should always be conscious of such automatic scaling. On the one hand, this scaling makes the upward trend very clearly identifiable. However, there are some very good arguments against scaling such axes to anything besides zero because it can exaggerate trends. For example, if we rescale the y-axis to start at zero in this case, the upward trend is still visible but is much flatter. Despite this, we might still choose to leave the axis starting point at 64 years on the grounds that, contextualized in terms of the length of human life, an increase of around six years is considerable and warrants this scaling. The point here is that you should always examine your axes and make a conscious decision about their scaling.

Using means makes sense with life expectancy because we are looking at the global average life expectancy. However, with some variables, we might be interested in adding up the results for all of our different cases. For example, there are several variables that report on refugee populations, in terms of both countries where they are living and countries where they came from. In this case, finding the global average would not be very meaningful. Instead, we might want to work with sums to find out the total population of refugees, asylum-seekers and other 'persons of concern' (as classified by the UN High Commissioner for Refugees) [refplushost] that countries in our dataset are hosting. We will start by producing a simple line chart with sums (Box 8.4) to show the total population of concern hosted in the 190 countries in our dataset. After that, we will produce a multiple line chart with sums to show the distribution of these refugee-like groups based on the World Bank income grouping [wbincome] to test the common claim that developed countries are overwhelmed by refugees and taking more than their fair share.

BOX 8.4 PRODUCING A SIMPLE LINE CHART WITH SUMS

This box shows you how to produce a simple line chart that portrays the results as a sum of all values across all cases for each value using a second continuous variable. This is most commonly done when time is the second continuous variable and there are multiple observations for a given point in time within the dataset. Here this is done to show the total population of concern (refugees plus other displaced persons) across 190 countries in any given year. The results are in Figure 8.5.

Menu instructions

Graphs > Chart Builder

Confirm that your variables have been set to the appropriate measurement level.

Press OK when you're sure, for example, that your two variables are set to scale to produce a simple line chart.

If you want to clear the settings from a previous chart, press Reset.

> Gallery tab > Line

Drag the first line chart option (Simple Line), with a single black line, onto the chart area. (If you have trouble distinguishing colours or are not sure which one is the simple line chart, SPSS will show you the label if you hover over the picture.)

> Variables

Drag Year [year] onto the X-Axis? box in the chart area.

Drag Total population of concern hosted (refugees, asylum-seekers, others of concern) [refplushost] onto the Y-Axis? box in the chart area.

> Element Properties > Statistics

Under Statistic, change the drop-down menu to Sum.

Click Apply at the bottom of the Element Properties window.

Click Paste to keep a copy in syntax. Then, in the Syntax window, select the block of text you have produced (starting with GGRAPH and ending with END GPL.) and press the green play triangle.

Or, press OK without pasting.

Syntax

```
GGRAPH

  /GRAPHDATASET NAME='graphdataset' VARIABLES=Year SUM(refplushost)
[name='SUM_refplushost']

  MISSING=LISTWISE REPORTMISSING=NO

  /GRAPHSPEC SOURCE=INLINE.

BEGIN GPL

  SOURCE: s=userSource(id('graphdataset'))

  DATA: Year=col(source(s), name('Year'))

  DATA: SUM_refplushost=col(source(s),
name('SUM_refplushost'))

  GUIDE: axis(dim(1), label('Year'))

  GUIDE: axis(dim(2), label('Sum Total population of concern hosted
(refugees, asylum-seekers, ',

    'others of concern)'))

  ELEMENT: line(position(Year*SUM_refplushost),
missing.wings())

END GPL.
```

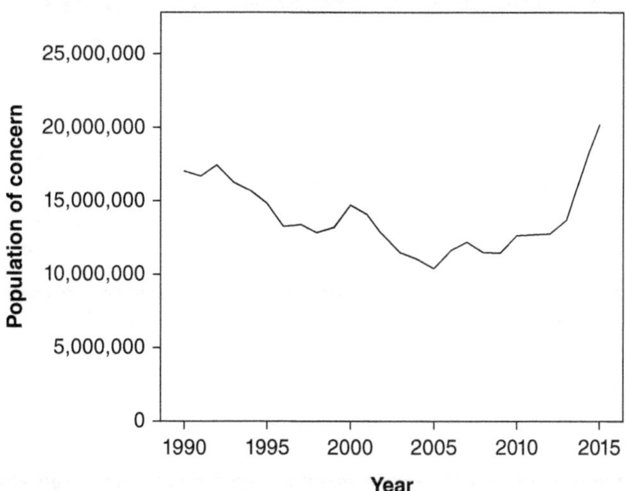

Figure 8.5 Simple line chart of population of concern [`refplushost`] in 190 countries

Figure 8.5 shows global trends in people who are recognized by the UN High Commissioner for Refugees as having crossed an international border fleeing persecution in their home country. In more recent years, the UNHCR has begun to tabulate data separately for asylum-seekers and 'other populations of concern'. In the earlier years of data, you should notice that there is no difference in the numbers reported for this variable and the variable that isolates refugees [`refhost`].

We can see some very clear trends in the chart, with a steady downward trend in populations of concern through the 1990s, a short spike around 2000, then nearly uninterrupted rises since 2015. The upward trend becomes especially steep after 2011, when the Arab Spring revolutions and the rise of Daesh in the Middle East, conflict in Central Africa and a return of instability in Afghanistan caused a drastic rise in the number of people fleeing across international borders. The upheaval since 2010 means that the number of people with refugee-like characteristics now exceeds the period following the breakdown of the Soviet Union.

This chart only gives us an indication of the worldwide numbers, however. It does not give us an indication of where these populations are hosted or what their financial capacity is to support these populations. We will test this using the World Bank's income group classification system, which splits countries into four categories according to their GNI per capita: high income, upper middle income, lower middle income and low income. There are claims by developed, mostly high-income countries that they are overburdened with refugees. To test this claim, albeit in a fairly simplistic manner, we will create a multiple line chart which allows us to create different lines based on a categorical variable (Box 8.5). We will use sums again so that we can see the total number of persons of concern hosted in countries in each of the income groupings.

BOX 8.5 PRODUCING A MULTIPLE LINE CHART WITH SUMS

This box shows you how to produce a multiple line chart that conveys the results as sums. This requires having two continuous variables (plotted on the x- and y-axis) and a categorical variable, which will split the results by category. In this example, we look at the same two continuous variables as Box 8.4: year and population of concern. This time, we add World Bank income group as the grouping variable, which will result in separate lines representing the total population of concern in each year within each World Bank income group. The results are in Figure 8.6.

Menu instructions

Graphs > Chart Builder

Confirm that your variables have been set to the appropriate measurement level.

Press OK when you're sure, for example, that your two variables are set to scale, in addition to one variable set to nominal or ordinal, to produce a multiple line chart.

If you want to clear the settings from a previous chart, press Reset.

> Gallery tab > Line

Drag the second line chart option (Multiple Line), with three lines in blue, green and beige, onto the chart area. (If you have trouble distinguishing colours or are not sure which one is the multiple line chart, SPSS will show you the label if you hover over the picture.)

> Variables

Drag Year [year] onto the X-Axis? box in the chart area.

Drag Total population of concern hosted (refugees, asylum-seekers, others of concern) [refplushost] onto the Y-Axis? box in the chart area.

Drag World Bank income group [wbincome] onto the Set pattern box in the chart area.

> Element Properties > Statistics

Under Statistic, change the drop-down menu to Sum.

Click Apply at the bottom of the Element Properties window.

Click Paste to keep a copy in syntax. Then, in the Syntax window, select the block of text you have produced (starting with GGRAPH and ending with END GPL.) and press the green play triangle.

Or, press OK without pasting.

Syntax

```
GGRAPH
  /GRAPHDATASET NAME='graphdataset' VARIABLES=Year SUM(refplushost)
[name='SUM_refplushost']
    wbincome MISSING=LISTWISE REPORTMISSING=NO
  /GRAPHSPEC SOURCE=INLINE.
BEGIN GPL
  SOURCE: s=userSource(id('graphdataset'))
  DATA: Year=col(source(s), name('Year'))
  DATA: SUM_refplushost=col(source(s), name('SUM_refplushost'))
  DATA: wbincome=col(source(s), name('wbincome'), unit.category())
  GUIDE: axis(dim(1), label('Year'))
  GUIDE: axis(dim(2), label('Sum Total population of concern hosted
(refugees, asylum-seekers, ',
```

(Continued)

```
  'others of concern)'))

GUIDE: legend(aesthetic(aesthetic.shape.interior), label('World Bank
income group'))

SCALE: cat(aesthetic(aesthetic.shape.interior), include('1', '2',
'3', '4'))

ELEMENT: line(position(Year*SUM_refplushost), shape.interior(wbincome),
missing.wings())

END GPL.
```

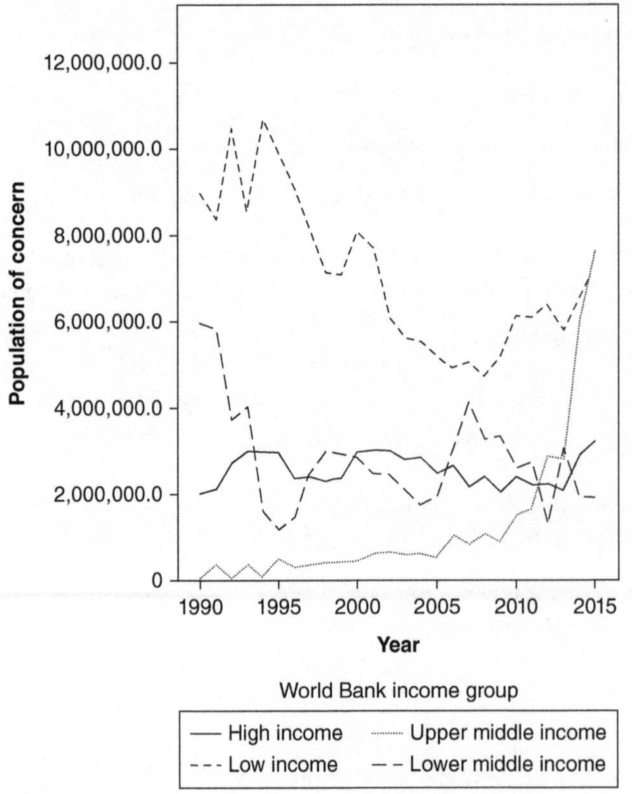

Figure 8.6 Population of concern [`refplushost`] by World Bank income group [`wbincome`]

Figure 8.6 shows the total number of refugees, asylum-seekers and 'others of concern' hosted in each of the different income groupings. What is clear from the chart is that countries classed as 'low income' consistently host the majority of the world's populations of concern. However, we can also see a sharp rise in the number of refugees hosted by upper middle income countries in a pattern that parallels the sudden rise in populations of concern after 2010 from our simple line graph, a trend that is not mirrored by any of the other income groups. This initial evidence offers mixed results about whether rich countries are now hosting more than their fair share of refugees and populations of concern. On the one hand, there has been a significant rise in the number of persons of concern hosted in upper middle-income countries; on the other hand, this is not reflected in a similar rise in high-income countries, a category that encompasses all EU member states except Bulgaria, Croatia and Romania, none of which takes a large number of refugees. In fact, the sharp rise in the upper middle-income group is driven almost entirely by Turkey.

SCATTERPLOTS

Scatterplots show joint variation of continuous variables. A simple scatterplot plots two continuous variables, with one dot to represent each answer pairing. Variants of scatterplots include a grouped scatterplot, which adds a third, categorical variable, and bubble plots, which add a third, continuous variable. Bubble plots involve rescaling the size of the dots in proportion to the third continuous variable, such as the population of a country. Bubble plots are popular with infographics and work well with mapping. Such graphics have been popularized over recent times by Hans Rosling, in an application known as Gapminder, which provides intuitive tools to find out about inequalities around the world (Gapminder Foundation, n.d.).

Unlike with a line chart, where there needs to be a logical order to the variable values, such as using time, scatterplots are useful for plotting pairs of answers that do not necessarily follow a tidy linear or time-bound progression. For example, Figure 8.7 looks very messy as a line chart because there is considerable variation in the data pairings, resulting in a lot

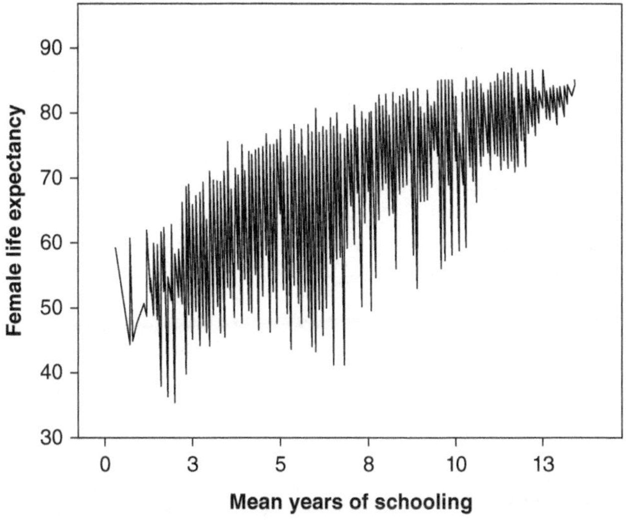

Figure 8.7 Simple line chart of mean years of schooling [meanschyrs] and female life expectancy [femlifeexpect]

of vertical 'noise'. We can simplify this by showing it as the mean, but we might not wish to hide the considerable variation between countries, and this still does not make a smooth, tidy line. Instead, we can plot the same variables as a simple scatterplot. This allows us to see much more information about the shape of our data than a line chart. For example, a scatterplot can identify potential outliers and will give us a reasonable impression of possible underlying patterns and how closely clustered the cases are around a trend line. Box 8.6 shows you how to produce a simple scatterplot.

BOX 8.6 PRODUCING A SIMPLE SCATTERPLOT

This box shows you how to produce a simple scatterplot with two continuous variables. The results are in Figure 8.8.

Menu instructions

Graphs > Chart Builder

Confirm that your variables have been set to the appropriate measurement level.

Press OK when you're sure, for example, that your two variables are set to scale, to produce a scatterplot.

If you want to clear the settings from a previous chart, press Reset.

> Gallery tab > Scatter/Dot

Drag the first scatterplot option (Simple Scatter), with black circles, onto the chart area. (If you have trouble distinguishing colours or are not sure which one is the simple scatterplot, SPSS will show you the label if you hover over the picture.)

> Variables

Drag Public health expenditure (% of GDP) [`healthspend`] onto the X-Axis? box in the chart area.

Drag Female life expectancy [`femlifeexpect`] onto the Y-Axis? box in the chart area.

Click Paste to keep a copy in syntax. Then, in the Syntax window, select the block of text you have produced (starting with `GGRAPH` and ending with `END GPL.`) and press the green play triangle.

Or, press OK without pasting.

Syntax

```
GGRAPH
  /GRAPHDATASET NAME='graphdataset' VARIABLES=healthspend femlifeexpect
MISSING=LISTWISE
    REPORTMISSING=NO
```

```
  /GRAPHSPEC SOURCE=INLINE.
BEGIN GPL
  SOURCE: s=userSource(id('graphdataset'))
  DATA: healthspend=col(source(s), name('healthspend'))
  DATA: femlifeexpect=col(source(s),
name('femlifeexpect'))
  GUIDE: axis(dim(1), label('Public health expenditure (% of GDP)'))
  GUIDE: axis(dim(2), label('Female life expectancy'))
  ELEMENT: point(position(healthspend*femlifeexpect))
END GPL.
```

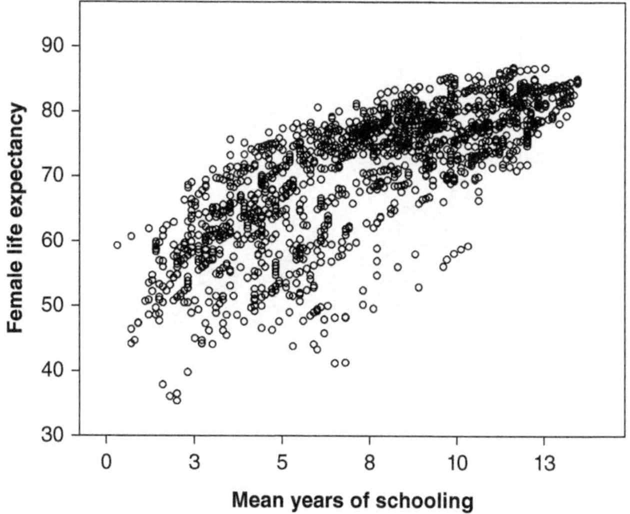

Figure 8.8 Scatterplot of mean years of schooling [`meanschyrs`] and female life expectancy [`femlifeexpect`]

Figure 8.8 shows a fairly straight upward trend that is somewhat cone-shaped. We can also see some dots that lie apart from the main clusters (outliers). We will talk through each of these characteristics in turn. First, the scatterplot shows a clear *positive* relationship. In the statistical sense of the word, this is not a value judgement; rather, it means that, as one variable increases, the other does as well. This is called a positive relationship because, if we drew a best fit line through the data, the slope of the line would be a positive number.

Now, look at the shape formed by the dots. This conic shape is known as heteroscedasticity, which was discussed in Chapter 7. This cone shape tells us that there is greater variation in female life expectancy among countries with lower average levels of schooling; this variation decreases considerably as the mean years of schooling rises until there is strong clustering of female life expectancies for countries at the upper end of average years of schooling. This is probably unsurprising, given that countries where 13 years is the mean for years of schooling are also likely to be richer countries with better access to healthcare, lower maternal mortality and lower total fertility rates. In fact, plotting mean years of schooling against maternal mortality ratios (Figure 8.9) is an example of a *negative* relationship. With a negative relationship, as one number increases, the other decreases. In this case, as average years of schooling rises, the number of deaths due to pregnancy-related causes per 100,000 live births decreases considerably.

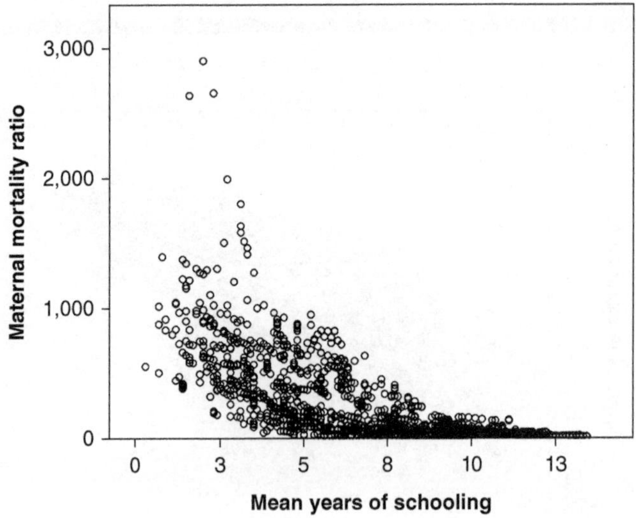

Figure 8.9 Example of mean years of schooling [meanschyrs] and maternal mortality [matmort]

Finally, look at the outliers in both of the scatterplots. There are some clear outliers, indicated by isolated dots, and some general trends, indicated by the thicker clusters of dots. Outliers are cases that we should always give extra attention to. If they contain very unusual characteristics, we might want to check for data entry errors. Or, even if they have been entered accurately, we might want to explore them more to identify if they are unusual to the point of wishing to exclude them, because their values are likely to distort calculations involving means, such as having a single respondent with an income exceeding £1,000,000 per week, when the next highest value is £5,000. If the cases are countries, we might decide to exclude a particular country and year from our analysis because it was a year of significant political upheaval, and the results are unlikely to contribute to our overall understanding of a question we are exploring. Alternatively, identifying outliers can also create worthwhile research projects by trying to explain the exceptions that prove the general rule. Returning to Figure 8.9, we might want to identify the three outlying cases that have much higher maternal mortality ratios than any of the other countries to try to identify if there were any policies or external factors that could explain such outlying results. The easiest way to identify these cases is to use the Chart Editor interactively (Box 8.7).

BOX 8.7 USING A SCATTERPLOT TO IDENTIFY OUTLIER CASES

This box shows you how to use a scatterplot interactively in the Chart Editor to identify particular outlier cases. This example uses Figure 8.9 for the scatterplot.

Menu instructions

Duplicate the scatterplot in Figure 8.9.

> Double click the chart in the Output window to open the Chart Editor.
>
> Click on the dot with the highest maternal mortality ratio value twice. It will be more likely to work if you pause briefly between clicks instead of double clicking.
>
>> Make sure that only one dot is circled by the beige ring to indicate that it is active. If all of the dots are activated, you will not be able to identify the single case.
>>
>> Right click on the dot after you have isolated it. Choose Go to case (CTRL + G) from the menu options. This will highlight the case in the Data View tab of the Data Editor window.

Syntax

```
GGRAPH
  /GRAPHDATASET NAME='graphdataset' VARIABLES=meanschyrs matmort
MISSING=LISTWISE REPORTMISSING=NO
  /GRAPHSPEC SOURCE=INLINE.
BEGIN GPL
  SOURCE: s=userSource(id('graphdataset'))
  DATA: meanschyrs=col(source(s), name('meanschyrs'))
  DATA: matmort=col(source(s), name('matmort'))
  GUIDE: axis(dim(1), label('Mean years of schooling'))
  GUIDE: axis(dim(2), label('Maternal mortality ratio'))
  ELEMENT: point(position(meanschyrs*matmort))
END GPL.
```

When you isolate the case with the highest maternal mortality ratio, you should find that it represents Sierra Leone in 1995. The next two highest values for maternal mortality also come from Sierra Leone, in 2000 and 1990. This is perhaps not entirely surprising, given that Sierra Leone endured a bloody civil war lasting from 1991 to 2002, which included widespread use of rape as a weapon of war and abduction of women as sex slaves. However, this still cannot entirely explain why Sierra Leone's maternal mortality exceeds that of any other country by more than 1,000 women per 100,000 births (in other words, more than 1 per cent), including other countries that have endured civil wars that also weaponized women's bodies. Researchers exploring Sierra Leone's extremely high figures more recently have raised significant questions about the quality of data collected, though some have claimed the numbers underestimate maternal mortality, while others have found them to overestimate it (WHO, 2015; Young, 2016). The (fairly obvious) takeaway point from this is to use development-related figures with caution, and follow up outliers to determine whether they merit exclusion from further analysis.

As with the other types of charts we have looked at, it is possible to create a scatterplot that splits the results according to a categorical variable, called a grouped scatterplot. Grouped scatterplots are useful for comparing two groups whose values for the continuous variables are fairly distinct from each other. Just as you should severely limit the number of groups you use in a pie chart to achieve maximum visual clarity, this is very important for grouped scatterplots. However, there is an option within the Chart Builder settings to exclude some groups from analysis to achieve this, so you do not have to worry about recoding variables or using the Select Cases command. If using a scatterplot to explore your data, a grouped scatterplot can help you to identify whether your groups appear to exhibit different characteristics before running further tests like comparison of means or regression. Box 8.8 shows you how to produce a grouped scatterplot with limited groups.

BOX 8.8 PRODUCING A GROUPED SCATTERPLOT WITH LIMITED GROUPS

This box explains how to produce a grouped scatterplot that excludes some categories from the grouping variable. This technique for excluding some categories can be applied to all of the other chart types. The results are in Figure 8.10.

Menu instructions

Graphs > Chart Builder

Confirm that your variables have been set to the appropriate measurement level.

Press OK when you're sure, for example, that your two variables are set to scale and one to categorical, to produce a grouped scatterplot.

If you want to clear the settings from a previous chart, press Reset.

> Gallery tab > Scatter/Dot

Drag the second scatterplot option (Grouped Scatter), with green, blue and beige circles, onto the chart area. (If you have trouble distinguishing colours or are not sure which one is the grouped scatterplot, SPSS will show you the label if you hover over the picture.)

> Variables

Drag Human Development Index [hdi] onto the X-Axis? box in the chart area.

Drag Gender Inequality Index [gii] onto the Y-Axis? box in the chart area.

Drag World Bank income group [wbincome] onto the Set pattern box in the chart area.

> Element Properties (use this option to exclude some groups from analysis)

> Edit Properties of > select Group Pattern (Point 1).

> Categories > Order.

Move Upper middle income and Lower middle income into Excluded.

Click Apply.

Click Paste to keep a copy in syntax. Then, in the Syntax window, select the block of text you have produced (starting with GGRAPH and ending with END GPL.) and press the green play triangle.

Or, press OK without pasting.

Syntax

```
GGRAPH
  /GRAPHDATASET NAME='graphdataset' VARIABLES=HDI GII wbincome
MISSING=LISTWISE REPORTMISSING=NO
  /GRAPHSPEC SOURCE=INLINE.
BEGIN GPL
  SOURCE: s=userSource(id('graphdataset'))
  DATA: HDI=col(source(s), name('HDI'))
  DATA: GII=col(source(s), name('GII'))
  DATA: wbincome=col(source(s), name('wbincome'),
notIn('2', '3'), unit.category())
  GUIDE: axis(dim(1), label('Human Development Index (HDI)'))
  GUIDE: axis(dim(2), label('Gender Inequality Index'))
```

(Continued)

```
  GUIDE: legend(aesthetic(aesthetic.shape.interior), label('World Bank
income group'))

  SCALE: cat(aesthetic(aesthetic.shape.interior), include('1', '4'))

  ELEMENT: point(position(HDI*GII), shape.interior(wbincome))

END GPL.
```

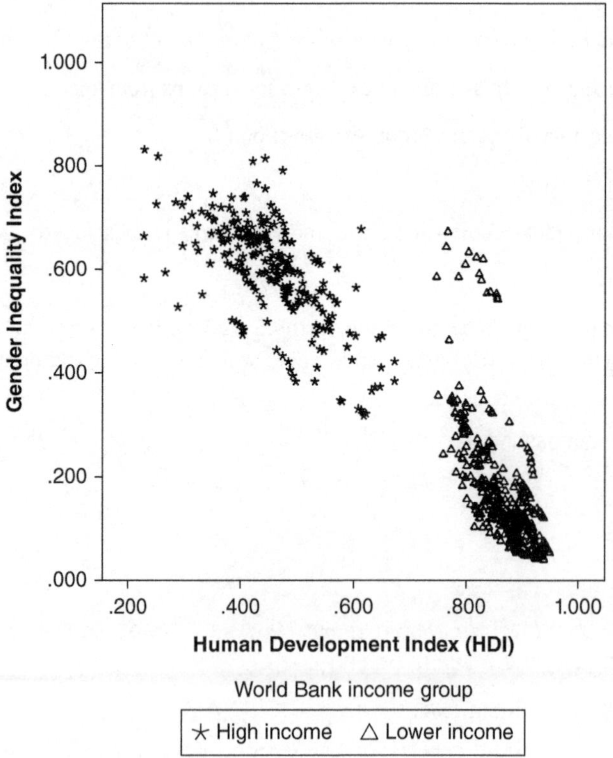

Figure 8.10 Grouped scatterplot of gender inequality [`gii`] and human development [`hdi`], highest and lowest income groups [`wbincome`]

Figure 8.10 shows a comparison of human development and gender inequality between the highest and lowest income groups. This grouped scatterplot conveys a fairly clear pattern: countries classed as low income by the World Bank have noticeably lower levels of human development and higher gender inequality than countries in the highest income group. There is an identifiable cluster of high-income countries that have a high level of human development but also much higher levels of gender inequality than most of the other high-income country results. If you identify these cases, however, you should find that this cluster is composed of various years of results for Saudi Arabia, the United Arab

Emirates, Kuwait and Qatar. The difference in gender inequality of these four countries compared to other high-income countries is perhaps unsurprising, given the socially conservative societies represented in these countries. Much has been written elsewhere about the possible restraining influence of natural-resource-based (in this case, oil) wealth on the social and democratic development of countries (see, for example, Ross, 2012).

BOXPLOTS

Although boxplots are relatively common in the natural sciences and medicine, they are the least common in political research of all of the charts discussed here. This is partially a reflection on the fact that much public-opinion-based quantitative data is overwhelmingly categorical, but for datasets that do contain continuous variables, boxplots can be a very useful tool for comparing means between different groups of results. Boxplots are very rich in information but take some unpicking to digest.

A boxplot requires one categorical and one continuous variable. Results for the continuous variable are reported for each category in the categorical variable (such as income groups [`wbincome`] or geographic regions [`georegion`] in the UN dataset). The boxplot contains a thick line that shows the median of all results in that category, a symbol indicating the mean, a box that shows the range covering the middle 50 per cent of values (called the *interquartile range* because it extends from the first quartile, or first 25 per cent of values, through the third quartile, or 75 per cent of values), the minimum and maximum (excluding outliers), and outliers.

It is important to understand how SPSS defines outliers in the boxplot, which is somewhat complicated, so we will explore this for a moment before moving on to produce and interpret an example boxplot. The underlying definition of outlying cases that SPSS applies to boxplots is those that are more than 1.5 box lengths lower or higher than the interquartile values. To illustrate this, let's use gross national income (Table 8.2). We have 4,436 observations of gross national income, per capita (purchasing power parity) in our dataset, across all countries and years. The 25th percentile (or first quartile) value is USD 2,426.75, and the 75th percentile (or third quartile) value is USD 18,414.75. (We can learn all this using the Frequencies command.) This means that the box length is USD 15,988, so SPSS would class as outliers values that are more than 1.5 times the box length (USD 23,982) below USD 2,426.75, which would be –USD 21,555.25, but we cannot have negative gross national income, so we would just call this 0; or more than 1.5 times the box length above USD 18,414.75, which would be USD 23,982 more than USD 18,414.75, or USD 42,396.75. SPSS defines as 'extreme outliers' values that lie more than 3 box lengths (in this case, USD 47,964) from the upper or lower boundary of the box. There are, of course, other ways of defining and measuring outliers, but it is important to know how SPSS has calculated them as part of understanding a boxplot. With this overview of the elements of the boxplot in mind, we will work through an example using GNI per capita [`gnipcppp`] as the continuous variable and Freedom House status [e_fh_status] as the categorical variable to explore what, if any, trends there are about income and democratization.

Box 8.9 shows you how to produce a boxplot using one categorical and one continuous variable

Table 8.2 Descriptive statistics for gross national income

N	Valid	4436
	Missing	26
Mean		14053.69
Median		7396.50
Std. dev.		17541.283
Minimum		178
Maximum		129916
Percentiles	25	2426.75
	50	7396.50
	75	18414.75

BOX 8.9 PRODUCING A BOXPLOT

This box shows you how to produce a boxplot using one categorical and one continuous variable. This example uses gross national income per capita, purchasing power parity [gnipcppp] and Freedom House status [e_fh_status]. The results are in Figure 8.11.

Menu instructions

Graphs > Chart Builder

Confirm that your variables have been set to the appropriate measurement level.

Press OK when you're sure, for example, that your one variable is set to scale and one to categorical, to produce a boxplot.

If you want to clear the settings from a previous chart, press Reset.

> Gallery tab > Boxplot.

Drag the first boxplot option (Simple Boxplot), with beige bars, onto the chart area. (If you have trouble distinguishing colours or are not sure which one is the simple boxplot, SPSS will show you the label if you hover over the picture.)

> Variables

Drag Freedom House status [e_fh_status] onto the X-Axis? box in the chart area.

Drag Gross National Income per capita, purchasing power parity [gnipcppp] onto the Y-Axis? box in the chart area.

Click Paste to keep a copy in syntax. Then, in the Syntax window, select the block of text you have produced (starting with GGRAPH and ending with END GPL.) and press the green play triangle.

Or, press OK without pasting.

Syntax

```
GGRAPH

  /GRAPHDATASET NAME='graphdataset' VARIABLES=e_fh_status GNIpcPPP
MISSING=LISTWISE REPORTMISSING=NO

  /GRAPHSPEC SOURCE=INLINE.

BEGIN GPL

  SOURCE: s=userSource(id('graphdataset'))

  DATA: e_fh_status=col(source(s), name('e_fh_status'), unit.category())

  DATA: GNIpcPPP=col(source(s), name('GNIpcPPP'))

  DATA: id=col(source(s), name('$CASENUM'), unit.category())

  GUIDE: axis(dim(1), label('Freedom House status'))

  GUIDE: axis(dim(2), label('Gross National Income per capita, purchasing
 power parity (USD)'))

  SCALE: cat(dim(1), include('1', '2', '3'))

  SCALE: linear(dim(2), include(0))

  ELEMENT:
schema(position(bin.quantile.letter(e_fh_status*GNIpcPPP)), label(id))

END GPL.
```

Figure 8.11 shows distinctly different income profiles between the different Freedom House democracy levels. First, looking at the boxes, we can see that the box is much larger for Free than Partly Free and Not Free. This shows us that the range of incomes covering the middle 50 per cent of results is wider than the other two categories. The lines running through the boxes report the medians for each group, which is the same thing as the 50th percentile, with half of cases falling above the line and half below. To find the exact values for these, you will need to split the file by Freedom House status, then produce the descriptive statistics (Box 8.10).

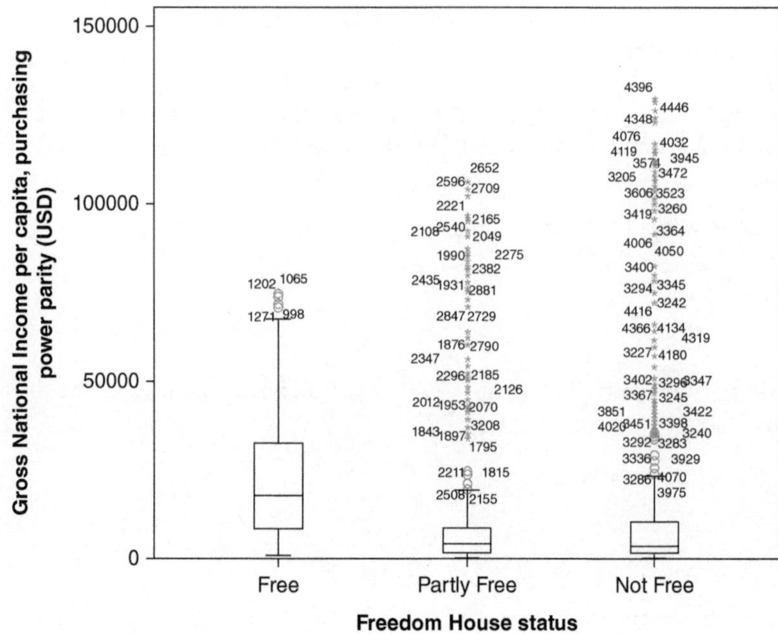

Figure 8.11 Boxplot of GNI [`gnipcppp`] by Freedom House democracy rating [`e_fh_status`]

BOX 8.10 PRODUCING DESCRIPTIVE STATISTICS WITH SPLIT FILE

To produce the descriptive statistics that correspond to the boxplot, you first need to split the file by your categorical variable, then produce the statistical table. The results are in Table 8.3.

Syntax

```
*Split file by Freedom House ratings [e_fh_status].

SORT CASES

BY e_fh_status.

SPLIT FILE LAYERED BY e_fh_status.


*Table 8.3 Descriptives for gross national income [gnipcppp], split by
Freedom House rating [e_fh_status].

FREQUENCIES VARIABLES=GNIpcPPP

  /FORMAT=NOTABLE

  /NTILES=4
```

```
  /STATISTICS=STDDEV MINIMUM MAXIMUM MEAN MEDIAN
  /ORDER=ANALYSIS.


*Turn split file off when finished.
SPLIT FILE OFF.
```

Menu instructions

> Data > Split File

Select Compare groups.

Drag Freedom House status [`e_fh_status`] into Groups Based on box.

Click Paste to keep a copy in syntax. Or, press OK without pasting.

> Analyze > Descriptive Statistics > Frequencies

Drag Gross National Income per capita, purchasing power parity [`gnipcppp`] into Variables box.

Untick Display frequency tables. Press OK if it warns you that you have turned off all output.

> Statistics

Percentiles Values: select Quartiles.

Central Tendency: select Mean and Median.

Dispersion: select Std. deviation, Minimum and Maximum.

Click Continue.

Click Paste to keep a copy in syntax.

Then, in the Syntax window, select the block of text you have produced (starting with `SORT CASES` and ending with `/ORDER=ANALYSIS.`) and press the green play triangle.

Or, press OK without pasting.

Remember to turn Split File off (Data > Split File > Analyze all cases, do not create groups > OK) when you are finished, or it will continue to produce each of your results separately.

Table 8.3 shows that the differences in median incomes between the three different Freedom House groups are substantial: 'Free' countries have a median income (in 2011 USD) of USD 17,930; for 'Partly Free' countries, this drops drastically to USD 4,203.50; and for 'Not Free' countries, it is only USD 3,492. In fact, the lower quartile boundary for the Free countries (USD 8,585) is roughly double the median income of the less free countries.

Table 8.3 Descriptives for gross national income [gnipcppp], split by Freedom House rating [e_fh_status]

		Free	Partly Free	Not Free
N	**Valid**	**1649**	**1462**	**1185**
	Missing	**0**	**0**	**26**
Mean		21258.25	8096.45	11490.98
Median		17930.00	4203.50	3492.00
Std. Deviation		15205.679	13730.712	21274.135
Minimum		904	332	178
Maximum		74725	106549	129916
Percentiles	25	8585.00	1680.00	1605.50
	50	17930.00	4203.50	3492.00
	75	32397.50	8835.00	10406.50

All three groups have so many outliers that it is difficult to discern the symbols denoting them. Given how small the boxes are for Partly Free and Not Free, it is probably unsurprising that there are so many cases that fall outside of 1.5 or 3 box lengths beyond the 75th percentile. If you look at the numbers next to the outliers, these are identifying the row numbers of each outlier so that you can follow them up (if desired). You can do this interactively through the Chart Editor or manually by navigating to the corresponding row number in the Data View tab of the Data Editor window. You must keep in mind, though, that these only point to the relevant row as long as you do not re-sort your data according to any other variable. For example, if you carry out some later analysis using the Select Cases function, which will re-sort your data, the boxplot outlier numbers will no longer point you to the correct data rows, and you will need to rerun it to identify the outlier cases. If you want to follow up outliers at a later point, it is a better idea to take note of the corresponding unique case identifier, rather than relying on the rows being correct.

ADJUSTING CHART APPEARANCE IN THE CHART EDITOR

There are a few additional ways of customizing your chart appearance that we did not cover in Chapter 5. This section highlights some additional customizations that are more likely to be relevant to visualizations of continuous data. To open the Chart Editor, double click on your chart in the Output window. When the Chart Editor window opens, click on the chart to open the Properties window. If the Properties window does not open automatically, or you close it by accident, you can always open it again in Chart Editor > Edit > Properties. Some options that are more likely to be useful with continuous data include:

- You can transpose a chart (e.g. turning a column chart into a bar chart) by Options > Transpose Chart.
- You can add labels to a line chart by clicking Elements > Add Markers.
- When showing means on bar charts with one categorical and one continuous variable, you can add error bars through Elements > Show Error Bars.
- You can add gridlines by Options > Show Grid Lines. This can be useful with scatter-plots, histograms and population pyramids to make it easier to interpret the position of data.

Rescaling axes

Sometimes you may wish to rescale the axes, for example to exclude outliers from a histogram where there are so few respondents at the extremes that the bars are not visible to the naked eye. For example, Figure 8.12 shows a population pyramid of birth year and

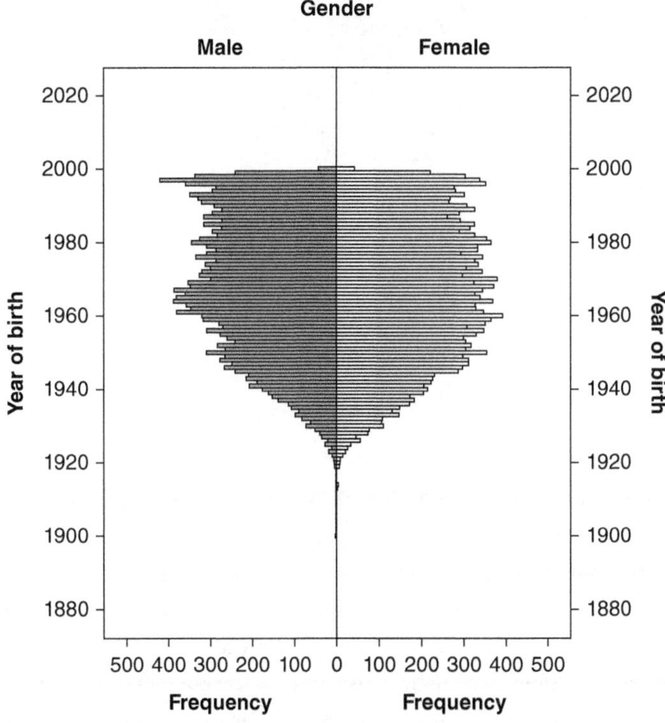

Figure 8.12 Population pyramid of birth year [`yrbrn`] by sex [`gndr`]

sex for the ESS dataset. There are very few respondents born after 2000 or before 1920, and rescaling the axis will make it easier to absorb the information about the rest of the years by spreading them out more (Figure 8.13). You can change the axes by opening Chart Editor and clicking on the y-axis labels. In the Properties window, go to the Scale tab. Change Minimum to 1910 and Maximum to 2000, then click Apply. This makes it easier to see the results. You can also specify the axis range when you are producing the chart through Element Properties > Edit Properties of > X-Axis 1 (Pyramid 1), then changing the Scale Range > Minimum 1920; Maximum 2000 > Apply > OK.

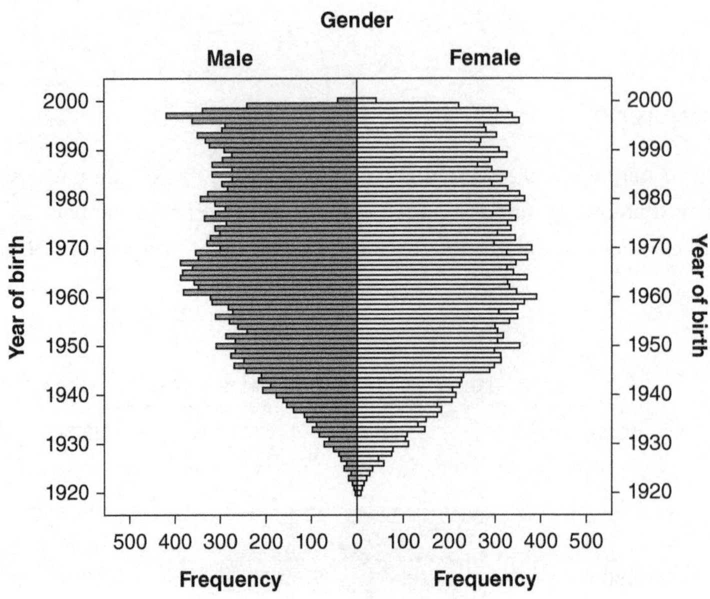

Figure 8.13 Population pyramid of birth year [`yrbrn`] by sex [`gndr`], axes rescaled

Alternative instructions for excluding categories within Chart Editor

You may find that the tool to identify outlier cases for scatterplots works imperfectly if you exclude categories at the Chart Builder stage; or you might decide that your chart is visually confusing and that several of the categories included do not add materially to your understanding of the data. You can exclude categories after producing a chart through Chart Editor by clicking on the data, then selecting the Categories tab in the Properties window. You can move the categories you wish to discard into the Excluded box, then click Apply to activate the changes. Equally, if you wish to reorder the categories, you can do so manually in this tab.

ACTIVITIES

Activity 8.1

RQ: Is democracy increasing globally?

1. Write a hypothesis.
2. Create a simple line chart with means. Place Year [year] on the x-axis and Freedom House average score [fhavg] on the y-axis. Rescale the y-axis to run from 1 (completely free) to 7 (not free). Set the major increment to 1. Add major gridlines to box the x- and y-axis. Look at your result. What does this mean for the spread of democracy in the world? In what year was democracy most widespread?
3. Create a multiple line chart with means. Place Year [year] on the x-axis and Freedom House average score [fhavg] on the y-axis. Place World Bank income group [wbincome] in the Set pattern box. Look at your result, keeping in mind that a score of 1 is completely free and 7 is not free. What does this mean for theories, such as economic modernization theory, that link higher economic development with higher support for democracy?
4. Repeat these steps using Revised combined Polity score [polity2] instead of Freedom House scores. The Polity measure of democracy runs from -10 (strongly autocratic) to +10 (strongly democratic). How do the results compare to the results using Freedom House data?

Activity 8.2

RQ: How have the numbers and locations of refugees and other populations of concern changed over time?

1. Create a multiple line chart with sums. Place Year [year] on the x-axis and Total population of concern hosted (refugees, asylum-seekers, others of concern) [refplushost] on the y-axis. Place Geographical grouping (UN) [georegion] in the Set pattern box. Which region hosts the most refugees? Does this vary at different points in time?
2. Repeat the chart using Freedom House status [e_fh_status] instead of geographic region. Which Freedom House group (not free, partly free or free) hosted the greatest number of people of concern? Does this vary at different points in time?

Activity 8.3

RQ: How are human development, gender inequality and democracy related?

Create a grouped scatterplot with the Human Development Index [hdi] and Gender Inequality Index [gii], grouped by Freedom House status [fhstatus]. Exclude results for 'partly free'.

1. What do the results show? Is there a positive or negative relationship between gender inequality and human development? Do democratic countries tend to have higher or lower gender inequality and human development in comparison to autocracies? What cases are exceptions from the 'free' group?

(Continued)

2. Run a correlation between human development and gender inequality with the file split by Freedom House status. Are the correlations statistically significant? Which group's correlation is strongest?

FURTHER READING

A comprehensive book on data visualization in SPSS is:

Aldrich, J.O. and Rodriguez, H.M. (2013) *Building SPSS Graphs to Understand Data*. London: Sage.

REFERENCES

Gapminder Foundation (n.d.) (https://www.gapminder.org).

Ross, M.L. (2012) *The Oil Curse: How Petroleum Wealth Shapes the Development of Nations*. Oxford: Princeton University Press.

WHO (2015) *Trends in Maternal Mortality: 1990 to 2015*. Geneva: World Health Organization. (https://www.refworld.org/pdfid/5645ae384.pdf).

Young, F. (2016, 17 Nov) 'The slow road to progress: why is Sierra Leone's maternal mortality rate so high?', *Financial Times*. (https://www.ft.com/content/8205b21e-7b44-11e6-ae24-f193b105145e).

9

COMPARING GROUP MEANS

CHAPTER SUMMARY

Thus far, most of the statistics we have looked at have only worked with one type of variable at a time-either categorical or continuous-with the exception of some of the more advanced data visualizations. This chapter introduces techniques for testing a categorical independent variable with a continuous dependent variable by performing a comparison of means. The chapter introduces the basic comparison of means test as well as inferential tests that allow you to test the significance and strength of differences between different groups.

OBJECTIVES

In this chapter, you will learn:

- What a comparison of means is
- Four different tests to compare means (comparison of means, independent samples t-test, ANOVA and Mann-Whitney U)
- What the underlying assumptions of these tests are and when it is appropriate to use them.

INTRODUCTION

You have already encountered means in Chapter 7 as a measure of central tendency that we can use to describe the characteristics of a single variable. In Chapters 7 and 8, you learned how to visualize this in the form of a histogram, and you learned how to visualize a comparison of means between different categories using a boxplot. This chapter starts with an introduction to the idea of comparison of means before teaching you how to test these relationships using inferential statistics. These inferential statistics allow you to test for the significance and strength of the differences between the groups.

COMPARISON OF MEANS

A comparison of means calculates means separately according to the grouping (categorical) variable. The comparison of means test is appropriate for testing categorical variables against one continuous variable. The categorical variable should normally be your independent (predictor) variable, and the continuous variable should normally be the dependent (outcome) variable. For cases where the reverse is true, it is still possible to run a comparison of means, but the more robust test would be logistic regression (covered in Chapter 10). The inferential statistics taught in this chapter will only work with one independent variable, although you will learn to create a descriptive comparison of means table with more than one categorical variable.

To illustrate what this means and how it works in application, this chapter starts with the research question, Why are Conservatives happier than Liberals? (Napier and Jost, 2008). This research is drawn from a range of studies across many countries that have consistently shown that people with more conservative political views are happier, although the greatest body of research is specific to the United States. This is a finding that has perplexed many and has received periodic attention in the news media (Brooks, 2012; Cooper-White, 2014; Morgan, 2017). We then expand this question to look at other drivers of happiness.

This chapter grapples with several related questions, using the ESS data to explore answers:

- Does the UK fit this trend?
- Why are Conservatives happier?
- Are there alternative explanations that better address the underlying causality?

For example, to answer our first question, we need one categorical variable (Which party feel closer to, United Kingdom `[prtclbgb]`) and one continuous variable (How happy are you `[happy]`). Here, the political parties are the categories, and the comparison of means will calculate the mean happiness for each group. Strictly speaking, happiness is an ordinal variable on an 11-point scale (0 = extremely unhappy; 10 = extremely happy). In practice, researchers tend to treat such large scales as continuous for the sake of analysis, and we will do so here. Think about it this way: it is very difficult to look at a table of percentages with more than 70 cells of numbers for the above two variables; it is much easier to absorb the information portrayed with a single mean for each political party.

We will start with a data visualization to understand comparison of means better. Bar charts are frequently used to portray this kind of information, with the categorical variable on the horizontal (x-)axis and the mean or count of the continuous variable portrayed on the vertical (y-)axis. By creating a bar chart, we can quickly see whether there does appear to be a difference between those who identify with different political parties, thereby forming a preliminary answer to our research question (Box 9.1).

BOX 9.1 BAR CHART COMPARING MEAN HAPPINESS BY POLITICAL PARTY IDENTIFICATION

This box shows you how to create a bar chart with means using Which party feel closer to, UK `[prtclbgb]` and How happy are you `[happy]`. Results are filtered only to include the main national parties: Conservative (1), Labour (2), Liberal Democrat (3), Green (6), UKIP (7) and Not applicable (no party affiliation, 66). Make sure that 'not applicable' has been reclassified so that it is not a missing value. The results are in Figure 9.1.

Menu instructions

Graphs > Chart Builder

(Continued)

Confirm that your variables have been set to the appropriate measurement level.

Press OK when you're sure, for example, that one of your variables is set as scale and one is set as nominal or ordinal for a bar chart with means. You may need to change the setting on `happy` from ordinal to scale.

If you want to clear the settings from a previous chart, press Reset.

> Gallery tab > Bar

Drag the first bar chart option (Simple Bar), with beige bars, onto the chart area. (If you have trouble distinguishing colours or are not sure which one is the simple bar chart, IBM SPSS Statistics ('SPSS') will show you the label if you hover over the picture.)

> Variables

Drag Which party feel closer to, United Kingdom [`prtclbgb`] onto the X-Axis? box in the chart area.

Drag How happy are you [`happy`] onto the y-axis (where it says Count) in the chart area.

> Element Properties

> Edit Properties of: Select Bar1. Under Statistic, make sure the drop-down menu is set to Mean, not Value.

> Edit Properties of: Select X-Axis1. Under Categories > Order: move all parties except Conservative, Labour, Liberal Democrat, Green, UK Independence Party and Not applicable to Excluded box.

Click Apply at the bottom of the Element Properties window.

Click Paste to keep a copy in syntax. Then, in the Syntax window, select the block of text you have produced and press the green play triangle.

Or, press OK without pasting.

Syntax

```
GGRAPH

  /GRAPHDATASET NAME='graphdataset' VARIABLES=prtclbgb MEAN(happy)
[name='MEAN_happy']

  MISSING=LISTWISE REPORTMISSING=NO

  /GRAPHSPEC SOURCE=INLINE.

BEGIN GPL

  SOURCE: s=userSource(id('graphdataset'))

  DATA: prtclbgb=col(source(s), name('prtclbgb'),

notIn('5', '4', '18', '17', '16', '15', '14', '13', '12', '11', '10',
'9', '8'),unit.category())
```

```
  DATA: MEAN_happy=col(source(s), name('MEAN_happy'))
  GUIDE: axis(dim(1), label('Which party feel closer to, United Kingdom'))
  GUIDE: axis(dim(2), label('Mean How happy are you'))
  SCALE: cat(dim(1), include('1', '2', '3', '6', '7', '66'))
  SCALE: linear(dim(2), include(0))
  ELEMENT: interval(position(prtclbgb*MEAN_happy), shape.interior(shape.
square))
END GPL.
```

Add data labels by opening the Chart Editor.

Elements > Show Data Labels

Click once on one of the labels to open the Data Value Labels options.

To place the labels at the end of the bars:

Data Value Labels > Label Position > Custom

Select the grid option that has the text box at the top of the bar.

Apply.

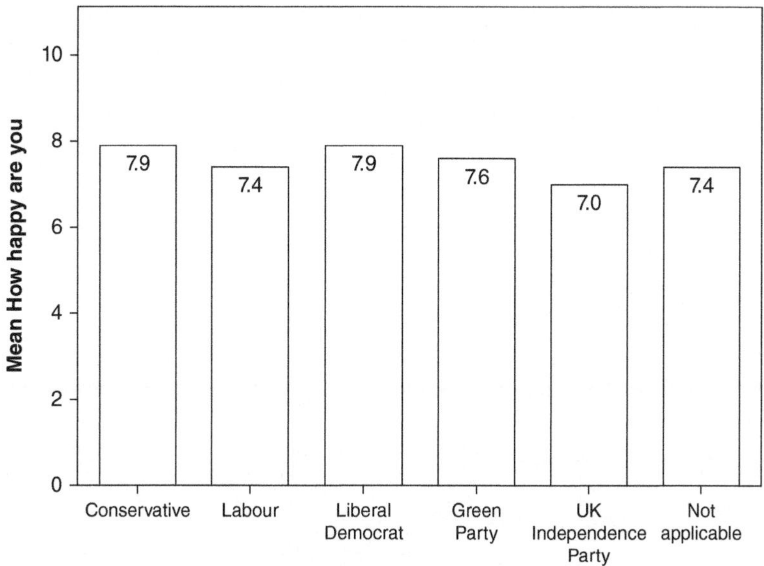

Figure 9.1 Mean happiness by political party identification

A quick look at the resulting chart (Figure 9.1) seems to indicate that Conservatives and Lib Dems are the happiest, and UKIP supporters are the least happy, but this is only a visual estimate. We must also keep in mind that this does not tell us whether the difference between groups is significant or whether the data in the different categories is actually suitable for comparison. We will take the first step towards checking this by running a descriptive comparison of means test. This test will produce information about the mean, count and standard deviation but will not give us information about statistical significance or strength of relationship.

BOX 9.2 BIVARIATE DESCRIPTIVE COMPARISON OF MEANS

This box shows you how to run a descriptive comparison of means using one categorical predictor and one continuous outcome variable. You can add additional categorical variables to add to the complexity (Box 9.3), but you can only work with one continuous variable at a time. This example uses Which party feel closer to, United Kingdom [prtclbgb] and How happy are you [happy].

Syntax

Filter results only to use the main national parties (Conservatives=1, Labour=2, Liberal Democrat=3, Green=6, UKIP=7) and respondents with no political affiliation (not applicable=66). The filter here has been renamed from filter_$ to filter_party.

```
USE ALL.

COMPUTE filter_party=(prtclbgb=1 OR prtclbgb=2 OR prtclbgb=3 OR
prtclbgb=6 OR prtclbgb=7 OR prtclbgb=66).

VARIABLE LABELS filter_party 'Main UK national parties (FILTER)'.

VALUE LABELS filter_party 0 'Not Selected' 1 'Selected'.

FORMATS filter_party (f1.0).

FILTER BY filter_party.

EXECUTE.
```

Produce comparison of means table.

```
MEANS TABLES=happy BY prtclbgb

  /CELLS=MEAN COUNT STDDEV.
```

Menu instructions

Filter results only to main national parties and no political affiliation.

Data > Select Cases > If condition is satisfied > If

Find the filtering variable [prtclbgb] in the list of variables and drag it into the main box or just type 'prtclbgb' in the main box to the right of the arrow, followed by = and the first party's value (1 for Conservative):

prtclbgb=1

Follow each value with OR to include responses matching any of the selected parties until it reads:

prtclbgb = 1 OR prtclbgb = 2 OR prtclbgb = 3 OR prtclbgb = 6 OR prtclbgb = 7 OR prtclbgb=66

Click Continue.

Click Paste to keep a copy in syntax. Then, in the Syntax window, select the block of text you have produced and press the green play triangle.

Or, press OK without pasting.

Produce comparison of means table.

Analyze > Compare Means > Means

Continuous variable (How happy are you [happy]) > Dependent List

Categorical variable (Which party feel closer to, United Kingdom [prtclbgb]) > Layer 1 of 1

Click Paste to keep a copy in syntax. Then, in the Syntax window, select the block of text you have produced and press the green play triangle.

Or, press OK without pasting.

Table 9.1 shows us the same mean as we saw in the labels on the bar chart but also gives us the number of respondents and the standard deviation for each group's mean. These are very important for satisfying the assumptions of the inferential tests we will learn in the rest of this chapter. We will first interpret the means, however, before we address the other two columns.

Remembering that our scale ran from 0 (least happy) to 10 (happiest), we can see that the mean for these UK respondents was 7.48. Of the selected UK parties shown here, Conservatives are happiest, at 7.95. Though there is a difference between our groups–as we already noted from the chart–the difference is not huge, with the UKIP supporters coming in least happy but still only 0.91 points behind the Conservatives. Thus far, the table does not offer any more information than the chart. However, the table shows that the number of respondents varies considerably between the different groups, with the Conservative and Labour groups having many times the number of respondents of the Liberal Democrats and Greens, and far more people expressing no political affiliation (1057) than identification with any of the parties. We can also see that the standard deviation is greater among the two groups who seem to be the least happy: Labour and UKIP. This indicates that there is much more variation within those two groups than within the other four groups, who all have much smaller standard deviations.

Table 9.1 Mean happiness [happy] by UK political party identification [prtclbgb], selected parties

Political affiliation	Mean	N	Std. dev.
Conservative	7.95	371	1.711
Labour	7.38	415	2.091
Liberal Democrat	7.88	64	1.609
Green Party	7.64	56	1.623
UKIP	7.04	166	2.292
Not applicable	7.39	1057	2.009
Total	7.48	2129	1.995

What could be other explanations for variations in happiness? Some of the most obvious would be explanations based on employment (see, for example, Main activity, last 7 days. All respondents. Post coded [mnactic]), general health (see the series of health-related variables starting with hltpr) and income [hinctnta]. Let's take a moment to look at the results for happiness based on the subjective income variable, feeling about household income [hinfel] (Table 9.2). Here we can see that those who said they were 'living comfortably on present income' were much happier (mean 8.15 out of 10) than those who were finding it 'very difficult on present income' (mean 4.96 out of 10), and each increase in subjective income category is accompanied by a noticeable increase in reported happiness.

This would seem to indicate that, contrary to the popular adage, money can buy you a certain amount of happiness. The differences in means between these groups appear to be much larger than the differences in means between different political affiliations, so we will expect from our inferential statistics that there might be a stronger relationship between these two variables. We can also see that the standard deviation is lower for each increase in income groups, as are the group sizes: there were far fewer people who placed themselves in the categories of life being difficult (301)/very difficult (96), compared to living comfortably (883) and coping (967) on present income.

Table 9.2 Mean happiness by feeling about household income, UK respondents

Feeling about household's income	Mean	N	Std. dev.
Living comfortably on present income	8.15	883	1.463
Coping on present income	7.39	967	1.842
Difficult on present income	6.55	301	2.409
Very difficult on present income	4.96	96	2.824
Total	7.47	2247	1.996

Returning to our original question, though, we can ask to what extent subjective household income is a mitigating factor, or whether Conservatives (but not conservatives) in the UK are happier, regardless of income. One way to test this would be to create a multivariate comparison of means test, using two categorical variables (political party identification and feeling about household income) and one continuous variable (happiness). Box 9.3 shows you how to do this.

BOX 9.3 MULTIVARIATE COMPARISON OF MEANS

This box shows you how to run a multivariate comparison of means with two categorical predictors and one continuous outcome variable. This example uses Feeling about household income nowadays [hincfel], Which party feel closer to, United Kingdom [prtclbgb] and How happy are you [happy]. The results are in Table 9.3.

Syntax

Follow the instructions in Box 9.2 to filter results for the main UK national political parties and no political affiliation.

```
MEANS TABLES=happy BY hincfel BY prtclbgb

  /CELLS=MEAN COUNT STDDEV.
```

In the syntax, when adding additional categorical variables to the same table, add BY before each categorical variable. Without BY, SPSS will interpret it as a command to create separate tables.

Menu instructions

Follow instructions in Box 9.2 to filter results to supporters of UK national parties.

Analyze > Compare Means > Means

Continuous variable (How happy are you [happy]) > Dependent List.

First categorical variable (Feeling about household income nowadays [hincfel]) > Layer 1 of 1.

Click Next.

Categorical variable (Which party feel closer to, United Kingdom [prtclbgb]) > Layer 2 of 2.

Click Paste to keep a copy in syntax. Then, in the Syntax window, select the block of text you have produced and press the green play triangle.

Or, press OK without pasting.

Table 9.3 Happiness by political party affiliation and feeling about household income

	Party affiliation	Living comfortably on present income	Coping on present income	Difficult on present income	Very difficult on present income	Total
Mean	Conservative	8.40	7.36	7.63	3.67	7.95
	Labour	8.18	7.44	6.56	4.88	7.38
	Liberal Democrat	8.31	7.50	6.75	6.00	7.88
	Green Party	7.71	7.95	6.80	7.00	7.60
	UKIP	8.03	6.93	5.64	5.25	7.04
	Not applicable	8.02	7.41	6.52	5.13	7.39
	Total	8.15	7.39	6.56	5.07	7.48
N	Conservative	214	130	24	3	371
	Labour	132	191	63	26	412
	Liberal Democrat	35	24	4	1	64
	Green Party	24	19	10	2	55
	UKIP	58	74	25	8	165
	Not applicable	370	472	162	46	1050
	Total	833	910	288	86	2117
Std. dev.	Conservative	1.258	2.015	1.765	1.528	1.711
	Labour	1.629	1.755	2.340	3.011	2.086
	Liberal Democrat	1.078	2.085	1.258	.	1.609
	Green Party	1.429	1.682	1.619	2.828	1.606
	UKIP	1.825	2.096	2.580	3.012	2.299
	Not applicable	1.513	1.779	2.545	2.786	2.009
	Total	1.484	1.845	2.427	2.802	1.993

In Table 9.3 (which has been rearranged after production to make comparison easier), we can see that Conservatives appear to be happier than other respondents across different subjective income levels. We will discount the results for the column 'Very difficult on present income' because the number of respondents from all parties except Labour and no affiliation are so small. Focusing particularly on the comparison between Conservative, Labour and UKIP, which are the three with the greatest number of respondents, there is an inconsistent trend of Conservatives being happier than Labourites, with Conservatives happier on 'living comfortably' and 'difficult' but Labourites happier on 'coping'. UKIP supporters are least happy of these three at each income level. This does not precisely align with the theory that conservatives (with a small c) are happier, since UKIP is generally classed as falling on the right of the political spectrum, but it does give some support for the idea that Conservatives (with a large C) are happier.

INFERENTIAL TESTS FOR COMPARISON OF MEANS

Thus far, we can see what looks like a difference in happiness between our groups, but we cannot be sure whether these differences are statistically significant or how consistent or strong these differences might be. We saw, for example, relatively minor differences between our political affiliation groups, with the least happy people being UKIP supporters and the happiest being Conservatives; but this difference was less than 1, and the difference between Labour supporters and UKIP supporters was only 0.3. So how do we know whether this actually means something–that the groups actually have different levels of happiness? We will start by looking at a visualization of what we mean when we're looking for statistically significant differences between groups. We can do this by producing a special kind of bar chart called a simple error bar. To do this, follow the instructions in Box 9.4.

BOX 9.4 SIMPLE ERROR BAR CHART OF HAPPINESS BY POLITICAL PARTY IDENTIFICATION

This box shows you how to create a simple error bar chart with using Which party feel closer to, UK [prtclbgb] and How happy are you [happy]. This chart will visually show means and

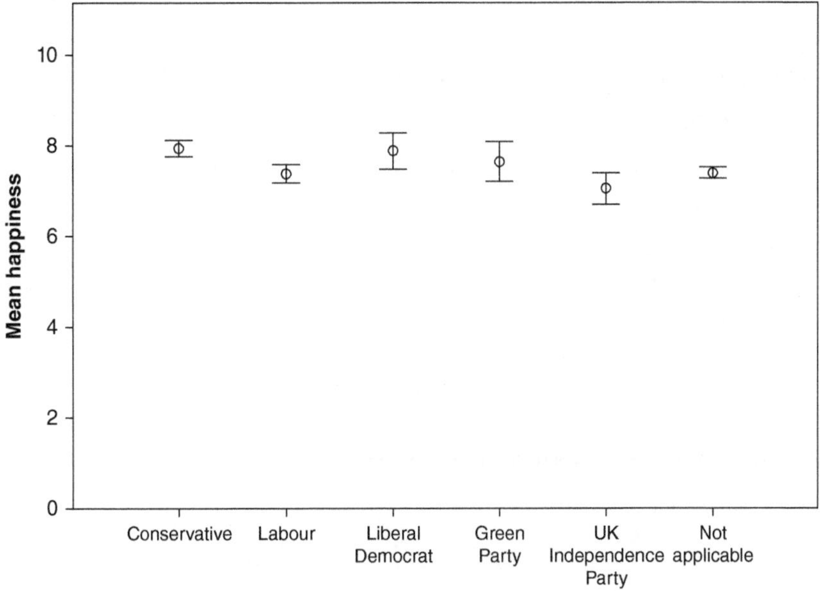

Figure 9.2 Error bar chart of happiness by political party identification, UK

(Continued)

confidence intervals. Results are filtered only to include the main national parties: Conservative (1), Labour (2), Liberal Democrat (3), Green (6), UKIP (7) and Not applicable (no party affiliation, 66). Make sure that 'not applicable' has been reclassified so that it is not a missing value. The results are in Figure 9.2.

Menu instructions

Graphs > Chart Builder

Confirm that your variables have been set to the appropriate measurement level.

Press OK when you're sure, for example, that one of your variables is set as scale and one is set as nominal or ordinal for a bar chart with means. You may need to change the setting on `happy` from ordinal to scale.

If you want to clear the settings from a previous chart, press Reset.

> Gallery tab > Bar

Drag the bar chart option towards the end of the list that looks like circles with lines running vertically through them (Simple Error Bar) onto the chart area. (If you are not sure which one is the simple error bar chart, SPSS will show you the label if you hover over the picture.)

> Variables

Drag Which party feel closer to, United Kingdom [`prtclbgb`] onto the X-Axis? box in the chart area.

Drag How happy are you [`happy`] onto the y-axis (where it says Mean) in the chart area.

> Element Properties

> Edit Properties of: Select Point1. Under Statistic, make sure the drop-down menu is set to Mean, not Value.

> Edit Properties of: Select X-Axis1. Under Categories > Order: move all parties except Conservative, Labour, Liberal Democrat, Green, 'UK Independence Party' and Not applicable to Excluded box.

Click Apply at the bottom of the Element Properties window.

Click Paste to keep a copy in syntax. Then, in the Syntax window, select the block of text you have produced and press the green play triangle.

Or, press OK without pasting.

Syntax

```
GGRAPH

  /GRAPHDATASET NAME='graphdataset' VARIABLES=prtclbgb MEANCI(happy,
95)[name='MEAN_happy'
```

```
  LOW='MEAN_happy_LOW' HIGH='MEAN_happy_HIGH'] MISSING=LISTWISE RE-
PORTMISSING=NO
 /GRAPHSPEC SOURCE=INLINE.
BEGIN GPL
 SOURCE: s=userSource(id('graphdataset'))
 DATA: prtclbgb=col(source(s), name('prtclbgb'),
notIn('4', '5', '8', '9', '10', '11', '12', '13', '14', '15', '16',
'17', '18'), unit.category())
 DATA: MEAN_happy=col(source(s), name('MEAN_happy'))
 DATA: LOW=col(source(s), name('MEAN_happy_LOW'))
 DATA: HIGH=col(source(s), name('MEAN_happy_HIGH'))
 GUIDE: axis(dim(1), label('Which party feel closer to, United Kingdom'))
 GUIDE: axis(dim(2), label('Mean How happy are you'))
 GUIDE: text.footnote(label('Error Bars: 95% CI'))
 SCALE: cat(dim(1), include('1', '2', '3', '6', '7', '66'))
 SCALE: linear(dim(2), include(0))
 ELEMENT: point(position(prtclbgb*MEAN_happy))
 ELEMENT:
interval(position(region.spread.range(prtclbgb*(LOW+HIGH))),shape.interior
(shape.ibeam))
END GPL.
```

Figure 9.2 represents the mean with a circle and portrays the range within which we would expect the mean to fall 95 per cent of the time if we kept resampling the same population (the 95 per cent confidence interval). To be completely confident that the results are truly different between groups, we would want not only for the mean (circles) to be different but also that the error bars of each category would not overlap each other at all. Figure 9.2 includes gridlines to make it easier to figure out whether this is the case. Let's look at the results for Conservatives and Labourites. We can see that the mean is noticeably higher for Conservative than Labour. We can also see that the lower end of the Conservative error bar is slightly higher than the upper end of the Labour error bar. This indicates to us a high degree of confidence that Conservatives really are happier than Labourites. If, however, we compare Labour to any of the other categories, we can see that there are overlaps between the heights of the various error bars. We also see that the error bars are longer for Liberal Democrat, Green and UKIP than for Conservative, Labour and None; this is also reflective of the fact that these are smaller samples, so unless they have a very clear, consistent result, we will be less confident of where the real population mean falls.

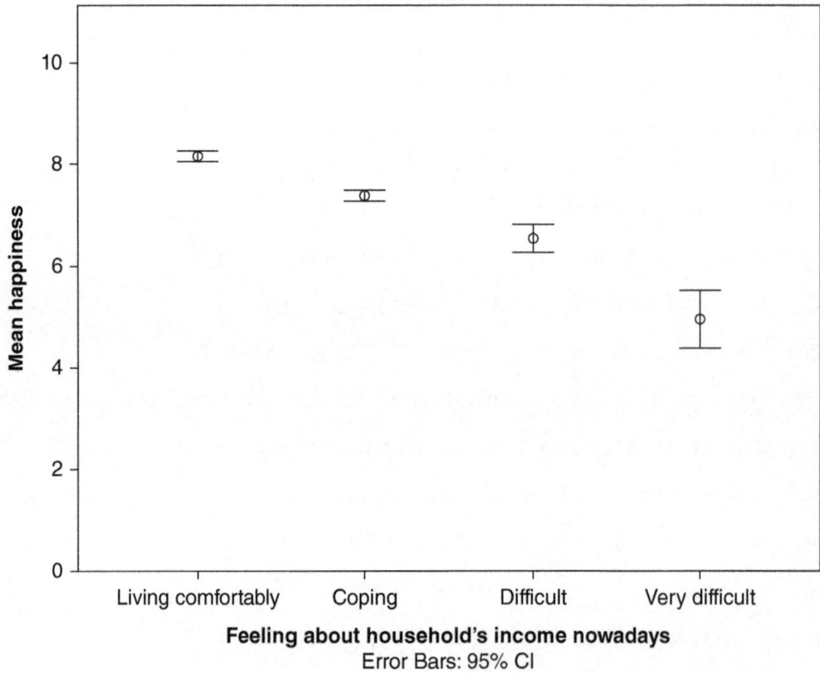

Figure 9.3 Error bar chart of happiness by subjective income, UK

For comparison, look at Figure 9.3. In this case, none of the error bars overlaps at all with any of the other categories. As we would expect from the smaller sample sizes and larger standard deviations in the lower income groups, the error bars are longer, with the largest range of possible values of the mean for 'very difficult'. We have now visually confirmed statistically significant differences between Conservatives, on the one hand, and Labour, UKIP and no party affiliation, on the other, but not between any of the other party affiliations. And we have visually confirmed statistically significant differences between different levels of subjective household income. If we want to report the numerical values accompanying these visual representations, however, we will need to run a statistical test. The next section discusses the various merits of the most common tests before showing you how to do them, continuing with the same examples.

T-test vs one-way ANOVA

To check for statistically significant differences between means, the classic statistical method taught for generations of students was the t-test. Because of its continued dominance in statistics teaching, we will address the t-test in this section, but we make a strong argument in favour of skipping the t-test entirely and using analysis of variance (ANOVA), if you have a choice. Both the t-test and ANOVA are parametric tests, which means that they make certain assumptions about the data. If these assumptions are violated, then you would need to look at comparing means using a non-parametric technique, such as bootstrapping, a Mann–Whitney U test or Kruskal–Wallis test. We will deal first with parametric tests (t-test and ANOVA) and then with non-parametric tests (bootstrapping, Mann–Whitney U and Kruskal–Wallis tests).

Until recently, the t-test was such a staple of introductory statistics teaching that it is also referred to as Student's t-test. A t-test is used to compare the means between precisely two groups of similar size. (This is the first, major limitation.) The t-test also produces a series of statistics in SPSS that require further manipulation to calculate the strength of the difference. (This is the second, major limitation.) While it is relatively straightforward to determine whether there is a statistically significant difference between the groups, the necessity of undertaking further calculations to determine the strength of the relationship means this element is frequently neglected, resulting in incomplete analysis of the meaningfulness of the results.

As we have argued elsewhere, the strength of the relationship is, in nearly all cases, the more important piece of information because you can have a statistically significant but incredibly weak result (who cares?), but you cannot have a strong result that is not statistically significant. The sensitivity of statistical significance to sample sizes further limits its utility. This is compounded by reports in the natural sciences of researchers manipulating their p-values to show statistical significance in order to get their research published (Resnick, 2017). The final nail in the coffin for overreliance on p-values is that rejecting data that is statistically insignificant can actually lead to the non-reporting of real results, as vocal Null Hypothesis Significance Test critic Andy Field has demonstrated repeatedly (Field, 2011, 2012, 2013b).

ASSUMPTIONS

T-tests and ANOVA share most of their underlying assumptions about the data. The shared assumptions are:

1. Categorical predictor (independent) variable.
2. Continuous outcome (dependent) variable.
3. Independent observations.
4. Normal distribution.
5. Equal variances (homogeneity of variances, homoscedasticity).

Variables

Let's look in greater detail at each of these assumptions in turn. First, the predictor variable must be categorical. This is a much easier assumption to meet because continuous variables can always be recoded into categories. The key difference between the t-test and ANOVA regards the number of categories: the t-test will only work with two categories, while ANOVA works with two or more categories. If using a t-test, this often means recoding categories into two groups, or selecting only two groups at a time, before running the test. Second, the dependent variable should be continuous. As we have discussed elsewhere, there are relatively few truly continuous variables when working with public opinion data; instead, many Likert scales with seven or more categories are treated as continuous for analysis.

Third, the observations must be independent. This means that respondents cannot be included in more than one group. This is relatively rare but could occur, for example, in response to a survey question that prompts respondents to 'tick all that apply'. This parameter is more applicable in experimental settings, where it is important to ensure that the participants are separated and that no participant appears in both groups.

Normality and homogeneity of variance

Fourth, these tests assume that the data is normally distributed. This is the same assumption of normality that we have encountered elsewhere, which is based on the central limit theorem. For sample data, the assumption is that experimental errors (measured as residuals) will be evenly distributed. This assumption is based on trying to estimate that the mean in your sample actually occurs within the population as a whole. In practice if your data is roughly normally distributed, the errors will probably be normally distributed as well, so judging by the shape of your data will be sufficient. Normal distribution of errors is also only relevant for sample data but not for census data. For large sample sizes and whole-population data (e.g. census data or a dataset about democracies that includes all democracies in the world), this assumption is about the data itself being normally distributed rather than the errors.

An important point about the assumption of normality when undertaking a comparison of means is that it assumes the data for the continuous variable is normally distributed *within each group*, not across groups. This is important because your data might not have a normal distribution when all of the groups are merged, but when the data is separated out into groups, the distribution might be completely normal. In fact, tests from statisticians have shown that ANOVA is relatively accurate even with somewhat skewed data, though you should still consider excluding outliers and will have trouble if using data that does not have an inverted u-shape. For example, the data for total household income [`hinctnta`] (Figure 9.4) shows that the distribution of responses within various groups is not normal, especially for respondents with no political party affiliation. This means it would not be an eligible continuous variable to use for ANOVA. Box 9.5 shows you how to create this specialized type of histogram to run a visual check for normality.

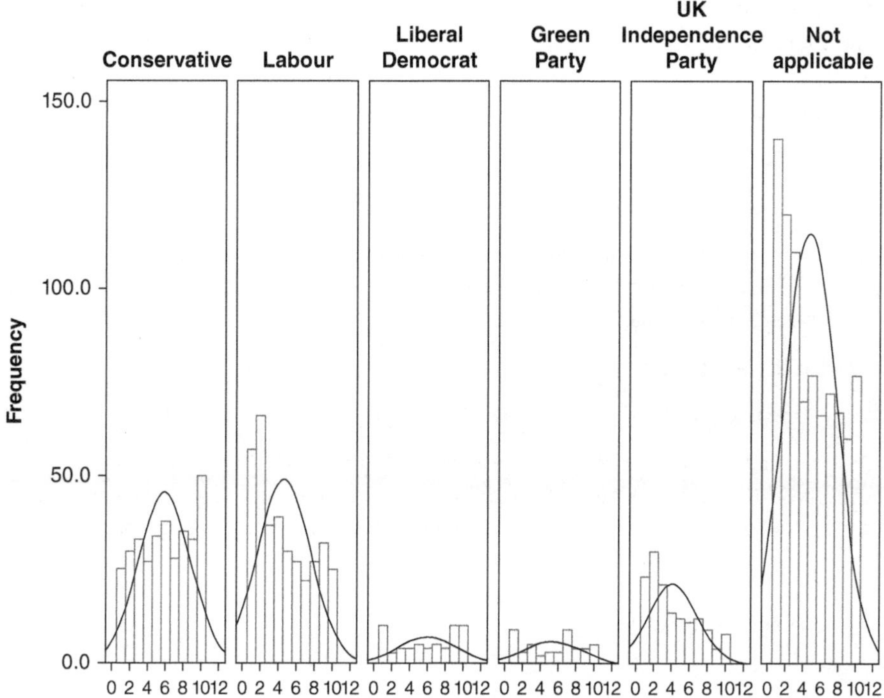

Figure 9.4 Column panel histogram of household income [hinctnta] by party affiliation

The assumption of normality is only truly important for ANOVA when you have a very small *N* (less than 40, as a rule of thumb), a very non-normal distribution, or a small effect size. (Remember how we keep going on about effect sizes being more important than statistical significance?) There is reasonable evidence that ANOVA even holds up well when the data is not normally distributed if group sizes are fairly equal, but errors creep in when the comparison groups are considerably different in size.

BOX 9.5 COLUMN PANEL HISTOGRAM FOR CHECKING NORMALITY

This box shows you how to produce a panel of histograms for a continuous variable that splits the results using a categorical variable. This test is appropriate for one categorical independent (predictor) variable and one continuous dependent (outcome) variable. This example uses Which party closer to, UK [prtclbgb] as the categorical predictor variable and How happy are you [happy] as the continuous outcome variable. Results with UK party affiliation have been

(Continued)

filtered to include national parties and no party affiliation ('not applicable'). The results can be found in Figure 9.5.

Menu instructions

Graphs > Chart Builder

Confirm that your variables have been set to the appropriate measurement level.

Press OK when you're sure, for example, that one of your variables is set as scale and one is set as nominal or ordinal for a bar chart with means. You may need to change the setting on `happy` from ordinal to scale.

If you want to clear the settings from a previous chart, press Reset.

> Gallery tab > Histogram

Drag the first histogram chart option (Simple Histogram), with beige bars, onto the chart area. (If you have trouble distinguishing colours or are not sure which one is the simple histogram, SPSS will show you the label if you hover over the picture.)

> Groups/Point ID

Tick Columns panel variable.

> Variables

Drag How happy are you [`happy`] onto the X-Axis? box in the chart area.

Drag Which party feel closer to, United Kingdom [`prtclbgb`] onto the Panel? box in the chart area.

> Element Properties

> Edit Properties of: Select Bar1. Under Statistic, make sure the drop-down menu is set to Histogram. Tick Display normal curve.

> Edit Properties of: Select Columns Panel (Bar 1). Under Categories > Order: move all parties except Conservative, Labour, Liberal Democrat, Green, 'UK Independence Party' and Not applicable to Excluded box.

Click Apply at the bottom of the Element Properties window.

Click Paste to keep a copy in syntax. Then, in the Syntax window, select the block of text you have produced and press the green play triangle.

Or, press OK without pasting.

Syntax

```
GGRAPH

  /GRAPHDATASET NAME='graphdataset' VARIABLES=happy prtclbgb MISSING=
LISTWISE REPORTMISSING=NO

  /GRAPHSPEC SOURCE=INLINE.
```

```
BEGIN GPL
  SOURCE: s=userSource(id('graphdataset'))
  DATA: happy=col(source(s), name('happy'))
  DATA: prtclbgb=col(source(s), name('prtclbgb'),
notIn('4', '5', '6', '8', '9', '10', '11', '12', '13', '14', '15', '16',
'17', '18'),
    unit.category())
  GUIDE: axis(dim(1), label('How happy are you'))
  GUIDE: axis(dim(2), label('Frequency'))
  GUIDE: axis(dim(3), label('Which party feel closer to, United Kingdom'),
opposite())
  SCALE: cat(dim(3), include('1', '2', '3', '7', '66'))
  ELEMENT: interval(position(summary.count(bin.rect(happy*1*prtclbgb))),
  shape.interior(shape.square))
  ELEMENT: line(position(density.normal(happy*1*prtclbgb)), color
('Normal'))
END GPL.
```

In comparison to Figure 9.4, we can see that the data for happiness is fairly normally distributed within each group for happiness (Figure 9.5). There is a slight skew towards being more happy than neutral, but there is a clear u-shaped distribution.

Finally, these tests assume equal variances. This means that deviation from the mean should not be vastly different within each of the categories. You can get a general idea by checking the column panel histogram when you check for normality. The more robust check is to consult the variance statistics, which you can produce at the same time as a descriptive comparison of means. One rule of thumb to follow to determine whether you have violated the equal variances assumption is to calculate the ratio of the largest variance to the smallest (largest/smallest = variance ratio). If the ratio exceeds 9, then you have violated the assumption of equal variance. You might notice from this ratio that this actually allows for considerable variation between groups: one group is allowed to have a spread that is nine times greater than the group with the least variation! Some statisticians advocate a ratio of 4. A classic way of testing for the violation of this assumption is to use Levene's test. However, others (Field, 2013a: 194; Zimmerman, 2004) have made good arguments against employing this test because the test is more likely to indicate a problem if there is a slight variation between groups in large samples; and it does not work well with small sample sizes or unequal group sizes. As you can see, academics rarely agree on

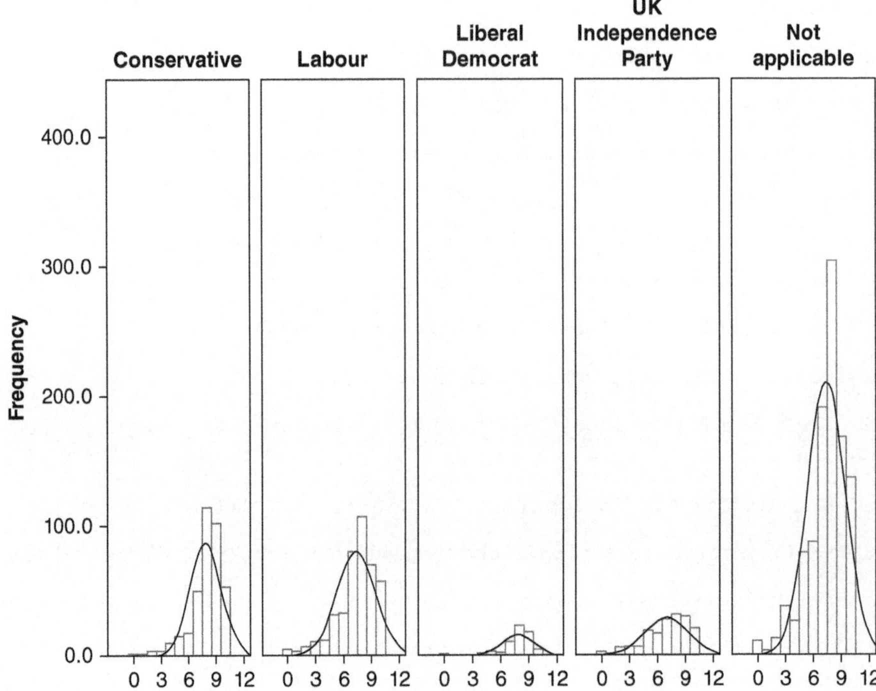

Figure 9.5 Column panel histogram of happiness by political party affiliation, UK

anything, even mathematics. Whatever threshold or test you choose, if this assumption is violated, you will need to transform your data or exclude some observations, as this will influence your results.

BOX 9.6 BIVARIATE DESCRIPTIVE COMPARISON OF MEANS WITH VARIANCE

This box shows you how to produce a descriptive comparison of means with variance statistics. The results can be found in Table 9.4.

Syntax

The syntax for this is very simple: just add VAR to the cell statistics from the table we produced in Box 9.2. Follow the instructions in Box 9.2 to filter results for the main UK national political parties and no political affiliation.

```
MEANS TABLES=happy BY prtclbgb

  /CELLS=MEAN COUNT STDDEV VAR.
```

Menu instructions

Follow the instructions in Box 9.2 to filter results for the main UK national political parties and no political affiliation.

Analyze > Compare Means > Means

Continuous variable (How happy are you [happy]) > Dependent List.

Categorical variable (Which party feel closer to, United Kingdom [prtclbgb]). > Layer 1 of 1

> Options

Add Variance to Cell Statistics.

Click Continue.

Click Paste to keep a copy in syntax. Then, in the Syntax window, select the block of text you have produced and press the green play triangle.

Or, press OK without pasting.

Table 9.4 Mean happiness by political party affiliation, including variance

Party affiliation	Mean	N	Std. dev.	Variance
Conservative	7.95	371	1.711	2.927
Labour	7.38	415	2.091	4.370
Liberal Democrat	7.88	64	1.609	2.587
Green Party	7.64	56	1.623	2.634
UKIP	7.04	166	2.292	5.253
Not applicable	7.39	1057	2.009	4.036
Total	7.48	2129	1.995	3.978

Follow the instructions in Box 9.6 to produce a comparison of means with the variance statistics. (You can calculate this yourself by squaring the standard deviation.) In Table 9.4, the highest variance is for UKIP supporters (5.253). The smallest is for Conservative supporters (2.927). The ratio of these variances is 1.794 (5.253/1.794), which satisfies even the stricter ratio of 4:1, so we will conclude that we have not violated the assumption of equal variances with this example. If we check this for our other variable pair (happiness and subjective household income), there is greater variance between our groups (Table 9.5). Here the largest ratio is between living comfortably (2.142) and very difficult on present income (7.977). This makes a ratio of 3.724, which still meets the stricter rule of thumb of a ratio of 4:1. If we had mildly violated the 4:1 ratio but not the 9:1 ratio, we might choose to exclude this most volatile group(s) from further analysis. Here, we might choose to exclude 'very difficult' in any case because the sample size is so much smaller than the other groups.

Table 9.5 Mean happiness by subjective household income, including variance, UK

Feeling about household's income	Mean	N	Std. dev.	Variance
Living comfortably on present income	8.15	883	1.463	2.142
Coping on present income	7.39	967	1.842	3.393
Difficult on present income	6.55	301	2.409	5.802
Very difficult on present income	4.96	96	2.824	7.977
Total	7.47	2247	1.996	3.982

ONE-WAY ANOVA AND ETA

Now that you understand the assumptions behind the inferential tests for comparisons of means and how to test whether you have violated them, we can move on to the inferential tests themselves. Because ANOVA can compare two or more groups, thereby covering what the t-test can do, is less sensitive to differences in group size (as long as the data is not very abnormally distributed) and is much more user-friendly, we will introduce ANOVA as the preferred inferential statistic and will only discuss t-tests thereafter to support those of you who encounter them in the classroom. We can produce an ANOVA table and/or eta with a comparison of means test. This provides us with a set of inferential statistics to evaluate whether the differences in means between groups are statistically significant and how strong the relationship is. See Box 9.7 for instructions to produce ANOVA and eta results. After understanding these outputs, we will look at the full one-way ANOVA test.

To provide a comparison to illustrate differences in strength of relationship, we will produce two sets of inferential statistics for happiness: one using political party affiliation for the UK [`prtclbgb`], one using feeling about household income [`hincfel`]. Our hypotheses, based on the data we encountered earlier in our error bar charts, are:

H1. The relationship between subjective income and happiness will be stronger than the relationship between party affiliation and happiness.

H2a. Conservatives are happier than Labour, UKIP and no party supporters.

H2b. There is no significant difference between the other groups' mean happiness.

BOX 9.7 BIVARIATE COMPARISON OF MEANS WITH ANOVA AND ETA

This box shows you how to produce a comparison of means table with accompanying ANOVA and eta (η) statistics. This test is appropriate for one categorical independent (predictor) variable and one continuous dependent (outcome) variable. This example uses Which party closer to, UK [prtclbgb] as the categorical predictor variable and How happy are you [happy] as the continuous outcome variable. Results with UK party affiliation have been filtered to include national parties and no party affiliation ('not applicable'). Comparison of means results can be found in Tables 9.4 and 9.5. ANOVA results can be found in Table 9.6. Eta results can be found in Table 9.7.

Syntax

Follow the instructions in Box 9.2 to filter results for the main UK national political parties and no political affiliation.

```
MEANS TABLES=happy BY prtclbgb
  /CELLS=MEAN COUNT STDDEV
  /STATISTICS ANOVA.
```

Remove filter when finished.

```
FILTER off.
```

Menu instructions

Follow the instructions in Box 9.2 to filter results for the main UK national political parties and no political affiliation.

Analyze > Compare Means > Means

Drag How happy are you [happy] into Dependent List.

Drag Which party feel closer to, United Kingdom [prtclbgb] into Layer 1 of 1.

> Options

Cell statistics: Confirm that mean, number of cases and standard deviation are in the Cell Statistics box.

Statistics for First Layer: tick Anova table and eta.

Click Continue.

Click Paste to keep a copy in syntax. Then, in the Syntax window, select the block of text you have produced and press the green play triangle.

Or, press OK without pasting.

To produce the results for feeling about household's income [hincfel], remove the party filter and filter results for UK respondents, then replace UK political party affiliation with subjective household income in the instructions above.

Table 9.6 ANOVA results for happiness by political party affiliation and subjective income

Predictor	Comparison	Sum of squares	df	Mean square	F	Sig.
Party affiliation	Between groups	136.283	5	27.257	6.947	.000
	Within groups	8329.119	2123	3.923		
	Total	8465.402	2128			
Subjective household income	Between groups	1278.868	3	426.289	124.739	.000
	Within groups	7665.359	2243	3.417		
	Total	8944.227	2246			

Let's look at the ANOVA table results (Table 9.6), which combine the results for a one-way ANOVA using UK party affiliation as the predictor with a separate test using subjective household income as the predictor. Start with the statistical significance (Sig.) and the F-ratio (F). We interpret statistical significance using the same thresholds as always, so in both of these tests we would report that the test is statistically significant ($p<0.001$). The F-ratio indicates to us how good our predictor variable is at explaining variation in the outcome variable. It is calculated by dividing the amount of variance the calculation *does* explain by the amount of variance it *doesn't* explain. For the result to be statistically significant, F will have to be at least 1; if it falls below 1, you will see that the significance score will exceed the threshold for statistical significance. Higher F-ratios indicate that the predictor explains more of the variation in the outcome variable. For example, the F-ratio for a test of the relationship between UK political party identification [`prtclbgb`] (limited to the five parties with more than 50 responses and respondents with no political affiliation) and happiness [`happy`] is 6.947. However, F for the relationship between feeling about household income [`hincfel`] and happiness is 426.289, indicating that feeling about household income is a much better predictor of happiness than political party affiliation.

Table 9.7 Measures of association for happiness, UK

	Eta	Eta squared
Party affiliation	0.127	0.016
Subjective household income	0.378	0.143

This same information about which variable is a better predictor that we gleaned from the F-ratio is presented in a more accessible format with eta and eta squared, which are standardized to run from 0 to 1. Eta can be interpreted using the same guidance as other measures of strength of association (≥0.1=small, ≥0.3=medium, ≥0.5=large; some authors use ≥0.25 as the threshold for medium with eta). In this case, eta for political party affiliation and happiness is 0.127 (weak relationship), while it is 0.378 (moderate) for feeling about household income and happiness (Table 9.7). As you can see, both eta and the F-statistic give us the same result (subjective income is a better predictor of happiness), but it is easier to interpret the result of eta because it is standardized.

If we look at eta squared (which really is the value of eta, squared), we can interpret this as the percentage of variation in the outcome variable that change in the predictor variable can explain. This is the same way that we interpret r squared in regression results. When we interpret eta squared or r squared, we convert it into a percentage. For political party affiliation, eta squared is 0.016, which means that political party affiliation can explain about 1.6 per cent (0.016 × 100) of variation in happiness. For feeling about household income, eta squared is 0.128, which means subjective income can explain about 14.3 per cent (0.143 × 100) of variation in happiness. Neither of these figures might seem particularly large (and is why they are classed as small and medium, not large, effects), but in social statistics, we get excited if we can explain 25 per cent of variation in the outcome variable (equating to eta/r of 0.50), so explaining 14.3 per cent is a decent result.

Our results so far have confirmed H1: F, eta and eta squared are all noticeably higher for subjective household income than for party affiliation. However, to test H2, we need to run some further tests using the full one-way ANOVA options rather than the add-on options available in the comparison of means test. For instructions on carrying out a full one-way ANOVA, see Box 9.8.

BOX 9.8 ONE-WAY ANOVA WITH COMPARISON OF MEANS AND POST HOC TESTS

This box shows you how to carry out a one-way ANOVA with descriptive statistics, tests of homogeneity of variance and post hoc tests. This test is appropriate for one categorical independent (predictor) variable and one continuous dependent (outcome) variable. This example uses Which party closer to, UK [`prtclbgb`] as the categorical predictor variable and How happy are you [`happy`] as the continuous outcome variable. Results with UK party affiliation have been filtered to include national parties and no party affiliation ('not applicable'). The results can be found in Table 9.8.

Syntax

Follow the instructions in Box 9.2 to filter results for the main UK national political parties and no political affiliation.

```
ONEWAY happy BY prtclbgb
  /STATISTICS DESCRIPTIVES
  /MISSING ANALYSIS
  /POSTHOC=TUKEY ALPHA(0.05).
```

(Continued)

Menu instructions

Follow the instructions in Box 9.2 to filter results for the main UK national political parties and no political affiliation.

Analyze > Compare Means > One-way ANOVA

Drag How happy are you [happy] into Dependent List.

Drag Which party feel closer to, United Kingdom [prtclbgb] into Factor.

> Options

> Tick Descriptive to get the table of comparison of means, count and standard deviation that you produced through the simple comparison of means before. This set of descriptives also includes standard error, confidence intervals (represented by the error bars in the error bar chart), minimum and maximum values. Producing your descriptives through the one-way ANOVA options does not allow you to choose which descriptives are included in the output table the way that you can choose in the simple comparison of means.

> If you tick Means plot, it will plot the means as a line graph. There is not really any gain in doing this, as you can do this better yourself using Chart Builder.

> Missing values: if you are running more than one test at a time, the recommended setting would be Excluded cases analysis by analysis. However, you should be careful about running an ANOVA with more than one categorical and one continuous variable at a time to make sure that your results don't get confused.

> Post hoc

Tick Tukey. This will give you information about which groups are significantly different from one another by pitting the categories against each other one at a time.

Click Paste to keep a copy in syntax. Then, in the Syntax window, select the block of text you have produced and press the green play triangle.

Or, press OK without pasting.

Table 9.8 One-way ANOVA results for happiness by UK political party affiliation

	N	Mean	Std. dev.	Std. error	95% confidence interval for mean		Minimum	Maximum
					Lower bound	Upper bound		
Conservative	371	7.95	1.711	.089	7.77	8.12	0	10
Labour	415	7.38	2.091	.103	7.17	7.58	0	10
Liberal Democrat	64	7.88	1.609	.201	7.47	8.28	0	10
Green Party	56	7.64	1.623	.217	7.21	8.08	3	10

	N	Mean	Std. dev.	Std. error	95% confidence interval for mean		Minimum	Maximum
					Lower bound	Upper bound		
UKIP	166	7.04	2.292	.178	6.69	7.39	0	10
Not applicable	1057	7.39	2.009	.062	7.27	7.51	0	10
Total	2129	7.48	1.995	.043	7.40	7.56	0	10

ANOVA

	Sum of squares	df	Mean square	F	Sig.
Between groups	136.283	5	27.257	6.947	.000
Within groups	8329.119	2123	3.923		
Total	8465.402	2128			

You should notice in the outputs (Table 9.8) that you have already produced many of these results before using the comparison of means function. We have seen the N, mean and standard deviation in Table 9.1. We have seen the ANOVA results in Table 9.6. The new additions of note are the lower and upper boundaries for the confidence interval, which show us the range where we would expect to find the population mean in 95 per cent of samples taken from the same population. (This is the information that was expressed by the error bars in the error bar chart.) The other main outputs are from the Tukey post hoc test (Table 9.9).

Table 9.9 Tukey post hoc test results for happiness by political party affiliation

(I) Which party feel closer to, UK	(J) Which party feel closer to, UK	Mean difference (I–J)	Std. error	Sig.	95% Confidence interval	
					Lower bound	Upper bound
Conservative	Labour	.570*	.142	.001	.17	.97
	Liberal Democrat	.071	.268	1.000	−.69	.84
	Green Party	.303	.284	.894	−.51	1.11
	UKIP	.904*	.185	.000	.38	1.43
	Not applicable	.553*	.120	.000	.21	.89

(Continued)

Table 9.9 (Continued)

(I) Which party feel closer to, UK	(J) Which party feel closer to, UK	Mean difference (I–J)	Std. error	Sig.	95% Confidence interval	
					Lower bound	Upper bound
Labour	Conservative	–.570*	.142	.001	–.97	–.17
	Liberal Democrat	–.499	.266	.417	–1.26	.26
	Green Party	–.267	.282	.934	–1.07	.54
	UKIP	.334	.182	.443	–.19	.85
	Not applicable	–.018	.115	1.000	–.34	.31
Liberal Democrat	Conservative	–.071	.268	1.000	–.84	.69
	Labour	.499	.266	.417	–.26	1.26
	Green Party	.232	.362	.988	–.80	1.27
	UKIP	.833*	.291	.049	.00	1.66
	Not applicable	.481	.255	.410	–.25	1.21
Green Party	Conservative	–.303	.284	.894	–1.11	.51
	Labour	.267	.282	.934	–.54	1.07
	Liberal Democrat	–.232	.362	.988	–1.27	.80
	UKIP P	.601	.306	.364	–.27	1.47
	Not applicable	.249	.272	.942	–.53	1.02
UKIP	Conservative	–.904*	.185	.000	–1.43	–.38
	Labour	–.334	.182	.443	–.85	.19
	Liberal Democrat	–.833*	.291	.049	–1.66	.00
	Green Party	–.601	.306	.364	–1.47	.27
	Not applicable	–.351	.165	.275	–.82	.12
Not applicable	Conservative	–.553*	.120	.000	–.89	–.21
	Labour	.018	.115	1.000	–.31	.34
	Liberal Democrat	–.481	.255	.410	–1.21	.25
	Green Party	–.249	.272	.942	–1.02	.53
	UKIP	.351	.165	.275	–.12	.82

* The mean difference is significant at the 0.05 level.

The Tukey results pit each category pairing against each other in turn to determine whether there are statistically significant differences between the two groups. This is the information we need to test our second hypothesis. To find this information, we need to look at the significance results first. The p-value is given in the 'Sig.' column; statistically significant results (by default, $p<0.05$) are flagged with an asterisk in the 'Mean difference' column. If we start with the block of results compared to Conservatives, we can see flags for statistical significance for comparison with Labour, UKIP and no party affiliation but not for Liberal Democrat or Green. This is precisely what we expected to find based on the error bar chart and confirms H2a. Turning to the differences between the other groups, a quick scan for flags in the mean difference column confirms that almost all results flagged as significant are the comparisons with Conservatives, with the exception of Lib Dem–UKIP. This confirms our finding from the error bar charts and H2b: the differences in happiness between other party affiliations, except the difference between Lib Dem and UKIP supporters, are not statistically significant. The values in the mean difference column are simply the difference in the means, which we could also figure out from the descriptive statistics. For example, in the Tukey table, the mean difference between Conservative and Labour is 0.570. This is simply the Conservative mean happiness (7.95) minus the Labour mean happiness (7.38).

Table 9.10 Tukey post hoc test results for happiness by subjective household income

(I) Feeling about household's income nowadays	(J) Feeling about household's income nowadays	Mean difference (I–J)	Std. error	Sig.	95% Confidence interval	
					Lower bound	Upper bound
Living comfortably on present income	Coping on present income	.764*	.086	.000	.54	.99
	Difficult on present income	1.603*	.123	.000	1.29	1.92
	Very difficult on present income	3.196*	.199	.000	2.68	3.71
Coping on present income	Living comfortably on present income	–.764*	.086	.000	–.99	–.54
	Difficult on present income	.838*	.122	.000	.52	1.15
	Very difficult on present income	2.432*	.198	.000	1.92	2.94
Difficult on present income	Living comfortably on present income	–1.603*	.123	.000	–1.92	–1.29
	Coping on present income	–.838*	.122	.000	–1.15	–.52
	Very difficult on present income	1.593*	.217	.000	1.04	2.15

(Continued)

Table 9.10 (Continued)

(I) Feeling about household's income nowadays	(J) Feeling about household's income nowadays	Mean difference (I–J)	Std. error	Sig.	95% Confidence interval	
					Lower bound	Upper bound
Very difficult on present income	Living comfortably on present income	−3.196*	.199	.000	−3.71	−2.68
	Coping on present income	−2.432*	.198	.000	−2.94	−1.92
	Difficult on present income	−1.593*	.217	.000	−2.15	−1.04

* The mean difference is significant at the 0.05 level.

If we compare this to results for the Tukey post hoc test for subjective household income (Table 9.10), we can identify the same difference in explanatory power of the two categorical variables as we predicted based on the error bar chart and the eta results. We can see that the difference between groups is significant for every category pairing.

T-test

The t-test is another way of conducting a comparison of group means, but only between two groups at a time. The independent samples t-test is the equivalent of the one-way ANOVA you have conducted in the previous section and compares two groups, with any given case only occurring in one group. This is the main form of analysis possible in cross-sectional survey data: this data only looks at each case (e.g. survey respondent) at one point in time. The ESS data is cross-sectional. Survey data that looks at the same individuals at different points in time is called panel data and is far less common because it costs a lot more to follow the same people over time, and drop-out rates mean that you have to start with a much larger sample than for a cross-sectional study in the hope that you will still have enough respondents by the end of the study. Follow the instructions in Box 9.9 to run an independent samples t-test using the same variables in the ESS dataset as we worked with for ANOVA. Because we can only compare groups, we will focus our comparison on Conservatives and Labourites. These are well suited to comparison using a t-test because the group sizes are very similar.

BOX 9.9 INDEPENDENT SAMPLES T-TEST

This box shows you how to carry out an independent samples t-test using two categories from a categorical variable and one continuous variable. The categories in this test must be independent: cases cannot fall into more than one category for this test to be appropriate. This example compares Conservative and Labour supporters' average happiness. The results can be found in Table 9.11.

Before conducting an independent samples t-test, you need to know the values of the two groups you are comparing, as you will have to type the numbers representing the groups as part of the test. In this case, we are comparing Conservative (1) and Labour (2). If we wanted to compare Labour and UKIP, we would need 2 and 7.

Syntax

```
T-TEST GROUPS=prtclbgb(1 2)
  /MISSING=ANALYSIS
  /VARIABLES=happy
  /CRITERIA=CI(.95).
```

Menu instructions

Analyze > Compare Means > Independent Samples T-Test

Drag the continuous variable (How happy are you [happy]) into the Test Variable box.

Drag the categorical variable (Which party feel closer to, United Kingdom [prtclbgb]) into the Grouping Variable box.

> Define Groups

Group 1: Enter the value of the first group (Conservative = 1).

Group 2: Enter the value of the second group (Labour = 2).

Click Continue.

Click Paste to keep a copy in syntax. Then, in the Syntax window, select the block of text you have produced and press the green play triangle.

Or, press OK without pasting.

You will recognize the values in the first output table ('Group Statistics' in SPSS) (Table 9.11), as we have already seen them several times in this chapter. The statistics contained here are the same count, mean, standard deviation and standard error that we have already seen. To interpret our results, we start with the significance result for Levene's test for equality of variances.

Table 9.11 Independent samples t-test of average happiness, Conservative and Labour supporters

Party affiliation	N	Mean	Std. dev.	Std. error mean
Conservative	371	7.95	1.711	.089
Labour	415	7.38	2.091	.103

(Continued)

(Continued)

	Levene's test for equality of variances		t-test for equality of means						
	F	Sig.	t	df	Sig. (2-tailed)	Mean difference	Std. error difference	95% confidence interval of the difference	
								Lower	Upper
Equal variances assumed	17.948	.000	4.155	784	.000	.570	.137	.301	.840
Equal variances not assumed			4.201	778.049	.000	.570	.136	.304	.837

If the significance is less than 0.05, read the rest of the results in the bottom row, 'Equal variances not assumed'. If the significance is greater than or equal to 0.05, read the rest of the statistics for the top row, 'Equal variances assumed'. In this case, the Levene's test significance is less than 0.05 (p=0.000), so we will read the rest of the results from the bottom row of the table. The Levene's significance *only* relates to the test of the assumption of equal variances; it does *not* tell us whether there is a statistically significant difference between the groups. That information is contained in the column 'Sig. (2-tailed)'. Here we have a statistically significant difference between the two groups (p=0.000, so p<0.001), and the mean difference is 0.570 (average Conservative happiness of 7.95 minus average Labour happiness of 7.38). We can see that F (17.948) is much larger than the F we produced in the one-way ANOVA with more groups (6.947). This is because we are only looking at a comparison of Conservative and Labour supporters. If we filter our results before running an ANOVA to only include Conservatives and Labourites, we get a similar F (17.263).

You can calculate the effect size (*r*) for the t-test results using t and df from the appropriate row of the table. In this case, because we are reading 'equal variances not assumed', we would use t=4.201 and df=778.049. You can find handy effect size calculators on the internet (search for 't-test effect size calculator'), but if you want to do it yourself, the equation is:

$$r = \sqrt{\frac{t^2}{(t^2 + df)}}$$

With these results, this gives us an effect size of $r = 0.149$, or a small effect. You should notice that this corroborates all of our previous findings about the relationship between political party affiliation and happiness.

Table 9.12 Independent samples t-test of average happiness, Labour and UKIP supporters

Party affiliation	N	Mean	Std. dev.	Std. error mean
Labour	415	7.38	2.091	.103
UKIP	166	7.04	2.292	.178

	Levene's test for equality of variances		t-test for equality of means						
	F	Sig.	t	df	Sig. (2-tailed)	Mean difference	Std. error difference	95% confidence interval of the difference	
								Lower	Upper
Equal variances assumed	3.167	.076	1.690	579	.091	.334	.197	−.054	.722
Equal variances not assumed			1.625	280.711	.105	.334	.205	−.071	.738

Now produce another independent samples t-test comparing Labour and UKIP supporters. Based on our previous results, we would expect the difference between these groups not to be statistically significant. We can see from the results that, this time, Levene's test for equality of variances is not significant, so we will read the results from the 'Equal variances assumed' row (Table 9.12). We can see that F is above 1, but the difference between groups (2-tailed significance) is only statistically significant at $p<0.10$. This confirms the results that we had from our previous tests: the difference in happiness between Labour and UKIP supporters is only statistically significant using the highest threshold.

NON-PARAMETRIC TESTS

Sometimes your data does not fit the assumptions about the population from which your data is taken (the parameter). One of the key assumptions of parametric tests, which you have encountered many times already in this book, is about normal distribution of data. Non-parametric tests are not reliant on this assumption, which makes them a good choice when your data violates the assumption of normality in a way that you cannot correct through other manipulations. Non-parametric tests are, however, less powerful than parametric tests, so you should aim to use parametric tests whenever possible. Non-parametric tests still rely on meeting the assumptions that your sample is random and that you have independent observations–each case cannot occur in more than one group in the test.

Mann–Whitney U test

The Mann–Whitney U test is the non-parametric equivalent of an independent samples t-test. The key difference is that it compares the groups based on median values instead of means. This helps the test results to compensate for abnormal distribution and outliers. As with an independent samples t-test, you will need one categorical variable that has two groups and one continuous variable. A Mann–Whitney U test essentially puts all of the uous variable values in order from smallest to largest, then looks at which group categorical variable each of the observations of the continuous value belongs to. If is no real difference between the groups, then the groups from the categorical variable should be roughly evenly mixed in the rankings of the observations of the continuous variable. If, however, there is a difference between the groups, then we would expect more of the lower observations of the continuous variable to belong to one group and more of the higher observations to belong to the other group. The Mann–Whitney U results confirm whether the difference between your two groups is statistically significant. To interpret your results meaningfully, you should produce a Mann–Whitney U test alongside a descriptive comparison of means table that shows the median instead of mean value. We will apply this idea to looking at whether carbon emissions are lower in low-income countries than high-income countries, using the UN dataset. Follow the instructions in Box 9.10 to produce results to test the statistical significance of any difference between groups and Box 9.11 to produce the accompanying information about medians.

BOX 9.10 MANN-WHITNEY U TEST

This box shows you how to produce a Mann-Whitney U test. This test is appropriate for using one categorical predictor variable with two categories and one continuous outcome variable. This test should only be used when the data violates the assumption of normality in a way that you cannot manipulate to use a parametric test (ANOVA or t-test) because it is less powerful than the parametric alternatives. This example uses the UN dataset, comparing Carbon dioxide emissions per capita (tonnes) [`emissions`] by high-and low-income groups [`wbincome`]. To compare these groups, you will first need to use Select Cases to choose the two groups for comparison, in this case 1 ('high income') and 4 ('low income'). The results can be found in Figures 9.6 and 9.7.

Syntax

Select World Bank income groups 1 and 4.

```
USE ALL.

COMPUTE filter_$=(wbincome=1 OR wbincome=4).

VARIABLE LABELS filter_$ 'wbincome=1 OR wbincome=4 (FILTER)'.

VALUE LABELS filter_$ 0 'Not Selected' 1 'Selected'.

FORMATS filter_$ (f1.0).

FILTER BY filter_$.

EXECUTE.
```

Produce a non-parametric independent samples test with Mann-Whitney U results.

```
NPTESTS
```

```
/INDEPENDENT TEST (emissions) GROUP (wbincome) MANN_WHITNEY
/MISSING SCOPE=ANALYSIS USERMISSING=EXCLUDE
/CRITERIA ALPHA=0.05
CILEVEL=95.
```

Menu instructions

Select World Bank income groups 1 and 4.

Data > Select Cases > If condition is satisfied > If

Type: 'wbincome = 1 OR wbincome = 4' in the box.

Continue.

OK/Paste.

Produce a non-parametric independent samples test with Mann-Whitney U results.

Analyze > Nonparametric Tests > Independent Samples

Objective tab: Select Compare medians across groups.

Fields tab

Put the continuous variable (Carbon dioxide emissions per capita (tonnes) [`emissions`]) in Test Fields.

Put the grouping variable (World Bank income group [`wbincome`]) in Groups.

Settings tab

Choose tests: Customize tests.

Compare Distributions across Groups: Select Mann-Whitney U (2 samples).

Run/Paste.

You will need to double click on the Hypothesis Test Summary table to open the full results and see the Mann-Whitney U test results.

Hypothesis test summary

	Null hypothesis	Test	Sig.	Decision
1	The distribution of carbon dioxide emissions per capita (tonnes) is the same across categories of World Bank income group	Independent samples Mann–Whitney U test	.000	Reject the null hypothesis

Asymptotic significances are displayed. The Significance level is .05.

Figure 9.6 Mann–Whitney U summary results for GNI by World Bank high-and low-income groups

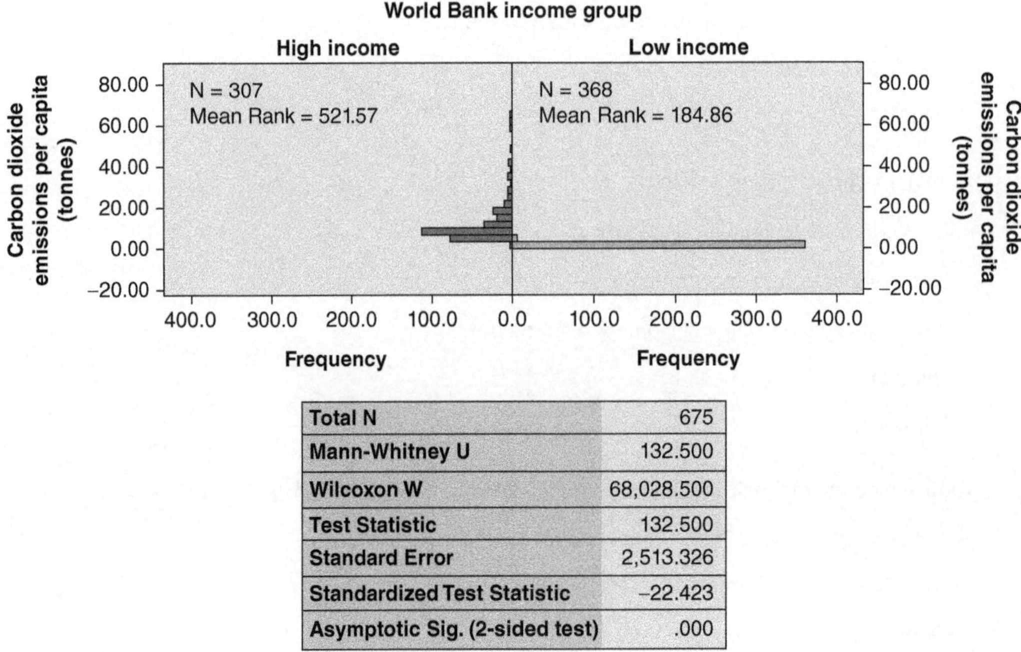

Total N	675
Mann-Whitney U	132.500
Wilcoxon W	68,028.500
Test Statistic	132.500
Standard Error	2,513.326
Standardized Test Statistic	−22.423
Asymptotic Sig. (2-sided test)	.000

Figure 9.7 Mann–Whitney U test statistics

The only result you will see in the Output viewer is the Hypothesis Test Summary (Figure 9.6). This summary tells you whether or not there is a statistically significant difference between the two groups. In this case, there is a significant difference ($p<0.001$), which the summary table tells us should lead us to reject the hypothesis that the distribution of carbon dioxide emissions per capita is the same across World Bank income groups. When you double click on the Hypothesis Test Summary table, you will open the full model viewer to see the independent samples Mann–Whitney U test results (Figure 9.7).

In this table the total N shows us the total number of cases assessed (675), which we can see in the accompanying histogram breaks down into 307 high-income countries and 368 low-income countries. The Mann–Whitney U statistic (132.5) summarizes the mean difference in ranks between the two groups. When reporting the results, you should report the U and the significance. In this case, you could write, 'A Mann–Whitney U test shows there is a significant difference in carbon emissions between high-and low-income countries (U 132.5, $p<0.001$).' If you have a sample size over 40, the significance will be provided as the asymptotic significance; if it is less than 40, you will see an additional row in your table named 'Exact significance'. You should accompany this with a comparison of *medians* (not means), which you can produce following the procedure for a descriptive comparison of means, simply selecting medians instead of means (Box 9.11). We would report this alongside our test results: 'Median carbon dioxide emissions were 8.9 tonnes per capita in high-income countries but only 0.2 tonnes per capita in low-income countries'.

BOX 9.11 BIVARIATE DESCRIPTIVE COMPARISON OF MEDIANS

This box shows you how to produce a comparison of medians. This test is appropriate for one categorical predictor variable and one continuous outcome variable. This example follows the example in Box 9.10, using the UN dataset, comparing Carbon dioxide emissions per capita (tonnes) [emissions] by high-and low-income groups [wbincome]. The categorical variable has been filtered here only to show the high-and low-income groups to align with the Mann-Whitney U comparison of two groups. The results can be found in Table 9.13.

Table 9.13 Comparison of median carbon emissions between high-and low-income groups

	Carbon dioxide emissions per capita (tonnes)	
World Bank income group	**N**	**Median**
High income	307	8.900
Low income	368	.200
Total	675	1.000

Syntax

The syntax follows the same pattern as a descriptive comparison of means but includes median and leaves out mean and standard deviation.

```
MEANS TABLES=emissions BY wbincome
  /CELLS=COUNT MEDIAN.
```

Menu instructions

Analyze > Compare means > Means

Place the continuous variable ('Carbon dioxide emissions per capita (tonnes)' [emissions]) in the Dependent List box.

Place the categorical variable (World Bank income group [wbincome]) in the Layer 1 of 1 box.

> Options

Remove mean and standard deviation from Cell Statistics.

Add Median to Cell Statistics.

Continue.

OK/Paste.

Thus far, we have learned how to check descriptive statistics by comparing group medians and how to test statistically significant differences between groups using the Mann–Whitney U test. You might have noticed by now how many steps you have to go through to produce a full set of results for a non-parametric comparison of groups–and we have not even looked at the strength of relationship. Unfortunately, SPSS does not calculate this for you, but you can calculate the effect size for a Mann–Whitney U test using the total N and the standardized test statistic (z) from your results. The effect size calculation is:

$$r = \frac{z}{\sqrt{N}}$$

In this example, our standardized test statistic was –22.423, and the total N was 675. This gives us an effect size of –0.856 ($r = -22.423/\sqrt{675}$), which we interpret the same as *r* elsewhere. This is a very strong relationship, which should not surprise us, given the substantial difference in median carbon dioxide emissions between the two income groups.

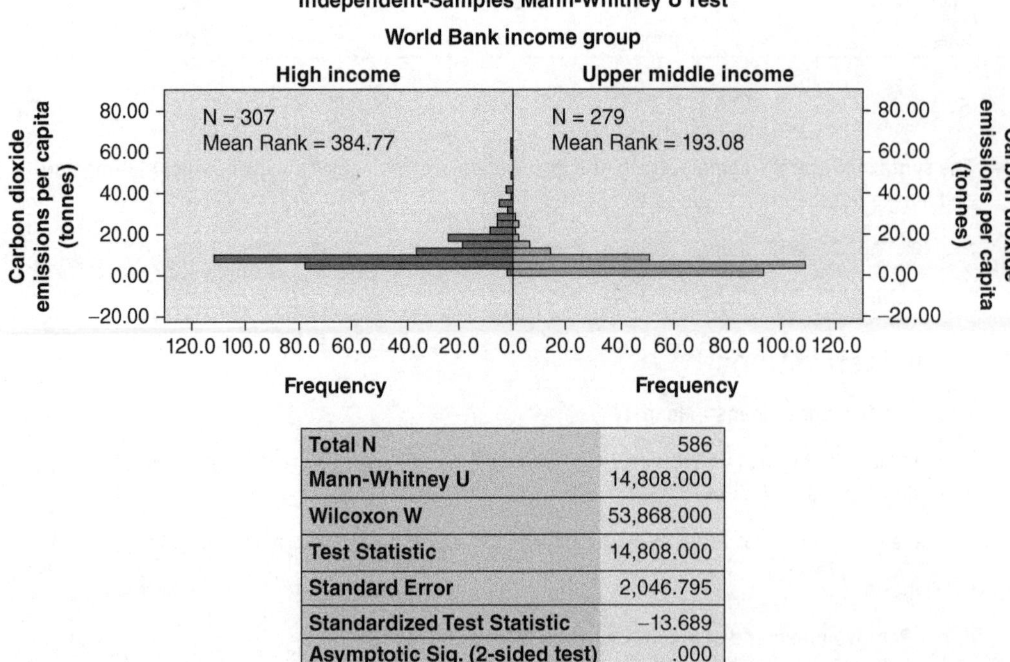

Total N	586
Mann-Whitney U	14,808.000
Wilcoxon W	53,868.000
Test Statistic	14,808.000
Standard Error	2,046.795
Standardized Test Statistic	–13.689
Asymptotic Sig. (2-sided test)	.000

Figure 9.8 Mann–Whitney U comparison of carbon emissions between high-income and upper middle-income countries

Table 9.14 Median carbon emissions (tonnes per capita) by income group

World Bank income group	N	Median
High income	307	8.9000
Upper middle income	279	4.2000
Total	586	6.8000

We could instead compare the two income groups we would expect to show the most similar carbon dioxide emissions to see to what extent income makes a difference in carbon emissions. We could do this either through a comparison of high-income to upper middle-income countries; or of lower middle-income to low-income countries. A comparison of high-income and middle-income countries indicates a statistically significant difference between the groups (U 14,808, $p<0.001$) (Figure 9.8). Median carbon emissions are much higher in high-income countries (8.9 tonnes per capita) than upper middle-income countries (4.2 tonnes per capita) (Table 9.14). The effect size is large ($r = -0.566$). If you do not calculate the effect size yourself, you should include the standardized test statistic (reported as z) to enable interested readers to calculate the effect size themselves.

CONCLUSIONS

This chapter has introduced you to ways of testing relationships between a categorical predictor variable and a continuous outcome variable. You have learned how to produce a descriptive comparison of means and medians. You have also learned a series of inferential tests, looking at the parametric one-way ANOVA and independent samples t-tests and the non-parametric Mann–Whitney U test. The next chapter shows you how to combine one or more continuous predictors with a continuous outcome variable in linear regression, or with a categorical outcome variable in logistic regression.

ACTIVITIES

Activity 9.1

RQ: To what extent is party affiliation reflected in support for immigration?
Dataset: ESS.

1. Create a bivariate descriptive comparison of means table using Country's cultural life undermined or enriched by immigrants [`imueclt`] and Which party feel closer to, Denmark [`prtclcdk`]. Include the mean, count and standard deviation.

(Continued)

2. What are the three largest parties? Look up some background information about each of them. Where would they be placed on the left-right spectrum? Based on this information, which parties' supporters would you expect to be the most and least hostile to immigration? Formulate your answer as two hypotheses.

3. Look at the means. Which groups are the most pro-immigration? How does this compare to your expectations based on the party's placement on the left-right spectrum?

4. Create an error bar chart for these two variables, limiting your output to the main three parties. You may need to reclassify the immigration variable as scale before generating the chart. Based on the chart, do you expect to find statistically significant differences between these groups?

5. Run a bivariate comparison of means with ANOVA and eta, filtering your results to the three largest parties. Is the difference between the groups statistically significant? How strong is the relationship between the two variables?

6. Run a one-way ANOVA with a Tukey post hoc test. Are the differences significant between each of the groups?

Activity 9.2

RQ: How does female representation in legislatures differ between democracies and autocracies?

Dataset: UN.

1. Formulate a hypothesis for your expectation of whether democracies or autocracies will have higher female representation in the legislature.

2. Create a bivariate descriptive comparison of means table using Female share of parliamentary seats [`femleg`] and Democracy-Dictatorship classification [`e_regime`]. Include the mean, count and standard deviation. Look at the means. Which group has the largest share of female legislators? How does this compare to your expectation?

3. Create an error bar chart for these two variables. Based on the chart, do you expect to find a statistically significant difference between the groups?

4. Run a bivariate comparison of means with ANOVA and eta, filtering your results to the three largest parties. Is the difference between the groups statistically significant? How strong is the relationship between the two variables?

5. Produce the same results, this time comparing groups by Freedom House status [`e_fh_status`]. Do the results indicate the same trend when using a different measure of democracy?

6. Run a one-way ANOVA with a Tukey post hoc test using Freedom House status [`e_fh_status`] and Female share of legislative seats [`femleg`]. Are the differences significant between each of the groups?

Activity 9.3

RQ: How does income affect homicide rates?

Dataset: UN.

Compare homicide rates [homicides] between World Bank income [wbincome] groups 1 (high income) and 2 (upper middle income).

1. Produce a column panel histogram to check for violations of the assumptions of normality and homogeneity of variance.
2. Based on the outcome of your histogram, decide whether a parametric test (ANOVA or independent samples t-test) or non-parametric test (Mann-Whitney U test) is more suitable. Produce the appropriate test and any necessary additional statistics.
3. Is the difference between groups statistically significant? Report the appropriate statistics to indicate this.
4. What is the difference between the groups? (Report the appropriate numbers, e.g. median, mean.)
5. If the difference is statistically significant, how strong is the effect of the difference?

Activity 9.4

RQ: How does democracy affect gender inequality?

Dataset: UN.

Compare Gender Inequality Index [gii] scores between Freedom House status [fhstatus] groups 1 (free) and 2 (partly free).

1. Produce a column panel histogram to check for violations of the assumptions of normality and homogeneity of variance.
2. Based on the outcome of your histogram, decide whether a parametric test (ANOVA or independent samples t-test) or non-parametric test (Mann-Whitney U test) is more suitable. Produce the appropriate test and any necessary additional statistics.
3. Is the difference between groups statistically significant? Report the appropriate statistics to indicate this.
4. What is the difference between the groups? (Report the appropriate numbers, e.g. median, mean.)
5. If the difference is statistically significant, how strong is the effect of the difference?

FURTHER READING

Aldrich, J.O. and Rodriguez, H.M. (2013) *Building SPSS Graphs to Understand Data*. London: Sage.

See chapter 16 ('Paneling on one dimension') for an overview of panelled charts, which can be used to create panelled histograms.

Marchant-Shapiro, T. (2015) *Statistics for Political Analysis: Understanding the Numbers*. London: Sage/CQ Press.

This book includes some basic instructions for using SPSS to conduct data analysis, and the examples are from political science. See chapter 7 ('Hypothesis testing: Examining relationships'), particularly the section 'Analysis of variance' for ANOVA.

Pallant, J. (2016) *SPSS Survival Manual*. Maidenhead: Open University Press/McGraw-Hill Education.
This book provides a functional overview of how to produce statistics in SPSS. See various chapters in Part 5 ('Statistical techniques to compare groups') for coverage of comparison of means, t-tests, ANOVA and Mann-Whitney U tests.

REFERENCES

Brooks, A.C. (2012, 7 Jul) 'Why conservatives are happier than liberals', *New York Times*. (http://www.nytimes.com/2012/07/08/opinion/sunday/conservatives-are-happier-and-extremists-are-happiest-of-all.html?mcubz=0).

Cooper-White, M. (2014, 11 Sept) 'The surprising reason conservatives are happier than liberals', *Huffington Post*. (http://www.huffingtonpost.com/2014/09/11/conservatives-happier-liberal-countries_n_5797938.html).

Field, A. (2011, 11 Oct) 'Top 5 statistical faux pas', *MethodSpace*. (https://www.methodspace.com/top-5-statistical-fax-pas/).

Field, A. (2012, 18 Jul) 'The joy of confidence intervals', *Discovering Statistics*. (https://www.discoveringstatistics.com/2012/07/18/the-joy-of-confidence-intervals).

Field, A. (2013a) *Discovering Statistics Using IBM SPSS Statistics*, 3rd edn. London: Sage.

Field, A. (2013b, 8 Jul) 'Making statistics easy by getting your PENIS out in the classroom', *Workshop for Teachers of Quantitative Methods*. Oxford: University of Oxford. (https://www.sociology.ox.ac.uk/materials/qm/field.pdf).

Morgan, E. (2017, 21 Mar) 'Are conservatives really happier than liberals?', *Vice*. (https://www.vice.com/en_uk/article/gv33pw/are-conservatives-really-happier-than-liberals).

Napier, J.L. and Jost, J.T. (2008) 'Why are conservatives happier than liberals?', *Psychological Science*, 19 (6): 565–72.

Resnick, B. (2017, 31 Jul) 'What a nerdy debate about p-values shows about science: and how to fix it–the case for, and against, redefining "statistical significance"', *Vox*. (https://www.vox.com/science-and-health/2017/7/31/16021654/p-values-statistical-significance-redefine-0005).

Zimmerman, D.W. (2004) 'A note on preliminary tests of equality of variances', *British Journal of Mathematical and Statistical Psychology*, 57: 173–81.

10

INFERENCE WITH CONTINUOUS DATA

CHAPTER SUMMARY

In Chapter 7, we worked with descriptive statistics for continuous data, introducing one bivariate inferential test - correlation - at the end. This chapter introduces regression, an inferential technique that allows you to test the relative impact of several independent variables to create a linear model of the result. The first part of the chapter introduces the most common multivariate inferential test for continuous data: linear regression. The second part of the chapter looks at logistic regression, a test that combines continuous, ordinal or binary categorical predictors with a binary categorical outcome variable. These tests allow you to identify the most influential predictors and to determine how much variation in the outcome they can explain.

OBJECTIVES

In this chapter, you will learn:

- What linear regression is, and how to produce and interpret the results
- What logistic regression is, and how to produce and interpret the results
- How to recode data to make 'dummy' variables
- How to compute an index variable that combines the results of several variables.

INTRODUCTION

In Chapter 7, we looked at the research question What is the relationship between gender inequality and development?, testing five different hypotheses to see the association between the GII and trade, foreign direct investment, GNI (per capita, purchasing power parity), income inequality and education. However, we were only able to look at one predictor and one outcome variable at a time. In this chapter, we look at linear regression (also called ordinary least squares, or OLS regression) to allow us to use several predictor variables at a time to determine which ones are the most influential in explaining the outcome variable. We start by looking at what linear regression is, the underlying assumptions and finally how to produce and interpret the results. In the second part of the chapter, we look at logistic regression, which uses one or more continuous predictors (like linear regression) with a two-category categorical variable (unlike linear regression). We work through how to produce and interpret the resulting odds ratios. This chapter also includes some more advanced computation of variables, creating index variables to combine the results of several variables into a single, new variable.

The section on linear regression uses the UN dataset. The section on logistic regression uses the ESS dataset.

LINEAR REGRESSION

Linear regression is a measure of a linear relationship between one or more predictor variables and one outcome variable. The main product of linear regression is the equation of a straight line that best fits the data. To illustrate this, let's start with the scatterplot from Chapter 7 showing the relationship between gender inequality (which is measured on the dimensions of reproductive health (maternal mortality and adolescent fertility), empowerment (share of female parliamentary seats and higher education attainment levels) and labour market participation (female labour market participation rates)) and mean years of schooling. We will add a line of best fit to this scatterplot. A line of best fit is exactly that: the line that comes as close as possible to the greatest number of dots on the scatterplot. This is also called a trend line, or a fit line in IBM SPSS Statistics ('SPSS'). (For instructions on how to add a fit line to your graph, see the instructions in Box 7.3.) This line is calculated using the 'ordinary least squares' method, which is why linear regression is also referred to as ordinary least squares (or OLS) regression. This is simply the way of calculating that you have the best possible line that is as close as possible to the data points.

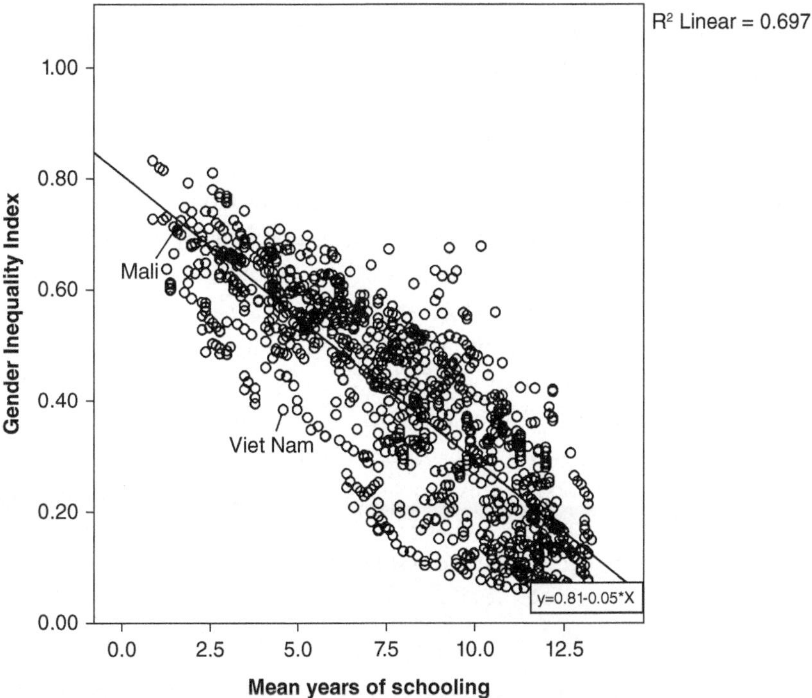

Figure 10.1 Scatterplot of mean years of schooling and gender inequality with best fit line

Look at the best fit line in Figure 10.1. First, we can see the line has a negative slope because there is a negative relationship between the two variables: as mean years of schooling increases, gender inequality decreases. This relationship is expressed in the equation of the line. The slope and intercept of the line (given in the bottom right-hand corner of the scatterplot) and r squared (given at the side of the scatterplot) form two of the core elements of a regression output. It is often helpful to return to a graphical portrayal of this data when you get confused by the outputs of a linear regression test. This slope and intercept of the line follow the form:

$$y = a + Bx$$

Where '*y*' is the outcome variable, '*a*' is the intercept with the y-axis, '*B*' is the slope of the line and '*x*' is the predictor variable. So in this example, the equation is:

$$\text{Gender inequality} = 0.81 - 0.05 \times \text{mean years of schooling}$$

This equation means that, for every one-unit increase in education (in this case, for every one year of extra education, on average), we expect gender inequality to decrease by 0.05 units (measured on a scale of 0 to 1). For cases that lie directly on the line, we should be able to calculate the gender inequality value based on the known mean years of schooling value. The scatterplot has highlighted Mali as a case that lies directly on the best fit line. This particular observation is from 2005, when Mali's mean years of schooling was 1.7. Using the equation from the best fit line, Mali's gender inequality should be:

$$0.81 - 0.05 \times 1.7 = 0.725$$

In the dataset, the value given for Mali in 2005 is 0.723. The 0.002 difference between our calculation and the given value could be because it is not perfectly centred on the line or because of rounding. For comparison, let's look at the case of Viet Nam, which clearly does not lie on the best fit line. This is an observation from 1995, when Viet Nam's mean years of schooling was 4.6. From the best fit line, we would predict the gender inequality score to be 0.580, but the actual score that year was 0.383. This means that Viet Nam did better than expected on gender inequality, based on its average education level. We can see that r squared is 0.697, which means we can explain 69.7 per cent of variance in gender inequality using average years of schooling; this also means that 30.3 per cent of variance in gender equality is not explained. Vietnam would be one of the cases contributing to that 30.3 per cent, since it does not fall precisely on the best fit line.

Assumptions

Linear regression follows the assumptions that we encountered in Chapter 7:

1. Both variables are continuous.

2. The relationship is linear.
3. There are pairs of observations.
4. Extreme outliers are excluded.
5. The data is homoscedastic.

Linear regression adds another layer to these assumptions: your predictor variables should not be too perfectly related to each other (multicollinearity). This is because, if you use two (or more) variables that are essentially measuring the same trend, SPSS gets confused and ends up telling you none of them is important because it cannot adequately distinguish between them. For example, if you wanted to run a regression using both the Human Development Index (HDI) and life expectancy as predictors, you would be likely to end up with problems with your model because life expectancy is one of the indicators included in the HDI. As a consequence, there is a strong correlation between them ($r=0.868$). Including both of them in a regression model would result in worse outputs. One rule of thumb is not to include any two predictors that have $r>0.80$. (Others say only to exclude variables when $r>0.90$. As you can see, statisticians rarely agree on the rules of the game, and they also violate their own assumptions quite frequently.) At the same time, you want to make sure that each of your predictors *is* correlated with your output variable, otherwise you will not achieve anything by including it in your model. It is, therefore, usually a good idea to check the relationship between your predictors and each other, and between each predictor and the outcome variable, before setting off on a meaningful regression.

You will also find that there may be times when you violate the other assumptions. Many researchers, for example, will use two-category nominal variables, normally coded '1' and '0', and treat them as continuous for the sake of regression. You might also take the decision to keep extreme outliers within your analysis because, while they are outliers, they are also important cases and should not be excluded from analysis. This is more likely to be the case if you are using whole-population data (such as the UN dataset, which includes most countries; or census data), but there are reasons why you could logically justify the inclusion of outliers even in sample data. You may also take the decision to include a variable that exhibits some level of uncorrected heteroscedasticity (fan-shape) because a linear model still tells you *something*, even though the results will not be perfect because of the underlying shape of the data.

Running linear regression

When we introduced linear regression earlier, we performed a bivariate linear regression using a line of best fit overlaid on a scatterplot of mean years of schooling and gender inequality, and we assured you that the equation of the line and the r squared result presented you with most of the output from a linear regression. To prove this, follow the instructions in Box 10.1 to produce a bivariate linear regression using these two variables.

BOX 10.1 BIVARIATE LINEAR REGRESSION

This box shows you how to produce a bivariate linear regression with the default statistical outputs. It is appropriate for one or more continuous predictor variables and one continuous output variable. This example uses human development and gender inequality. The results can be found in Table 10.1.

Syntax

```
REGRESSION
  /MISSING LISTWISE
  /STATISTICS COEFF OUTS R ANOVA
  /CRITERIA=PIN(.05) POUT(.10)
  /NOORIGIN
  /DEPENDENT GII
  /METHOD=ENTER meanschyrs.
```

If you only want to include the default statistics, as we do in this example, you can shorten the regression syntax to:

```
REGRESSION
/dependent GII
/method=enter meanschyrs.
```

Menu instructions

Analyze > Regression > Linear

Place the outcome variable (Gender Inequality Index [GII]) in the Dependent box.

Place the predictor variable (Mean years of schooling [meanschyrs]) in the Block 1 of 1 box.

OK/Paste.

Table 10.1 Bivariate regression results for mean years of schooling and gender inequality

Model summary				
Model	**R**	**R Square**	**Adjusted R Square**	**Std. error of the estimate**
1	.835	.697	.697	.107375

ANOVA						
Model		**Sum of squares**	**df**	**Mean square**	**F**	**Sig.**
1	Regression	29.026	1	29.026	2517.592	.000
	Residual	12.590	1092	.012		
	Total	41.616	1093			

Coefficients						
Model		**Unstandardized coefficients**		**Standardized coefficients**	**t**	**Sig.**
		B	**Std. error**	**Beta**		
1	(Constant)	.807	.009		91.460	.000
	Mean years of schooling	-.051	.001	-.835	-50.176	.000

You should see that there is very little you have not already encountered in the results from the bivariate linear regression. In the 'Model summary' table, we have the information about r (0.835, the same result we produced in Chapter 7 in the correlation test) and r squared (0.697, the same result we produced by adding a best fit line to our scatterplot in Figure 10.1). The adjusted r squared will be the same as r squared when we are only using one predictor variable. In the ANOVA table, we see the degrees of freedom (1093), F (2517.592) and significance (0.000), all of which we encountered in Chapter 9, when we looked at analysis of variance. As a reminder, the degrees of freedom tell us how much the values can vary. The df is not important for interpreting a regression result because we are already provided with r and r squared to give us the strength of relationship. F gives us a combined indication of whether the model as a whole is statistically significant (if F exceeds 1) and how strong the relationship is (the larger, the better). The overall significance of our result is also given to us in the ANOVA significance. In the Coefficients table, we encounter the equation of the line from our scatterplot by reading the Unstandardized Coefficients B column: the constant shows us the y-intercept (0.807, which the equation on the scatterplot rounded to 0.81), and the slope of the line (–0.051, which the scatterplot displayed as –0.05). In the Coefficients table, we are given the significance for each variable pairing individually, rather than for the model as a whole, which was given in the ANOVA table. This becomes more important when we conduct multiple regression, that is regression involving more than one independent variable; it does not give us a different result from the model as a whole when we are only using one predictor variable.

We could repeat each of our correlations from Chapter 7 using regression or adding a best fit line to the scatterplot, making sure that we apply our transformations to compensate for outliers on trade, FDI and logged GNI. (We will leave out income inequality because, even after limiting outliers, it still does not meet the assumption of homoscedasticity.) The results of this are shown in Figures 10.2 to 10.4. From these (and our previous correlation results), we see that the strongest predictors are average education and logged GNI, and the weakest are trade and FDI.

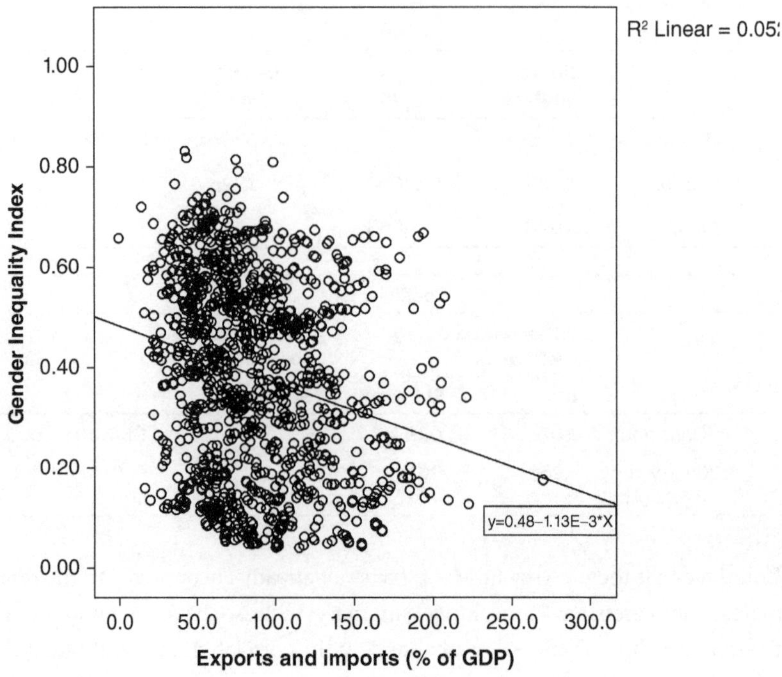

Figure 10.2 Scatterplot of trade and gender inequality with best fit line

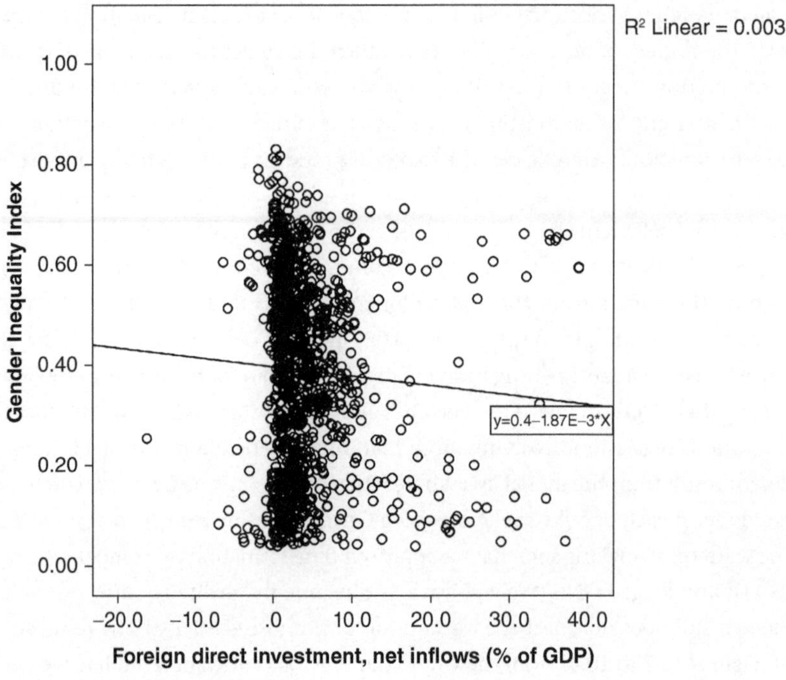

Figure 10.3 Scatterplot of FDI and gender inequality with best fit line

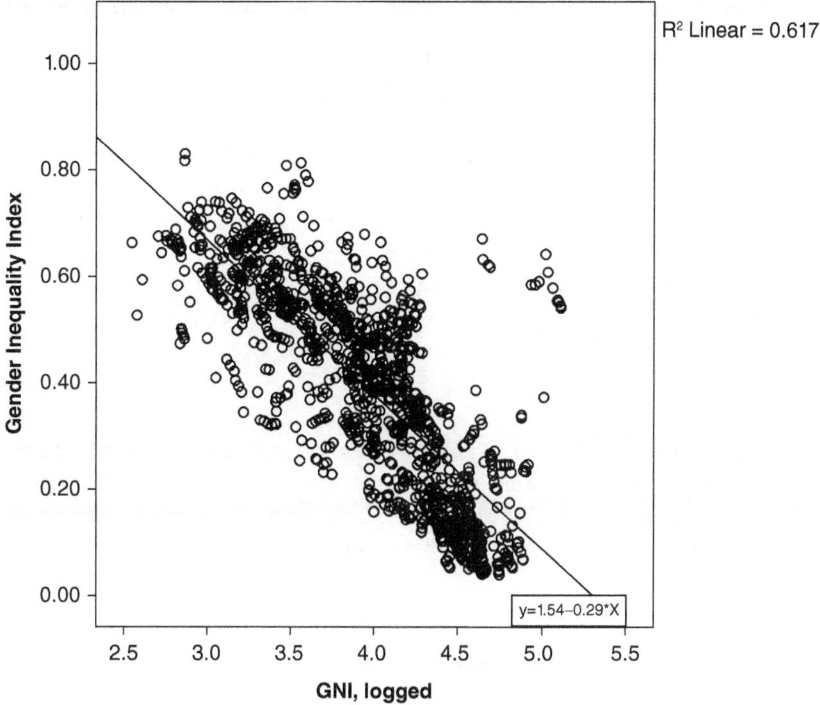

Figure 10.4 Scatterplot of logged GNI and gender inequality with best fit line

But what if we want to know how much each contributes to our overall understanding? For this, we need multiple regression, where we include multiple predictors to explain the outcome variable. Multivariate regression is also based on the equation of a line, just a more complex one. This time, the equation is:

$$y = a + B_1x_1 + B_2x_2 + B_3x_3 + \ldots + \varepsilon$$

In words, this means:

Outcome = Intercept + (B*first predictor) + (B*second predictor) + (B*third predictor) + ... + Random error

For this example, it would be:

Gender inequality = Constant + B*trade + B*FDI + B*Logged GNI + B*Education

The intercept and all of the B values in the equation are taken from the unstandardized B coefficients in the regression outputs. To apply this to our example, follow the instructions in Box 10.2 to run a multiple regression.

BOX 10.2 MULTIPLE REGRESSION WITH DEFAULT STATISTICS

This box shows you how to produce a multiple regression. This test uses more than one continuous predictor variable and one continuous outcome variable. This example uses Exports and imports (% of GDP) [trade], Foreign direct investment, net inflows (% of GDP) [FDIinflow], GNI, logged [loggni] and Mean years of schooling [meanschyrs] as predictors and gender inequality [GII] as the outcome. It applies filters to remove outliers. The results can be found in Table 10.2.

Syntax

Apply filters to outliers from trade and FDI. This time, we need several AND (&) statements in the filter. This ensures that we only include cases that meet every criterion. This is the opposite to the filters that we used in Chapter 6, where we used 'or' to select cases that met any of the criteria - in that case, any of the political parties of interest.

```
USE ALL.

COMPUTE filter_regressionoutliers=(trade <=269.311 & fdiinflow >=-30.947
& fdiinflow <=40.229).

VARIABLE LABELS filter_regressionoutliers 'trade <=269.311 & fdiinflow
>=-30.947 & fdiinflow <=40.229 (FILTER)'.

VALUE LABELS filter_regressionoutliers 0 'Not Selected' 1 'Selected'.

FORMATS filter_regressionoutliers (f1.0).

FILTER BY filter_regressionoutliers.

EXECUTE.
```

Produce regression. Full syntax:

```
REGRESSION

  /MISSING LISTWISE

  /STATISTICS COEFF OUTS R ANOVA

  /CRITERIA=PIN(.05) POUT(.10)

  /NOORIGIN

  /DEPENDENT GII

  /METHOD=ENTER FDIinflow loggni meanschyrs.
```

This can be shortened to:

```
REGRESSION
/dependent GII
/method=enter trade FDIinflow loggni meanschyrs.
```

The default settings for linear regression have quite a few more options than you have encountered in the syntax for most other tests so far. If you do not include the subcommands `MISSING` or `STATISTICS`, SPSS will include the default options. Some of the options for these subcommands include:

> `/MISSING` You can choose between `LISTWISE` (a case is excluded from all analysis if there is a missing value in any of the variables you are analysing) or `PAIRWISE` (a case is only excluded in parts of the analysis where a variable is included that has missing data). Listwise deletion is the default because you will otherwise be analysing different sets of cases for each part of the test in multiple regression. This is generally the more advisable choice.
>
> `/STATISTICS` The default is to include the regression coefficients (`COEFF`), standard outputs table (`OUTS`), r and r squared (`R`), and `ANOVA`. If you do not include this subcommand in your syntax, it will produce these default outputs.

Menu instructions

Apply outlier filter.

> Data > Select Cases > If condition is satisfied > If
>
> Type: trade <= 269.311 & fdiinflow >=-30.947 & fdiinflow <=40.229 in the equation box.
>
> Continue.
>
> OK/Paste.

Analyze > Regression > Linear

> Place the outcome variable (Gender inequality index [`GII`]) in the Dependent box.
>
> Place the predictor variables (Exports and imports (% of GDP) [`trade`], Foreign direct investment, net inflows (% of GDP) [`FDIinflow`], GNI, logged [`loggni`], Mean years of schooling [`meanschyrs`]) in the Block 1 of 1 box.
>
> OK/Paste.

Table 10.2 Multiple regression results for gender inequality

Model summary				
Model	**R**	**R Square**	**Adjusted R Square**	**Std. error of the estimate**
1	.860	.739	.738	.098827

(Continued)

Table 10.2 (Continued)

			ANOVA			
Model		**Sum of squares**	**df**	**Mean square**	**F**	**Sig.**
1	Regression	27.914	4	6.978	714.512	.000[b]
	Residual	9.855	1009	.010		
	Total	37.769	1013			

	Unstandardized coefficients		**Standardized coefficients**	**t**	**Sig.**
	B	**Std. error**	**Beta**		
(Constant)	1.194	.030		40.170	.000
Trade (% of GDP)	−0.00003	.000	−.007	−.383	.702
FDI inflows (% of GDP)	−.001	.001	−.020	−1.157	.248
GNI, logged	−.133	.010	−.357	−13.942	.000
Mean years of schooling	−.034	.002	−.550	−21.217	.000

Let's start with the 'Model summary' results. We have an r of 0.860, which translates into an r squared of 0.739, meaning our predictors can explain 73.9 per cent of variance in gender inequality. You might notice that this is only marginally higher than the r squared result for our bivariate regression between average education and gender inequality (r squared 0.697). This tells us that adding three more variables (trade, FDI and GNI) only increases the amount of variance in gender inequality that we can explain by 4.2 per cent. The adjusted r squared is very slightly lower than r squared (0.738 versus 0.739). As we add more predictors, the adjusted r squared will begin to differ from r squared, as it adjusts r squared for the number of predictors included in the analysis. The adjusted r squared will be higher than r squared when adding extra predictors increases the explanatory power of our test by more than would be expected by chance. If, however, adding extra predictors does not add any more to our explanation of variance in the outcome than we would expect from chance, the adjusted r squared will be smaller than r squared.

Turning to the ANOVA results, we see that we have 1013 degrees of freedom, and F is 714.512. When we compare that to the F statistics we produced in Chapter 9, we can see that this is a very high value, and the result is statistically significant ($F>1$, $p<0.001$). This reflects similar information to us as that in r squared: these predictors can explain a large amount of variation in the outcome. Finally, we look at the Coefficients table. Looking at B from the unstandardized coefficients, we can construct the equation of our line of best fit:

Gender inequality = 1.194 – 0.00003*trade – 0.001*FDI – 0.133*GNI, logged – 0.034*mean years of schooling + Random error

Do you see how small B is for trade and FDI? This should not come as a surprise, given how weak the correlations were and how small r squared was on the scatterplots that we produced with the fit lines. We can see from Sig. that we have statistically insignificant results for trade ($p=0.702$, so $p>0.10$) and FDI ($p=0.248$, so $p>0.10$); logged GNI and mean years of schooling are both statistically significant ($p<0.001$). The unstandardized coefficients give us the rate of change in the outcome variable for every one-unit change in the predictor variable. Taking mean years of schooling, this means that, for every additional year of schooling, we would expect a 0.034-unit decrease in gender inequality. For every one-unit increase in logged GNI, we would expect to find a 0.133-unit decrease in GII. But how do we know which of these exerts a stronger influence? We might be tempted to claim that GNI is more important because the unstandardized B for GNI is –0.133, which is a steeper slope than mean years of schooling, which has an unstandardized B of –0.034. However, we would be wrong because we are not comparing the same units to each other.

It is much easier to look at the standardized coefficients when we want to see which variables are the most important. Being standardized means that the results have been manipulated so that they are all presented on the same scale, so instead of trade and FDI being represented as a percentage of GDP and mean years of schooling being measured in years, they are all represented on comparable scales. This makes it immediately obvious that the standardized Beta is highest for mean years of schooling (–0.550), followed by logged GNI (–0.357); trade (–0.007) and FDI (–0.020) are both much weaker and statistically insignificant. From these results, we would conclude that, given a choice of these four variables, investing in general education is the best way to decrease gender inequality.

Additional statistics for linear regression

Now that you have encountered multiple regression, it is worth mentioning that there are some additional features that you can add to your results. If, however, you are already feeling overwhelmed with the number of tables you have produced, do not feel that this section is essential when you are starting out. For more advanced users, this section discusses the addition of descriptive statistics, collinearity diagnostics, residual plots and confidence intervals (Box 10.3). There are even more (such as part and partial correlations, casewise diagnostics and outlier identification, and Mahalanobis and Cook's tests), which we will not look at, as these are more advanced features than are intended to be addressed in this book. If you are undecided about whether you should look into these, here is a brief description of what each of these additional statistics tells you.

Descriptive statistics for linear regression include a correlation table between all of the variables. These results are used in conjunction with collinearity diagnostics to test for the problem of multicollinearity mentioned above: when the predictor variables vary too much with each other, this results in a worse overall model. Residual plots will provide you with information about outliers and deviations from normality. Confidence intervals take into account the sample size and variance to give us a lower and upper range in which we are 95 per cent certain we will find the actual value. In the case of regression, the confidence intervals give us a range within which we would expect to find the unstandardized B coefficient. This adds extra nuance to our interpretation of our results: having a very wide range of values for our confidence intervals gives us a warning that we may not want to overinterpret our results.

BOX 10.3 MULTIPLE REGRESSION WITH ADDITIONAL TESTS

This box shows you how to produce a multiple regression with descriptive statistics, collinearity diagnostics, residual plots and confidence intervals. This test uses more than one continuous predictor variable and one continuous outcome variable. The example uses Exports and imports (% of GDP) [trade], Foreign direct investment, net inflows (% of GDP) [FDIinflow], GNI, logged [loggni] and Mean years of schooling [meanschyrs] as predictors and gender inequality [GII] as the outcome. It applies filters to remove outliers. The results can be found in Table 10.3.

Syntax

```
REGRESSION
  /DESCRIPTIVES MEAN STDDEV CORR SIG N
  /MISSING LISTWISE
  /STATISTICS COEFF OUTS CI(95) R ANOVA COLLIN TOL
  /CRITERIA=PIN(.05) POUT(.10)
  /NOORIGIN
  /DEPENDENT GII
  /METHOD=ENTER trade FDIinflow loggni meanschyrs
  /SCATTERPLOT=(*ZRESID ,*ZPRED)
  /RESIDUALS NORMPROB(ZRESID).
```

Menu instructions

Analyze > Regression > Linear

Place the outcome variable (Gender inequality index [GII]) in the Dependent box.

Place the predictor variables (Exports and imports (% of GDP) [trade], Foreign direct investment, net inflows (% of GDP) [FDIinflow], GNI, logged [loggni], Mean years of schooling [meanschyrs]) in the Block 1 of 1 box.

> Statistics

Regression Coefficients: Select Estimates and Confidence Intervals.

Also tick Model fit, Descriptives and Collinearity diagnostics from the choices in the right-hand column.

Continue.

> Plots

Move *ZRESID into the Y box.

Move *ZPRED into the X box.

Standardized Residual Plots: Select Normal probability plot.

OK/Paste.

Table 10.3 Multiple regression results with additional statistics, selected tables

Correlations

		Gender Inequality Index	**Exports and imports (% of GDP)**	**Foreign direct investment, net inflows (% of GDP)**	**GNI, logged**	**Mean years of schooling**
Pearson correlation	Gender Inequality Index	1.000	−.255	−.061	−.792	−.833
	Exports and imports (% of GDP)	−.255	1.000	.363	.238	.250
	Foreign direct investment, net inflows (% of GDP)	−.061	.363	1.000	.025	.053
	GNI, logged	−.792	.238	.025	1.000	.778
	Mean years of schooling	−.833	.250	.053	.778	1.000
Sig. (1-tailed)	Gender Inequality Index	.	.000	.025	.000	.000
	Exports and imports (% of GDP)	.000	.	.000	.000	.000
	Foreign direct investment, net inflows (% of GDP)	.025	.000	.	.210	.044
	GNI, logged	.000	.000	.210	.	.000
	Mean years of schooling	.000	.000	.044	.000	.
N	Gender Inequality Index	1036	1036	1036	1036	1036
	Exports and imports (% of GDP)	1036	1036	1036	1036	1036
	Foreign direct investment, net inflows (% of GDP)	1036	1036	1036	1036	1036
	GNI, logged	1036	1036	1036	1036	1036
	Mean years of schooling	1036	1036	1036	1036	1036

(Continued)

Table 10.3 (Continued)

Model		Unstandardized coefficients		Standardized coefficients	t	Sig.	95.0% confidence interval for B		Collinearity statistics	
		B	Std. error	Beta			Lower bound	Upper bound	Tolerance	VIF
1	(Constant)	1.200	.028		42.705	.000	1.145	1.255		
	Exports and imports (% of GDP)	.000	.000	−.029	−1.661	.097	.000	.000	.809	1.236
	Foreign direct investment, net inflows (% of GDP)	.000	.000	−.012	−.738	.461	−.001	.000	.864	1.157
	GNI, logged	−.133	.009	−.362	−14.476	.000	−.151	−.115	.391	2.555
	Mean years of schooling	−.033	.002	−.543	−21.675	.000	−.037	−.030	.390	2.564

Coefficients[a]

a. Dependent variable: Gender Inequality Index

Let's start with the Correlations table. We use these statistics, alongside the Collinearity statistics column from the Coefficients table and the Collinearity diagnostics table, to test for multicollinearity. What we want to see is that each of our predictors has a relationship with the outcome variable, looking for a correlation (ideally above 0.30); but we do not want any of the predictors to be too strongly related to each other (generally below 0.7 or 0.8, depending on who you ask). Look at the column for 'Gender Inequality Index' in the Correlations table. We can see that the correlation between trade and gender inequality is –0.255. This falls below the ideal threshold of 0.3, but not irretrievably. However, the correlation with FDI – as we have encountered before – is very weak: –0.061. This variable would be better excluded from the analysis, as it is unlikely to add predictive value. Logged GNI and mean years of schooling both show correlations well above the 0.30 threshold (–0.792 and –0.833, respectively). Based on these results, we would want to drop FDI from the model as having very little explanatory value; here, we will keep it in the discussion so that we talk through a single set of results.

Now we turn to the correlations between the various predictors. Here we *don't* want to find a strong correlation. The only correlation that potentially poses problems for covariance here is between logged GNI and mean years of schooling (r=0.778). We can then investigate this potential conflict in greater detail by consulting the Collinearity statistics columns in the Coefficients table. Here, we have two statistics: Tolerance and VIF. Tolerance gives us an indication of the additional explanatory value of that variable in the model.

If the tolerance is below 0.10, then there is likely to be multicollinearity, and that variable does not add anything to the model that the other variables do not already provide. The tolerance statistics indicate that we should not be excessively concerned about the correlation between logged GNI and mean years of schooling, as the tolerance is nowhere near 0.10 (0.391 and 0.390, respectively). The variance inflation factor (VIF) contains the same information as the tolerance statistic but is the inverse (VIF = 1/tolerance). For example, the tolerance for trade is 0.809; thus 1/0.809 = 1.236, which is the VIF. Because it is the inverse, you are looking for a value over 10 (= 1/0.1) if you are looking for potentially problematic variables. If you exceed the collinearity statistics and have a strong correlation between two or more of your predictors, you should consider removing some of the strongly related predictors. When trying to decide which to remove or whether to remove borderline variables, it is worth running the regression with and without each of these to see whether adding the other variable adds materially to the explanatory power of the model.

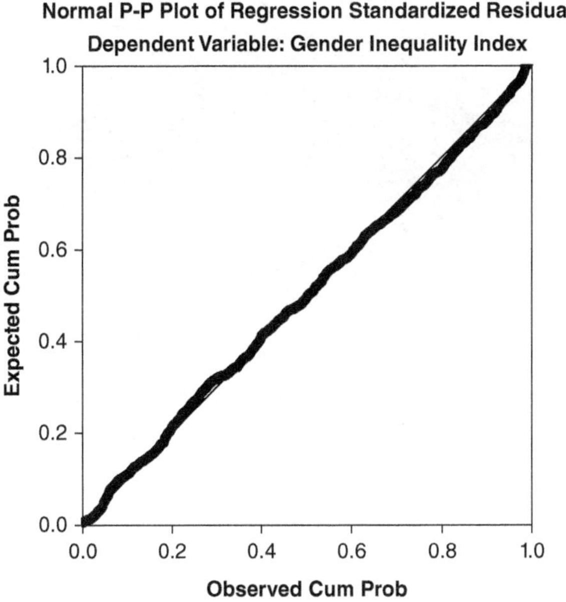

Figure 10.5 Normal P-P Plot

Next we turn to the tests of the assumption of normality, looking at the Normal P-P (Probability) Plot (Figure 10.5) and the scatterplot (Figure 10.6). You want your results to lie as close as possible to the diagonal line on a Normal P-P Plot. The closer the results are to this line, the more your data fits the assumption of normality. In this case, our data fits this assumption very well. The scatterplot shows the distribution of the standardized residuals.

You want them to be distributed in a rectangular shape without any clear pattern. If there is a clear pattern or skew to the distribution of the dots, then your data probably violates the assumptions of linear regression. You should also check whether you have standardized residual results that lie outside of ±3.3, which would indicate that you have outliers that should be considered for exclusion. If there are not many outliers in a fairly large sample, and they do not fall very far outside of the cut-off, then they are unlikely to pose a problem and can be included.

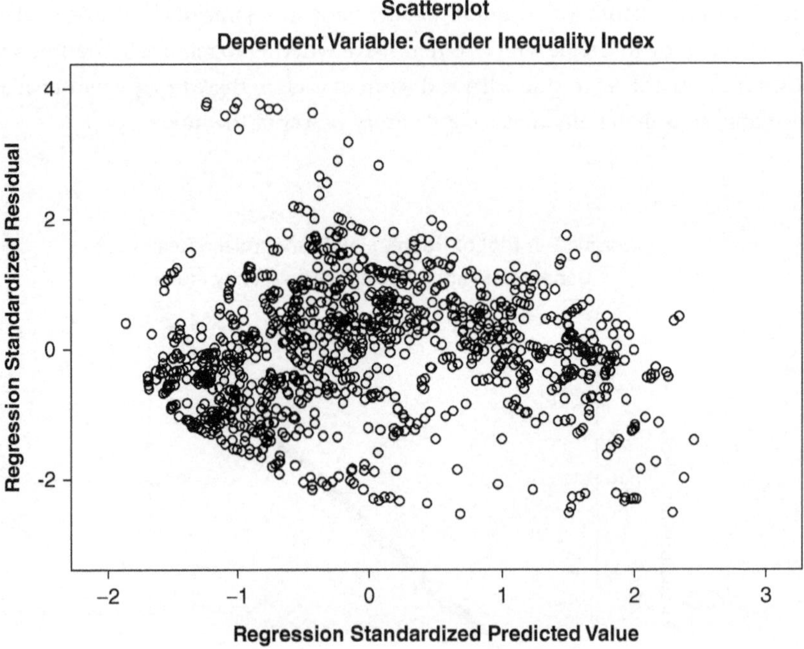

Figure 10.6 Residual scatterplot

Finally, we look at the confidence intervals in the Coefficients table. Rather than just reporting the unstandardized B coefficient, the confidence interval shows us the range in which we can express a high degree of confidence (95 per cent) that the actual value falls. This is only relevant for sample data, as it is another expression of how likely our sample is to represent the wider population from which it is taken. A 95 per cent confidence interval tells us the range in which we would expect to find the value in 95 per cent of samples drawn from the same population; in the other 5 per cent of samples, we might get a value that falls outside of this range, and the result would be unlikely to be representative of the population. With large samples or very consistent patterns, the confidence interval will be much smaller. For smaller samples or cases where the observations are much less consistent, the interval will be much wider. We see that the unstandardized B for both trade and FDI is

0.000. We have previously analysed this result and interpreted the significance, which shows that neither of these variables is statistically significant (trade p=0.097; FDI p=0.461). For logged GNI, the unstandardized B is –0.133, and the confidence interval runs from –0.151 to –0.115, which equates to –0.133 ± 0.018. For mean years of schooling, the confidence interval runs from –0.037 to –0.030, or –0.033 ± 0.003. In practical terms, this means that, for each additional year of school in a country, we would expect to see a decrease in gender inequality of 0.033 ± 0.003.

Let's apply these ideas to answering the question, 'How does the level of democracy in a country affect the level of gender equality?' We could start by using the Polity democracy/autocracy score (`e_polity2`, running from –10 to +10), treating it as a continuous variable and adding it to our previous multiple regression, leaving out trade and FDI this time because they were statistically insignificant in our previous model (Table 10.4). We can see from the correlations that all of the variables are associated with the GII at r>0.30. As we already know, there is a suspicion of multicollinearity between logged GNI and mean years of schooling (r=0.767) but not between the other predictors. The tolerance values are all above 0.10 (0.410, 0.378, 0.869), indicating that we do not have significant cause for concern, so we turn to the main results, keeping all three predictors.

Table 10.4 Multiple regression, impact of democracy on gender inequality

Descriptive statistics			
	Mean	**Std. dev.**	**N**
GII	.39636	.195654	1034
GNI, logged	3.9675	.53107	1034
Mean years of schooling	8.072	3.1561	1034
e_polity2	4.50	6.038	1034

Correlations					
		Gender Inequality Index	**GNI, logged**	**Mean years of schooling**	**e_ polity2**
Pearson correlation	Gender Inequality Index	1.000	–.784	–.838	–.400
	GNI, logged	–.784	1.000	.767	.233
	Mean years of schooling	–.838	.767	1.000	.356
	e_polity2	–.400	.233	.356	1.000
Sig. (1-tailed)	Gender Inequality Index	.	.000	.000	.000
	GNI, logged	.000	.	.000	.000

(Continued)

Table 10.4 (Continued)

Correlations

		Gender Inequality Index	GNI, logged	Mean years of schooling	e_ polity2
	Mean years of schooling	.000	.000	.	.000
	e_polity2	.000	.000	.000	.
N	Gender Inequality Index	1034	1034	1034	1034
	GNI, logged	1034	1034	1034	1034
	Mean years of schooling	1034	1034	1034	1034
	e_polity2	1034	1034	1034	1034

Model summary[b]

Model	R	R Square	Adjusted R Square	Std. error of the estimate
1	.875[a]	.766	.765	.094873

a. Predictors: (Constant), e_polity2, GNI, logged, Mean years of schooling

b. Dependent variable: Gender Inequality Index

ANOVA[a]

Model		Sum of squares	df	Mean square	F	Sig.
1	Regression	30.273	3	10.091	1121.105	.000[b]
	Residual	9.271	1030	.009		
	Total	39.544	1033			

a. Dependent variable: Gender Inequality Index

b. Predictors: (Constant), e_polity2, GNI, logged, Mean years of schooling

Coefficients[a]

Model		Unstandardized coefficients		Standardized coefficients	t	Sig.	95.0% confidence interval for B		Collinearity statistics	
		B	Std. error	Beta			Lower bound	Upper bound	Tolerance	VIF
1	(Constant)	1.194	.027		44.835	.000	1.142	1.247		
	GNI, logged	−.131	.009	−.355	−15.075	.000	−.148	−.114	.410	2.440

Coefficients[a]										
Model	Unstandardized coefficients		Standardized coefficients	t	Sig.	95.0% confidence interval for B		Collinearity statistics	
	B	Std. error	Beta			Lower bound	Upper bound	Tolerance	VIF
Mean years of schooling	−.032	.002	−.518	−21.123	.000	−.035	−.029	.378	2.643
Polity2	−.004	.001	−.133	−8.199	.000	−.005	−.003	.869	1.151

a. Dependent variable: Gender Inequality Index

We can see from the Model summary that the predictors explain 76.5 per cent of variance in the level of gender inequality. The model as a whole is statistically significant (F 1121.105, p<0.001). The Coefficients results show us that all three predictors are statistically significant. The standardized Beta coefficients show that mean years of schooling is the best predictor of gender inequality (Beta –0.355); the level of democracy in a country is the weakest (Beta –0.133). The confidence intervals indicate that a one-unit increase in logged GNI results in a decrease between –0.148 and –0.114 units in gender inequality. A one-year increase in mean years of schooling results in a decrease of 0.035 to 0.029 units in gender inequality, while a one-unit increase in Polity score results in a decrease of 0.005 to 0.003 units in gender inequality.

Multiple regression with dummy variables

What if we wanted to see whether these results are also true if we use a different measure of democracy? We might think of testing it against Freedom House scores, but we are not sure whether we should treat a 1 to 7 ordinal scale as a continuous variable, and Freedom House statuses are categorical (free, partly free, not free). To include such a categorical variable in a regression analysis, we need to create a series of 'dummy' variables. Dummy variables are coded 1 or 0, with a value of 1 indicating that a case possesses a specific characteristic and 0 being applied to all the cases without this characteristic. The coding essentially makes a statement about whether a case does or does not fall into the category of interest. This is straightforward with cases where the categories are mutually exclusive, such as Freedom House status, where a country can only fall into one category at any given time. This style of coding is also often applied, for example, to survey questions where respondents are allowed to tick multiple boxes, such as indicating which news sources they use. This would result in a series of variables with a value of 1 each time someone indicated they use that news outlet and a 0 when they do not. When converting a categorical variable with multiple categories into a dummy variable, we would need to create a separate dummy variable for each category. So, using the Freedom House status variable [e_fh_status], we would need one variable for 'free' (free=1; all other categories=0); one for 'partly free' (partly free=1; all other categories=0); and one for 'not free' (not free=1; all other categories=0). We would then include all three of these dummy variables in our regression analysis to see whether any of them made a difference. This is very laborious to do by hand, but if you are lucky enough to have a version of SPSS that includes Python Essentials, there is a tool for creating a series of dummy variables. Follow the instructions in Box 10.4 to create your dummy variables using this tool; or follow the instructions in Box 10.5 if you do not have a licence with Python.

BOX 10.4 CREATING DUMMY VARIABLES USING AUTOMATED TOOL

This box shows you how to create dummy variables from a categorical variable using the dummy variable tool. For this to work, you must have a Python Essentials licence, which may require separate installation. This is appropriate for one categorical variable with discrete categories. If you are converting a range of values or a continuous variable into dummy variables, you should use recoding, not the dummy variable tool. This example uses Freedom House status [e_fh_status].

Syntax

```
SPSSINC CREATE DUMMIES VARIABLE=e_fh_status

ROOTNAME1=e_fh_status

/OPTIONS ORDER=A USEVALUELABELS=YES USEML=YES OMITFIRST=NO.
```

Menu instructions

Transform > Create dummy variables

Move Freedom House status [e_fh_status] into Create Dummy Variables for: box.

Give a root name that will prefix your dummy variable, if desired (such as e_fh_status); this will then be put at the beginning of each dummy.

OK/Paste.

Check the success of your recoding by running a crosstab of the original variable against the dummy variables.

BOX 10.5 MANUALLY CREATING DUMMY VARIABLES

This box shows you how to create a series of dummy variables from a categorical variable using recoding. You can also use this to recode continuous variables, such as making any values greater than 0 a positive result and any 0 values negative. This can be useful if you simply want to know whether or not a case has a particular characteristic rather than exploring the value of that characteristic. This example uses Freedom House status [`e_fh_status`]. You need to know how many categories you have before starting.

Syntax

```
RECODE e_fh_status (1=1) (2 thru 3=0) into fhfree.

RECODE e_fh_status (2=1) (1=0) (3=0) into fhpartlyfree.

RECODE e_fh_status (3=1) (1 thru 2=0) into fhnotfree.

EXECUTE.

VARIABLE LABELS

fhfree 'Freedom House free dummy'

fhpartlyfree 'Freedom House partly free dummy'

fhnotfree 'Freedom House not free dummy'.

VALUE LABELS

fhfree 1 'Free' 0 'Other'

/fhpartlyfree 1 'Partly free' 0 'Other'

/fhnotfree 1 'Not free' 0 'Other'.
```

Menu instructions

Transform > Recode into Different Variables

Move the original variable (Freedom House status [`e_fh_status`]) into the middle box (labelled Numeric Variable -> Output Variable).

In the Output Variable section on the right, fill in the Name of the new variable (`fhfree`) and the Label (Freedom House free dummy).

Click Change. (This should replace the ? in the middle box with the name of the new variable.)

(Continued)

> Old and New Values.

Old Value: Value

Fill in the category value for Free (1) from the existing `e_fh_status` variable.

Put the new category value (1) in the New Value box on the left.

Click Add. Each time you fill in the Old and New Values, you must press Add so that the transformation appears in the Old -> New box on the right.

Old Value: Value or Range.

Range: 2 through 3; New Value 0. Add.

OR

Old Value 2, New Value 0, Add.

Old Value 3, New Value 0, Add.

Click Continue.

OK/Paste.

Table 10.5 Multiple regression results for gender inequality, using FH dummies

Descriptive statistics

	Mean	**Std. dev.**	**N**
GII	.39547	.195128	1094
GNI, logged	3.9583	.52846	1094
Mean years of schooling	8.001	3.1656	1094
Freedom House free dummy	.4479	.49751	1094
Freedom House not free dummy	.2358	.42471	1094

Correlations

		Gender Inequality Index	**GNI, logged**	**Mean years of schooling**	**Freedom House free dummy**	**Freedom House not free dummy**
Pearson correlation	Gender Inequality Index	1.000	−.783	−.835	−.559	.277
	GNI, logged	−.783	1.000	.773	.507	−.192

Correlations

	Mean years of schooling	−.835	.773	1.000	.515	−.238
	Freedom House free dummy	−.559	.507	.515	1.000	−.500
	Freedom House not free dummy	.277	−.192	−.238	−.500	1.000
Sig. (1-tailed)	Gender Inequality Index	.	.000	.000	.000	.000
	GNI, logged	.000	.	.000	.000	.000
	Mean years of schooling	.000	.000	.	.000	.000
	Freedom House free dummy	.000	.000	.000	.	.000
	Freedom House not free dummy	.000	.000	.000	.000	.
N	Gender Inequality Index	1094	1094	1094	1094	1094
	GNI, logged	1094	1094	1094	1094	1094
	Mean years of schooling	1094	1094	1094	1094	1094
	Freedom House free dummy	1094	1094	1094	1094	1094
	Freedom House not free dummy	1094	1094	1094	1094	1094

Model summary[b]

Model	R	R Square	Adjusted R Square	Std. error of the estimate
1	.870[a]	.757	.757	.096274

a. Predictors: (Constant), Freedom House not free dummy, GNI, logged, Freedom House free dummy, Mean years of schooling

b. Dependent variable: Gender Inequality Index

(Continued)

Table 10.5 (Continued)

ANOVA[a]						
Model		**Sum of squares**	**df**	**Mean square**	**F**	**Sig.**
1	Regression	31.520	4	7.880	849.999	.000[b]
	Residual	10.096	1089	.009		
	Total	41.616	1093			

a. Dependent variable: Gender Inequality Index

b. Predictors: (Constant), Freedom House not free dummy, GNI, logged, Freedom House free dummy, Mean years of schooling

Coefficients[a]										
Model		**Unstandardized coefficients**		**Standardized coefficients**	**t**	**Sig.**	**95.0% confidence interval for B**		**Collinearity statistics**	
		B	**Std. error**	**Beta**			**Lower bound**	**Upper bound**	**Tolerance**	**VIF**
1	(Constant)	1.128	.027		41.102	.000	1.074	1.182		
	GNI, logged	−.115	.009	−.312	−12.915	.000	−.133	−.098	.382	2.618
	Mean years of schooling	−.033	.001	−.528	−21.839	.000	−.035	−.030	.381	2.627
	Freedom House free dummy	−.044	.008	−.112	−5.589	.000	−.059	−.028	.555	1.800
	Freedom House not free dummy	.016	.008	.034	1.983	.048	.000	.031	.745	1.342

a. Dependent variable: Gender Inequality Index

Once you have created your dummy variables, try including them in a regression. This time, we will leave out trade and FDI, since we know they were statistically insignificant. That leaves us with logged GNI, mean years of schooling and the Freedom House status dummies as predictors and gender inequality as the outcome variable. You will see that it leaves out one of the Freedom House dummies automatically from the analysis, since the three categories cover all possible variations. Here we have reported the results using the 'free' and 'not free' dummies (Table 10.5). The correlation and tolerance statistics do not pose any particular problems, just flagging again the relationship between logged GNI and mean years of schooling. We can see that removing the trade and FDI variables and adding the Freedom House status dummy variables does result in an increase (albeit a modest one) in the explanatory power of our model compared to not including a measure of democracy: our r squared has increased to 0.757. However, perhaps unsurprisingly because of its greater level of nuance, the model with the Polity score has greater explanatory power than using the Freedom House dummy variables (r squared 0.766 versus 0.757). Turning to the Coefficients table, we can see that all of the variables except 'not free' are statistically significant at $p<0.001$; 'not free' is significant at $p<0.05$. This might be because there is less of a clear trend for 'not free' countries than 'free' countries. The standardized Beta results show that mean years of schooling still has the greatest effect in reducing gender inequality. Being rated 'not free' causes an increase in gender inequality (Beta 0.035). 'Free' countries have a much greater impact in reducing gender inequality (Beta –0.111). These results mean that greater political and civil liberties are associated with positive gains for gender equality, even controlling for gross national income and education levels.

LOGISTIC REGRESSION

Logistic regression, like linear regression, is an attempt to build a model of what happens to the outcome variable when one or more predictors change. Both tests use continuous variables for the predictors. However, while linear regression also uses a continuous variable for the outcome, logistic regression uses a binary categorical variable for the outcome. A binary (also sometimes called binomial, binominal or dichotomous) categorical variable is one that only has two categories, like the dummy variables we created earlier in the chapter. Other examples of binary variables include traditional questions about sex and gender (which is reflected, for example, in people identifying as non-binary when rejecting this two-category classification) and questions that can be answered yes or no (such as whether someone voted in the last national election). The binary categories must be mutually exclusive: any given case can only fall into one category or the other. For categorical outcome variables with more than two categories, you would need to use multinomial logistic regression.

While linear regression's results are interpreted as how much change you would expect to observe in the outcome variable based on a one-unit change in the predictor variable, logistic regression's results are interpreted as a probability of the outcome occurring. With linear regression, we saw this expressed as the equation:

$$y = a + Bx$$

This translates into words:

Outcome variable value = Constant + (unstandardized B coefficient*predictor variable value)

With logistic regression, the model is expressed with the equation:

$$\text{Log-odds} = a + Bx$$

SPSS then helps us by converting log-odds back to normal odds so that we can interpret our results. (Do you remember how hard it was to make sense of the logged values of 'GNI, logged' when we manipulated it for linear regression?) With logistic regression, this means that we are presenting the odds of our outcome being the characteristic specified by our binary output variable. For example, we might want to form a prediction about someone's likelihood to vote. In this case, we are trying to predict the likelihood of someone either being a voter or not. Using the ESS dataset, we would need to convert Voted last national election [`vote`] from the ESS dataset into a binary variable (yes/no), excluding answers of 'not eligible' and missing answers to use this as the outcome variable. Then we could look at a series of continuous predictors, such as age, years of full-time education completed, weekly hours worked and income. Or we could also look at voting behaviour more specifically by looking at voting for or identification with a particular party. We could do this by taking one of the variables from the series Party voted for in last national election or Which party feel closer to, then creating a dummy variable. For example, if we pose the question, 'Who is likely to identify with UKIP?', we could start with Which party feel closer to, United Kingdom [`prtclbgb`] because it has a larger sample of UKIP supporters than the voting variable as a consequence of the impact of first-past-the-post voting driving voters away from fringe parties as a 'wasted' vote. We could then recode this into a binary variable with two categories: voted for UKIP (1), did not vote for UKIP (0). To understand this in application, follow the instructions in Box 10.6 to run a binary logistic regression using likelihood of having voted in the last national election.

BOX 10.6 BINARY LOGISTIC REGRESSION WITH DEFAULT STATISTICS

This box shows you how to produce a binary logistic regression. This test is appropriate for one or more continuous predictor variables and one binary outcome variable. This example uses Age of respondent, calculated [`agea`], Years of full-time education completed [`eduyrs`] and Total hours normally worked per week in main job, overtime included [`wkhtot`] as the predictor variables and Voted last national election [`vote`] as the outcome variable. Voting is reclassified for this example so that 'not eligible' is classed as a missing answer. The results can be found in Table 10.6.

Syntax

Reclassify missing values for voting to exclude 'not eligible'.

```
MISSING VALUES vote (3 thru HIGHEST).
```

Binary logistic regression with default options.

```
LOGISTIC REGRESSION VARIABLES vote
  /METHOD=ENTER agea eduyrs wkhtot
  /CRITERIA=PIN(.05) POUT(.10) ITERATE(20) CUT(.5).
```

Menu instructions

Analyze > Regression > Binary Logistic

Put the binary dependent variable (Voted last national election [vote]) in the Dependent box.

Put the continuous independent variables (Age of respondent, calculated [agea], Years of full-time education completed [eduyrs] and Total hours normally worked per week in main job, overtime included [wkhtot]) in the Block 1 of 1 box.

OK/Paste.

Table 10.6 Binary logistic regression results for likelihood to vote

Case processing summary			
Unweighted cases[a]		**N**	**Per cent**
Selected cases	Included in analysis	32450	80.8
	Missing cases	7735	19.2
	Total	40185	100.0
Unselected cases		0	.0
Total		40185	100.0

a. If weight is in effect, see classification table for the total number of cases

Dependent variable encoding	
Original value	**Internal value**
Yes	0
No	1

(Continued)

Table 10.6 (Continued)

Block 0: Beginning block

Classification table[a,b]

	Observed		Predicted		
			Voted last national election		Percentage correct
			Yes	No	
Step 0	Voted last national election	Yes	25358	0	100.0
		No	7092	0	.0
	Overall percentage				78.1

a. Constant is included in the model

b. The cut value is .500

Variables in the equation

		B	S.E.	Wald	df	Sig.	Exp(B)
Step 0	Constant	−1.274	.013	8996.931	1	.000	.280

Variables not in the equation

			Score	df	Sig.
Step 0	Variables	Age of respondent, calculated	695.502	1	.000
		Years of full-time education completed	408.208	1	.000
		Total hours normally worked per week in main job overtime included	.410	1	.522
	Overall statistics		1556.078	1556.662	3	.000

Block 1: Method = Enter

Omnibus tests of model coefficients

		Chi squared	df	Sig.
Step 1	Step	1642.403	3	.000
	Block	1642.403	3	.000
	Model	1642.403	3	.000

Model summary

Step	−2 Log likelihood	Cox & Snell R Squared	Nagelkerke R Squared
1	32434.554[a]	.049	.076

a. Estimation terminated at iteration number 5 because parameter estimates changed by less than .001

Classification table[a]

	Observed		Predicted		
			Voted last national election		Percentage correct
			Yes	No	
Step 1	Voted last national election	Yes	25247	111	99.6
		No	7000	92	1.3
	Overall percentage				78.1

a. The cut value is .500

Variables in the equation

		B	S.E.	Wald	df	Sig.	Exp(B)
Step 1[a]	Age of respondent, calculated	−.030	.001	1159.062	1	.000	.971
	Years of full-time education completed	−.120	.004	862.982	1	.000	.887
	Total hours normally worked per week in main job overtime included	.003	.001	7.661	1	.006	1.003
	Constant	1.646	.086	368.065	1	.000	5.185

a. Variable(s) entered on step 1: Age of respondent, calculated, Years of full-time education completed, Total hours normally worked per week in main job overtime included

Start by looking at the Case processing summary table. Make sure that the number of cases looks like what you were expecting. If not, check whether you have large amounts of missing data or if you have any unintentional filters applied to your data. Next, check the Dependent variable encoding. It is important for interpreting the rest of your results that you know which category of your outcome variable is coded '1', as this is your reference group, and all of the other odds are produced in comparison to this group. In this case, because we are using the original voting variable and have simply manipulated our missing values, we have ended up with 'No' coded as 1: this means our reference group is people who *didn't* vote. If you want to make sure that your reference group is 'Yes', then recode vote into a new variable, with 'Yes' coded '1' and 'No' coded '0'.

The results in Block 0 are our 'control' results: they give us the results without including any of the predictor variables. In the Block 0 classification table, the overall percentage in the Percentage correct column gives a baseline for accuracy of predicting correctly whether someone had voted based on SPSS's attempt at classification. In this case, the prediction is correct 78.1 per cent of the time, so we hope to achieve higher than 78.1 per cent accuracy when we add the predictor variables to the model. What we see is that SPSS's classification was that everyone would have voted in the last national election, so the error in the classification that reduces the percentage correct is arising from not having predicted non-voting.

The results in Block 1 are the results including the predictor variables. The Omnibus tests of model coefficients tells us how our model performs when the predictors are included, compared to the baseline we established in Block 0. This is a test of 'goodness of fit': if the result is statistically significant, then including our predictor variables results in a better accuracy of prediction than the random guess in Block 0. Here, our significance is very close to 0 ($p<0.001$), so we can conclude that our predictor variables are better at predicting someone's likelihood to vote than random chance. The Model summary provides us with further information about the amount of variation in the outcome variable that the predictors can explain, like other measures of explanatory power we have encountered, such as r squared and eta squared. Although the Cox & Snell R Squared and Nagelkerke R Squared each contain 'R Squared' in the name, they are not calculated the same way as the r squared result in linear regression results, so they are sometimes called 'pseudo r squared' results. We still interpret them the same way as r squared results, however. We express them as a percentage of variance explained. The Cox & Snell result will always be lower than the Nagelkerke result because the Cox & Snell calculation can never reach the theoretical maximum of 1, while Nagelkerke's can. The Cox & Snell result is therefore a conservative estimate of variance explained, while Nagelkerke's is a more generous correction based on Cox & Snell's underlying calculation. In this case, the Cox & Snell R Squared is 0.049, equating to explaining about 5 per cent of variance; the Nagelkerke R Squared is 0.076, explaining about 7.6 per cent of variance. This means that the predictors explain somewhere between 5 and 7.6 per cent of variance in likelihood to vote – which you might say is not very much, but you should always interpret this in context: many elections are won and lost on such margins. The Block 1 classification table tells us that our model correctly classifies people 78.1 per cent of the time, which is the same as we got in Block 0, when SPSS was just guessing that everyone would vote. The lack of difference in correct classification between the model with (Block 1) and without (Block 0) our predictors is a further reflection of the relatively low pseudo r squared values.

The Variables in the equation table partially resembles the results we encountered in linear regression: we have B, standard error and significance for each variable. Check for statistical significance first to identify any variables whose effect can be ruled out. In this case, all three of our predictors are statistically significant ($p<0.001$ for age and years of full-time education; $p<0.01$ for weekly hours normally worked). The B values are like those from linear regression. Looking at whether they are positive or negative will tell you the direction of the relationship. Remember, in this case, non-voting is our reference category, so having a negative B for age (–0.030) means that as age increases, non-voting decreases – which we would expect based on a large amount of voter turnout data that indicates voting rates are higher among older people. We also see a negative B for years of full-time education completed (–0.120), meaning that more years of education is associated with lower likelihood of not voting. We have a positive B for weekly hours worked (0.003), which means working more hours increases the likelihood of not voting. This might be because people working high numbers of hours find it more difficult to make it to the polls.

Like the unstandardized B in linear regression, it is difficult to compare the B results between different variables to interpret which ones are exerting the strongest effect on the outcome. For this, we need the Exp(B) column, which serves a similar purpose to the standardized betas in linear regression, providing us with information that we can compare between variables that are measured in different units. These values are odds ratios, which tell us the change in odds of being in the reference outcome category when the value of the predictor changes by one unit. If the odds ratio (Exp(B)) is 1, then the predictor makes no difference to the outcome. If it is greater than 1, then a one-unit increase in the predictor will result in an increased likelihood of belonging to the reference category of the outcome variable (in this case, non-voting). If it is less than 1, then a one-unit increase in the predictor will mean a case is less likely to belong to the reference category of the outcome variable.

So far, this gives us the same information as simply interpreting whether B was positive or negative. Exp(B) is expressed as odds, however. This means, for example, that for every additional hour normally worked per week, someone is 1.003 times more likely not to vote (which we can see is barely above 1 – no effect). On the other hand, for each year older the respondent is, the odds of not voting decrease by 0.971. When the value is less than 1, we usually report it by reporting the value of 1/odds ratio to make it easier to understand. For age, this means that we would report someone is 1.030 times less likely (1/0.971) to be a non-voter for each additional year older. We would also report that someone is 1.127 times less likely to be a non-voter for each additional year of full-time education completed (1.127 = 1/0.887). As we can see from these, total hours worked has the least impact; years of full-time education completed has the most.

BOX 10.7 COMPUTING AN INDEX VARIABLE

This box shows you how to combine the values of multiple variables to create an index variable. This is appropriate for ordinal variables with at least four (preferably more) categories or continuous variables. This example uses a series of variables about immigration that are measured on a scale of 0 (most negative) to 10 (most positive). The variables used are:

- Immigration bad or good for country's economy [`imbgeco`]
- Country's cultural life undermined or enriched by immigrants [`imueclt`]

(Continued)

- Immigrants make country worse or better place to live [imwbcnt]
- Immigrants take jobs away in country or create new jobs [imtcjob]
- Taxes and services: immigrants take out more than they put in or less [imbleco]
- Immigrants make country's crime problems worse or better [imwbcrm].

Before combining variables for an index, you need to verify that all of the scales run in the same direction. For example, if you have one variable where the low value means hostility to immigration but another where the high value means hostility, you would need to recode one of the variables to make sure that the low value means the same thing consistently across variables. You also need to check whether you are using variables with different lengths of scales. For example, there are some immigration-related variables in the ESS that are measured on a five-point scale (agree strongly to disagree strongly), while others are measured from 0 to 10. If this is the case, then you will want to transform each scale into a percentage to make sure that each variable is given the same weight in the index variable. Otherwise, the variables with a 0-10 scale will have a much greater influence on the result than those with a 1-5 scale. For information on how to fix these problems, see Box 10.9 at the end of the chapter.

Once you have verified that the scales run in the same direction and that you know how long the scale (if relevant) is on each variable, the syntax itself is very straightforward.

Syntax

Use the COMPUTE command, followed by the name of the new variable you want to create, then '=', followed by the name of each variable you want to add together, separated with +. If you are using syntax, make sure you also apply variable and value labels to remember how to interpret your new variable.

```
COMPUTE imindex=imbgeco + imueclt + imwbcnt + imtcjob + imbleco +
imwbcrm.

VARIABLE LABELS imindex 'Openness to immigration index'.

VALUE LABELS imindex 60 'Strongly pro-immigrant' 0 'Strongly hostile'.
```

Menu instructions

Transform > Compute Variable

Type the name of the new variable [imindex] in Target Variable, then click Type & Label.

Write the variable label (Openness to immigration index) in the Label box, then click Continue.

Type the name of or add the first index variable (Immigration bad or good for country's economy [imbgeco]) to the Numeric Expression box, then type or click +. Add each of the other index variables. (It should read imbgeco + imueclt + imwbcnt + imtcjob + imbleco + imwbcrm when you are finished.)

OK/Paste.

Thus far, our results have been (mostly) statistically significant but not very strong or insightful. Now we turn to more sophisticated testing to answer the question, 'Who is likely to identify with UKIP?' We will test this using the hypothesis:

> H1. People who identify with UKIP are more likely to be male, older, white, with lower educational qualifications and greater hostility to immigration.

This hypothesis is based on stereotypes of an older, white male bias among right-wing voters and the anti-immigration policy stance taken by the party. Testing education is related to anti-immigration stance, as research has shown that people with lower educational qualifications are also more likely to hold anti-immigration views. There are various explanations for this, from perceived economic threat to workers who hold more precarious employment (which is more likely to be the case with lower educational qualifications) to lower educational qualifications being associated with higher national identity and in-group solidarity (see, for example, Ford and Goodwin, 2014; Kunovich, 2009). To test this hypothesis, we will start by computing an index variable that combines the answers to six different questions about immigration (Box 10.7), then run a logistic regression that incorporates categorical predictors: gender and ethnicity (Box 10.8).

BOX 10.8 BINARY LOGISTIC REGRESSION WITH ADDITIONAL STATISTICS

This box shows you how to produce a binary logistic regression with additional statistics to calculate confidence intervals for the odds ratios, Hosmer-Lemeshow goodness of fit test and a casewise listing of residuals to identify possible outlier cases. This test is appropriate for one or more continuous predictor variables and one binary outcome variable. This example uses Openness to immigration index [`imindex`] (created in Box 10.7), Age of respondent, calculated [`agea`], Years of full-time education completed [`eduyrs`], Gender [`gndr`] and Belong to minority ethnic group in country [`blgetmg`] as the predictor variables and a dummy variable for identification with UKIP (based on `prtclbgb` and called `prtclbgb_7` here) as the outcome variable. We have introduced a binary categorical predictor here (sex) to demonstrate how to work with categorical data. The results can be found in Table 10.7.

Syntax

```
LOGISTIC REGRESSION VARIABLES prtclbgb_7

  /METHOD=ENTER imindex agea eduyrs gndr blgetmg

  /CONTRAST (gndr)=Indicator

  /CONTRAST (blgetmg)=Indicator(1)

  /CASEWISE OUTLIER(3)
```

(Continued)

```
/PRINT=GOODFIT CI(95)
/CRITERIA=PIN(0.05) POUT(0.10) ITERATE(20) CUT(0.5).
```

The /CONTRAST subcommand is used with categorical predictors. Each categorical predictor is entered on a new line, each time starting with /CONTRAST. The /CASEWISE subcommand allows you to specify how many standard deviations should be used as a cut-off for identifying potential outlier cases. Here we have specified 3 standard deviations. The /PRINT options include the Hosmer-Lemeshow goodness of fit test ('goodfit') and the confidence intervals for the odds ratios (CI), here specified at the 95 per cent CI.

Menu instructions

Analyze > Regression > Logistic Regression

Put the binary dependent variable (Political party affiliation=UKIP [prtclbgb_7]) in the Dependent box. (Your variable may have a different name and label. This should be a binary variable you have produced from Which party feel closest to, UK [prtclbgb], with UKIP coded as 1 and all others as 0.)

Put the independent variables (Openness to immigration index [imindex], Age of respondent, calculated [agea], Years of full-time education completed [eduyrs] and Gender [gndr]) in the Block 1 of 1 box.

When using any categorical predictors, click Categorical, then move all categorical variables into the Categorical Covariates box. (In this example, move Gender [gndr] and Belong to minority ethnic group in country [blgetmg].) You can choose between the Last and First category as the reference category for each categorical variable. This means that the statistics produced will be in comparison to this group. For sex, 'male' is the first category ('1') and female is the last category ('2'), so if you choose 'last', the results will be in comparison to female respondents. Belonging to an ethnic minority group is coded 'Yes' ('1') and 'No' ('2'). For this example, we want to compare the non-minorities to the minorities, so change the reference group for ethnic group to First, then click Change to apply the change. It should now show 'blgetmg(Indicator(first))'. Click Continue.

Open Options. Choose Hosmer-Lemeshow goodness-of-fit, Casewise listing of residuals (choose between 2 and 3 standard deviations for identifying outliers) and CI for Exp(B) (which produces the confidence intervals for the odds ratios. Click Continue.

OK/Paste.

Table 10.7 Logistic regression results for identification with UKIP

Case processing summary			
Unweighted cases[a]		**N**	**Per cent**
Selected cases	Included in analysis	1985	4.9
	Missing cases	38200	95.1
	Total	40185	100.0

Case processing summary		
Unselected cases	**0**	**.0**
Total	40185	100.0
a. If weight is in effect, see classification table for the total number of cases		

Categorical variables codings			
		Frequency	**Parameter coding**
			(1)
Belong to minority ethnic group in country	Yes	173	.000
	No	1812	1.000
Gender	Male	921	1.000
	Female	1064	.000

Block 0: Beginning block

Classification table[a,b]					
Observed			**Predicted**		
			prtclbgb=UK Independence Party		**Percentage correct**
			.00	**1.00**	
Step 0	prtclbgb=UK Independence Party	.00	1833	0	100.0
		1.00	152	0	.0
	Overall percentage				92.3

a. Constant is included in the model

b. The cut value is .500

Block 1: Method = Enter

Omnibus tests of model coefficients				
		Chi squared	**df**	**Sig.**
Step 1	Step	196.012	5	.000
	Block	196.012	5	.000
	Model	196.012	5	.000

(Continued)

Table 10.7 (Continued)

Model summary			
Step	**−2 Log likelihood**	**Cox & Snell R Squared**	**Nagelkerke R Squared**
1	877.166[a]	.094	.225

a. Estimation terminated at iteration number 8 because parameter estimates changed by less than .001

Hosmer and Lemeshow test			
Step	**Chi squared**	**df**	**Sig.**
1	8.597	8	.377

Contingency table for Hosmer and Lemeshow test						
		prtclbgb=UK Independence Party = .00		**prtclbgb=UK Independence Party = 1.00**		**Total**
		Observed	**Expected**	**Observed**	**Expected**	
Step 1	1	199	198.209	0	.791	199
	2	199	196.970	0	2.030	199
	3	198	195.661	1	3.339	199
	4	196	195.066	4	4.934	200
	5	190	192.126	9	6.874	199
	6	188	189.395	11	9.605	199
	7	188	185.503	11	13.497	199
	8	173	179.296	26	19.704	199
	9	167	168.564	32	30.436	199
	10	135	132.209	58	60.791	193

Classification table[a]					
Observed			**Predicted**		
			prtclbgb=UK Independence Party		**Percentage correct**
			.00	**1.00**	
Step 1	prtclbgb=UK Independence Party	.00	1824	9	99.5
		1.00	148	4	2.6
	Overall percentage				92.1

a. The cut value is .500

Variables in the equation

		B	S.E.	Wald	df	Sig.	Exp(B)	95% C.I. for EXP(B)	
								Lower	Upper
Step 1[a]	Openness to immigration index	−.089	.009	109.866	1	.000	.915	.899	.930
	Age of respondent, calculated	.009	.005	2.704	1	.100	1.009	.998	1.019
	Years of full-time education completed	−.058	.031	3.497	1	.061	.944	.888	1.003
	Gender(1)	.915	.186	24.163	1	.000	2.497	1.733	3.595
	Belong to minority ethnic group in country(1)	1.672	.738	5.130	1	.024	5.325	1.253	22.641
	Constant	−2.346	.878	7.136	1	.008	.096		

a. Variable(s) entered on step 1: Openness to immigration index, Age of respondent, calculated, Years of full-time education completed, Gender, Belong to minority ethnic group in country

Casewise list[a]
a. The casewise plot is not produced because no outliers were found

We can see from the Case processing summary (Table 10.7) that there are 1,985 cases included in this analysis, which is what we would expect, since the UKIP variable is based on UK political party affiliation. In the Categorical variables codings table, we can confirm that belonging to an ethnic minority group and being female are being treated as the reference groups (coded as 0), so our odds ratios for these should be interpreted as the likelihood in contrast to these two groups. Our B block 0 results indicate that SPSS classified 92.3 per cent of cases correctly by assuming that none of the cases would indicate identification with UKIP (since there are only 152 respondents in this test who did identify with UKIP). Turning to the model itself (Block 1), we see that the model as a whole is significant ($p<0.001$) and explains between 9.4 (Cox & Snell R Squared) and 22.5 per cent (Nagelkerke R Squared) of variance in identification with UKIP – substantially higher than our predictions in our previous test about whether someone voted in the last national election.

The Hosmer and Lemeshow test of goodness of fit provides another indication that our model holds explanatory power but also tells us whether the underlying assumption in logistic regression of independence of errors is violated. In this table, the significance results are interpreted the opposite to the interpretation of the Omnibus tests: we are looking for significance that *exceeds* the threshold $p>0.05$, which our model easily does ($p=0.377$). We are likely to have violated the assumption of independence of errors if the ratio of the Hosmer and Lemeshow chi squared statistic to the degrees of freedom is greater than 1. In this case, the Hosmer and Lemeshow chi squared result is 8.597, and we have 8 degrees of freedom. Because 8.597/8 is slightly higher than 1, we conclude that we may have violated the assumption of independence of errors; for the purposes of working through the interpretation of results, however, we will pretend that this has not flagged a potential concern.

Turning to our results, we find all of the variables significant, depending on the threshold applied: openness to immigration and sex are both significant at $p<0.001$; belonging to a minority ethnic group is significant at $p<0.05$; and age and years of full-time education completed are significant at $p<0.1$. We see from the negative B coefficients as well as the odds ratios (Exp(B)) below 1 that our immigration index and years of full-time education have a negative impact on identifying with UKIP, which is what we would expect: higher values on the immigration index mean greater positivity towards immigration, and higher numbers of years of full-time education completed mean (normally) higher educational qualifications, both of which we would expect to decrease the likelihood of identifying with UKIP. If we look at the odds ratios, the lowest odds ratio is openness to immigration: a one-unit increase in openness to immigration decreases the likelihood of identifying with UKIP by 1.093 times. Given that this would mean only a one-point change on a single answer to one of the six survey questions in the index, this is actually fairly substantial. With each additional year of full-time education, respondents are 1.059 (= 1/0.944) times less likely to identify with UKIP; each additional year of age makes someone 1.009 times more likely to identify with UKIP.

Now we look at the odds ratios for the two categorical variables. When interpreting results for categorical variables you need to remember which group is your reference group in order to interpret who is more/less likely to exhibit the outcome characteristic. Looking at gender, our reference group is women because we wanted to see if men were more likely to identify with UKIP. The results confirm this: men are 2.497 times more likely to identify with UKIP than women. For ethnicity, our reference group is people belonging to an ethnic minority group in the UK because we wanted to see whether people from the majority ethnicity (white British) are more likely to identify with UKIP than other groups. Again, our results confirm this: white British respondents are 5.325 times more likely to identify with UKIP than ethnic minorities.

The confidence intervals give us the range in which we expect the true value to fall with 95 per cent confidence. (Think of this like when you see public opinion polling results reported with a ± margin of error: we report the value given, but, in truth, we would only expect our result to be present in a resampling of the population 95 times out of 100.) For age, the lower confidence interval is 0.998: barely below 1 and therefore extremely close to having no effect at all; the upper boundary is at 1.019. When the lower and upper confidence intervals span across 1, this is another indication of statistical insignificance.

Confidence intervals will be wider when there are small sample sizes and/or high levels of variance in the data. For example, we see that the confidence intervals for belonging to an ethnic minority group run from 1.253 to 22.641. The former is a fairly small odds ratio, the latter is huge: this would mean that white respondents are nearly 23 times more likely to identify with UKIP than ethnic minority respondents! You might also notice that the lower confidence interval for ethnicity is below that of gender, but the upper confidence interval for ethnicity is much higher than gender. All of these observations could be reflective of a relatively small number of ethnic minority respondents and/or greater variation in responses.

Our final result is the Casewise list. This tells us that none of our cases was classed as outliers when using a threshold of 3 standard deviations to define outliers. If you decrease this threshold to 2 standard deviations, the casewise list result identifies 69 cases of potential outliers, all of which SPSS expected to be non-UKIP but who actually were UKIP supporters. Given that we only had 152 respondents who identified with UKIP, this is a substantial number of cases. This may indicate that, rather than those cases being outliers, our model is missing some key variables to explain support for UKIP.

BOX 10.9 CREATING AN INDEX VARIABLE WITH VARIABLES WITH DIFFERENT SCALES

This box builds on the example in Box 10.7 about building an index variable by combining the values for several variables. This box expands the example of the openness to immigration index, adding four variables that are measured on a 1-4 scale to the original six variables measured on a 0-10 scale.

You will often find when creating an index variable that different variables will use different scales. For example, you might want to include Allow many/few immigrants of same race/ethnic group as majority [`imsmetn`], Allow many/few immigrants of different race/ethnic group from majority [`imdfetn`], Allow many/few immigrants from poorer countries in Europe [`eimpcnt`] and Allow many/few immigrants from poorer countries outside Europe [`impcntr`] to the index above; but these four variables are measured from 1 ('allow many') to 4 '(allow none). Here we would encounter several problems. First, the scales run in the opposite direction to our other index variables: for 1-4 scales, low values are positive towards immigrants; for the 0-10 scales, low values are negative. Second, the lowest value is 1, while it is 0 on the other scales. Third, these are measured on a 4-point scale, while the others are measured on an 11-point scale. This means that, if we simply added them together, we would not get an accurate reading of the responses. To address this, we need to do two things:

1. Recode our variables to reverse the scale and make the lowest value 0. (In this case, we would recode 4 into 0, 3 into 1, 2 into 2, and 1 into 3.)

(Continued)

2. Apply some fractions to our index equation to revalue the answers as if they ran from 0 to 10 instead of 0 to 3. To do this, we simply need to divide the variable by its current number of categories (3) and multiply by the number of categories we want it to have (10), such as 'imsmetnrecoded/3*10'.

Syntax

First we need to recode all of the variables to reverse the scales and start at 0.

```
RECODE imsmetn imdfetn eimpcnt impcntr (4=0) (3=1) (1=3) (else=copy)

into imsmetnr imdfetnr eimpcntr impcntrr.

EXECUTE.
```

Add variable labels, value labels and set missing values.

```
VARIABLE LABELS imsmetnr 'Allow many/few immigrants of same race/ethnic group as majority (scale reversed)'

imdfetnr 'Allow many/few immigrants of different race/ethnic group from majority (scale reversed)'

eimpcntr 'Allow many/few immigrants from poorer countries in Europe (scale reversed)'

impcntrr 'Allow many/few immigrants from poorer countries outside Europe (scale reversed)'.


VALUE LABELS imsmetnr imdfetnr eimpcntr impcntrr 0 'Allow many' 1 'Allow some' 2 'Allow a few'

3 'Allow none' 7 'Refusal' 8 'Dont know' 9 'No answer'.


MISSING VALUES imsmetnr

imdfetnr

eimpcntr

impcntrr (7 thru 9).
```

Compute index variable, adding mathematical manipulation to the four-point scales.

```
COMPUTE imindex2=imbgeco + imueclt + imwbcnt + imtcjob + imbleco + imwbcrm + imsmetnr/3*10 + imdfetnr/3*10 + eimpcntr/3*10 + impcntrr/3*10.

EXECUTE.

VARIABLE LABELS imindex2 'Openness to immigration index, 10 items'.

VALUE LABELS imindex2 0 'Strongly hostile' 100 'Strongly pro-immigrant'.
```

Menu instructions

Follow the instructions in Box 10.5 for more on recoding and Box 10.7 for computing the first half of the index variable, this time naming the new variable Openness to immigration index, 10 items [imindex2]. At the end of the calculation from Box 10.7, add each of the four-point scale variables, with /3*10 for each; or put all of them in one set of parentheses, with /3*10 after the closed parenthesis:

```
... + imsmetnr/3*10 + imdfetnr/3*10 + eimpcntr/3*10 + impcntrr/3*10
```

OR

```
...+ (imsmetnr + imdfetnr + eimpcntr + impcntrr)/3*10
```

OK/Paste.

ACTIVITIES

Activity 10.1

RQ: How can we explain openness to immigration?

Dataset: ESS.

You will need the variable Openness to immigration index [imindex] created in Box 10.7 to answer this question. Create an index variable Trust in institutions index [trustindex] using the series of variables relating to trust in institutions (trstprl, trstlgl, trstplc, trstplt, trstprt, trstep, trstun). Use Openness to immigration index [imindex] as the outcome variable and Trust in institutions index [trustindex], Age of respondent, calculated [agea] and Years of full-time education completed [eduyrs] as the predictor variables.

1. Develop some hypotheses about the expected relationships. (See, for example, Herreros and Criado, (2009) for an exploration of the relationship between trust and views of immigration.)
2. Which test is appropriate for this combination of variables? Produce the appropriate test.
3. Is the model as a whole statistically significant? At what level?
4. How much variance in the outcome variable can be explained by the predictors?
5. Are all of the predictors statistically significant? At what level?
6. What is the direction of the relationship with each of the variables?
7. Rank the influence of each predictor, from strongest to weakest.
8. What do your results mean for your hypotheses?

(Continued)

Activity 10.2

RQ: 'How can we explain likelihood to vote in France?'

Dataset: ESS.

Select only respondents from France. Use Age of respondent, calculated [`agea`], Years of full-time education completed [`eduyrs`] and Total hours normally worked per week in main job, overtime included [`wkhtot`] as the predictors and Voted last national election [`vote`] as the outcome variable. Make sure that you have reclassified the missing values for `vote` to exclude 'not eligible' from analysis; alternatively, recode vote into a dummy variable, keeping only 'yes' and 'no'.

1. Which test is appropriate for this combination of variables? Produce the appropriate test.
2. Is the model statistically significant?
3. What proportion of variation in the outcome variable can these predictors explain?
4. What is the direction of the relationship between each predictor and the outcome?
5. Which predictor has the greatest explanatory power? How would you report the odds ratios of each variable?
6. How does the explanatory power of France's results compare to the results for the whole survey (refer to the outputs from Box 10.6)?

Activity 10.3

RQ: Who is likely to identify with the Austrian FPÖ?

Dataset: ESS.

Recode Which party feel closer to, Austria [`prtclcat`] into a binary variable with FPÖ as 1 and all other parties as 0. Make sure that you have properly classified any missing values in the dummy variable. Use Openness to immigration index [`imindex`] (created in Box 10.7), Age of respondent, calculated [`agea`], Years of full-time education completed [`eduyrs`], Gender [`gndr`] and Belong to minority ethnic group in country [`blgetmg`] as the predictors and the FPÖ binary variable as the outcome variable. Set female and ethnic minority as the categorical reference groups. Include a goodness of fit test and 95 per cent confidence intervals.

1. Which test is appropriate for this combination of variables? Produce the appropriate test.
2. Is the model statistically significant?
3. What proportion of variation in the outcome variable can these predictors explain?
4. Which predictors have a statistically significant effect on identifying with the FPÖ?
5. What is the direction of the relationship between each predictor and the outcome?
6. Which predictor has the greatest explanatory power? How would you report the odds ratios of each variable?
7. How do these results compare to the results for explaining identification with UKIP in the UK?

Activity 10.4

RQ: To what extent are higher homicide rates driven by income inequality?

Dataset: UN.

In *The Spirit Level*, Wilkinson and Pickett (2010: 129-44) propose that increased inequality increases the importance of status, resulting, among other things, in higher homicide rates in more unequal societies. However, their data only covers 23 highly developed countries. Test this theory against a larger pool of countries. Use homicide rate (per 100,000 people) [`homicides`] as the outcome variable and gender inequality [`gii`], mean years of schooling [`meanschyrs`], Polity score [`e_polity2`], logged GNI [`loggni`] and income inequality [`incomeineq`] as the predictors.

Part A: Default statistics.

1. Which test is appropriate for this combination of variables? Produce the appropriate test.
2. Is the model statistically significant?
3. What proportion of variation in the outcome variable can these predictors explain?
4. Which predictors have a statistically significant effect on homicide rates?
5. For the statistically significant predictors, what is the direction of the relationship between each predictor and the outcome?
6. Which predictor has the greatest explanatory power?

Part B: Additional statistics:

7. Produce the appropriate test, this time including the relevant additional statistics.
8. Check the additional statistics. Are any of the assumptions violated? What steps can you take to correct any violations? Take any necessary corrective steps, then rerun the test.
9. Now answer questions 2 to 6 using the modified results.
10. How would you interpret the confidence intervals for the results?
11. What do these results mean for Wilkinson and Pickett's theory?

FURTHER READING

As with the other chapters on continuous data, there are far more resources for these topics than for categorical data.

Marchant-Shapiro, T. (2015) *Statistics for Political Analysis: Understanding the Numbers*. London: Sage/CQ Press.

This book includes some basic instructions for using SPSS to conduct data analysis, and the examples are from political science. See chapter 12 ('Bivariate regression: Putting your ducks in a line') and chapter 13 ('Multiple regression: The final frontier') for a discussion of linear regression. This book does not cover logistic regression. For a discussion of dummy variables, see the section 'Gauss-Markov assumption 1: Interval-level variables' in chapter 13 ('Multiple regression').

Pallant, J. (2016) *SPSS Survival Manual*. Maidenhead: Open University Press/McGraw-Hill Education.

This book provides a functional overview of how to produce statistics in SPSS. See chapter 13 ('Multiple regression') for coverage of linear regression and chapter 14 ('Logistic regression') for logistic regression.

Urdan, T.C. (2017) *Statistics in Plain English*, 4th edn. Abingdon: Routledge.

This book discusses statistical concepts in much more accessible language than most. See chapter 13 ('Regression') for a discussion of the statistical ideas behind regression.

REFERENCES

Ford, R. and Goodwin, M. (2014) 'Understanding UKIP: identity, social change and the left behind', *The Political Quarterly*, 85 (3): 277–84.

Herreros, F. and Criado, H. (2009) 'Social trust, social capital and perceptions of immigration', *Political Studies*, 57 (2): 337–55.

Kunovich, R. (2009) 'The sources and consequences of national identification', *American Sociological Review*, 74 (4): 573–93.

Wilkinson, R. and Pickett, K. (2010) *The Spirit Level*. Harmondsworth: Penguin.

11

WRITING ABOUT DATA

CHAPTER SUMMARY

This chapter covers the final step of any research project: writing about data. Now that you have learned how to conduct appropriate statistical tests, you need to be able to convey your findings clearly and effectively. This requires you to be able to talk about your data, knowing what information to highlight in your discussion and what information to present in tables and charts. The first part of this chapter looks at the main components of a dissertation or quantitative data report, walking through the contents of each section. Even if you are not undertaking a dissertation, quantitative data reports will normally include all of these elements, so this information should be applicable to anyone writing a data report. The second part looks at how to format your work according to professional standards.

OBJECTIVES

In this chapter, you will learn:

- The main components of a data report or quantitative dissertation
- How to write up findings
- How to present your results professionally.

INTRODUCTION

For most researchers, producing a series of data outputs is only one part of the process. Most researchers will then need to present their findings, accompanied by written and/or verbal explanations interpreting the outputs. Most students will be used to writing essays based on compiling information from a variety of text-based sources, but they are much less confident when writing about tables and charts. Yet the way you talk about data is not fundamentally different from the way that you might use quotes or paraphrases from the academic literature. This chapter walks you through some of the things to keep in mind when reporting quantitative findings. We will start with the professional conventions around formatting your tables and charts; then we will walk through some guidelines for how to talk about the data; and finally, we will look at the general structure of a quantitative dissertation.

DISSERTATIONS AND DATA REPORTS

Quantitative data reports and dissertations generally contain the same elements, but the word count dedicated to each element varies in proportion to the total length of the work.

Data reports will often range from 1,000 to 8,000 words; undergraduate dissertations are typically 8,000–12,000 words, with Master's dissertations ranging from 10,000 to 40,000 words and doctoral theses normally 60,000–100,000 words. Most undergraduate students in Europe, and some in the United States, are expected to write a long essay, or dissertation, towards the end of their studies. A dissertation or thesis is a coherent and original examination of a particular topic, generally of your choosing. You should always consult your local guidance to ensure that you meet the requirements of your dissertation or data report in your department. Your department or university is likely to have a handbook or other document that lays out the requirements, with regards to both topic and content, and style, format, length and presentation. The process will be much easier if you read the guidance carefully at the start of your project, as this should affect how you plan both time and content.

Selecting your topic

Deciding on your topic is often one of the hardest parts of the process. You will probably find this task is actually harder, the shorter the word limit. Students often underestimate the amount of time and effort required to narrow down their topic and choose their research question(s). This can be a very frustrating process, where you may feel that you undertake a significant amount of 'wasted' reading because it does not make the final cut – but this is all part of establishing your background in the topic and deciding on your primary focus. This work may feel wasted, but without this developmental process, you cannot get to the end point of a completed piece of original research.

It is helpful if you have at least a topic of interest to start with, such as voter behaviour, democratization in the Middle East and North Africa, clash of civilizations or support for gender equality in authoritarian states. Whatever topic, you need to make sure that you have a personal interest in researching it. It should be something that you are keen to learn more about and want to spend time reading about it and discussing. Without this spark of enthusiasm at the start of the project, you will find it very hard to maintain motivation and focus as your project progresses. If you are really struggling to identify a topic, think about the topics you have encountered so far on your degree course. Are there any that particularly appealed to or excited you? If this does not help, think about the world you live in. Is there something you have noticed in the community where you live? This was the way I arrived at my dissertation topic as an undergraduate. I was studying abroad at the time when I had to submit a proposal, and, looking around for ideas, I became interested in the relationship between the country where I was living and its immigrant populations. It became a topic that I was passionately interested in, which made the dissertation research a much better experience than some students who choose a topic too quickly and find that their enthusiasm is exhausted within the first few weeks, but it is then too late to change.

If none of these techniques works to help you identify a topic to start with, some universities make past dissertations and theses available for you to consult, and you could get ideas by looking at what former students have done. For postgraduate degrees, these will often be publicly available, either in a university library or through a thesis repository. This is less common for undergraduate dissertations, but you may find that your department keeps some copies of good past examples that you can read through. It is a good idea to dip into these examples at several points during your dissertation. You should try to skim two or three examples at the start of your dissertation to give you an idea of what a dissertation looks like and what kinds of topics might be appropriate for the length and timeframe. This can be a very useful exercise to help you understand the guidelines in application and may give you some inspiration. You should try to look at particular sections of the dissertation when you are taking them on yourself, such as examples of literature reviews when you are writing your own literature review or how students have written up their data when you are doing your data analysis. You should have another look at the very end with a sharp eye to presentation and formatting, making sure that your dissertation looks professional and conforms to the expectations of your institution. Do, however, treat any examples with caution: relying too much on examples of previous students' work may limit how you conceive of your own project. You may also find that your department has fewer examples of quantitative dissertations than more theoretical, historical or qualitative research, depending on what the most common topics and methods are in your department.

Main components of dissertations and data reports

Once you have an idea of your topic, you can embark on the process of the project itself. Most dissertations and data reports will contain some key elements:

- Introduction (~10 per cent of the word count)
- Literature review (20–25 per cent)
- Methodology (5–15 per cent, depending on complexity)
- Substantive/data analysis chapters (40–50 per cent)
- Conclusions (10–15 per cent).

If you break these sections up into discrete pieces of work, you will probably find the word count much less daunting, and it will help you to develop some interim deadlines rather than looking at the dissertation as a whole. When undertaking a quantitative dissertation, you will generally follow the order listed above for your writing as well, though I would always recommend writing the introduction as the absolute last element: you cannot write a good introduction that lays out your structure and key arguments until you know what those are, and you will not know what those are until you write them.

Introduction

When structuring writing in political science and IR, you might follow the mantra: say what you're going to say (introduction); say it (body); say what you said (conclusion). The introduction serves the purpose of 'say what you're going to say': it gives the reader a clear overview of the work as a whole, which is why I would recommend only drafting a couple of sentences on your topic to keep you focused, saving the real writing of your introduction to last. Your introduction will usually be quite short, often starting by giving the reader an overview of your topic, situating it perhaps within some relevant historical context or current affairs. You should always include a few sentences outlining what your key arguments are. Unless otherwise instructed, your reader should have a very good idea of what your ultimate conclusions are from reading the introduction. Most political science/IR readers do not want to wait for the conclusions to find out what the answer to your question is; and being presented with an overview at the beginning can also help the readers to orientate themselves within each chapter by identifying how the information they encounter fits into the bigger picture. For example, if I were exploring the question, 'To what extent does immigration affect support for the radical right?', my overall argument could be, 'This dissertation finds that, while immigration is often portrayed as a catalyst for support for the radical right, it is clear that perceptions of immigrants play a greater role in support for the radical right than objective immigration levels.' You should also briefly outline the structure of the rest of the work, such as, 'This dissertation/data report begins with an overview of key arguments relating to the rise of the radical right in Western Europe. This is followed by a discussion of the case selection, datasets and measurement of key concepts. The substantive chapters look at two case studies in turn: France, a country with high levels of immigration and a long history of immigration; and Hungary, a history with very low levels of immigration and small immigrant populations.'

Literature review and research question(s)

Quantitative dissertations, because they are generally taking a deductive approach to research (see more about the distinction between inductive and deductive research in Chapter 2), will usually follow a theory-driven approach. This means that the first steps with your dissertation will be identifying your topic, reading around the literature, using the literature to develop a research question, then writing a literature review. This makes it sound simple, though the process is often far messier: you start with one topic, start reading the literature, fall down a rabbit hole in one sub-theme of the literature, come out the other side with a new/altered focus, read some more, change your mind again, etc. There are two things to remember in this process:

1. This is both normal and necessary for defining your topic and research question.
2. You should not underestimate the amount of time this process takes to be done well.

Topic selection, identification of research questions and reviewing the literature are undertaken together as one part of the research cycle. Students often feel that they have 'wasted' their time by going through this cycle several times, especially when they may end up reading a whole stack of sources that do not make the final cut. Excellent dissertations will probably use less than one-third of the sources read. But the process of reading and responding to these sources is important for developing your knowledge of the field and helping you to identify your position in the literature. You should allow yourself plenty of time to do this, probably around one-third of the total time you have for your project.

Once you have defined your topic, you should start to read the literature with a view to formulating your research question(s), which will focus your project. Reviewing the literature is a process of learning more about a topic (expanding your general knowledge of the field), critically analysing what other people have already said on the topic, identifying your research question(s), checking whether someone else has already answered your chosen research question(s) and gleaning inspiration for how to go about your data analysis by seeing how other people have done it. When you are reading, think about the following questions:

- What have other people already said? Are there flaws in their arguments? Did they miss something? What are the major points of agreement/disagreement between authors? Who agrees/disagrees with whom? Why?
- Based on the literature, what is a preliminary answer to your research question(s)? What do you expect to find in the data? What hypotheses does the literature lead you to?
- How have other people researched this topic? What methods did they use (surveys, interviews, archival research, etc.)? If they used secondary data, which datasets did they use?
- How is the literature connected to what you are planning to do in the rest of your dissertation?

As you read, you should also look at the questions that other researchers have asked, keeping a note of any that you find interesting. As you begin to formulate your own questions, try to create questions that are open-ended, explanatory questions, such as questions beginning with 'how', 'why' and 'to what extent'. Question phrasing is very important because it will influence your focus. If you ask a basic, descriptive question or a question that can be answered yes or no, you will more easily fall into the trap of description instead of analysis, and you may find that you run out of things to say. Prompting yourself with a question that is more complex and requires a more nuanced answer will help you to avoid this common pitfall.

Some examples of explanatory, complex, open-ended research questions from academic publications include:

- Why would religiosity have a greater effect on happiness for political conservatives compared to political liberals? (Bixter, 2015).

- Why do some societies have a pattern of mass political values that seems supportive of stable democracy while others do not? (Reisinger et al., 1994: 183).

Academic publications do not always contain well-formulated research questions, and some do not contain a research question at all, so you should not expect that all published examples are good examples. Some examples that should not be emulated include:

- Are predominantly Muslim societies distinctly disadvantaged in democratization? (Fish, 2002). This question prompts a yes or no answer and also indicates some bias in the phrasing; it is also difficult to conceptualize 'distinctly disadvantaged'.
- Will more countries become democratic? (Huntington, 1984). This question cannot be empirically answered because it is a question trying to predict the future. You can, of course, use data to make a prediction about the future, but the danger of choosing such a question for a dissertation is that you will be prompted to deviate from an evidence-based argument.

Conducting a literature review for your dissertation will test your academic skills severely. You will need to keep careful notes of all the sources you have read, key arguments and their full citation information, especially noting page numbers for any key ideas and quotes. A dissertation is usually the point where using referencing software can start to make a big difference in your ability to organize so many sources. Whether you use a reference manager or not, careful notes are important to avoiding academic misconduct or having to remove entire ideas at the end of your dissertation because you can no longer find their original source. Careful notes are also important because, after reading more than 50 sources – which you should plan to do as a minimum for an undergraduate dissertation, likely more for postgraduate – you will begin to forget who said what and what you have read.

There is a difference between the process of reviewing the literature (reading around and familiarizing yourself with the topic, the key authors and main debates) and writing a literature review (an argumentative piece of writing that provides a preliminary answer to the research question based on what other people have already found). You are at a good point to slow down your search for literature when you reach saturation: this is when you have read enough sources that you notice repetition of authors and ideas and are not gleaning anything more than very minor additions to your knowledge with new sources. When you reach this point, you should start to structure your written literature review.

The literature review has several purposes. First, as mentioned already, it is an important part of the development of your topic, questions and the scope of your project. Second, you need to demonstrate that you are aware of existing research and to make sure that you are not planning to duplicate someone else's research. Third, you should highlight flaws, omissions and gaps in existing research. Fourth, you need to take a stance by identifying the major debates on the topic, then stating your position on these debates. (Academics are guaranteed to disagree with each other about everything, so if you have not found some debates in the literature, then you should ask your supervisor or a specialist librarian for help with your literature searching skills.) Finally, you should identify what you are going to add to the literature with your study (your original contribution). The bar for originality is actually much lower than students often think. Originality can come from applying existing ideas or theories to a new case, updated time period or different dataset; it can come from combining two bodies of literature that do not tend to speak to one another; or by identifying a flaw in a common argument.

The key to a good written literature review is *critical analysis*. Critical analysis is a tricky concept to explain. Unlike casual usage of the term, 'critical' in this context actually means approaching a topic with an open mind and recognizing both strengths and weaknesses in an argument. Criticism is not inherently negative: it can be based on recognizing the validity of a claim. Criticality is the difference between simply accepting or describing what other people have said and probing the validity or coherence of their arguments. The first step to developing criticality is to read more, as this will help you to develop an idea of the differences of opinion on the topic. Analysis means subjecting ideas and theories to questions to see how they hold up, testing whether the evidence supports the findings given and evaluating the coherence and logic of the argument. This does not necessarily mean that the arguments will not withstand the tests, but you need to show the process of testing and application of those ideas or theories to other contexts. Analysis can also come from noticing where scholars agree and disagree.

If you are struggling to develop critiques of the literature, try using other sources to help you. Find your main source with a search tool like Google Scholar or Web of Science, then look at 'cited by' sources. This will show you authors who have published later works that have referred back to the source you are trying to critique. Articles with phrases like 'A response to...', 'A critique of...' and 'reply' in the title are very likely to be critical of the original source; 'in defence of...' and other variants will indicate a counterargument against critics.

You may want to use a large piece of paper or mind-mapping software to help you map and link ideas between different authors. Think about making a spider diagram, looking for groups of arguments. Start to position your sources according to common ideas and arguments rather than according to sources, identifying the points of commonality and difference. Good literature reviews are structured thematically, approaching the literature argumentatively, rather than analysing one source at a time. Ideally, you should, when relevant, deal with more than one source at a time by *synthesizing* the ideas. Synthesizing the literature means identifying common arguments in the literature and putting all/the most important (if there are many) authors in a single citation, such as this example from Ariely (2012: 461): 'Some consider [globalisation] a force that undermines national identity, while others argue that globalisation trends reinforce national feelings (Calhoun, 2007; Guibernau, 2001; Kaldor, 2004; Kymlicka, 2003; Tonnesson, 2004; Zuelow et al., 2007).' When synthesizing multiple sources into a single citation, you should either alphabetize them, as in this example, or list them chronologically; unless otherwise specified, you can choose which system to follow, but use it consistently.

Synthesizing the literature will make your writing more concise and argumentative and will demonstrate your analytical skills in identifying commonalities across a range of authors, bringing them together. Ariely had not synthesized all of these sources; his writing would have been a descriptive, long-winded list of who said what and agreed with whom, along the lines of, 'Guibernau (2001) argues that globalisation trends reinforce national feelings. Calhoun (2007) agrees with this, saying that globalisation has made national belonging more important. Kymlicka (2003) also agrees…', etc. After providing a long list that essentially repeats the same point made by many people, you would finally arrive at your critique towards the end of the paragraph. This is one of the things that your tutors mean if they complain that your writing is too descriptive. To solve this, you will need to return to the planning stage, looking again at your spider diagram and notes about the literature to help you build this synthesis.

In summary, your literature review should have a clear argument running through it that, as a whole, adds up to a preliminary answer to your research question. You should establish what other people have already said and where the gaps are in the literature, and position yourself around key debates.

Hypotheses

Because quantitative dissertations are usually taking a deductive, theory-testing approach, and you are starting with a literature review, you should develop some hypotheses from the literature. (Quick tip: 'hypothesis' is the singular – one hypothesis; 'hypotheses' is the plural – two or more hypotheses.) 'Hypothesis' can sound quite intimidating, but it is actually just a clearly formulated 'hunch, assumption, suspicion, assertion or an idea about a phenomenon, relationship or situation, the reality or truth of which you do not know' (Kumar, 2011: 82). Hypotheses are tentative propositions whose validity is unknown. Drafting hypotheses can be a good exercise to test whether you have been able to apply the theoretical debates in the literature to data. They can also provide you with a focus when collecting and analysing data. You may need to reformulate your hypotheses as you explore your evidence and your research question evolves.

Hypotheses can be used in both qualitative and quantitative research, but when used in quantitative research, they are usually formulated according to natural science norms. This means numbering the hypotheses consecutively as H1, H2, etc., and specifying an empirically testable relationship between two or more variables. Taken together, your hypotheses should test your research question(s). The results of your tests should clearly lead you to an answer to your question(s). They must be empirically testable and falsifiable (can be proved wrong). In shorter pieces of work, such as data reports, hypotheses should be directly testable: it should be clear precisely which variables you are examining for a relationship, such as:

H1. People who identify with a political party are more interested in politics than those who do not.

When writing something of dissertation length, however, your hypotheses sometimes become more complex and include concepts (such as nationalism, authoritarian values, environmentalism) that need to be broken down into measures, such as these examples from Buttice and Milazzo (2011: 850–1):

H1. As the constituency becomes more competitive, the policy contrast between candidates will decline.

H2. As the experience contrast between the candidates increases, the policy contrast will decrease.

These hypotheses should then be accompanied by paragraphs explaining how the concepts (competitiveness, policy contrast, experience contrast) were broken down into empirically testable measures, either in the literature review or in the methodology section. Whether you have simple or complex hypotheses, you need to make it absolutely clear to the reader:

- How your hypotheses are drawn from the literature.
- How your hypotheses can be tested with data.

There are two approaches to the placement of your hypotheses: they can be spread throughout your literature review, or they can be focused at the end. There is not a right or wrong choice between these approaches. Instead, you should think carefully about the structure and flow of your literature review and use the approach that is the most logical for your argument. If your literature breaks up very clearly into discrete 'chunks', such as when there are multiple explanations of the phenomenon, or when you are bringing together multiple distinct clusters of the literature, it can make the most sense to spread your hypotheses across your literature review, presenting each hypothesis as close as possible to the section of literature that led you to it. If, on the other hand, there are no clear breaking points or subsections in your literature review, with the whole review focused on the same theoretical explanations, it may make the most sense to place your hypotheses at the end of your literature review. Whichever approach you take, your hypotheses should never precede the literature supporting them: you should discuss the literature first, then propose the hypothesis/hypotheses the sources lead you to.

Methodology

The literature review should transition naturally into the methodology section. It should identify for the reader *what* you are going to do in the rest of the dissertation; the methodology tells the reader *how* and *why* you are going to do it. You should spend time explaining your case selection, answering questions like:

- Why did you choose these cases? Have you used a particular framework for selecting them?
- What are the strengths and weaknesses of your case selection?
- Were there other cases that might have been useful but were not included? If they were excluded, what were the reasons? (These might be pragmatic, such as limitations of time and resources, or missing data; or they might be theory driven, such as arguing that one case has been over-studied.)

You will also need to talk about your data sources. If you are using primary data (data you collected), you should explain how and when you collected it, what sampling method you used, potential problems with the sample and a justification for why it is still a useful dataset. If you are using secondary data (data someone else collected), you should give some background information about the dataset, which wave(s) you are using if it is a dataset collected at multiple points in time, information about its sample, and possible strengths and weaknesses.

You then need to spend time talking about your concepts and measurement. Discussing your conceptualization and measurement is referred to as the process of operationalization: making your ideas into something that you can use and test. You will need to break down complex concepts into dimensions (if necessary) and then specific measures (variables). Concepts are ideas that exist at a very broad level but can rarely be directly measured. The problem with empirically testing concepts is that their meaning can vary considerably between different researchers. The key question to answer when operationalizing your concepts is, 'How do I know it when I see it?' You need to be clear and specific enough in your conceptualization and measurement that another researcher could apply the information you have given and arrive at the same result. Your reader must be able to clearly see how you got from an abstract idea in your literature review ('nationalism') to specific measures (Some cultures: much better or all equal [`smctmbe`], ESS). You will need to bridge this gap using logic and the academic literature. In this example, I would break down nationalism into two dimensions: cultural superiority and in-group solidarity, modelled on Mudde's conceptualization (2010). I can then justify the choice of the survey question, 'Thinking about the world today, would you say that some cultures are much better than others or that all cultures are equal?', from the ESS (round 7). I should then provide the further information that this variable is nominal, with the answer options being: Some cultures are much better than others and All cultures are equal. To measure in-group solidarity, I could look for evidence of trying to protect the in-group (natives), such as Immigrants take jobs away in country or create new jobs [`imtcjob`] or Law against ethnic discrimination in workplace good/bad for a country [`lwdscwp`].

You will need not only to explain your logic and how you moved from concept to measures, but also to provide a justification for *why* you did it that way. Your justifications might be pragmatic: there was only one variable available in your dataset that could reasonably be used as a measure for your concept; or you chose a series of variables measured on ordinal scales, rather than the nominal alternatives, so that you could run some of the more advanced multivariate inferential tests or construct an index variable. Or your justifications might be theoretical: you rejected some of the alternatives because you disagree with the way some of the literature has gone about breaking down your key concepts, and you are consciously rejecting their conceptualization. Whatever the reasons, it is important to make clear to the reader that your decisions were conscious and that you had good reasons for handling your data the way you did. This justification is another aspect of showing off your critical analysis skills by showing that you can think critically about your own choices with the data.

Data analysis

Once you have produced a series of results, look at them and think about which pieces of information best help you to answer your research question and test your hypotheses. You are unlikely to include every output that you produce, so you will need to be judicious in your choice. You should include the data in the order of your hypotheses, so that you are testing each hypothesis in the same order as they are numbered and the order in which they were presented in the literature review. Sometimes you will test more than one hypothesis at once, such as when you are testing competing explanations from the literature.

Once you have made your initial selection of results and have reordered them, write up some preliminary analysis. Learning how to write about data can feel foreign and confusing, but it really is straightforward. Try to strike a balance between not packing every piece of data from every table into your written analysis at one extreme, and only referring vaguely to a table full of data with no discussion of specific numbers at the other extreme. When trying to assess whether you have reached a good balance of detail, read your write-up, asking yourself, 'If my readers did not look at the tables and charts at all, would they be able to pick up enough information from reading my analysis to understand my results and agree with my conclusions?' Make sure that it is clear, after you discuss each set of results, whether the evidence leads you to confirm your hypothesis or reject it, or whether the results are inconclusive and can neither confirm nor reject.

You should also think about the intended audience you are writing for. The intended audience of this book is students; if that is you, you are probably writing about data for some form of assessment, and, as such, your teacher will be looking for you to demonstrate that you understand your results well enough to write about them – this is an element of testing in your data report. If you are writing for other audiences or in a non-assessment context, think about your reader when you decide where to place yourself on the spectrum of detail in reporting your results. If you are writing for a lay audience, you will usually include less detail about your methodology and the finer points of data analysis (such as statistical significance and confidence intervals), focusing on the broad findings. If you are writing for an academic audience, you will need to provide a much more robust justification of your choices with data and a more nuanced reporting and interpretation of your findings.

The conventional way of writing about data is to discuss key figures in the body of your writing, then put a reference to the appropriate table or figure number in parentheses, just as you would cite a text-based source. For example, we could write about the results from the comparison of means from Chapter 9 (which we label here Tables 11.1 to 11.3):

> There is a statistically significant difference between subjective income groups' mean happiness levels, with those who were living comfortably on their present income reporting mean happiness of 8.18 on a scale 0–10, compared with a mean happiness of only 5.20 for those who were finding it very difficult on their present income (Table 11.1). The difference between groups is statistically significant (p<0.001), and the effect size is moderate (eta 0.358), with subjective household income explaining 12.8 per cent of variance in happiness levels.

You would only need to include Table 11.1 within the body of your report, as you have reported the key information from Table 11.2 and 11.3 by including the statistical significance result from the ANOVA table and the effect size from the eta results in the text of your analysis.

Table 11.1 Mean happiness by subjective household income, including variance, UK

Feeling about household's income	Mean	N	Std. dev.	Variance
Living comfortably	8.18	902	1.408	1.984
Coping	7.50	954	1.754	3.075
Difficult	6.75	303	2.315	5.357
Very difficult	5.20	87	2.863	8.200
Total	7.58	2247	1.897	3.597

Source: ESS (round 7). Variables: `hincfel, happy`.

Table 11.2 ANOVA results for happiness by political party affiliation and subjective income

	Sum of squares	df	Mean square	F	Sig.
Between groups	1035.088	3	345.029	109.858	.000
Within groups	7043.908	2243	3.141		
Total	8078.996	2246			

Table 11.3 Measures of association for happiness, UK

	Eta	Eta squared
Subjective household income	0.358	0.128

Writing up your results is only half of the process of data analysis. The other half of data analysis is thinking about the causality, explanation and implications: the interpretation and application of your results. To write high-quality analysis, you then need to think about a qualitative, contextualized explanation of your findings: What alternative explanations might there be? What do my findings *not* tell me? How do my results align with other literature? You should have references back to some of the key sources from your literature review, and you will likely need to include some additional sources that did not appear in your literature review to help you justify your interpretation of your findings. Finally, you need to identify the implications of your findings: what do they mean for the theory/theories you are testing? If they are theory-infirming, what else might need to be tested to verify that the problem is with the theory itself and not with your data or case(s)?

Conclusions

Writing the conclusions for a dissertation often goes beyond the simple recap of arguments in shorter pieces of work. Dissertation conclusions should, of course, revisit your key arguments and findings; but you also have the opportunity to identify the questions the dissertation leaves unexplored. Most students will find that, in the end, a dissertation raises more questions than it answers: you may have unexpected or equivocal findings, for example. These unanswered questions are sometimes referred to as 'avenues for further research': if you (or someone else) were going to continue this research, what should they look at next? The conclusions are also an opportunity to think about the generalizability and real-world application of your findings. This aspect of the conclusions should answer the question, 'So what?' You have provided lots of evidence and answered your narrow research question, but why should other researchers care about your findings? Why are they important? What can they teach us about the social world?

When to use an appendix

It can be confusing to try to figure out when you should use an appendix with data. There are two main reasons to use one. The first reason is to provide further insights into data handling. You should consider including an appendix to provide information about any variables you recoded, showing their original groups and which groups you recoded them into; or providing information about variables you manipulated in other ways, such as specifying how you computed an index variable, showing which variables were included and any weightings that were applied if variables were measured using different scales. See Norris and Inglehart (2012) for an example of a measurement-related appendix. The second reason for an appendix is to include other interesting results that are not core to your argument. In this usage, an appendix functions as a footnote for data: the data can provide further information to the interested reader, but the reader should be able to digest all of your arguments and evidence in the main body of your text without missing any key points by not reading the appendix. Sometimes authors will include full tables of results in an appendix, for example, while providing selected or summary results in the main body of the report. This is often done by international organizations: see UNHCR (2018), for instance.

Effective supervision

Dissertation students are usually allocated a supervisor, who provides one-to-one or small-group guidance on the progress of the project. Your supervisor may or may not have a subject background in the field you are exploring, but they will usually have experience both of having been supervised and of supervising students through an extended piece of independent research. Thus, your supervisor may not always be able to point you to specific literature on your topic, especially as you progress in the development of it and reach a level of specialism that makes you an expert on your topic. However, the supervisor will be able to advise you on the process of research, giving you tips for practical skills like literature searching, helping you to navigate common pitfalls in the dissertation process and giving you feedback on your work. Your dissertation supervisor should also be able to point you towards your department and institution's requirements for the dissertation.

One of the common differences between dissertations and your average taught content is the emphasis on independent study with less guidance on the use of your time. Because of this independence, many students find it all too easy to let their dissertation slip down the list of priorities, especially if they have half a year or more to complete it. You will rarely find that dissertation supervisors will be proactive in chasing you down if you have not been in touch, so you will need to make sure that you put mechanisms in place to avoid finding yourself nearly at the end of the supervision period with nothing to show for it. You will need to be aware of how you work, how your supervisor works and how to compensate for your weaknesses in order to get the most effective supervision. There are some key questions that you should answer as early as possible into the supervision period to support your success:

- How many hours of supervision am I expected to receive?
- How often should I expect to be meeting with my supervisor?
- What are the key deadlines and milestones in the dissertation (e.g. submission of a dissertation proposal, research ethics approval, submission of draft materials)?
- How much of my dissertation content can my supervisor read and comment on before final submission?
- How long in advance of a supervision does my supervisor require to read any materials?

To use your supervision effectively, you will need to prepare for every session, just as you would(should) prepare for every classroom session you attend. Do your reading, write up notes and questions and, preferably, come with an agenda of items you want to discuss. You will also need to plan your supervision and dissertation in the context of your other commitments. This will require significant personal organization and advance planning. As soon as you have information about your other commitments (both for your degree and your extracurricular activities), plot your key deadlines and periods of more intense activity. When are your other coursework and exam deadlines? When do you have key meetings or events? When do you need to take time off? When is your dissertation due? What intermediate deadlines do you need to meet? When you have worked out the answers to these questions, work backwards to determine how many hours you will have available in any given week to dedicate to your dissertation, and be realistic about some weeks when you will not be able to make any progress on it at all. Check over your plan with your dissertation supervisor to get their feedback about whether you have been realistic and whether you have planned enough time to achieve a good end result.

Make sure, at the very least, that you schedule your next supervision at the end of each meeting. Your supervisor may take a relaxed approach to supervision, encouraging you to get in touch as and when you need to, but this can be a trap for most dissertation students by allowing them to push their dissertation down the priority list. You may also find it harder to get a time in your supervisor's diary than expected, adding further delays to supervision. It may be best to book your supervisions on a consistent day and time (even if you are only meeting every two to four weeks) to ensure that you are in your supervisor's diary and that you keep the pressure on yourself to keep up with your work. You should also agree targets with your supervisor at the end of each session, setting goals about what you are going to accomplish before the next meeting and identifying any materials or results that you will commit to sending your supervisor in advance of the meeting.

You may find that you and your supervisor are kindred spirits, agreeing on many things and developing a very agreeable way of communicating. Or you may find that you have a personality clash with your supervisor. You might find them too harsh and critical, leaving you demoralized after every supervision; or too vague and philosophical, leaving every session with more questions than answers. If you are confident enough, you can respond to this by opening a dialogue with your supervisor. Try to use sentence formulation that focuses on you and your goals rather than on your supervisor's failings so that you do not start by making them feel defensive. 'I feel really unsure about what I am doing right when I get feedback from you. You are really good at identifying my weaknesses, but I need some help in identifying what I'm doing well'; or 'I'm really struggling to identify my research question and argument. Can you help me to summarize these?' This is much more likely to engage their help than, 'You only criticize me all the time. Stop being so harsh!' or 'Can you please stop responding to my questions with more questions? I need you to be more concrete.'

You should also consider forming a group with other students undertaking a dissertation. You can compare with each other the tips and tricks you have gleaned, and you can create peer pressure to make progress on your dissertation. Very few students, especially at the undergraduate level, have the study skills and personal organization to make a success of a dissertation without peer or supervisor support. The majority will need to create a series of external points where you can check in, compare progress and push yourself to keep working, especially when you reach the inevitable points in the dissertation process when you are demotivated. Boxes 11.1 and 11.2 give my side of the story – as a student myself and then as a supervisor.

BOX 11.1 MY STORY: THE STUDENT

In the interests of full disclosure, and maybe to make you feel better, I should say that most of these tips are based on my poor track record as a dissertation student. I fell into nearly every trap as an undergraduate dissertation student. I think I saw my supervisors twice in the year. I did not form a peer study group, which, combined with my heavy extracurricular commitments and a period of significant illness, meant that I fell so far behind on my dissertation that I was downgraded to a half-dissertation partway through the year. I managed to scrape a good grade in the end, but that was based on spending an entire holiday writing eight to ten hours per day by myself. As a Master's student, I learned some of my lessons: I went to see my supervisor more, I occasionally compared progress with some of my peers and I started well in advance of the deadline. However, I did not start early enough to raise the right questions during the supervision period, and I changed topics entirely partway through, so I was not able to get feedback on some of my later ideas. As a PhD student, I started with a supervisor who was good at supervision. He laid out clear guidelines, expectations and deadlines. He helped me to set interim targets, gave me concrete feedback about my ideas that was not demoralizing and helped me to develop my project into an achievable thesis. I made friends with some of the other PhD students, especially those ahead of me, which allowed me to learn from some of their experiences. Because of my supervisor's good example and my engagement with peers, I was in a much better position to manage my project successfully. I also knew much better how to ask questions, and, by the end of my PhD, I had become adept at planning ahead around my teaching commitments to identify the points in the year when I would and would not be able to make progress. As you can see, it took me three degrees to learn how to navigate supervision effectively.

BOX 11.2 MY STORY: THE SUPERVISOR

As a supervisor, the perspective is a bit different, of course. Most academics genuinely enjoy supervision. It is a rare opportunity to work very closely with a student to explore their ideas in a way that we are not normally able to in the classroom. I love being able to help students develop their ideas and work through particularly knotty problems. The best supervisees manage me, booking my time in advance, sending me information in advance of a meeting, identifying questions and problems they need help with. Supervision works best when a

(Continued)

student books a consistent time in my diary that is sacrosanct, and we are able to engage in the journey together. One of my biggest frustrations as a supervisor is to have a supervisee who never comes to see me (just as I did as a student) and then submits a final product that contains misunderstandings of the literature or methodological flaws that I could have foreseen months in advance – if I had ever seen their ideas or their work. The weeks slip by very quickly without realizing that I have not seen or contacted some of my dissertation students, which sometimes results in a feeling of guilt, but there are often so many demands on my time that I am most likely to deal with the students on my doorstep rather than chasing the ones I have not seen. The other bugbear is students who seem unaware of the number of other demands on supervisors' time and email substantial pieces of work with feedback requested 'ASAP'. Be conscious that, just as you will have points in the year when your workload is much higher, so will your supervisor. There might be periods with heavy marking loads to turn around or high numbers of letters of recommendation to write, or your supervisor may be under significant pressure from deadlines for funding or publications.

FORMATTING YOUR WORK

Presenting your work to a professional standard is perhaps even more important for data reports and dissertations than for standard coursework. Haphazard or IBM SPSS Statistics ('SPSS') default formatting of tables and charts, and missing labels and section headers, not only make the overall effect of your work less professional but can also actually make it harder to interpret your findings. This section gives you guidance based on what is commonly expected for presenting data, but you should always follow your local guidance on all formatting elements as well as considering the audience for whom you are writing: presenting your data to an academic reader will look different from writing for a lay audience or an NGO, for example.

Spacing, indentations and section headings

Most institutions will have a requirement for expanded line spacing for the sake of your readers: reading a dissertation that is single-spaced, especially if read on a screen, can be very challenging on a reader's eyes. While it may look less professional, since books are usually published with 1.0–1.2 line spacing, consider this a kindness to your reader. You will also need to think about your spacing between paragraphs to make sure that it is visually clear where your paragraph breaks are, especially if you are using full justification so that the text is stretched across the full width of the page. The most common systems for distinguishing paragraphs are either to leave an extra gap between paragraphs or to use tab indentation at the beginning of a new paragraph; you would not normally combine both.

You should also be comfortable with creating page and section breaks, which will force the text to start at the top of a new page. For instance, each new section or chapter of the dissertation (Introduction, Literature Review, Methodology, etc.) might require a new page. Repeated use of the Enter key is not the best way to achieve this, as later editing might change the position of relevant text. Instead use CTRL (PC)/CMND (Mac) + Enter to force a page break. This keeps the same header and footer content, margins, etc., but starts your text on a new page. You might have times when you need a section break, which not only starts content on a new page but can also allow you to change the orientation from portrait to landscape, change the margin width and alter the contents or formatting of the headers and footers (if desired). You are most likely to use this feature if you want to include a large table or figure that is best displayed in landscape form, or when you do not want page numbering to include your title page, abstract and table of contents.

Data reports and dissertations commonly use section headings to signal clearly the main components. The headings should signal to the reader when you have a distinct change in focus but should not break up the flow of your writing. For data reports, the most common headings are Introduction, Literature review, Methodology, Results/data analysis, Conclusion. This differs from most essays, where, unless they are longer, using headings is uncommon. For dissertations, you are likely to use a system of headings (chapter titles) and sub-headings (sections within chapters). Whatever the length of your report or dissertation, you should use headings to add clarity but not to the point where you are adding a heading to nearly every paragraph. In general, you would not want to have more than one heading per page in a shorter report; in dissertations, you should aim for at least two pages between most of the sub-headings, and you should keep your main chapters roughly equal in length, with each representing around one-quarter of the total word count.

Presenting data

Once you have produced all of the data outputs you want for your report, sift through them to identify which tables need to be included in their entirety (such as the main crosstab results); which tables need to have some contents removed (such as correlations, where you will normally delete all of the results either above or below the diagonal line where the results repeat to make the table easier to read); and which tables will not be included, but their results will be reported in the text of your analysis (such as significance readings for crosstabs, ANOVA and regression, and F values for various tests). It is a good idea to sort through this before you go to the effort of reformatting every table of your output unnecessarily. For more guidance on what information should be included or excluded in reporting each test, see the discussion around the relevant test in the main chapters of this book. You can also find published examples by searching for the name of a statistical test and a keyword, such as 'ANOVA' and 'nationalism', which would lead you to sources like Kemmelmeier and Winter (2008), who use this test to look at the effect of exposure to US flag imagery on patriotism and nationalism. Doing test-specific results searches can help you become more comfortable with writing about data.

When you know which tables will be included in the body of your analysis, you will need to make sure they are formatted according to professional norms. It is possible to produce all of your outputs pre-formatted to follow these norms by using the APA table template in SPSS (see instructions in Chapter 4), so if you have your full syntax saved, you can simply rerun all of your results with this template in place, and you will have very little post-production reformatting to undertake. However, this is not always possible, or you may sometimes need to make some final tweaks, so it is good to understand the professional norms around table presentation. Quantitative publications tend to follow the style of having a solid line across the top and bottom of the table. There should also be a full-width line across the bottom of the header row(s), and there may be a line across the top of a total line (if applicable) (Table 11.4). For more complex or long tables (such as a multivariate crosstab or a comparison of means with two or more categorical variables), authors will often insert a thin line or use indentation to separate sections of results (Table 11.5).

Table 11.4 Example of a simple table

	Voted	**Didn't vote**	**Total**
Male	76.0%	24.0%	100.0%
Female	75.2%	24.8%	100.0%
Total	75.6%	24.4%	100.0%

Source: ESS (round 7). Variables: `gndr, vote`.

Table 11.5 Example of a more complex table

Gender	**Age group**	**Voted**	**Didn't vote**	**Total**
Male	18–24	59.90%	40.10%	100.00%
	25–34	68.30%	31.70%	100.00%
	35–44	73.00%	27.00%	100.00%
	45–54	78.50%	21.50%	100.00%
	55–64	82.10%	17.90%	100.00%
	65+	86.00%	14.00%	100.00%
	Total	76.40%	23.60%	100.00%
Female	18–24	59.60%	40.40%	100.00%
	25–34	66.10%	33.90%	100.00%
	35–44	74.20%	25.80%	100.00%
	45–54	78.70%	21.30%	100.00%
	55–64	82.00%	18.00%	100.00%
	65+	80.60%	19.40%	100.00%

Gender	Age group	Voted	Didn't vote	Total
	Total	75.50%	24.50%	100.00%
Total	18–24	59.80%	40.20%	100.00%
	25–34	67.20%	32.80%	100.00%
	35–44	73.60%	26.40%	100.00%
	45–54	78.60%	21.40%	100.00%
	55–64	82.00%	18.00%	100.00%
	65+	83.00%	17.00%	100.00%
	Total	76.00%	24.00%	100.00%

Source: ESS (round 7). Variables: `gndr, agegrp (user generated), vote.`

After you have written up your analysis, position your tables and charts as close as possible to the section of text where you are discussing them. Try not to overwhelm your reader with results: choose your results judiciously, and generally aim to have one table or chart per page. This might be increased to two on some pages, but you absolutely want to avoid having a series of tables and charts, pasted one after the other, with no discussion of the results in between. This is especially important if your readers are going to be looking at your results on a screen: scrolling back and forth between a table on page 2 and the discussion on page 4 quickly becomes very laborious and irritating. Make sure you think about the experience of the reader and place your results for ease of being able to glance at your table/chart while reading your interpretation of the data. If you want to aim for fully professional appearance, then tables and charts should be positioned at the very top or bottom of a page. For examples, have a look at journal articles or books. You should notice that the typesetters have always anchored them to the top or bottom, and they never appear in the middle of the page. However, given how cumbersome it can be to set this positioning, most academics will be lenient on this – just make sure that you check with your teacher on their views!

When you have positioned all of your tables and charts, you need to label them. Do not use the chart title feature within SPSS (or a spreadsheet, if you have exported your data to chart in another program). Instead, all tables and charts should have a title, normally formatted in either bold (more common) or italics (less common) that is typed into the body of your writing rather than being embedded in the table or chart. The tables label should always be placed above the table, should start with the label 'Table', followed by consecutive numbering. If you are writing a report without chapters (such as a normal data report or a journal article), you should follow the simple numbering system 'Table 1', 'Table 2', etc. If you are writing a report with chapters (such as a dissertation, thesis or book), you should start the numbering with the chapter number, then number consecutively within the chapter, for example 'Table 11.1', 'Table 11.2', etc., and you should restart at 1 at the beginning of a new chapter. (This is the system used within this book.) If you are writing without chapter numbers, it is conventional to put a full stop after the number, followed by the description of the table, for example 'Table 1. Support for gender equality by sex, Austria'. If you are using chapter numbers, you do not normally follow the table number with a full stop, for example 'Table 11.1 Support for gender equality by sex, Austria'. Some publications will use a colon after the table number, regardless of whether you are using chapter numbers, such as 'Table 1: Support…' and 'Table 11.1: Support…'. Where relevant, you should include a line underneath the table indicating the p-thresholds for any stars used within the table, such as with correlation results.

Charts, graphics or other forms of pictures should be labelled using 'Figure' – they should not be labelled as 'Table'. The numbering conventions are the same for figures: number consecutively, include the chapter number if relevant, and put a full stop after the figure number if you are not using chapter numbers. Different journals use different conventions for the placement of figure labels: some follow the same formatting as tables, placing the label above the top of the figure, while others place the label underneath the figure. Be sure to consult any specific guidelines about the placement of the label.

The label should give a clear description of the substantive contents so that someone would be able to find the information they are looking for based solely on a list of the labels of your tables and figures. For example, if you simply use the label 'Table 1. Linear regression results', this would not be enough information for the reader to know whether that table will contain the results they are looking for. Instead, a label like 'Table 1. Regression coefficients for determinants of gender inequality' will be much more helpful. Best practice is to include information about the source of data underneath tables and figures, specifying the dataset and the variable codes, if you are using a publicly available dataset, for example 'Source: ESS (round 7), Germany. Variables: imueclt, gndr'. When you have all of your tables and figures labelled consecutively and placed in the text, you will need to insert references to the relevant tables in the body of your analysis, making sure that you update the numbers in your cross-references if you reposition your data.

Using paragraph styles for dissertations

A dissertation may well be the longest writing project on which you have embarked. You will normally use a word processing program to produce the final document. There are a range of word processing programs that will do the job, some proprietary (like Apple Pages and Microsoft Word), some free (such as Apache OpenOffice, IBM Lotus Symphony, LibreOffice, WPS Office Free and Neo Office – made for Mac users), and some online-based (such as Google Docs, Zoho and Microsoft Office Online). The free options offer similar functionality in word processing terms and may be particularly useful to those unable to access commercial products, or those committed to using free and/or open-access alternatives. Those trained in more scientific environments may be introduced to a document-formatting system called LaTeX (pronounced 'lay-tech'; the X is a representation of Greek letter 'chi'), but this would be unusual for students below doctoral level and is still relatively rare. In the sections below we look at how to apply formatting elements that are often required in dissertations, including a few tricks that will make your final submission look more professional and take far less time (such as the automated table of contents tool).

The single most helpful feature to use for dissertations is to apply style formatting to different text components. More powerful word processors normally come pre-programmed with a variety of styles of headings and text. If you use no other advanced features, simply applying heading formatting to your chapter and section titles will open a range of additional features to you, including automatic numbering of chapters, sections, tables and figures; automated table of contents; and navigation. To apply formatting, navigate to the text of your chapter or section title, and apply Heading 1 (chapter titles), Heading 2 (sections) or Heading 3 (subsections). You would not normally use more than three heading levels in a dissertation, as this would usually be accompanied by overuse of section headings, with too little content between sections. You can also make alterations to the styles to suit your needs. For example, if you need to increase the line spacing to 1.5–2.0, you can alter the normal paragraph text style.

When you have applied heading styles throughout your dissertation, many word processors (including Microsoft Word, Pages for Mac and LibreOffice) include a tool to automatically create a table of contents based on the headings. You are strongly advised to use this tool, as it will normally automatically indent based on the heading level, creating a nested effect for sub-headings that makes it clear which section they belong to; it will add a dotted line and right-align the page numbers; and it will automatically calculate the page number where the heading is located, updating as your text moves around. (Just make sure you update the TOC before your final submission!)

In some word processors, you can combine heading styles with multilevel (hierarchical) list numbering, which will then apply autonumbering to sections. For example, if you formatted all chapter titles as Heading 1, it would number the chapters consecutively. Subsections within each chapter would then be numbered, such as Chapter 9, Section 9.1, 9.1.1, and so on. The numbering will also then be applied to tables and figures that are labelled using the caption feature, and the numbers will auto-update if you move or delete chapters, tables or figures.

CONCLUSIONS

This chapter has walked through the main components of a data report or dissertation, outlining the contents of each section and suggesting some questions for you to answer in each. For students undertaking dissertations, this also included a discussion of how to use supervision effectively, looking at some of the common pitfalls for students undertaking an extended piece of independent research. This chapter also identified some key tips and tricks for formatting your work to make it look as professional as possible. You can find suggestions of other sources to consult for writing a dissertation in the Further reading below.

You have now reached the end of this book. Having survived an introduction to statistics, I hope that you now feel more confident in how to produce and interpret numbers to explore questions about the social world. My deepest desire is that you would be genuinely excited about data and numbers, but I would settle for you no longer feeling that you would rather have teeth drawn than look at statistics. I hope I have convinced you that learning applied statistics well has much more to do with exploring data, trying and often failing than with any innate mathematics ability, and I hope that the non-mathsy approach has made this book slightly less dry than some of the alternatives. There remains only to say: good luck!

FURTHER READING

If you are writing a dissertation or thesis in an educational institution, there is very likely to be guidance specific to your institution or department, including expectations and practice. This should be your most indispensable source.

For a very accessible, quick-reference guide to the research process, see:
Thomas, G. (2017) *Doing Research*, 2nd edn. London: Palgrave.

For a more in-depth discussion of the research process in political science, see:
Toshkov, D. (2016) *Research Design in Political Science*. London: Palgrave.

For a good discussion of research questions, hypotheses and the application of theory, see Part 2 ('How to do research: an overview') in:
Halperin, S. and Heath, O. (2017) *Political Research: Methods and Practical Skills*, 2nd edn. Oxford: Oxford University Press.

For more in-depth discussions of the process of an undergraduate dissertation or research projects:
Greetham, B. (2014) *How to Write Your Undergraduate Dissertation*, 3rd edn. London: Macmillan.
Thomas, G. (2017) *How to Do Your Research Project: A Guide for Students*, 3rd edn. London: Sage.
Walliman, N. (2014) *Your Undergraduate Dissertation: The Essential Guide for Success*, 2nd edn. London: Sage.
Whisker, G. (2014) *Dissertations and Project Reports: A Step by Step Guide*. London: Palgrave.
Whisker, G. (2019) *The Undergraduate Research Handbook*, 2nd edn. London: Macmillan.

REFERENCES

Ariely, G. (2012) 'Globalisation and the decline of national identity? An exploration across sixty-three countries', *Nations and Nationalism*, 18 (3): 461-82.

Bixter, M. (2015) 'Happiness, political orientation, and religiosity', *Personality and Individual Differences*, 72: 7-11.

Buttice, M.K. and Milazzo, C. (2011) 'Candidate positioning in Britain', *Electoral Studies*, 30: 848-57.

Fish, M.S. (2002) 'Islam and authoritarianism', *World Politics*, 55 (1): 4-37.

Huntington, S.P. (1984) 'Will more countries become democratic?', *Political Science Quarterly*, 99 (2): 193-218.

Kemmelmeier, M. and Winter, D. (2008) 'Sowing patriotism, but reaping nationalism? Consequences of exposure to the American flag', *Political Psychology*, 29 (6): 859-79.

Kumar, R. (2011) *Research Methodology: A Step-By-Step Guide for Beginners*, 3rd edn. London: Sage.

Mudde, C. (2010) 'The populist radical right: a pathological normalcy', *West European Politics*, 33 (6): 1167-86.

Norris, P. and Inglehart, R. (2012) 'Muslim integration into Western cultures: between origins and destinations', *Political Studies*, 60 (2): 228-51.

Reisinger, W.M., Miller, A.H., Hesli, V.L. and Maher, K.H. (1994) 'Political values in Russia, Ukraine and Lithuania: sources and implications for democracy', *British Journal of Political Science*, 24 (2): 183-223.

UNHCR (2018) *Global Trends 2017*. Geneva: UNHCR. (https://www.unhcr.org/globaltrends2017).

APPENDIX: ACTIVITY ANSWERS

CHAPTER 4

Activity 4.1

Run a frequency for which party the respondent feels closest to [prtclbgb].

```
freq prtclbgb.
```

Table A.4.1 Party identification, UK [prtclbgb]

		Frequency	Percent	Valid Percent	Cumulative Percent
Valid	Conservative	373	16.5	32.0	32.0
	Labour	415	18.3	35.6	67.6
	Liberal Democrat	64	2.8	5.5	73.1
	Scottish National Party	48	2.1	4.1	77.3
	Plaid Cymru	4	.2	.3	77.6
	Green Party	56	2.5	4.8	82.4
	UK Independence Party	166	7.3	14.2	96.7
	Other (inc. NIR)	39	1.7	3.3	100.0
	Total	1165	51.5	100.0	
Missing	Not applicable	1058	46.7		
	Refusal	33	1.5		
	Don't know	8	.4		
	Total	1099	48.5		
Total		2264	2264	100.0	

1. There are 1,058 valid responses and 1,099 missing responses.
2. The most common choice was Labour. The least common choice was Liberal Democrat. For other counts, see Table A.4.1 Party identification, UK [prtclbgb].
3. There is a considerable difference between the two columns, with the valid percent value being about double that of the percent value. This is because nearly half of the responses (48.5 percent) were not valid responses.

4. These numbers are reflected in wider trends of political apathy, low turnout and the breakdown of the two-party system, leading to more fragmented support for a wider range of political parties and disagreement about the direction of the country. The fact that 16.5 percent of respondents identified most closely with the Conservatives in a survey period when the Conservatives were in government is indicative of the challenge of governing a diverse electorate with often opposing positions on core policies, such as membership of the EU.

Activity 4.2

Select only UK cases (UK=11).

```
USE ALL.
COMPUTE filter_country=(country = 11).
VARIABLE LABELS filter_country 'country = 11 (FILTER)'.
VALUE LABELS filter_country 0 'Not Selected' 1 'Selected'.
FORMATS filter_country (f1.0).
FILTER BY filter_country.
EXECUTE.
```

Run a frequency table for 'How interested in politics [`polintr`]' for UK respondents.

```
freq polintr.
```

Remove filter after finishing the activity.

```
USE ALL.
EXECUTE.
```

Table A.4.2 Level of interest in politics [`polintr`], UK respondents

		Frequency	Percent	Valid Percent	Cumulative Percent
Valid	Very interested	367	16.2	16.2	16.2
	Quite interested	952	42.0	42.0	58.3
	Hardly interested	567	25.0	25.0	83.3
	Not at all interested	378	16.7	16.7	100.0
	Total	2264	100.0	100.0	

1. All responses (2,264) are valid. There are no missing responses to this question for UK respondents.
2. 'Quite interested' was the most common; 'very interested' was the least common. For other values, see Table A.4.2 Level of interest in politics [polintr], UK respondents.
3. There is no difference because all responses were valid.
4. The Cumulative Percent column indicates that slightly over half of respondents (58.3 percent) expressed some interest in politics ('very' or 'quite' interested). Nearly equal proportions of people said they were not at all interested (16.7 percent) as said they were very interested (16.2 percent). These are the strict numbers, but the way we write about them can change the way people see them. We could use these numbers to paint a picture of widespread political apathy by highlighting that only 16.2 percent of respondents were very interested in politics; or we could emphasise the fact that 83.3 percent of respondents expressed some level of political interest. The fact that we can use the same numbers to support very different conclusions is one reason why it is so important for politics students to be able to engage with numbers.

Activity 4.3

Create a crosstab for 'Which party feel closer to, Austria' [prtclcat] and 'How close to party' [prtdgcl]. Choose the appropriate percentages to show how close people feel within each party affiliation.

```
CROSSTABS prtclcat by prtdgcl

/cells=count row.
```

If you used prtdgcl first, you should have chosen column percentages. In this case, the syntax would be:

```
CROSSTABS prtdgcl by prtclcat

/cells=count column.
```

Table A.4.3 Party identification and closeness, Austria

		Very close	Quite close	Not close	Not at all close	Total
SPÖ	N	41	182	60	1	284
	%	14.4%	64.1%	21.1%	0.4%	100.0%
ÖVP	N	28	169	63	0	260
	%	10.8%	65.0%	24.2%	0.0%	100.0%

(Continued)

Table A.4.3 (Continued)

		Very close	Quite close	Not close	Not at all close	Total
FPÖ	N	18	88	21	0	127
	%	14.2%	69.3%	16.5%	0.0%	100.0%
BZÖ	N	3	1	1	0	5
	%	60.0%	20.0%	20.0%	0.0%	100.0%
Grüne	N	11	117	22	0	150
	%	7.3%	78.0%	14.7%	0.0%	100.0%
KPÖ	N	2	3	1	0	6
	%	33.3%	50.0%	16.7%	0.0%	100.0%
NEOS	N	4	16	6	0	26
	%	15.4%	61.5%	23.1%	0.0%	100.0%
Piratenpartei Österreich	N	0	1	1	0	2
	%	0.0%	50.0%	50.0%	0.0%	100.0%
Team Frank Stronach	N	0	2	0	0	2
	%	0.0%	100.0%	0.0%	0.0%	100.0%
Other	N	1	1	0	0	2
	%	50.0%	50.0%	0.0%	0.0%	100.0%
Total	N	108	580	175	1	864
	%	12.5%	67.1%	20.3%	0.1%	100.0%

1. SPÖ, ÖVP, FPÖ, Grüne
2. SPÖ (14.4%), though the FPÖ is very close (14.2%).
3. There is no clear pattern. The Greens have the lowest level of identification (7.3%), but the left-wing Social Democratic Party (SPÖ) is the highest (14.4%). The second-highest is the right-wing populist Freedom Party (FPÖ, 14.2%).

Activity 4.4

Select only responses from Germany.

```
USE ALL.

COMPUTE filter_$=(country = 5).
```

```
VARIABLE LABELS filter_$ 'country = 5 (FILTER)'.

VALUE LABELS filter_$ 0 'Not Selected' 1 'Selected'.

FORMATS filter_$ (f1.0).

FILTER BY filter_$.

EXECUTE.
```

Create a crosstab for 'Ever unemployed and seeking work for a period more than three months' [uemp3m] and 'Voted in the last national election' [vote]. Produce counts and appropriate percentages for showing voting patterns within different categories of experience of unemployment.

```
CROSSTABS uemp3m by vote

/cells=count row.
```

Table A.4.4 Voting by experience of long-term unemployment

	Yes		No		Not eligible to vote		Total	
Unemployed >3 mos	**N**	**%**	**N**	**%**	**N**	**%**	**N**	**%**
Yes	666	72.9%	196	21.4%	52	5.7%	914	100.0%
No	1676	79.1%	264	12.5%	178	8.4%	2118	100.0%
Total	2342	77.2%	460	15.2%	230	7.6%	3032	100.0%

1. 3,032.
2. 72.9 percent of people without experience of long-term unemployment reported voting in the last national election, compared to 79.1 percent of those who had experienced unemployment lasting more than three months.

CHAPTER 5

Activity 5.1

Create a simple bar chart for 'Better for a country if almost everyone shares customs and traditions' [pplstrd] with percentages (Element Properties > Bar1 > Statistic > Change from 'Count' to 'Percentage').

The largest category is 'Agree' (31.5%). The smallest category is 'Disagree strongly' (5.4%).

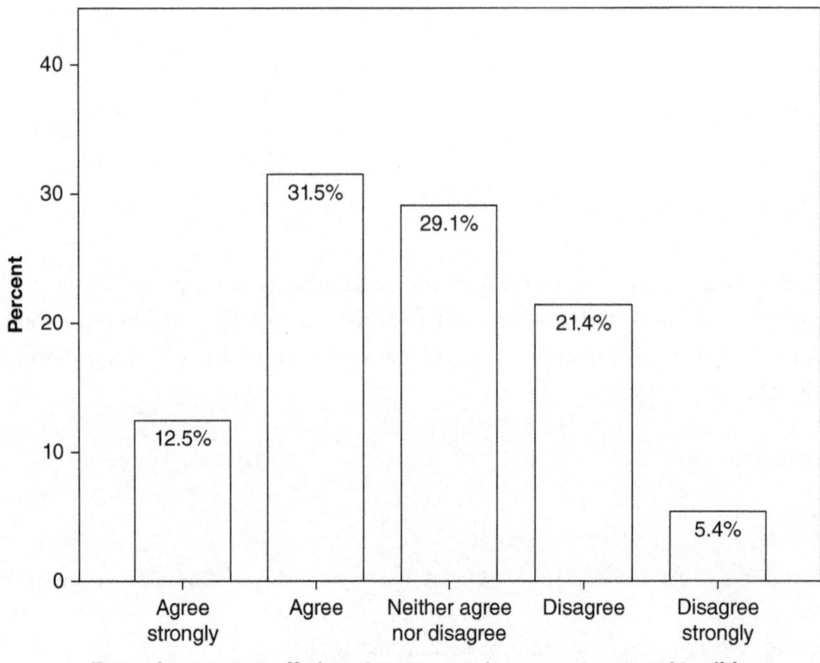

Figure A.5.1 Better to share customs and traditions, percentages

Activity 5.2

Select only responses from Spain (Spain=8).

```
USE ALL.

COMPUTE filter_$=(country = 8).

VARIABLE LABELS filter_$ 'country = 8 (FILTER)'.

VALUE LABELS filter_$ 0 'Not Selected' 1 'Selected'.

FORMATS filter_$ (f1.0).

FILTER BY filter_$.

EXECUTE.
```

Create another bar chart for 'Better for a country if almost everyone shares customs and traditions' [pplstrd] with percentages (Element Properties > Bar1 > Statistic > Change from 'Count' to 'Percentage').

```
GGRAPH

  /GRAPHDATASET NAME="graphdataset" VARIABLES=pplstrd COUNT()[name="COUNT"]
MISSING=LISTWISE

    REPORTMISSING=NO

  /GRAPHSPEC SOURCE=INLINE.

BEGIN GPL

  SOURCE: s=userSource(id("graphdataset"))

  DATA: pplstrd=col(source(s), name("pplstrd"), unit.category())

  DATA: COUNT=col(source(s), name("COUNT"))

  GUIDE: axis(dim(1), label("Better for a country if almost everyone
shares customs and ",

    "traditions"))

  GUIDE: axis(dim(2), label("Percent"))

  SCALE: cat(dim(1), include("1", "2", "3", "4", "5"))

  SCALE: linear(dim(2), include(0))

  ELEMENT: interval(position(summary.percent(pplstrd*COUNT, base.
all(acrossPanels()))),

    shape.interior(shape.square))

END GPL.
```

The largest category is 'Agree' (34.2%). The smallest category is 'Disagree strongly' (4.3%). A larger proportion of respondents in Spain agree with this statement than the survey as a whole.

Activity 5.3

Create a clustered bar chart for 'Were happy, how often past week' [`wrhpp`] with country as the clustering variable. Show the results as a percentage (Element Properties > Bar1 > Statistic > Change from 'Count' to 'Percentage'). Remove all of the countries from the chart except Denmark and Sweden (Element Properties > GroupColor > Categories > Press the red X to move countries to the Excluded box; apply changes).

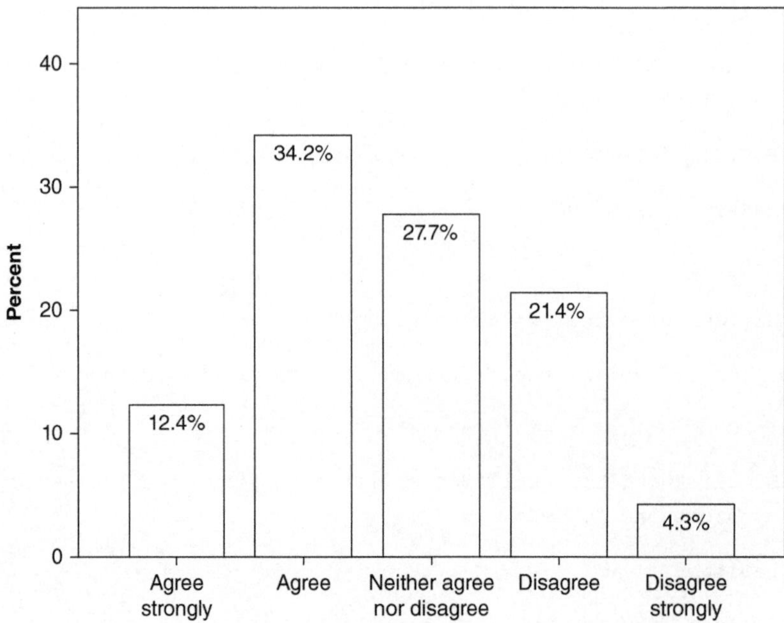

Figure A.5.2 Better to share customs and traditions, percentages, Spain respondents

```
GGRAPH
  /GRAPHDATASET NAME="graphdataset" VARIABLES=wrhpp COUNT()
[name="COUNT"] country MISSING=LISTWISE
    REPORTMISSING=NO
  /GRAPHSPEC SOURCE=INLINE.
BEGIN GPL
  SOURCE: s=userSource(id("graphdataset"))
  DATA: wrhpp=col(source(s), name("wrhpp"), unit.category())
  DATA: COUNT=col(source(s), name("COUNT"))
  DATA: country=col(source(s), name("country"),
notIn("15", "16", "17", "18", "19", "21", "11", "12", "13", "14", "1",
"2", "3", "4", "5"
, "7", "8", "9", "10"), unit.category())
  COORD: rect(dim(1,2), cluster(3,0))
  GUIDE: axis(dim(3), label("Were happy, how often past week"))
```

```
  GUIDE: axis(dim(2), label("Percent"))

  GUIDE: legend(aesthetic(aesthetic.color.interior), label("Country"))

  SCALE: cat(dim(3), include("1", "2", "3", "4"))

  SCALE: linear(dim(2), include(0))

  SCALE: cat(aesthetic(aesthetic.color.interior), include("20", "6"),
sort.values("20", "6"))

  SCALE: cat(dim(1), include("20", "6"), sort.values("20", "6"))

  ELEMENT:
interval(position(summary.percent(country*COUNT*wrhpp, base.
all(acrossPanels()))),

    color.interior(country), shape.interior(shape.square))

END GPL.
```

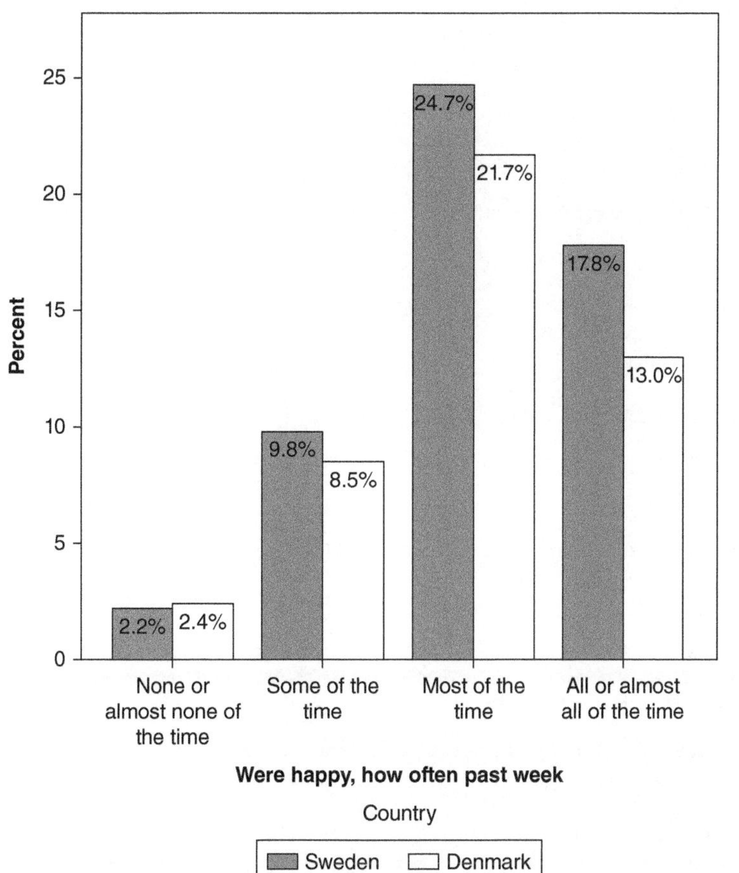

Figure A.5.3 Reported happiness in Sweden and Denmark

1. Sweden's residents are happier than Denmark's: the bars are higher for both 'most of the time' and 'all or almost all of the time'.
2. 17.8 percent of Swedish residents reported being happy all or almost all of the time in the week preceding the interview compared to 13.0 percent of Danes; this means there is slightly less than a 6 percent gap in the proportion of the population reporting the highest level of happiness.

Activity 5.4

Create a stacked bar chart with 'Which party feel closer to, France' [`prtcldfr`] on the x-axis and 'Important to care for nature and the environment' [`impenv`] as the stack colour. Limit the parties to the UMP (Union pour un Mouvement Populaire, centre–right), PS (Parti Socialiste, centre–left) and FN (Front National, right-wing) (Element Properties > GroupColor > Categories > Press the red X to move parties to the Excluded box; apply changes). Run the chart with counts.

```
GGRAPH

  /GRAPHDATASET NAME="graphdataset" VARIABLES= prtcldfr

COUNT()[name="COUNT"] impenv

    MISSING=LISTWISE REPORTMISSING=NO

  /GRAPHSPEC SOURCE=INLINE.

BEGIN GPL

  SOURCE: s=userSource(id("graphdataset"))

  DATA: prtcldfr=col(source(s), name("prtcldfr"),

notIn("16", "15", "14", "13", "10", "9", "8", "7", "6", "5", "4", "3",
"1"), unit.category())

  DATA: COUNT=col(source(s), name("COUNT"))

  DATA: impenv=col(source(s), name("impenv"), unit.category())

  GUIDE: axis(dim(1), label("Which party feel closer to, France"))

  GUIDE: axis(dim(2), label("Count"))

  GUIDE: legend(aesthetic(aesthetic.color.interior), label("Important
to care for nature and ",

    "environment"))

  SCALE: cat(dim(1), include("2", "12", "11"), sort.values("2", "12", "11"))

  SCALE: linear(dim(2), include(0))
```

```
  SCALE: cat(aesthetic(aesthetic.color.interior), include("1", "2",
"3", "4", "5", "6"))

  ELEMENT: interval.stack(position(prtcldfr*COUNT), color.interior
(impenv),

    shape.interior(shape.square))

END GPL.
```

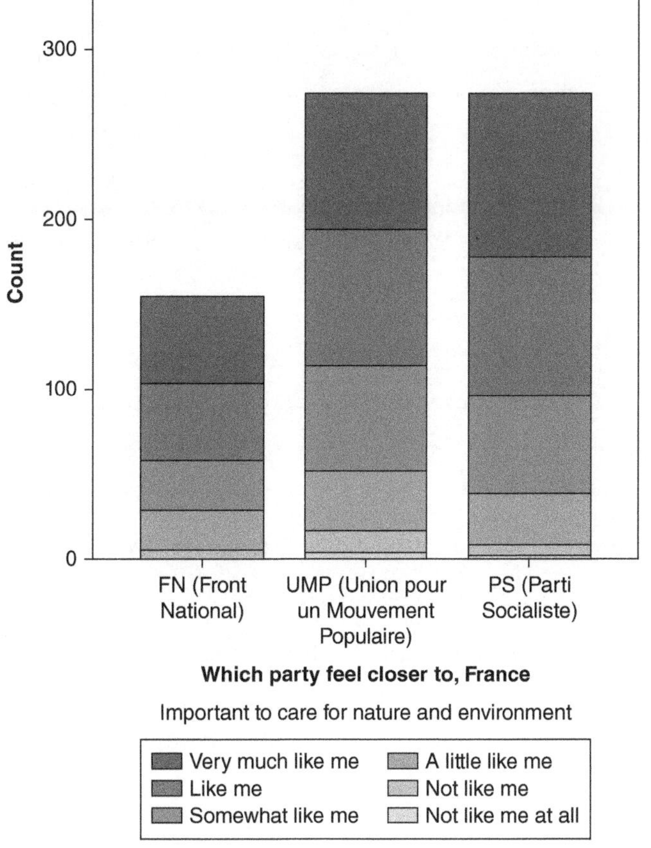

Figure A.5.4 Support for environmentalism [`impenv`] by party identification, France [`prtcldfr`], counts

Run the chart with percentages (Element Properties > Bar1 > Statistic > Change from 'Count' to 'Percentage'). For the percentages, set the parameters for the percentage to 'Total for Each X-Axis Category' (Element Properties > Bar1 > Statistic > Percentage > Set Parameters > Change Denominator for Computing Percentage from 'Grand Total' to 'Total for Each X-Axis Category'; apply changes). (This is the equivalent of using column percentages so that each column will add up to 100 percent.)

```
GGRAPH
  /GRAPHDATASET NAME="graphdataset" VARIABLES=prtcldfr COUNT()
[name="COUNT"] impenv
    MISSING=LISTWISE REPORTMISSING=NO
  /GRAPHSPEC SOURCE=INLINE.
BEGIN GPL
  SOURCE: s=userSource(id("graphdataset"))
  DATA: prtcldfr=col(source(s), name("prtcldfr"),
notIn("16", "15", "14", "13", "10", "9", "8", "7", "6", "5", "4", "3",
"1"), unit.category())
  DATA: COUNT=col(source(s), name("COUNT"))
  DATA: impenv=col(source(s), name("impenv"), unit.category())
  GUIDE: axis(dim(1), label("Which party feel closer to, France"))
  GUIDE: axis(dim(2), label("Percent"))
  GUIDE: legend(aesthetic(aesthetic.color.interior), label("Important
to care for nature and ",
    "environment"))
  SCALE: cat(dim(1), include("2", "12", "11"), sort.values("2", "12", "11"))
  SCALE: linear(dim(2), include(0))
  SCALE: cat(aesthetic(aesthetic.color.interior), include("1", "2",
"3", "4", "5", "6"))
  ELEMENT: interval.stack(position(summary.percent(prtcldfr*COUNT,
base.coordinate(dim(1)))),
    color.interior(impenv), shape.interior(shape.square))
END GPL.
```

1. H1. Supporters of the Parti Socialiste will have greater support for the environment than supporters of the right-wing parties.
2. PS supporters show the highest level of environmentalism, with more than 80 percent saying that caring for the environment is 'very', 'like' or 'somewhat' like them. Supporters of the FN have slightly higher levels of support for the environment than the UMP.

3. This confirms the hypothesis with regards to the PS, but it is unexpected that FN supporters show higher levels of environmentalism than UMP voters. This is surprising because environmentalism is usually associated with left-wing politics.

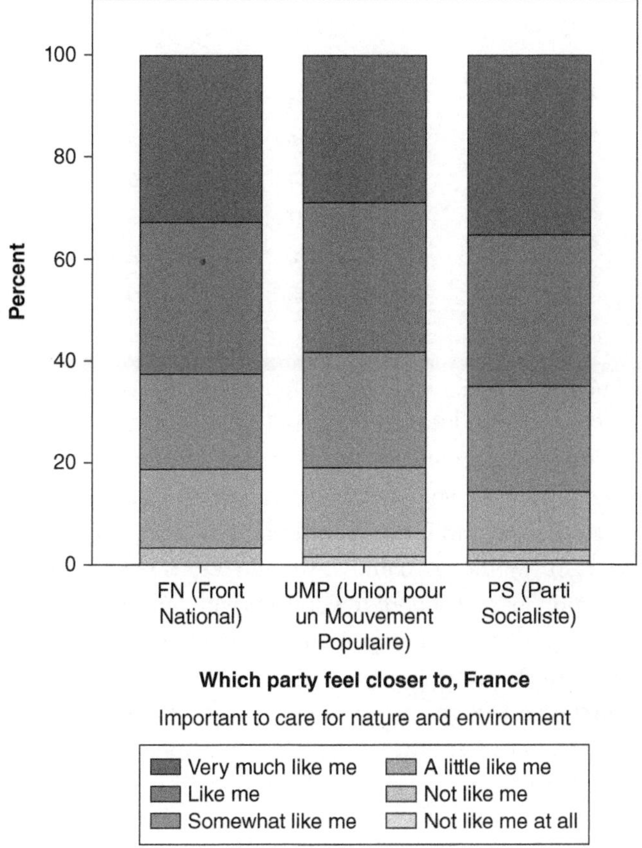

Figure A.5.5 Support for environmentalism [`impenv`] by party identification, France [`prtcldfr`], column percentages

CHAPTER 6

Activity 6.1

RQ: How many respondents in this dataset come from a migration background?

Create a multivariate crosstab with 'Born in country' [`brncntr`], 'Father born in country' [`facntr`] and 'Mother born in country' [`mocntr`]. Include observed counts.

```
CROSSTABS mocntr by facntr by brncntr

/cells=count.
```

Table A.6.1 Immigrant heritage of respondents

Respondent born in country	Mother born in country	Father born in country		Total
		Yes	No	
Yes	Yes	31512	1246	32758
	No	996	1632	2628
	Total	32508	2878	35386
No	Yes	325	181	506
	No	129	3878	4007
	Total	454	4059	4513
Total	Yes	31837	1427	33264
	No	1125	5510	6635
	Total	32962	6937	39899

1. 39,899. To find this answer, look at the bottom right-hand cell, where it shows the total of totals. You can also find this in the Case Processing Summary table in the output, which shows that 286 cases are classified as missing for this analysis.
2. 31,512. To find this answer, you need to find the cell that has 'yes' for all three questions'.
3. 1,632. To find this answer, you need the cell where the answer to 'Born in country' is yes, but the answers for 'Mother born in country' and 'Father born in country' are both no.
4. It is more common for native-born respondents with one immigrant parent to be born to a native-born mother and foreign-born father (1,246) than to a native-born father and a foreign-born mother (996).
5. 4,110. To find this answer, you need to add up the three cells where the answer to 'Born in country' is yes but where the answer for at least one of the parents was no. This means mother born in the country but father not (1,316), father born in the country but mother not (1,045) and neither of the parents born in the country (1,749).
6. 3,874. This is the total number of respondents who answered 'no' to being born in the country, regardless of their parents' birthplace. This constitutes about 9.7 percent (3874 / 39899 × 100) of respondents who answered all three of these questions.

Activity 6.2

RQ: Do supporters of the Front National hold more openly racist views than supporters of other French political parties?

Filter cases for the following parties for 'Which party feel closer to, France' [`prtcldfr`]: UMP (Union pour un Mouvement Populaire, centre–right), PS (Parti Socialiste, centre–left) and FN (Front National, right-wing).

```
USE ALL.

COMPUTE filter_$=(prtcldfr = 2 OR prtcldfr = 11 OR prtcldfr = 12).
```

```
VARIABLE LABELS filter_$ 'prtcldfr = 2 OR prtcldfr = 11 OR prtcldfr = 12
(FILTER)'.

VALUE LABELS filter_$ 0 'Not Selected' 1 'Selected'.

FORMATS filter_$ (f1.0).

FILTER BY filter_$.

EXECUTE.
```

Create a crosstab with 'Which party feel closer to, France' [`prtcldfr`] and 'Some races or ethnic groups: born less intelligent' [`smegbli`]. Choose the appropriate percentages to show results within each party affiliation. Include a chi squared test, Cramer's V and adjusted standardized residuals.

```
CROSSTABS prtcldfr by smegbli

/cells=count row asresid

/statistics=chisq phi.
```

Table A.6.2 Views on racial superiority by party affiliation, France

Party affiliation	Some races or ethnic groups: born less intelligent						Total	
	Yes			No				
	N	%	Adj. Res.	N	%	Adj. Res.	N	%
FN	41	27.2%	5.3	110	72.8%	–5.3	151	100.0%	100.0%
PS	17	6.3%	–4.7	254	93.7%	4.7	271	100.0%	100.0%
UMP	39	14.4%	.3	231	85.6%	–.3	270	100.0%	100.0%
Total	97	14.0%		595	86.0%		692	100.0%	100.0%

Chi-Square Tests

	Value	df	Asymptotic Significance (2-sided)
Pearson Chi-Square	35.141[a]	2	.000
Likelihood Ratio	34.259	2	.000
Linear-by-Linear Association	24.158	1	.000
N of Valid Cases	692		

a. 0 cells (0.0%) have expected count less than 5. The minimum expected count is 21.17.

(Continued)

Table A.6.2 (Continued)

Symmetric Measures			
		Value	**Approximate Significance**
Nominal by Nominal	Phi	.225	.000
	Cramer's V	.225	.000
N of Valid Cases		692	

1. The relationship is significant: the Pearson chi-square significance is 0.000. This would be reported as p<0.001.
2. The relationship has a medium effect. We can find this using the Cramer's V value (0.225) and the degrees of freedom (2), which tells us that it meets the threshold for a small effect (>0.21) but not for a medium effect (>0.35).
3. To find this, we need to look at our percentages. We can see that more than a quarter (27.2 percent) of FN supporters agreed with the statement in contrast to 93.7 percent of PS supporters who rejected it. UMP supporters lie between the two extremes with 14.4 percent agreement. This would align with our expectations based on the parties' left-right positioning: centre–left (PS) supporters are more open to immigration and multiculturalism than centre–right (UMP) supporters, and right-wing (FN) supporters show the greatest hostility to racial equality.
4. There are strong associations for FN and PS respondents, but the responses for UMP supporters show no relationship. We can find this in the adjusted standardized residuals: all of the cells for FN and PS responses exceed ±2, but those for the UMP are only ±0.3. The positive/negative split on the residuals shows us that FN respondents appear in the Yes column much more than expected (+5.3), while PS supporters appear here much less than expected (–4.7).
5. These results indicate that supporters of the right-wing FN are much more likely to hold views espousing racial superiority than supporters of the other parties.

Activity 6.3

Answers should follow the same pattern as above.

Activity 6.4

RQ: How does education affect national identity?

Run a crosstab with counts, appropriate percentages, a chi squared test, Cramer's V and adjusted standardized residuals.

```
CROSSTABS eisced by fclcntr
```

```
/cells=count row asresid

/statistics=chisq phi.
```

Table A.6.3 Feeling of closeness to country by highest educational qualification

Highest level of education		Very close	Close	Not very close	Not close at all	Total
Less than lower secondary	N	2328	1412	246	64	4050
	%	57.5%	34.9%	6.1%	1.6%	100.0%
	Adj. Res.	8.6	–7.3	–3.8	2.5	
Lower secondary	N	3276	2769	583	88	6716
	%	48.8%	41.2%	8.7%	1.3%	100.0%
	Adj. Res.	–4.1	1.9	3.8	1.1	
Lower tier upper secondary	N	3861	2753	493	69	7176
	%	53.8%	38.4%	6.9%	1.0%	100.0%
	Adj. Res.	5.2	–3.5	–2.4	–1.9	
Upper tier upper secondary	N	3385	2981	590	88	7044
	%	48.1%	42.3%	8.4%	1.2%	100.0%
	Adj. Res.	–5.5	4.0	2.9	.6	
Advanced vocational, sub-degree	N	2859	2272	429	76	5636
	%	50.7%	40.3%	7.6%	1.3%	100.0%
	Adj. Res.	–.5	.2	.2	1.3	
Lower tertiary education, BA level	N	2198	1765	339	43	4345
	%	50.6%	40.6%	7.8%	1.0%	100.0%
	Adj. Res.	–.6	.6	.6	–1.2	
Higher tertiary education, >= MA level	N	2341	2005	317	41	4704
	%	49.8%	42.6%	6.7%	0.9%	100.0%
	Adj. Res.	–1.9	3.6	–2.3	–2.1	
Other	N	64	46	12	1	123
	%	52.0%	37.4%	9.8%	0.8%	100.0%
	Adj. Res.	.2	–.6	.9	–.4	
Total	N	20312	16003	3009	470	39794
	%	51.0%	40.2%	7.6%	1.2%	100.0%

(Continued)

Table A.6.3 (Continued)

Chi-Square Tests			
	Value	**df**	**Asymptotic Significance (2-sided)**
Pearson Chi-Square	171.432[a]	21	.000
Likelihood Ratio	171.933	21	.000
Linear-by-Linear Association	2.513	1	.113
N of Valid Cases	39794		

a. 1 cells (3.1%) have expected count less than 5. The minimum expected count is 1.45.

Symmetric Measures			
		Value	**Approximate Significance**
Nominal by Nominal	Phi	.066	.000
	Cramer's V	.038	.000
N of Valid Cases		39794	

1. Is the relationship between these two variables statistically significant? What p-threshold would you use to report the results? The relationship is significant: the Pearson chi-square significance is 0.000. This would be reported as $p<0.001$.
2. The relationship has a small effect. We can find this using the Cramer's V value (0.038) and the degrees of freedom (21), which tells us that it meets the threshold for a small effect (>0.022) but not for a medium effect (>0.065).
3. Respondents with less than lower secondary qualifications have the highest proportion (57.5 percent) reporting that they feel 'very close' to their country. The greatest proportion of respondents (1.6 percent) saying they felt 'not close at all' was also within those with less than lower secondary education. The lowest proportion reporting they felt 'very close' (48.1 percent) is respondents with upper tier upper secondary education.
4. The answer pairings relating to educational qualifications from less than lower secondary through upper tier upper secondary have far stronger adjusted residuals than the answer pairings for advanced sub-vocational qualifications through higher tertiary education. Only one of the answer pairings for 'not close at all' has an adjusted residual exceeding ±2: 'not close at all' and less than lower secondary education (Adj. Res. 2.5).
5. There is some evidence that people with lower educational qualifications feel closer to their country, but the evidence is inconsistent, with respondents holding less than lower secondary and lower tier upper secondary qualifications exhibiting much greater closeness than those with lower secondary and upper tier upper secondary. There is no conclusive evidence either way for respondents with higher educational qualifications.

CHAPTER 7

Activity 7.1

Produce a table with appropriate measures of central tendency and dispersion for 'Net migration rate (per 1,000 people)' [netmig].

```
FREQUENCIES netmig

/format=notable

/statistics=stddev range minimum maximum mean median

/histogram normal.
```

Table A.7.1 Descriptive statistics for net migration rate [netmig]

Statistic		**Value**
N	**Valid**	**1026**
	Missing	**3436**
Mean		-.1521
Median		-.5000
Std. Deviation		10.32
Range		194.30
Minimum		-62.90
Maximum		131.40

1. There are 1,026 observations. Each observation represents one country in one year.
2. The lowest net migration rate is –62.90. This means that, for one country in one year, the number of people leaving the country exceeded the number of people moving to the country by 62.9 people per thousand, or 6.29%. This means that, for every one person who moved to the country, 6.29 left.
3. The observations appear to be normally distributed, though there are more observations exceeding +50 than –50.
4. There is a slight difference between the mean (–0.15) and the median (–0.50). This is likely to be explained by the few outlier cases at the high end of positive net migration, such as the case that had a net migration rate of +131.40. However, given that this is measured in people per thousand, this equates to a difference of 0.035 percent, which is very small, so the outliers have not skewed the data excessively. It is also noticeable how closely this is centred on a mean of 0; in other words, equal numbers of people leaving the country as arriving.

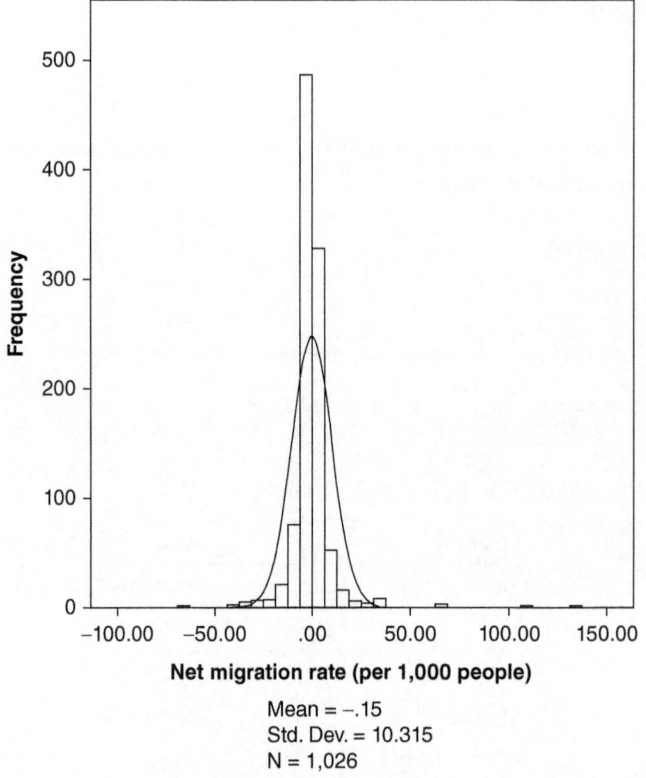

Figure A.7.1 Histogram of net migration rate [netmig]

Activity 7.2

Complete the following table for testing the relationship between logged gross national income [loggni] and mean years of schooling [meanschyrs], female life expectancy [femlifeexpect] and total unemployment rate [unemprate] testing for violation of the assumptions for a correlation.

Check for linearity and pairs by producing scatterplots:

```
GRAPH
  /scatterplot(bivar)=loggni with meanschyrs
  /missing=listwise.
GRAPH
  /scatterplot(bivar)=loggni with femlifeexpect
  /missing=listwise.
```

```
GRAPH
  /scatterplot(bivar)=loggni with unemprate
  /missing=listwise.
```

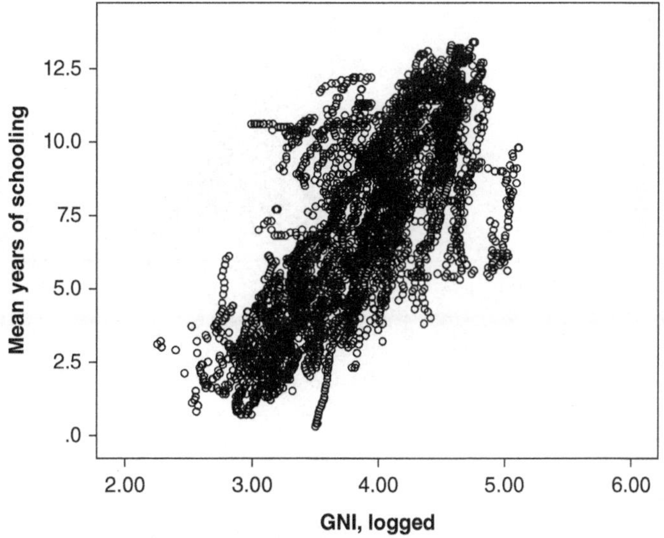

Figure A.7.2 Scatterplot of logged GNI and mean years of schooling

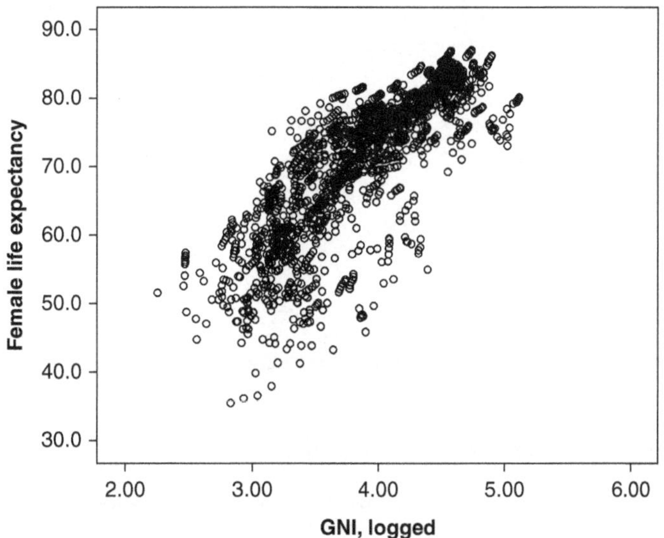

Figure A.7.3 Scatterplot of logged GNI and female life expectancy

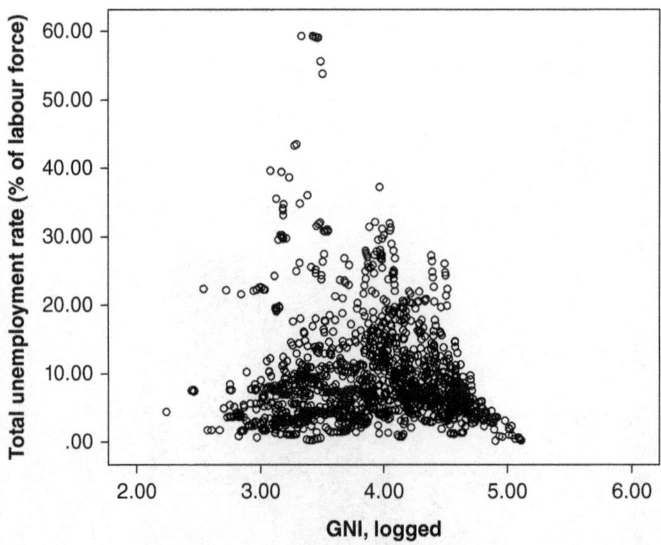

Figure A.7.4 Scatterplot of logged GNI and total unemployment rate

Calculate outlier thresholds:

```
FREQUENCIES loggni meanschyrs femlifeexpect unemprate
/format=notable
/statistics=stddev minimum maximum mean.
```

Table A.7.2 Summary of assumptions met by variable pair with logged GNI [`loggni`]

Variable paired with GNI pc, PPP	Continuous	Pairs	Linearity	Outliers	Homoscedasticity
Mean years of schooling [`meanschyrs`]	Met	Met	Met	Met	Met
Female life expectancy [`femlifeexpect`]	Met	Met	Met	Not met (minimum observation too low)	Met
Total unemployment rate [`unemprate`]	Met	Met	Not met (curvilinear)	Not met (maximum too high)	Not met

Table A.7.3 Summary statistics for calculating outliers

		GNI, logged	Mean years of schooling	Female life expectancy	Total unemployment rate
N	Valid	4436	3905	1719	1538
	Missing	26	557	2743	2924

	GNI, logged	Mean years of schooling	Female life expectancy	Total unemployment rate
Mean	3.84	7.15	70.83	9.52
Std. Deviation	0.56	3.19	10.32	7.66
3.29 SDs	1.83	10.50	33.96	25.20
Outlier minimum	2.01	–3.35	36.87	–15.69
Outlier maximum	5.66	17.65	104.79	34.72
Observed minimum	2.25	0.3	35.4	0.1
Observed maximum	5.11	13.4	87	59.4

Calculate the correlation coefficient for variable pairs that don't violate the outlier assumption.

```
CORRELATIONS
  /VARIABLES=loggni meanschyrs
  /PRINT=TWOTAIL NOSIG
  /MISSING=PAIRWISE.
```

For any variables where the only assumption violated is outliers, apply a filter. Exclude outliers for female life expectancy:

```
USE ALL.
COMPUTE filter_$=(femlifeexpect >= 36.87).
VARIABLE LABELS filter_$ 'femlifeexpect >= 36.87 (FILTER)'.
VALUE LABELS filter_$ 0 'Not Selected' 1 'Selected'.
FORMATS filter_$ (f1.0).
FILTER BY filter_$.
EXECUTE.
```

Remember to remove the filter when testing other variables.

```
FILTER off.
```

1. See Table A.7.2 Summary of assumptions met by variable pair with logged GNI [`loggni`] for overview of assumptions not met. For variables violating the assumption about outliers, the results can be filtered to exclude outliers. For violations of linearity and homoscedasticity, manipulations such as log transformations can be attempted.

2. See Table A.7.3 Summary statistics for calculating outliers for an overview of the calculations of mean, standard deviation, 3.29 standard deviations, and the minimums and maximums for outliers. Female life expectancy should have outliers excluded at the lower end of observations: the observed minimum is 35.4, but observations below 36.87 should be excluded. For total unemployment rate, outliers should be excluded above 34.72. However, unemployment rate violates other assumptions, and this should be taken into account in the approach.
3. Correlations have been run for mean years of schooling and female life expectancy; unemployment rate has been excluded because of violations of the assumptions of linearity and homoscedasticity. Both correlations are statistically significant ($p<0.001$). The correlation is strongest with female life expectancy ($r=0.801$), but the correlation with mean years of schooling is also very strong ($r=0.748$).

CHAPTER 8

Activity 8.1

RQ: Is democracy increasing globally?

1. H1. Democracy in the world has been steadily increasing.
2. Create a simple line chart with means. Place 'Year' [`year`] on the x-axis and 'Freedom House average score' [`fhavg`] on the y-axis.

```
GGRAPH

  /GRAPHDATASET NAME="graphdataset" VARIABLES=Year MEAN(FHavg)
[name="MEAN_FHavg"] MISSING=LISTWISE

    REPORTMISSING=NO

  /GRAPHSPEC SOURCE=INLINE.

BEGIN GPL

  SOURCE: s=userSource(id("graphdataset"))

  DATA: Year=col(source(s), name("Year"))

  DATA: MEAN_FHavg=col(source(s), name("MEAN_FHavg"))

  GUIDE: axis(dim(1), label("Year"))

  GUIDE: axis(dim(2), label("Mean Freedom House average score"))

  ELEMENT: line(position(Year*MEAN_FHavg), missing.wings())

END GPL.
```

Rescale the y-axis to run from 1 (completely free) to 7 (not free). Set the major increment to 1. Add major gridlines to box the x- and y-axis.

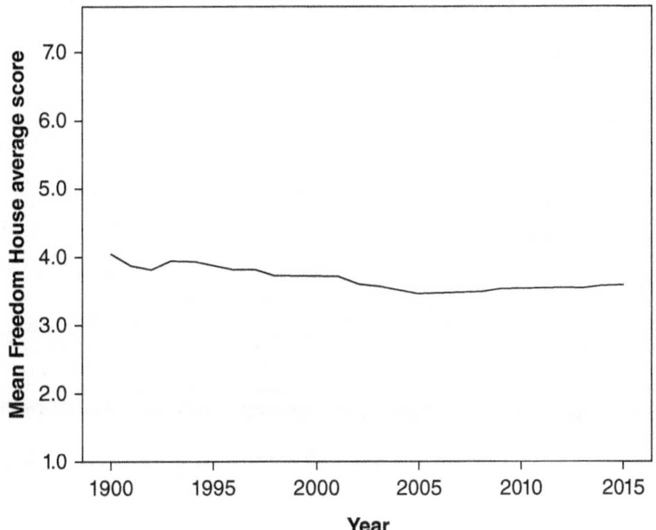

Figure A.8.1 Freedom in the world over time

Figure A.8.1 Freedom in the world over time shows that the mean Freedom House score is lower (=more free) now than it was in 1990. There was a steady decline from 1990 through 2005. However, after 2005, the mean Freedom House score increases (=less free). This means there has been democratic backsliding since 2005.

3. Create a multiple line chart with means. Place 'Year' [`year`] on the x-axis and 'Freedom House average score' [`fhavg`] on the y-axis. Place 'World Bank income group' [`wbincome`] in the 'Set pattern' box.

```
GGRAPH
  /GRAPHDATASET NAME="graphdataset" VARIABLES=Year MEAN(FHavg)
[name="MEAN_FHavg"] wbincome
    MISSING=LISTWISE REPORTMISSING=NO
  /GRAPHSPEC SOURCE=INLINE.
BEGIN GPL
  SOURCE: s=userSource(id("graphdataset"))
  DATA: Year=col(source(s), name("Year"))
  DATA: MEAN_FHavg=col(source(s), name("MEAN_FHavg"))
```

```
  DATA: wbincome=col(source(s), name("wbincome"), unit.category())

  GUIDE: axis(dim(1), label("Year"))

  GUIDE: axis(dim(2), label("Mean Freedom House average score"))

  GUIDE: legend(aesthetic(aesthetic.color.interior), label("World Bank
income group"))

  SCALE: cat(aesthetic(aesthetic.color.interior), include("1", "2",
"3", "4"))

  ELEMENT: line(position(Year*MEAN_FHavg), color.interior(wbincome),
missing.wings())

END GPL.
```

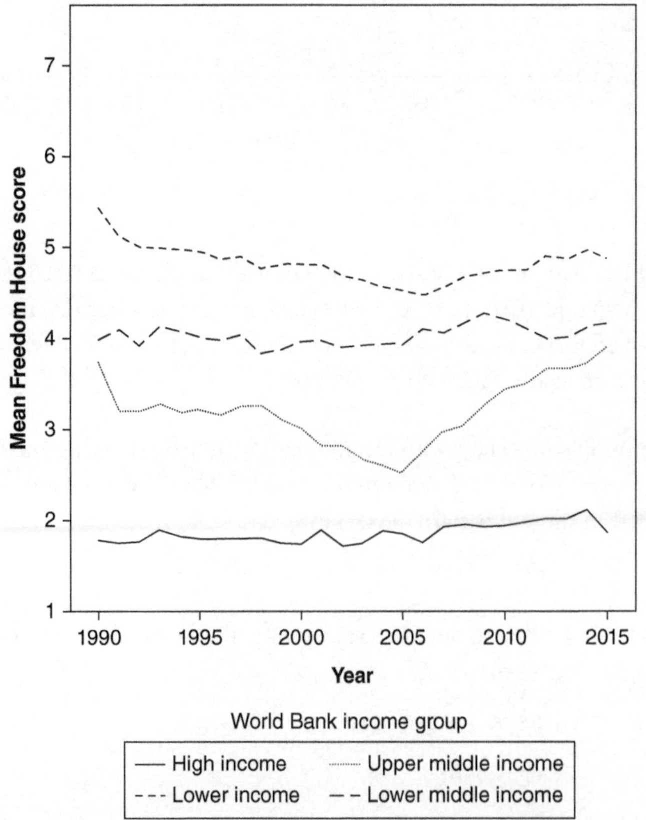

Figure A.8.2 Average Freedom House score by World Bank income groups

Look at your result, keeping in mind that a score of 1 is completely free and 7 is not free. What does this mean for theories, such as economic modernization theory, that link higher economic development with higher support for democracy? Figure A.8.2 Average Freedom House score by World Bank income groups shows a clear division in average Freedom House scores between different income groups. There is a clear progression with wealthier countries having greater levels of democracy. This would seem to indicate support for economic modernization theory. However, it is also clear that there has been considerable democratic backsliding that is almost entirely focused in the upper middle-income group.

4. Repeat these steps using 'Revised combined Polity score' [`polity2`] instead of Freedom House scores.

```
*4a. Simple line chart with means showing Polity scores over time.

GGRAPH

  /GRAPHDATASET NAME="graphdataset" VARIABLES=Year MEAN(polity2)
[name="MEAN_polity2"] MISSING=LISTWISE

    REPORTMISSING=NO

  /GRAPHSPEC SOURCE=INLINE.

BEGIN GPL

  SOURCE: s=userSource(id("graphdataset"))

  DATA: Year=col(source(s), name("Year"))

  DATA: MEAN_polity2=col(source(s), name("MEAN_polity2"))

  GUIDE: axis(dim(1), label("Year"))

  GUIDE: axis(dim(2), label("Polity score"))

  ELEMENT: line(position(Year*MEAN_polity2), missing.wings())

END GPL.


*4b. Multiple line chart with means showing Polity scores over time,
split by World Bank income groups.

GGRAPH

  /GRAPHDATASET NAME="graphdataset" VARIABLES=Year MEAN(polity2)
[name="MEAN_polity2"] wbincome

    MISSING=LISTWISE REPORTMISSING=NO

  /GRAPHSPEC SOURCE=INLINE.

BEGIN GPL

  SOURCE: s=userSource(id("graphdataset"))
```

```
DATA: Year=col(source(s), name("Year"))

DATA: MEAN_polity2=col(source(s), name("MEAN_polity2"))

DATA: wbincome=col(source(s), name("wbincome"), unit.category())

GUIDE: axis(dim(1), label("Year"))

GUIDE: axis(dim(2), label("Mean Polity score"))

GUIDE: legend(aesthetic(aesthetic.color.interior), label("World Bank
income group"))

SCALE: cat(aesthetic(aesthetic.color.interior), include("1", "2",
"3", "4"))

ELEMENT: line(position(Year*MEAN_polity2), color.interior(wbincome),
missing.wings())

END GPL.
```

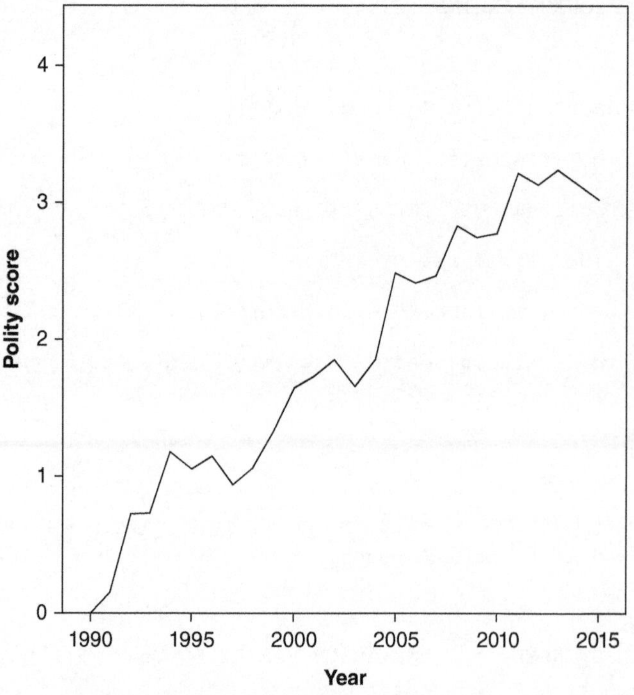

Figure A.8.3 Average Polity score over time

The overall trend in the Polity data over time shows a steady trend towards increasing democracy, albeit with occasional dips (Figure A.8.3 Average Polity score over time). This trend differs from the Freedom House average scores, which indicated that democracy has

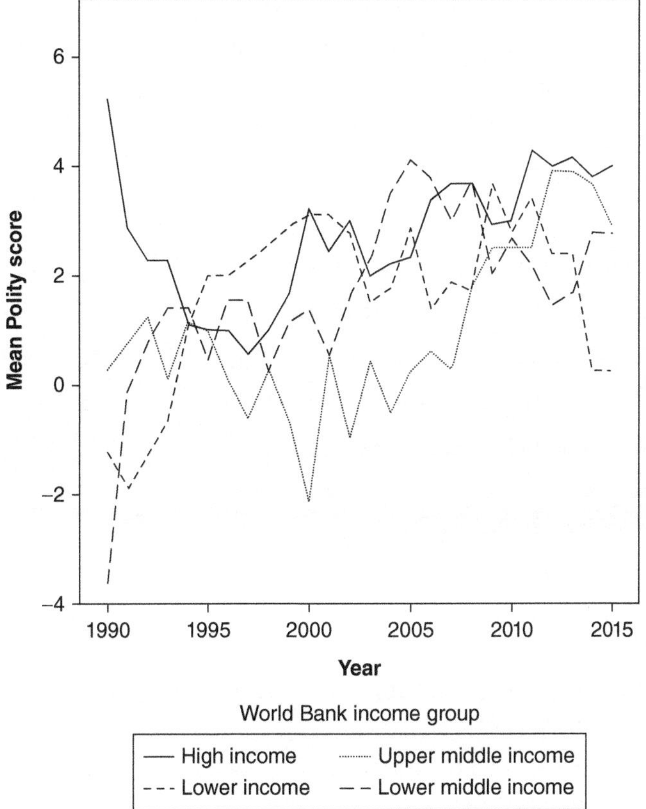

Figure A.8.4 Average Polity score by World Bank income group

been steadily declining since 2005; however, Polity does show a drop in democracy after 2010. When the data is divided by World Bank income groups (Figure A.8.4 Average Polity score by World Bank income group), the differences between groups are not as clear-cut as they were with the Freedom House scores. Both upper middle-income and low-income countries show a noticeable decline in quality of democracy post-2010.

Activity 8.2

RQ: How have the numbers and locations of refugees and other populations of concern changed over time?

1. Create a multiple line chart with sums. Place 'Year' [`year`] on the x-axis and 'Total population of concern hosted (refugees, asylum-seekers, others of concern)' [`refplushost`] on the y-axis. Place 'Geographical grouping (UN)' [`georegion`] in the 'Set pattern' box.

```
GGRAPH
  /GRAPHDATASET NAME="graphdataset" VARIABLES=Year SUM(refplushost)
[name="SUM_refplushost"]
    georegion MISSING=LISTWISE REPORTMISSING=NO
  /GRAPHSPEC SOURCE=INLINE.
BEGIN GPL
  SOURCE: s=userSource(id("graphdataset"))
  DATA: Year=col(source(s), name("Year"))
  DATA: SUM_refplushost=col(source(s), name("SUM_refplushost"))
  DATA: georegion=col(source(s), name("georegion"), unit.category())
  GUIDE: axis(dim(1), label("Year"))
  GUIDE: axis(dim(2), label("Sum Total population of concern hosted
(refugees, asylum-seekers, ",
    "others of concern)"))
  GUIDE: legend(aesthetic(aesthetic.color.interior), label("Geographi-
cal grouping (UN)"))
  SCALE: cat(aesthetic(aesthetic.color.interior), include("1", "2",
"3", "4", "5", "6", "7"))
   ELEMENT: line(position(Year*SUM_refplushost), color.interior(geore-
gion), missing.wings())
END GPL.
```

In the most recent year available (2015), Sub-Saharan Africa hosted the greatest number of people of concern; this is followed by Europe and Central Asia. This varies over time, however, with South Asia having been the top region from 2005 to 2012. The Middle East and North Africa have experienced considerable fluctuations in numbers.

2. Repeat the chart using Freedom House status [`e_fh_status`] instead of geographic region.

```
GGRAPH
  /GRAPHDATASET NAME="graphdataset" VARIABLES=Year SUM(refplushost)
[name="SUM_refplushost"]
    e_fh_status MISSING=LISTWISE REPORTMISSING=NO
  /GRAPHSPEC SOURCE=INLINE.
BEGIN GPL
  SOURCE: s=userSource(id("graphdataset"))
```

```
  DATA: Year=col(source(s), name("Year"))
DATA: SUM_refplushost=col(source(s), name("SUM_refplushost"))
  DATA: e_fh_status=col(source(s), name("e_fh_status"), unit.category())
  GUIDE: axis(dim(1), label("Year"))
  GUIDE: axis(dim(2), label("Sum Total population of concern hosted
(refugees, asylum-seekers, ",
  "others of concern)"))
  GUIDE: legend(aesthetic(aesthetic.color.interior), label("Freedom
House status"))
  SCALE: cat(aesthetic(aesthetic.color.interior), include("1", "2", "3"))
  ELEMENT: line(position(Year*SUM_refplushost), color.interior(e_fh_
status), missing.wings())
END GPL.
```

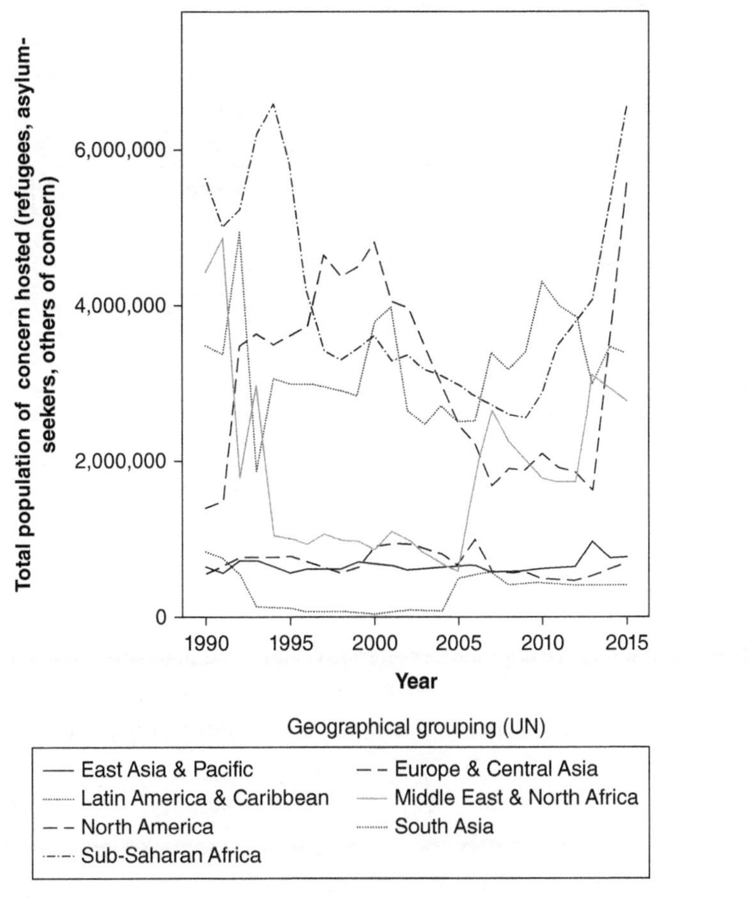

Figure A.8.5 Populations of concern by geographic region

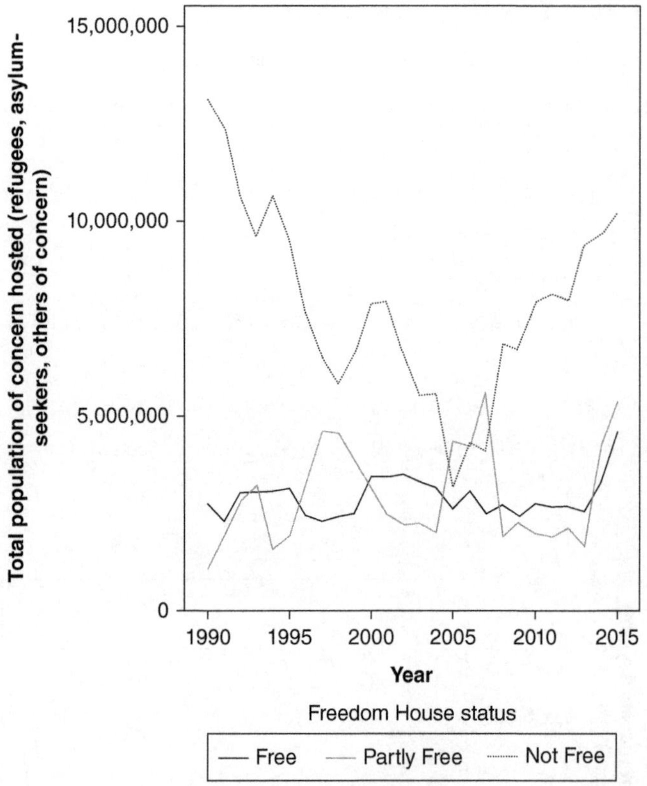

Figure A.8.6 Population of concern by Freedom House status

Countries rated 'not free' by Freedom House host far greater populations of concern than 'free' and 'partly free' countries. The only exception to this was a brief period after 2005, when 'partly free' countries narrowly surpassed 'not free' countries.

Activity 8.3

RQ: How are human development, gender inequality and democracy related?

Create a grouped scatterplot with the human development index [`hdi`] and gender inequality index [`gii`], grouped by Freedom House status [`e_fh_status`]. Exclude results for 'partly free'.

```
GGRAPH

  /GRAPHDATASET NAME="graphdataset" VARIABLES=HDI GII e_fh_status
MISSING=LISTWISE REPORTMISSING=NO

  /GRAPHSPEC SOURCE=INLINE.

BEGIN GPL

  SOURCE: s=userSource(id("graphdataset"))

  DATA: HDI=col(source(s), name("HDI"))

  DATA: GII=col(source(s), name("GII"))

  DATA: e_fh_status=col(source(s), name("e_fh_status"),

notIn("2"), unit.category())

  GUIDE: axis(dim(1), label("Human Development Index (HDI)"))

  GUIDE: axis(dim(2), label("Gender Inequality Index"))

  GUIDE: legend(aesthetic(aesthetic.color.exterior), label("Freedom
House status"))

  SCALE: cat(aesthetic(aesthetic.color.exterior), include("1", "3"))

  ELEMENT: point(position(HDI*GII), color.exterior(e_fh_status))

END GPL.
```

1. The results indicate a negative relationship between gender inequality and human development. This is what we would expect because a human development score of 1 equates to maximum development, while a gender inequality score of 1 equates to complete inequality. Free countries are more clustered at the bottom right of the chart, with higher levels of both gender equality and human development. An exception is Mali, which has a Freedom House status of 'free' but scores poorly on both human development and gender equality. An exception of the 'not free countries' is the Central African Republic, which scores well on both human development and gender equality but is rated 'not free'.
2. Run a correlation between human development and gender inequality with the file split by Freedom House status.

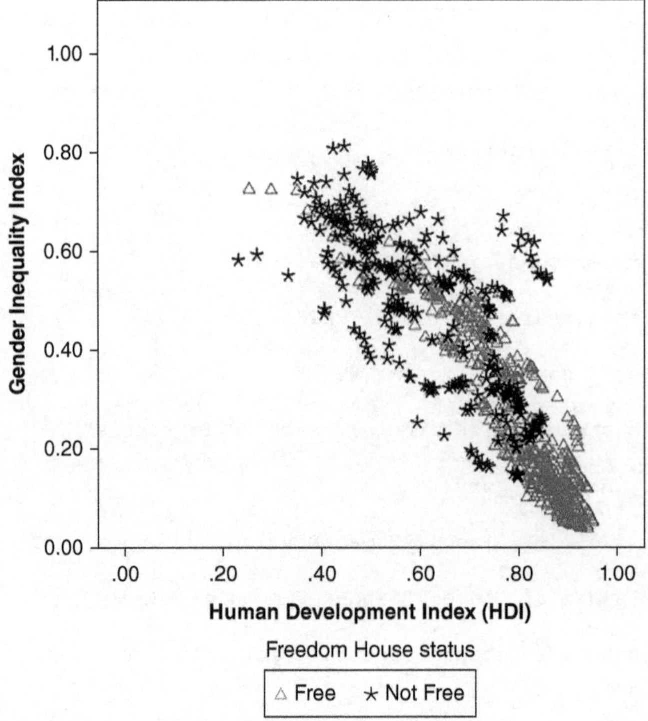

Figure A.8.7 Human development and gender inequality, grouped by Freedom House status

Split file by Freedom House status [`e_fh_status`].

```
SORT CASES BY e_fh_status.

SPLIT FILE LAYERED BY e_fh_status.
```

Correlation between HDI and GII.

```
CORRELATIONS
  /VARIABLES=HDI GII
  /PRINT=TWOTAIL NOSIG
  /MISSING=PAIRWISE.
```

Turn split file off when finished.

```
SPLIT FILE OFF.
```

Table A.8.1 Correlations between human development and gender inequality, split by Freedom House status

Freedom House status	Pearson Correlation	N
Free	–.917**	551
Partly Free	–.853**	396
Not Free	–.693**	297

** $p<0.01$

Are the correlations statistically significant? Which group's correlation is strongest? Table A.8.1 Correlations between human development and gender inequality, split by Freedom House status shows that all three correlations are statistically significant ($p<0.001$). The strongest correlation is for free countries, with a near-perfect correlation ($r=-0.917$). The weakest correlation is for 'not free' countries ($r=-0.693$). Although the relationship is weaker than the other two groups, this still constitutes a strong relationship.

CHAPTER 9

Activity 9.1

1. Bivariate descriptive comparison with mean, count and standard deviation.

```
MEANS imueclt by prtclcdk prtcldfr prtcldes

/cells=mean count stddev.
```

Table A.9.1 Mean 'immigrants enrich country's cultural life' by Danish party affiliation

Party affiliation	Mean	N	Std. Deviation
Socialdemokraterne - the Danish social democrats	6.52	191	2.115
Det Radikale Venstre - Danish Social-Liberal Party	7.66	83	1.625
Det Konservative Folkeparti - Conservative	6.22	50	2.359
SF Socialistisk Folkeparti - Socialist People's Party	7.40	94	1.839
Dansk Folkeparti - Danish peoples party	3.39	165	2.334
Kristendemokraterne - Christian democrats	6.50	10	1.434
Venstre, Danmarks Liberale Parti - Venstre	5.45	261	2.224
Liberal Alliance - Liberal Alliance	6.20	51	2.164
Enhedslisten - Unity List - The Red-Green Alliance	6.94	86	2.398
Andet - other	6.00	4	3.162
Total	5.90	995	2.527

2. The three largest parties are the Danish Social Democrats (N=191), the Danish People's Party (N=165) and Venstre (N=261). The Danish People's Party is a right-wing party; the Social Democrats are left-wing. This leads to two hypotheses:

H1. Supporters of the Danish People's Party will be the most hostile to immigration.

H2. Supporters of the Danish Social Democrats will be the most open to immigration.

3. The Social Democrats are the most pro-immigration (mean 6.52). The People's Party is the most anti-immigrant (mean 3.39). The conservative–liberal Venstre falls in the middle (mean 5.45). This aligns with expectations based on its general position on the left–right political spectrum.
4. The chart indicates that the difference between groups is statistically significant, as none of the confidence intervals overlap.

```
GGRAPH

  /GRAPHDATASET NAME="graphdataset" VARIABLES=prtclcdk MEANCI(imueclt,
95)[name="MEAN_imueclt"

    LOW="MEAN_imueclt_LOW" HIGH="MEAN_imueclt_HIGH"] MISSING=LISTWISE
REPORTMISSING=NO

  /GRAPHSPEC SOURCE=INLINE.

BEGIN GPL

  SOURCE: s=userSource(id("graphdataset"))

  DATA: prtclcdk=col(source(s), name("prtclcdk"),

notIn("2", "3", "4", "6", "8", "9", "10"), unit.category())

  DATA: MEAN_imueclt=col(source(s), name("MEAN_imueclt"))

  DATA: LOW=col(source(s), name("MEAN_imueclt_LOW"))

  DATA: HIGH=col(source(s), name("MEAN_imueclt_HIGH"))

  GUIDE: axis(dim(1), label("Which party feel closer to, Denmark"))

  GUIDE: axis(dim(2), label("Mean Country's cultural life undermined or
enriched by immigrants"))

  GUIDE: text.footnote(label("Error Bars: 95% CI"))

  SCALE: cat(dim(1), include("1", "5", "7"), sort.values("1", "5", "7"))

  SCALE: linear(dim(2), include(0))

  ELEMENT: point(position(prtclcdk*MEAN_imueclt))
```

```
  ELEMENT: interval(position(region.spread.range(prtclcdk*(LOW+HIGH))),
shape.interior(shape.ibeam))

END GPL.
```

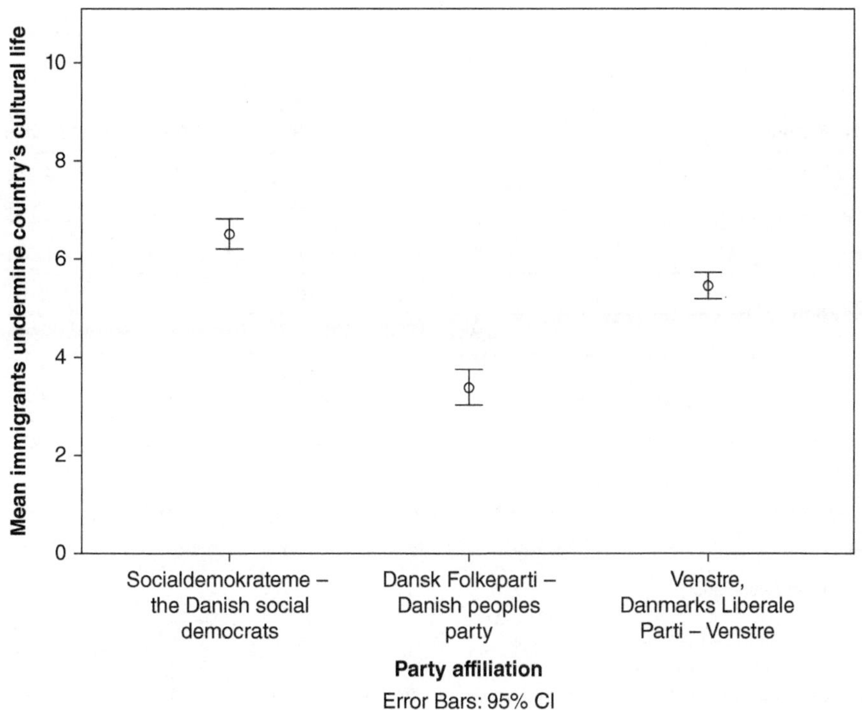

Figure A.9.1 Error bar chart of immigrants enrich country's cultural life, selected Danish parties

5. The difference between groups is statistically significant ($p<0.001$). The effect size is medium (eta 0.476).

```
USE ALL.

COMPUTE filter_$=(prtclcdk = 1 OR prtclcdk = 5 OR prtclcdk = 7).

VARIABLE LABELS filter_$ '3 largest Danish parties (FILTER)'.

VALUE LABELS filter_$ 0 'Not Selected' 1 'Selected'.

FORMATS filter_$ (f1.0).

FILTER BY filter_$.
```

```
EXECUTE.

MEANS TABLES=imueclt BY prtclcdk

  /CELLS=MEAN COUNT STDDEV VAR

  /STATISTICS ANOVA.
```

Table A.9.2 Strength of relationship between Danish party affiliation and immigrants enriching cultural life

Party affiliation	**Mean**	**N**	**Std. Deviation**	**Variance**
Danish social democrats	6.52	191	2.115	4.472
Danish people's party	3.39	165	2.334	5.446
Venstre	5.45	261	2.224	4.948
Total	5.23	617	2.522	6.362

ANOVA Table

		Sum of Squares	**df**	**Mean Square**	**F**	**Sig.**
Between Groups	(Combined)	889.365	2	444.682	90.128	.000
Within Groups		3051.549	3029.413	614	4.934	
Total		3868.447	3918.778	616		

Measures of Association

	Eta	Eta Squared
Country's cultural life undermined or enriched by immigrants * Which party feel closer to, Denmark	.476	.227

6. The Tukey post hoc comparisons confirm that the difference between all groups is statistically significant at p<0.001.

```
ONEWAY imueclt BY prtclcdk

  /STATISTICS DESCRIPTIVES

  /MISSING ANALYSIS

  /POSTHOC=TUKEY ALPHA(0.05).
```

Activity 9.2

1. H1. Democracies will have higher female representation in the legislature than autocracies.

Table A.9.3 Tukey post hoc comparison results, Danish party affiliation and immigrants enrich cultural life

(I) Which party feel closer to, Denmark	(J) Which party feel closer to, Denmark	Mean Difference (I-J)	Std. Error	Sig.	95% Confidence Interval Lower Bound	95% Confidence Interval Upper Bound
Socialdemokraterne – the Danish social democrats	Dansk Folkeparti – Danish peoples party	3.130*	.236	.000	2.58	3.69
	Venstre, Danmarks Liberale Parti – Venstre	1.070*	.212	.000	.57	1.57
Dansk Folkeparti – Danish peoples party	Socialdemokraterne – the Danish social democrats	−3.130*	.236	.000	−3.69	−2.58
	Venstre, Danmarks Liberale Parti – Venstre	−2.060*	.221	.000	−2.58	−1.54
Venstre, Danmarks Liberale Parti – Venstre	Socialdemokraterne – the Danish social democrats	−1.070*	.212	.000	−1.57	−.57
	Dansk Folkeparti – Danish peoples party	2.060*	.221	.000	1.54	2.58

*The mean difference is significant at the 0.05 level.

2. Create a bivariate descriptive comparison of means table using 'Female share of parliamentary seats' [femleg] and 'Democracy-Dictatorship score' [e_regime]. Include the mean, count and standard deviation.

```
MEANS TABLES=femleg BY e_regime
  /CELLS=MEAN COUNT STDDEV.
```

Table A.9.4 Female legislative representation by regime type

	Mean	N	Std. Deviation
Democratic	12.84	232	8.70
Autocratic	9.24	157	7.13
Total	11.39	389	8.28

Democratic countries have the larger share of female legislators with an average of 12.8 percent of legislators in democracies who are female compared to 9.2 percent in autocracies. However, the standard deviation indicates greater variability in democracies (8.70) than autocracies (7.13). This confirms the expectation from H1.

3. Based on the error bar chart, we should expect a statistically significant difference between the groups, as there is no overlap between the lower confidence interval of democracies and the upper confidence interval of autocracies.

```
GGRAPH
  /GRAPHDATASET NAME="graphdataset" VARIABLES=e_Regime MEANCI(femleg, 95)[name="MEAN_femleg"
    LOW="MEAN_femleg_LOW" HIGH="MEAN_femleg_HIGH"] MISSING=LISTWISE REPORTMISSING=NO
  /GRAPHSPEC SOURCE=INLINE.
BEGIN GPL
  SOURCE: s=userSource(id("graphdataset"))
  DATA: e_Regime=col(source(s), name("e_Regime"), unit.category())
  DATA: MEAN_femleg=col(source(s), name("MEAN_femleg"))
  DATA: LOW=col(source(s), name("MEAN_femleg_LOW"))
  DATA: HIGH=col(source(s), name("MEAN_femleg_HIGH"))
  GUIDE: axis(dim(1), label("Democracy-Dictatorship classification (Przeworski et al.)"))
  GUIDE: axis(dim(2), label("Mean Female share of parliamentary seats"))
  GUIDE: text.footnote(label("Error Bars: 95% CI"))
  SCALE: cat(dim(1), include("0", "1"))
  SCALE: linear(dim(2), include(0))
  ELEMENT: point(position(e_Regime*MEAN_femleg))
  ELEMENT: interval(position(region.spread.range(e_Regime*(LOW+HIGH))), shape.interior(shape.ibeam))
END GPL.
```

4. The difference between the groups is statistically significant ($p<0.001$). The effect size is medium (eta 0.213), indicating that regime type can explain 4.5 percent of variance in the share of legislative seats held by women.

```
MEANS TABLES=femleg BY e_regime
  /CELLS=MEAN COUNT STDDEV VAR
  /STATISTICS ANOVA.
```

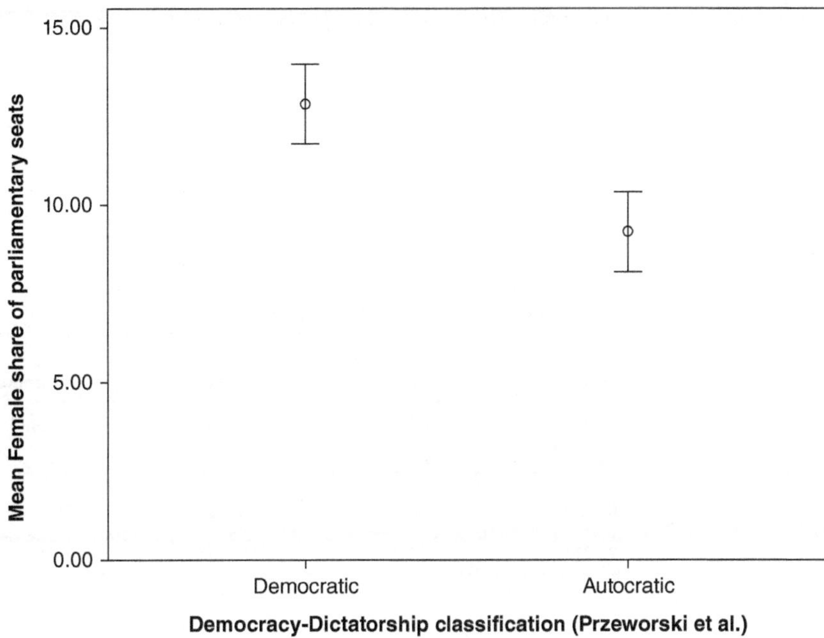

Figure A.9.2 Error bar chart of female share of legislative seats by regime type

Table A.9.5 ANOVA and eta results for female legislative seats by regime type

ANOVA Table

			Sum of Squares	df	Mean Square	F	Sig.
Female share of parliamentary seats * Democracy-Dictatorship classification	Between Groups	(Combined)	1208.737	1	1208.737	18.421	.000
	Within Groups		25393.872	387	65.617		
	Total		26602.608	388			

Measures of Association

	Eta	Eta Squared
Female share of parliamentary seats * Democracy-Dictatorship classification	.213	.045

5. The results still confirm that there is a difference in mean female legislative seats held depending on the level of democracy. However, the error bar chart indicates that the difference is only statistically significant for comparisons with countries rated 'free'; the difference between 'partly free' and 'not free' countries is not statistically significant.

Comparison of means female legislative seats by FH status.

```
MEANS TABLES=femleg BY e_fh_status
  /CELLS=MEAN COUNT STDDEV VAR
  /STATISTICS ANOVA.
```

Table A.9.6 Comparison of female legislative seats by Freedom House status

Female share of parliamentary seats				
Freedom House status	**Mean**	**N**	**Std. Deviation**	**Variance**
Free	20.8054	624	10.50376	110.329
Partly Free	14.9886	535	10.54925	111.287
Not Free	15.5165	417	10.84575	117.630
Total	17.4314	1576	10.95218	119.950

ANOVA Table

			Sum of Squares	df	Mean Square	F	Sig.
Female share of parliamentary seats * Freedom House status	Between Groups	(Combined)	11825.238	2	5912.619	52.517	.000
	Within Groups		177096.258	1573	112.585		
	Total		188921.495	1575			

Measures of Association

	Eta	Eta Squared
Female share of parliamentary seats * Freedom House status	.250	.063

Error bar chart female legislative seats by FH status.

```
GGRAPH
  /GRAPHDATASET NAME="graphdataset" VARIABLES=e_fh_status MEANCI
(femleg, 95)[name="MEAN_femleg"
    LOW="MEAN_femleg_LOW" HIGH="MEAN_femleg_HIGH"] MISSING=LISTWISE
REPORTMISSING=NO
  /GRAPHSPEC SOURCE=INLINE.
BEGIN GPL
```

```
SOURCE: s=userSource(id("graphdataset"))
DATA: e_fh_status=col(source(s), name("e_fh_status"), unit.category())
DATA: MEAN_femleg=col(source(s), name("MEAN_femleg"))
DATA: LOW=col(source(s), name("MEAN_femleg_LOW"))
DATA: HIGH=col(source(s), name("MEAN_femleg_HIGH"))
GUIDE: axis(dim(1), label("Freedom House status (V-Dem)"))
GUIDE: axis(dim(2), label("Mean Female share of parliamentary seats"))
GUIDE: text.footnote(label("Error Bars: 95% CI"))
SCALE: cat(dim(1), include("1", "2", "3"))
SCALE: linear(dim(2), include(0))
ELEMENT: point(position(e_fh_status*MEAN_femleg))
ELEMENT:
interval(position(region.spread.range(e_fh_status*(LOW+HIGH))),
shape.interior(shape.ibeam))
END GPL.
```

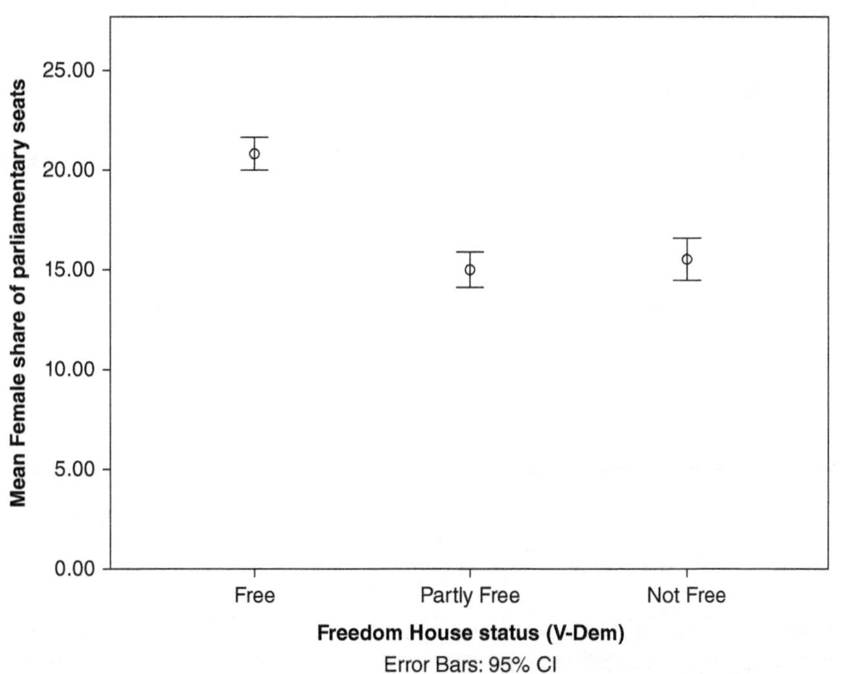

Figure A.9.3 Error bar chart of female share of legislative seats by Freedom House status

6. The post hoc tests confirm that the difference between free countries, on the one hand, and either partly free or not free countries, on the other hand, is statistically significant; but the difference between partly free and not free is not (p=0.727).

```
ONEWAY femleg BY e_fh_status
  /STATISTICS DESCRIPTIVES
  /MISSING ANALYSIS
  /POSTHOC=TUKEY ALPHA(0.05).
```

Table A.9.7 Tukey post hoc results for female legislative seats by Freedom House status

(I) Freedom House status (V-Dem)	(J) Freedom House status (V-Dem)	Mean Difference (I-J)	Std. Error	Sig.	95% Confidence Interval	
					Lower Bound	Upper Bound
Free	Partly Free	5.81685*	.62519	.000	4.3502	7.2835
	Not Free	5.28890*	.67113	.000	3.7145	6.8633
Partly Free	Free	−5.81685*	.62519	.000	−7.2835	−4.3502
	Not Free	−.52795	.69313	.727	−2.1540	1.0981
Not Free	Free	−5.28890*	.67113	.000	−6.8633	−3.7145
	Partly Free	.52795	.69313	.727	−1.0981	2.1540

*The mean difference is significant at the 0.05 level.

Activity 9.3

Compare homicide rates [homicides] between World Bank income [wbincome] groups 1 (high income) and 2 (upper middle income).

```
USE ALL.
COMPUTE filter_$=(wbincome = 1 OR wbincome=2).
VARIABLE LABELS filter_$ 'wbincome = 1 OR wbincome=2 (FILTER)'.
VALUE LABELS filter_$ 0 'Not Selected' 1 'Selected'.
FORMATS filter_$ (f1.0).
FILTER BY filter_$.
EXECUTE.
```

1. Produce a column panel histogram to check for violations of the assumptions of normality and homogeneity of variance.

```
GGRAPH
```

```
  /GRAPHDATASET NAME="graphdataset" VARIABLES=homicides wbincome MISS-
ING=LISTWISE REPORTMISSING=NO

  /GRAPHSPEC SOURCE=INLINE.

BEGIN GPL

  SOURCE: s=userSource(id("graphdataset"))

  DATA: homicides=col(source(s), name("homicides"))

  DATA: wbincome=col(source(s), name("wbincome"),
notIn("3", "4"), unit.category())

  GUIDE: axis(dim(1), label("Homicide rate (per 100,000 people)"))

  GUIDE: axis(dim(2), label("Frequency"))

  GUIDE: axis(dim(3), label("World Bank income group"), opposite())

  SCALE: cat(dim(3), include("1", "2"))

  ELEMENT:
interval(position(summary.count(bin.rect(homicides*1*wbincome))),
    shape.interior(shape.square))

END GPL.
```

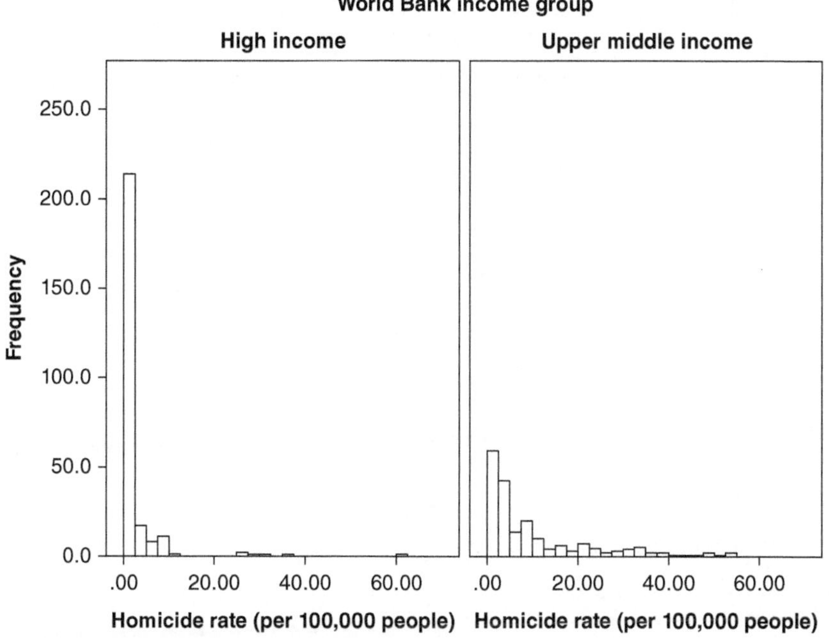

Figure A.9.4 Column panel histogram of homicide rates by income group

2. A non-parametric test is more appropriate for this data. It is not normally distributed, and there is not homogeneity of variance. Produce the appropriate test and any necessary additional statistics.

Mann–Whitney U test.

```
NPTESTS

  /INDEPENDENT TEST (homicides) GROUP (wbincome) MANN_WHITNEY

  /MISSING SCOPE=ANALYSIS USERMISSING=EXCLUDE

  /CRITERIA ALPHA=0.05 CILEVEL=95.
```

Independent-Samples Mann-Whitney U Test

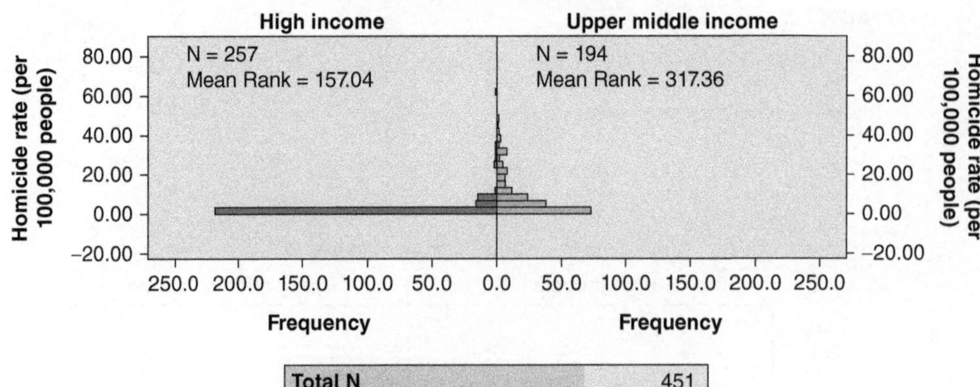

Total N	451
Mann-Whitney U	42,652.000
Wilcoxon W	61,567.000
Test Statistic	42,652.000
Standard Error	1,369.782
Standardized Test Statistic	12.939
Asymptotic Sig. (2-sided test)	.000

Figure A.9.5 Mann–Whitney U statistics for homicide rates by income group

Comparison of medians.

```
MEANS TABLES=homicides BY wbincome

  /CELLS=COUNT MEDIAN.
```

Table A.9.8 Median homicide rate (per 100,000 people) by income group

World Bank income group	N	Median
High income	257	1.1000
Upper middle income	194	4.7500
Total	451	1.7000

3. The difference between groups is statistically significant (U 42,652, p<0.001).
4. The median homicide rate in high-income countries is 1.1 homicides per 100,000 people. This is much lower than the median homicide rate of 4.75 homicides per 100,000 people in upper middle-income countries.
5. The effect size is large (r=0.609).

Activity 9.4

Compare gender inequality index [gii] scores between Freedom House status [e_fh_status] groups 1 (free) and 2 (partly free).

```
USE ALL.

COMPUTE filter_$=(e_fh_status = 1 OR e_fh_status = 2).

VARIABLE LABELS filter_$ 'e_fh_status = 1 OR e_fh_status = 2 (FILTER)'.

VALUE LABELS filter_$ 0 'Not Selected' 1 'Selected'.

FORMATS filter_$ (f1.0).

FILTER BY filter_$.

EXECUTE.
```

1. Produce a column panel histogram to check for violations of the assumptions of normality and homogeneity of variance.

```
GGRAPH

  /GRAPHDATASET NAME="graphdataset" VARIABLES=GII e_fh_status MISSING=
LISTWISE REPORTMISSING=NO

/GRAPHSPEC SOURCE=INLINE.

BEGIN GPL
```

```
  SOURCE: s=userSource(id("graphdataset"))
  DATA: GII=col(source(s), name("GII"))
  DATA: e_fh_status=col(source(s), name("e_fh_status"),
notIn("3"), unit.category())
  GUIDE: axis(dim(1), label("Gender Inequality Index"))
  GUIDE: axis(dim(2), label("Frequency"))
  GUIDE: axis(dim(3), label("Freedom House status"), opposite())
  SCALE: cat(dim(3), include("1", "2"), sort.values("1", "2"))
  ELEMENT:
interval(position(summary.count(bin.rect(GII*1*e_fh_status))), shape.
interior(shape.square))
END GPL.
```

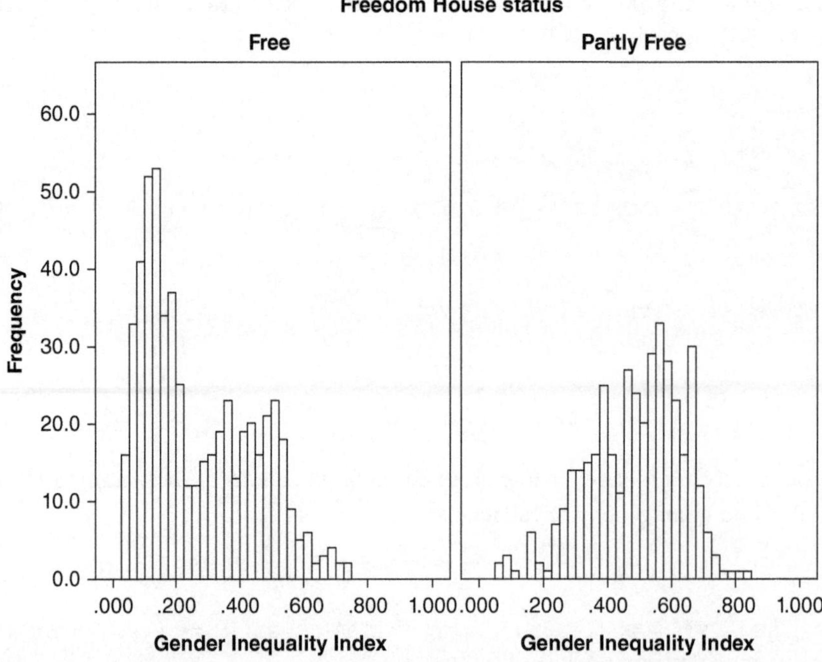

Figure A.9.6 Column panel histogram of gender inequality by Freedom House status

2. A Mann–Whitney U test is more suitable because the data is not normally distributed. The results for free have a multimodal distribution, while the partly free results are close to normally distributed.

Mann–Whitney U test of female legislative seats by FH status.

```
NPTESTS
  /INDEPENDENT TEST (gii) GROUP (e_fh_status) MANN_WHITNEY
  /MISSING SCOPE=ANALYSIS USERMISSING=EXCLUDE
  /CRITERIA ALPHA=0.05 CILEVEL=95.
```

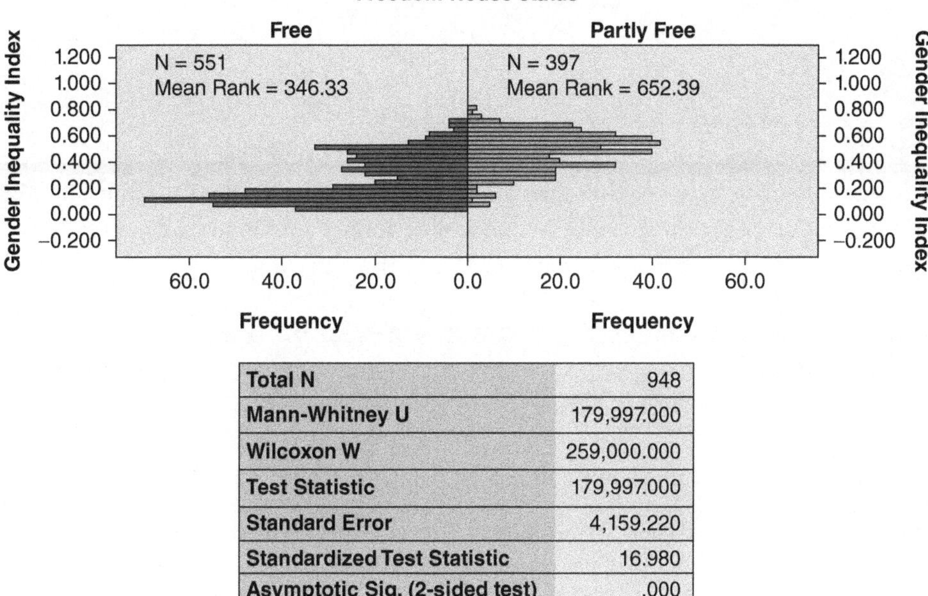

Total N	948
Mann-Whitney U	179,997.000
Wilcoxon W	259,000.000
Test Statistic	179,997.000
Standard Error	4,159.220
Standardized Test Statistic	16.980
Asymptotic Sig. (2-sided test)	.000

Figure A.9.7 Mann-Whitney U statistics for gender inequality by Freedom House status

Median female legislative representation by FH status.

```
MEANS TABLES=gii BY e_fh_status
  /CELLS=COUNT MEDIAN.
```

Table A.9.9 Median gender inequality index scores by Freedom House status

Freedom House status	N	Median
Free	551	.208
Partly Free	397	.504
Total	948	.373

3. The difference between the groups is statistically significant (U 179,997, $p<0.001$).
4. Countries rated 'free' by Freedom House have a much lower median gender inequality index score (0.208) than those rated 'partly free' (0.504). This would seem to indicate that democracies are better at reducing gender inequality than non-democracies.
5. The effect size of the difference between free and partly free countries is large ($r=0.551$).

CHAPTER 10

Activity 10.1

RQ: How can we explain openness to immigration?

Use the ESS dataset. You will need the variable 'Openness to immigration index' [`imindex`] created in Box 10.7 to answer this question. Create an index variable 'Trust in institutions index' [`trustindex`] using the series of variables relating to trust in institutions (`trstprl, trstlgl, trstplc, trstplt, trstprt, trstep, trstun`).

```
COMPUTE trustindex=trstprl + trstlgl + trstplc + trstplt + trstprt +
trstep + trstun.

EXECUTE.

VARIABLE LABELS trustindex 'Trust in institutions index'.

VALUE LABELS trustindex 0 'No trust at all' 70 'Complete trust'.
```

Use 'Openness to immigration index' [`imindex`] as the outcome variable and 'Trust in institutions index' [`trustindex`], 'Age of respondent, calculated' [`agea`] and 'Years of full-time education completed' [`eduyrs`] as the predictor variables.

Table A.10.1 Linear regression results for openness to immigration

Model summary				
Model	**R**	**R Square**	**Adjusted R Square**	**Std. Error of the Estimate**
1	.424[a]	.180	.179	9.39012

a. Predictors: (Constant), Years of full-time education completed, Trust in institutions index, Age of respondent, calculated

ANOVA[a]						
Model		Sum of Squares	df	Mean Square	F	Sig.
1	Regression	596552.363	3	198850.788	2255.200	.000[b]
	Residual	2726350.538	30920	88.174		
	Total	3322902.901	30923			

a. Dependent Variable: Openness to immigration index

b. Predictors: (Constant), Years of full-time education completed, Trust in institutions index, Age of respondent, calculated

Coefficients[a]						
Model		Unstandardized Coefficients		Standardized Coefficients	t	Sig.
		B	Std. Error	Beta		
1	(Constant)	13.737	.283		48.491	.000
	Trust in institutions index	.264	.004	.353	67.916	.000
	Age of respondent, calculated	−.006	.003	−.011	−2.030	.042
	Years of full-time education completed	.504	.014	.189	35.674	.000

a. Dependent Variable: Openness to immigration index

1. H1. An increase in trust will cause an increase in openness to immigration.

H2. The greater the level of a respondent's education, the more open they will be to immigration.

H3. Older respondents will have lower openness to immigration.

2. These variables are appropriate for linear regression, as all variables are continuous.

```
REGRESSION

/MISSING LISTWISE

/STATISTICS COEFF OUTS R ANOVA

/CRITERIA=PIN(.05) POUT(.10)

/NOORIGIN
```

```
/DEPENDENT imindex
/METHOD=ENTER trustindex agea eduyrs.
```

3. The model is statistically significant at $p<0.001$. (See ANOVA results table.)
4. 17.9 percent of variance in openness to immigration can be explained by these predictors. (See Model summary table.)
5. All of the predictors are statistically significant. (See Sig. column in Coefficients table.) Trust and years of full-time education completed are significant at $p<0.001$; age is significant at $p<0.05$.
6. Trust and years of full-time education completed are positively related to openness to immigration; age is negatively related.
7. Rank the influence of each predictor, from strongest to weakest. Trust in institutions is the strongest predictor (std. Beta 0.353). Every one-unit increase in trust results in a 0.264-unit increase in openness to immigration. The next strongest predictor is years of full-time education completed (std. Beta 0.189). For every additional year of education, openness to immigration increases by 0.504 units. This may seem larger than the impact of trust, but a one-unit increase on the 70-point trust scale equates to a 1.4 percent increase in trust, while an additional year of education equates to an approximately 7.7 percent increase in education. This is reflected in the lower std. Beta for education than for trust. Respondent age is the weakest predictor (std. Beta –0.011). For every additional year of age, there is a .006-unit decrease in openness to immigration.
8. These results confirm all three hypotheses, though it is somewhat surprising that age has such a weak effect.

Activity 10.2

Select only respondents from France.

```
USE ALL.
COMPUTE filter_$=(country=10).
VARIABLE LABELS filter_$ 'country=10 (FILTER)'.
VALUE LABELS filter_$ 0 'Not Selected' 1 'Selected'.
FORMATS filter_$ (f1.0).
FILTER BY filter_$.
EXECUTE.
```

Use 'Age of respondent, calculated' [agea], 'Years of full-time education completed' [eduyrs] and 'Total hours normally worked per week in main job, overtime included' [wkhtot] as the predictors and 'Voted last national election' [vote] as the outcome variable. Make sure that you have reclassified the missing values for vote to exclude 'not eligible' from analysis; alternatively, recode vote into a dummy variable, keeping only 'yes' and 'no'.

Table A.10.2 Selected outputs from binary logistic regression for voting in France

Case Processing Summary

Unweighted Cases[a]		N	Percent
Selected Cases	Included in Analysis	1523	79.4
	Missing Cases	394	20.6
	Total	1917	100.0
Unselected Cases		0	.0
Total		1917	100.0

a. If weight is in effect, see classification Table A. for the total number of cases.

Dependent Variable Encoding

Original Value	Internal Value
Yes	0
No	1

Block 0: Beginning Block

Classification Table[a,b]

	Observed		Predicted: Voted last national election – Yes	Predicted: Voted last national election – No	Percentage Correct
Step 0	Voted last national election	Yes	1053	0	100.0
		No	470	0	.0
	Overall Percentage				69.1

a. Constant is included in the model.

b. The cut value is .500

(Continued)

Table A.10.2 (Continued)

Block 1: Method = Enter

Omnibus Tests of Model Coefficients

		Chi-square	df	Sig.
Step 1	Step	221.928	3	.000
	Block	221.928	3	.000
	Model	221.928	3	.000

Model summary

Step	-2 Log likelihood	Cox & Snell R Square	Nagelkerke R Square
1	1660.430[a]	.136	.191

a. Estimation terminated at iteration number 5 because parameter estimates changed by less than .001.

Classification Table[a]

	Observed		Predicted		
			Voted last national election		Percentage Correct
			Yes	No	
Step 1	Voted last national election	Yes	961	92	91.3
		No	317	153	32.6
	Overall Percentage				73.1

a. The cut value is .500

Variables in the Equation

		B	S.E.	Wald	df	Sig.	Exp(B)
Step 1[a]	Age of respondent, calculated	–.058	.004	170.621	1	.000	.944
	Years of full-time education completed	–.121	.018	44.449	1	.000	.886
	Total hours normally worked per week in main job overtime included	–.007	.004	2.316	1	.128	.993
	Constant	3.869	.410	89.135	1	.000	47.877

a. Variable(s) entered on step 1: Age of respondent, calculated, Years of full-time education completed, Total hours normally worked per week in main job overtime included.

1. These variables are appropriate for binary logistic regression. The predictor variable is binary, and the outcome variables are all continuous.

```
LOGISTIC REGRESSION VARIABLES vote
  /METHOD=ENTER agea eduyrs wkhtot
  /CRITERIA=PIN(.05) POUT(.10) ITERATE(20) CUT(.5).
```

2. The model is statistically significant ($p<0.001$). (See significance results from Omnibus Tests of Model Coefficients table.)
3. Between 13.6 (Cox & Snell R Square) and 19.1 percent (Nagelkerke R Square) of variance in voting can be explained by these predictors.
4. The direction is negative for all three: as age increases, likelihood of non-voting decreases (B of –0.058); as years of full-time education completed increases, likelihood of non-voting decreases (B of –0.121); and as total hours worked per week increases, likelihood of non-voting decreases (–0.007).
5. Years of full-time education completed is the strongest predictor: for each additional year of education, someone is 1.129 times less likely (1/0.886) not to vote. Second strongest is age: for each additional year older, someone is 1.059 times less likely (1/0.944) to be a non-voter. Weakest is hours worked: for each additional hour worked, someone is 1.007 times less likely (1/0.944) to be a non-voter.
6. These predictors are much better at explaining non-voting in France (13.6–19.1 percent of variance explained) than in the survey as a whole (4.9–7.6 percent of variance explained).

Activity 10.3

Recode 'Which party feel closer to, Austria' [prtclcat] into a binary variable with FPÖ as 1 and all other parties as 0. Make sure that you have properly classified any missing values in the dummy variable.

```
RECODE prtclcat (1 thru 2=0) (3=1) (4 thru 10=0) (else=copy) into
prtclcatFPO.
EXECUTE.
VARIABLE LABELS prtclcatFPO 'Which party feel closer to, Austria: FPO'.
VALUE LABELS prtclcatFPO 1 'FPO' 0 'Other' 66 'Not applicable' 77
'Refusal' 88 'Dont know' 99 'No answer'.
MISSING VALUES prtclcatFPO (66 thru 99).
```

Use 'Openness to immigration index' [imindex] (created in Box 10.7), 'Age of respondent, calculated' [agea], 'Years of full-time education completed' [eduyrs], Gender [gndr] and 'Belong to minority ethnic group in country' [blgetmg] as the predictors and the FPÖ binary variable as the outcome variable. Set female and ethnic minority as the categorical reference groups. Include a goodness of fit test and 95 percent confidence intervals.

Table A.10.3 Selected outputs from binary logistic regression for voting for the Austrian FPÖ

Case Processing Summary

Unweighted Cases[a]		N	Percent
Selected Cases	Included in Analysis	767	1.9
	Missing Cases	39418	98.1
	Total	40185	100.0
Unselected Cases		0	.0
Total		40185	100.0

a. If weight is in effect, see classification Table A. for the total number of cases.

Dependent Variable Encoding

Original Value	Internal Value
Other	0
FPO	1

Categorical Variables Codings

		Frequency	Parameter coding
			(1)
Belong to minority ethnic group in country	Yes	35	.000
	No	732	1.000
Gender	Male	386	1.000
	Female	381	.000

Block 0: Beginning Block

Classification Table[a,b]

Observed			Predicted		
			Which party feel closer to, Austria: FPO		Percentage Correct
			Other	FPO	
Step 0	Which party feel closer to, Austria: FPO	Other	646	0	100.0
		FPO	121	0	.0
	Overall Percentage				84.2

a. Constant is included in the model.

b. The cut value is .500

Block 1: Method = Enter

Omnibus Tests of Model Coefficients

		Chi-square	df	Sig.
Step 1	Step	170.002	5	.000
	Block	170.002	5	.000
	Model	170.002	5	.000

Model summary

Step	-2 Log likelihood	Cox & Snell R Square	Nagelkerke R Square
1	498.719[a]	.199	.342

a. Estimation terminated at iteration number 7 because parameter estimates changed by less than .001.

Hosmer and Lemeshow Test

Step	Chi-square	df	Sig.
1	6.252	8	.619

Classification Table[a]

	Observed		Predicted		
			Which party feel closer to, Austria: FPO		Percentage Correct
			Other	FPO	
Step 1	Which party feel closer to, Austria: FPO	Other	624	22	96.6
		FPO	88	33	27.3
	Overall Percentage				85.7

a. The cut value is .500

(Continued)

Table A.10.3 (Continued)

		B	S.E.	Wald	df	Sig.	Exp(B)	95% C.I. for EXP(B)	
								Lower	Upper
Step 1[a]	Openness to immigration index	–.115	.012	91.695	1	.000	.891	.870	.912
	Age of respondent, calculated	–.027	.007	14.430	1	.000	.974	.960	.987
	Years of full-time education completed	–.072	.038	3.483	1	.062	.931	.863	1.004
	Gender(1)	.244	.238	1.048	1	.306	1.277	.800	2.037
	Belong to minority ethnic group in country(1)	1.929	1.137	2.877	1	.090	6.881	.741	63.906
	Constant	1.005	1.278	.618	1	.432	2.732		

Variables in the Equation

a. Variable(s) entered on step 1: Openness to immigration index, Age of respondent, calculated, Years of full-time education completed, Gender, Belong to minority ethnic group in country.

1. These variables are appropriate for binary logistic regression. The predictor variable is binary, and the outcome variables are all continuous.

```
LOGISTIC REGRESSION VARIABLES prtclcatFPO

  /METHOD=ENTER imindex agea eduyrs gndr blgetmg

  /CONTRAST (gndr)=Indicator

  /CONTRAST (blgetmg)=Indicator(1)

  /PRINT=GOODFIT CI(95)

  /CRITERIA=PIN(0.05) POUT(0.10) ITERATE(20) CUT(0.5).
```

2. The model is statistically significant at p<0.001 (chi-square 170.002, df 5). (See significance results from Omnibus Tests of Model Coefficients table.)
3. Between 19.9 (Cox & Snell R Square) and 34.2 percent (Nagelkerke R Square) of variation in voting for the FPÖ can be predicted with these variables.
4. Openness to immigration and age are statistically significant (p<0.001). Belonging to an ethnic minority group is statistically significant at p<0.10 but not at p<0.05. Gender and years of full-time education completed are not statistically significant (p>0.10).
5. Openness to immigration and age have a negative relationship, meaning that an increase in each of these leads to decreased likelihood of identifying with the FPÖ. Belonging to an ethnic minority group has a positive relationship: being from the majority ethnicity increases the likelihood of identifying with the FPÖ; but gender is not statistically significant.

6. Belonging to an ethnic minority group has a very high odds ratio: white Austrians are 7.320 times more likely to identify with the FPÖ than ethnic minorities; however, this has a very large confidence interval (0.885–60.542), likely reflective of the fact that there are only 35 people in this test who identified as belonging to an ethnic minority. Openness to immigration is a strong predictor of identification with the FPÖ: for each one-point increase on the immigration index, respondents are 1.127 times less likely to identify with the FPÖ. Each additional year older makes someone 1.045 times less likely to identify with the FPÖ.
7. Age has the opposite effect in Austrian identification with the FPÖ to British identification with Ukip. This is likely to reflect the FPÖ's young leader and modernization campaign, which appears to have been effective in appealing to younger voters. This campaign also seems to have been effective in drawing more women, since sex is not a statistically significant predictor of identification with the FPÖ, a very different pattern to that of Ukip support. In both cases, increased education and increased openness to immigration result in decreased likelihood to identify with these parties.

Activity 10.4

Part A: Default statistics.

Part A: Linear regression with default statistics.

Table A.10.4 Linear regression with default statistics

Model summary

Model	R	R Square	Adjusted R Square	Std. Error of the Estimate
1	.549[a]	.301	.293	11.29593

a. Predictors: (Constant), Income inequality %, Polity score, revised, GNI, logged, Mean years of schooling, Gender Inequality Index

ANOVA[a]

Model		Sum of Squares	df	Mean Square	F	Sig.
1	Regression	23407.329	5	4681.466	36.689	.000[b]
	Residual	54229.127	425	127.598		
	Total	77636.456	430			

a. Dependent Variable: Homicide rate (per 100,000 people)

b. Predictors: (Constant), Income inequality %, Polity score, revised, GNI, logged, Mean years of schooling, Gender Inequality Index

(Continued)

Table 10.4 (Continued)

Coefficients[a]						
Model		**Unstandardized Coefficients**		**Standardized Coefficients**	**t**	**Sig.**
		B	**Std. Error**	**Beta**		
1	(Constant)	−38.875	10.947		−3.551	.000
	Gender Inequality Index	26.694	7.113	.372	3.753	.000
	Mean years of schooling	.459	.374	.101	1.227	.220
	Polity score, revised	.099	.133	.034	.748	.455
	GNI, logged	5.107	2.463	.178	2.074	.039
	Income inequality %	.561	.063	.443	8.878	.000

a. Dependent Variable: Homicide rate (per 100,000 people)

1. These variables are all continuous variables, so a linear regression is the most appropriate test.

```
REGRESSION

  /DEPENDENT homicides

  /METHOD=ENTER gii meanschyrs e_polity2 loggni incomeineq.
```

2. The model is statistically significant (p<0.001, F 36.689). (See ANOVA results.)
3. The predictors can explain 29.3 percent of variance in the homicide rate. (See adjusted r-square in the Model summary.)
4. Gender inequality (p<0.001), logged GNI (p<0.05) and income inequality (p<0.001) all have a statistically significant effect on the homicide rate. Mean years of schooling (p=0.220) and Polity score (p=0.455) are both statistically insignificant.
5. There is a positive relationship between gender inequality, logged GNI, income inequality and homicides. For every one-unit increase in gender inequality, there is a 26.7-unit increase in the homicide rate. (In this case, a one-unit increase in the homicide rate means an increase in one homicide per 100,000 people.) For every one-unit increase in logged GNI, there is a 5.1-unit increase in the homicide rate. For every one-unit increase in income inequality (in this case, every 1 percent increase), there is a 0.56-unit increase in the homicide rate.
6. Income inequality has the greatest impact on the homicide rate (Beta 0.443), followed by gender inequality (Beta 0.372), then logged GNI (Beta 0.178).

Part B: Additional statistics:

7. Produce a linear regression with descriptive statistics, collinearity diagnostics, confidence intervals and diagnostic graphs.

```
REGRESSION
  /DESCRIPTIVES MEAN STDDEV CORR SIG N
  /MISSING LISTWISE
  /STATISTICS COEFF OUTS CI(95) R ANOVA COLLIN TOL
  /CRITERIA=PIN(.05) POUT(.10)
  /NOORIGIN
  /DEPENDENT homicides
  /METHOD=ENTER gii meanschyrs e_polity2 loggni incomeineq
  /SCATTERPLOT=(*ZRESID ,*ZPRED)
  /RESIDUALS NORMPROB(ZRESID).
```

Part B: Linear regression with additional statistics.

Table A.10.5 Linear regression with additional statistics for checking violations of assumptions

Correlations

		Homicide rate (per 100,000 people)	Gender Inequality Index	Mean years of schooling	Polity score, revised	GNI, logged	Income inequality %
Pearson Correlation	Homicide rate (per 100,000 people)	1.000	.350	–.264	–.030	–.192	.527
	Gender Inequality Index	.350	1.000	–.854	–.408	–.854	.521
	Mean years of schooling	–.264	–.854	1.000	.367	.814	–.464
	Polity score, revised	–.030	–.408	.367	1.000	.438	–.062
	GNI, logged	–.192	–.854	.814	.438	1.000	–.340
	Income inequality %	.527	.521	–.464	–.062	–.340	1.000

(Continued)

Table A.10.5 (Continued)

Correlations

		Homicide rate (per 100,000 people)	Gender Inequality Index	Mean years of schooling	Polity score, revised	GNI, logged	Income inequality %
Sig. (1–tailed)	Homicide rate (per 100,000 people)	.	.000	.000	.270	.000	.000
	Gender Inequality Index	.000	.	.000	.000	.000	.000
	Mean years of schooling	.000	.000	.	.000	.000	.000
	Polity score, revised	.270	.000	.000	.	.000	.101
	GNI, logged	.000	.000	.000	.000	.	.000
	Income inequality %	.000	.000	.000	.101	.000	.
N	Homicide rate (per 100,000 people)	431	431	431	431	431	431
	Gender Inequality Index	431	431	431	431	431	431
	Mean years of schooling	431	431	431	431	431	431
	Polity score, revised	431	431	431	431	431	431
	GNI, logged	431	431	431	431	431	431
	Income inequality %	431	431	431	431	431	431

Coefficients[a]

Model		Unstandardized Coefficients		Standardized Coefficients	t	Sig.	95.0% Confidence Interval for B		Collinearity Statistics	
		B	Std. Error	Beta			Lower Bound	Upper Bound	Tolerance	VIF
1	(Constant)	−38.875	10.947		−3.551	.000	−60.392	−17.359		
	Gender Inequality Index	26.694	7.113	.372	3.753	.000	12.713	40.675	.168	5.966
	Mean years of schooling	.459	.374	.101	1.227	.220	−.276	1.194	.240	4.160
	Polity score, revised	.099	.133	.034	.748	.455	−.162	.360	.784	1.275
	GNI, logged	5.107	2.463	.178	2.074	.039	.266	9.948	.222	4.495
	Income inequality %	.561	.063	.443	8.878	.000	.437	.685	.660	1.515

a. Dependent Variable: Homicide rate (per 100,000 people)

8. The Polity score poses a potential problem for inclusion because it has a very low correlation with the homicide rate (r=0.030). This will not add anything to the explanatory power of the model. The correlations with logged GNI (r±0.192) and mean years of schooling (r=–0.264) are also weak. We could consider excluding these variables from our model or running the model with and without them to determine their predictive power. There are potential violations of multicollinearity for gender inequality and mean years of schooling (r=–0.854) as well as between logged GNI and gender inequality (r=–0.854) and mean years of schooling (r=–0.814). However, none of these variables violates the tolerance threshold of 0.10 in the collinearity statistics. Greater concerns are raised about violations of normality for the dependent variable, judging by the normal P-P plot (Figure A.10.1 Normal P-P Plot for checking normality of homicide rate) and scatterplot (Figure A.10.2 Scatterplot for checking distribution of residuals of homicide rate). The best way to attempt to correct this shape is to create a logged variable for homicide. You might choose to exclude Polity score from analysis because of its lack of explanatory power and statistical insignificance.

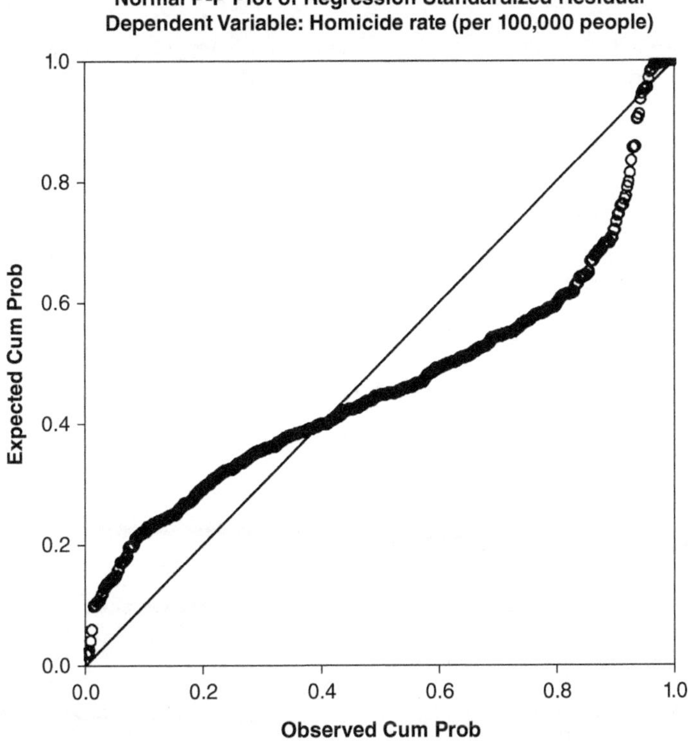

Figure A.10.1 Normal P-P Plot for checking normality of homicide rate

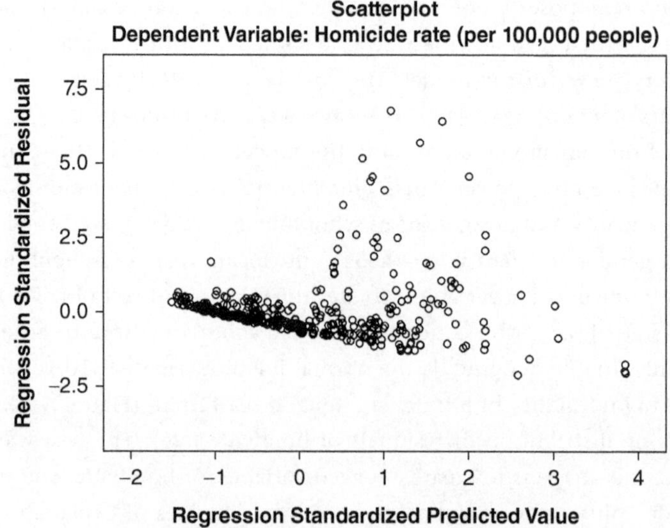

Figure A.10.2 Scatterplot for checking distribution of residuals of homicide rate

```
COMPUTE loghomicides=LN(homicides).
VARIABLE LABELS loghomicides 'Homicide rate per 100,000 people (natural
log)'.
EXECUTE.

REGRESSION
  /DESCRIPTIVES MEAN STDDEV CORR SIG N
  /MISSING LISTWISE
  /STATISTICS COEFF OUTS CI(95) R ANOVA COLLIN TOL
  /CRITERIA=PIN(.05) POUT(.10)
  /NOORIGIN
  /DEPENDENT loghomicides
  /METHOD=ENTER gii meanschyrs e_polity2 loggni incomeineq
  /SCATTERPLOT=(*ZRESID ,*ZPRED)
  /RESIDUALS NORMPROB(ZRESID).
```

Table A.10.6 Linear regression results for logged homicide rates

Model summary[b]

Model	R	R Square	Adjusted R Square	Std. Error of the Estimate
1	.728[a]	.530	.524	.39751

a. Predictors: (Constant), Income inequality %, Polity score, revised, GNI, logged, Mean years of schooling, Gender Inequality Index

b. Dependent Variable: Homicide rate per 100,000 people (natural log)

ANOVA[a]

Model		Sum of Squares	df	Mean Square	F	Sig.
1	Regression	75.671	5	15.134	95.778	.000[b]
	Residual	67.156	425	.158		
	Total	142.827	430			

a. Dependent Variable: Homicide rate per 100,000 people (natural log)

b. Predictors: (Constant), Income inequality %, Polity score, revised, GNI, logged, Mean years of schooling, Gender Inequality Index

Coefficients[a]

Model		Unstandardized Coefficients		Standardized Coefficients	t	Sig.	95.0% Confidence Interval for B		Collinearity Statistics	
		B	Std. Error	Beta			Lower Bound	Upper Bound	Tolerance	VIF
1	(Constant)	-1.671	.385		-4.337	.000	-2.428	-.913		
	Gender Inequality Index	2.194	.250	.712	8.767	.000	1.702	2.686	.168	5.966
	Mean years of schooling	.071	.013	.364	5.372	.000	.045	.097	.240	4.160
	Polity score, revised	-.001	.005	-.005	-.135	.893	-.010	.009	.784	1.275
	GNI, logged	.073	.087	.059	.839	.402	-.098	.243	.222	4.495
	Income inequality %	.024	.002	.449	10.955	.000	.020	.029	.660	1.515

a. Dependent Variable: Homicide rate per 100,000 people (natural log)

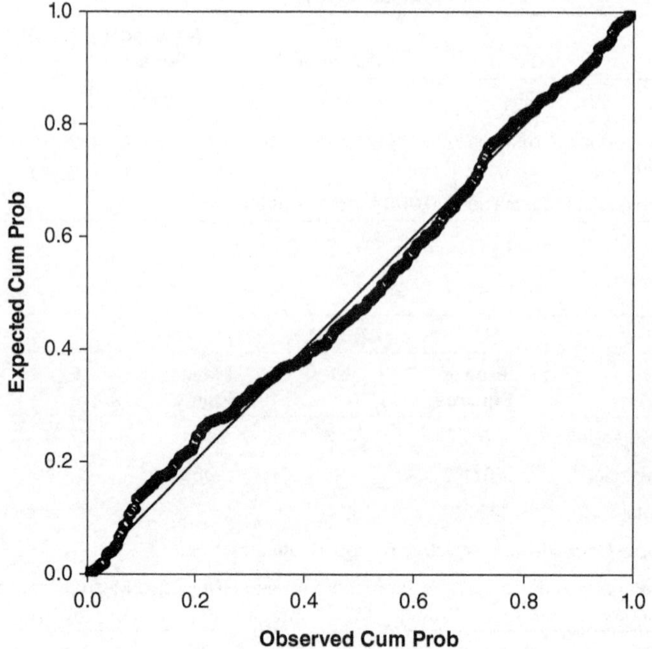

Figure A.10.3 Normal P-P Plot for checking normality of logged homicide rate

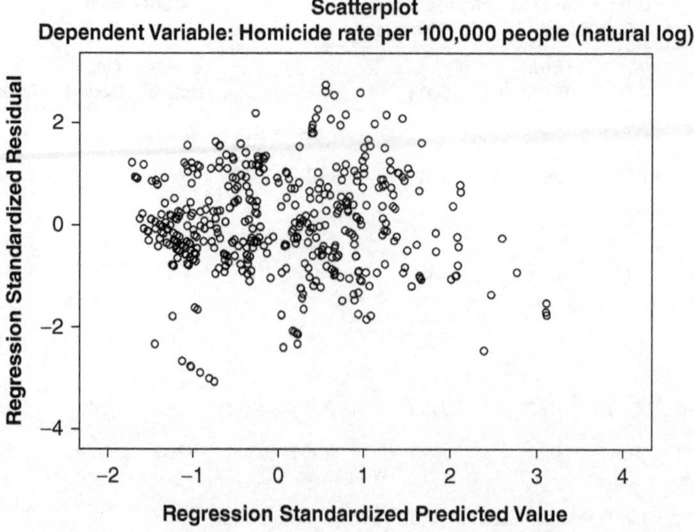

Figure A.10.4 Scatterplot for checking distribution of residuals of logged homicide rate

9. The model is statistically significant ($p<0.001$, F 95.778) (see ANOVA results). The predictors can explain 52.4 percent of variance in the homicide rate (see Model summary). Gender inequality, mean years of schooling and income inequality are all statistically significant ($p<0.001$). Each of these has a positive relationship with homicide rates: as each increases, so do homicide rates. When using logged homicide rates, gender inequality has the greatest explanatory power (Beta 0.712), followed by income inequality (Beta 0.449) and mean years of schooling (0.364). Neither logged GNI nor Polity score contributes to explaining variance in homicide rates.
10. How would you interpret the confidence intervals for the results? The confidence intervals indicate that, for every one-unit increase in gender inequality, the logged homicide rate increases between 1.702 and 2.686 units. For every one-unit increase in mean years of schooling, logged homicide rates increase between 0.045 and 0.097 units. For every 1 percent increase in income inequality, logged homicide rates increase between 0.020 and 0.029 units.
11. These results appear to support Wilkinson and Pickett's theory. They theorize that homicides are about status and power struggles; this would align with the importance of gender inequality, which could also be seen as an issue of status difference between men and women. It is remarkable that democracy and income are insignificant for predicting homicide rates. This indicates that the principle of equality in democracy does not shield populations from homicides, nor does living in a wealthier country. Instead, it is the distribution of wealth and power within a country that is more important.

INDEX

Note: Figures and tables are indicated by page numbers in bold print. The letter '*b*' after a page number refers to bibliographical information in a Further Reading section. Computer procedures described in BOXES are filed under the main heading 'IBM SPSS Statistics'.